# MindFitness Training

## Neurofeedback and the Process

Consciousness, Self-Renewal,
and
the Technology of Self-Knowledge

*R. Adam Crane BCIA, NRNP*
*and*
*Richard Soutar Ph.D.*

Writers Club Press
San Jose  New York  Lincoln  Shanghai

**MindFitness Training**
Neurofeedback and the Process

Published by Writers Club Press
an imprint of iUniverse.com, Inc.

For information address:
iUniverse.com, Inc.
620 North 48th Street
Suite 201
Lincoln, NE  68504-3467
www.iuniverse.com

ISBN: 0-595-09605-0

Printed in the United States of America

# Dedication

With gratitude to my mother, Lahoma Loveda who first taught me about love, to our wives, Barbara and Dagne who continue the teaching, the inspiration of our families, friends and teachers dead and alive and to those drawn to this book.

# Contents

# Preface

The successes of humanity are obvious. We have achieved astonishing technological development and, if anything, it appears to be accelerating so fast that we have had to invent the term 'super exponential' in order to attempt to describe it. We have been so successful as a species in terms of survival that we are approaching the limits of how many of us the planet can sustain. In fact, we have crowded and consumed so many species that the rate of extinction of other life forms is paralleling the rate of extinction in the catastrophic period which ended the dinosaurs. We are already seriously planning colonies on other planets, and some respected scientists believe we can eventually travel to other solar systems within our galaxy. In spite of persistent wars, starvation and brutality, wealth seems to be increasing around the world, and for the first time in history more than 50% of the world lives under some kind of a democratic government. Furthermore, non-democratic governments such as China appear to be on inexorable paths toward more democracy and free markets. So, one might ask oneself, "Why worry?"

I don't really think that worry is all that productive. But certainly concern for what happens is; and common sense must acknowledge that humanity is grappling with many crises. However, most would probably agree that the biggest, most dangerous crisis is the crisis in the consciousness of mankind. In fact, this crisis is so great that many feel we are in extreme danger of ending our species in spite of all of our achievements. They may be right. I don't know. But in my heart of hearts I believe we can make it. However, what does making it mean? It seems obvious that as we continue to solve the problem of providing for the reasonable material needs of a growing number of us, the next frontier to conquer is providing for our mental (some prefer the term spiritual) needs. I realize that there is still an appalling amount of starvation, poverty and suffering, but most experts are telling us that these problems are not caused by lack of resources so much as they are caused by the crisis in our collective consciousness.

In my part of the world most people are relatively wealthy. And most of us (including myself) would rather be wealthy than poor. However, isn't it obvious that once one has acquired food, clothing and shelter, the next challenge is how to live a meaningful, original life filled with caring relationships? This requires the development and sustaining of substantial mental and emotional (EQ) intelligence. We have coined the term MindFitness as a way of describing those robust qualities of mind (and heart) that bring about the miraculous unfoldment of aliveness that some have and we all hunger for. Those who can achieve this may be called artists of living. We believe the survival and flowering of our species (and probably many other species as well) depends on how well we practice this art of living.

Scientists, philosophers and quality thinkers of all kinds believe that the greatest new frontier we have is the human mind itself–the understanding and enhancement of consciousness. And we do not mean a mere scientific, intellectual, theoretical understanding, but a practical, applicable, real-world profitable and testable understanding of consciousness. Even those of us who are enthusiastic about the possibilities of extending ourselves into outer space realize that the fastest and best way to get there–indeed probably the only way to get there is to first master our own inner space.

Like most of you reading, this I have longed to make a contribution to those movements that are changing the world for the better, including but not limited to the women's movement, the spread of democracy, saving threatened species, developing sustainable agriculture, renewable energy sources, reduction of the world wide military dangers, the metaphysically sound harvesting of the benefits of outer space and the list goes on. As I meditated as deeply as I could on these issues it became clear to me that the question is not whether we can solve these problems. On the contrary, it is obvious that there are many brilliant and incredibly motivated people who know far better than I the exact steps to be taken in order to make vast strides towards the defining and solving of these huge challenges.

The question then became—what is holding these awesomely gifted individuals and organizations back? For me the answer is clear. The frustrating and dangerous drag on our problem solving and solution implementation is caused by the crisis in our consciousness. This crisis includes wrong conditioning which leads to wrong thinking and the suppression of natural qualities of consciousness and intelligence. This process in turn leads to fear, hyper—nationalism, greed, envy, lack of freedom, the desire to dominate others, and so on. The consequences that follow include squandering of our resources and a kind of collective exhaustion. Taken all together we have built a kind of barrier, a kind of mind unfitness, which slows and even prevents us from marshalling our vast resources. Should we be able to bring about adequate MindFitness we could make astonishing progress in a flood of creativity. Realizing our latent potential in this way would surely qualify as a golden age.

Therefore, I decided to devote all of the energy I could muster to resolving so much as I am able this crisis in my own consciousness. And in so much as I am able, passing on to anyone interested whatever I can in the hope that it will prove useful in heuristically discovering how to resolve their own barriers to unfoldment. This book is part of that effort. Dr. Richard Soutar's thinking had been developing along similar lines so he agreed to assist me in putting this book together. I am deeply indebted to him not only because he has added substantial and scholarly parts to the book but also because his own practice of those principles we agree upon and his application of them with his patients have been an encouragement and inspiration to me.

There has been a river of thinkers who have passionately spoken out on the need to transform our thinking and they have presented many means whereby this mind revolution can be accomplished. The work which Dr. Soutar and I are involved in deals more with making the way the mind works as understandable and practically applicable to as many as we can. The place to start then is with ourselves, and we feel we have both at least made a reasonable start, and are already personally reaping the benefits.

Making something useful like a tool may use science, but tool-making and use often precedes and goes beyond the theories and limitations imposed by much of modern reductionist, unholistic science. For example, most scientists agree that the most revolutionary discovery in the Decade of the Brain has been the realization that the human brain can grow new brain cells throughout life. Dr. Soutar and I have long suspected this was true; however, the greater challenge is to discover and make available those means whereby this brain cell growth can be most enhanced. We are not alone. Indeed, as ever-greater resources are devoted to the improvement of the mental (and spiritual) life of human beings, it can truly be said that the Decade of the Brain has opened the doorway to the Century of the Mind.

As we go deeper and deeper into our own minds we have come to the conviction that the potential for the unfoldment of intelligence in the human being is for all practical intents and purposes infinite. The down-to-earth, practical Process of unfolding these ever higher orders of intelligence (including emotional intelligence and health) is what we mean by MindFitness. Furthermore, we assert that millions of scientific, artistic, educational and spiritual developments worldwide have already guaranteed that this process of achieving and enhancing MindFitness is the most valuable mission we can undertake in the coming century. And in the centuries that follow (assuming we survive) the twenty-first century will look like a reasonable beginning—we hope and we pray.

Many of us dream that we will look back from 3000 and realize that a true neostasis (a new state), a New Mind has been born. No one expects it to be perfect. There will always be great struggles and problems to be solved. But at least we will have finally made it past this seemingly endless roll of the millennia in which we made fantastic technological breakthroughs, but could not improve the day to day quality of our consciousness and our relationships with one another. (I understand we've had 30,000 wars in 5 thousand years). There will be literally unimaginable discoveries in the centuries to come. Surely the greatest of these will nurture the flowering of the art of living, the enhancement of MindFitness in the New Millenium. The Process Project is our effort to make a small contribution to the unfoldment of the best in all of us who long for and believe can actually change—even at this late hour.

# Introduction

We all want to live our lives as fully as possible. We all want good health. We want to live creatively. We want to avoid suffering. We want deep personal relationships. We want time and opportunity to enjoy this marvelous earth. We want to be valued by society. What are we willing to do (or not do) to improve the quality of our day to day lives? The Process takes on the challenges of transforming the commonplace into the extraordinary, of bringing about healthy change in as many lives as possible, of learning and practicing together the art of adventuring into the unknown, of changing periods of second hand consciousness into a fuller awareness and expression of the original life, of allowing the greatest potentials of the mind/body to unfold.

The Process is a modern version, an evolution of ancient processes whereby human beings make the most of what we have, of what we are. It begins humbly, easily, and naturally, and then expands without end. Consciously or unconsciously, that which can be done, not done, undone, unfolds—allowing the natural, innocent, original, uniquely incomparable beauty and potential of each of us to come to pass. This book is meant to be a heuristic exploration, a friendly discussion of the study, the doing, the living of that Process.

From childhood I have been fascinated with the idea that at least a substantial percentage of human beings and even some animals have the relative freedom to transform and re-invent themselves. The possibility that this freedom can result in a wonderful life, even in the face of extreme adversity and challenge, must surely be one of the highest priorities for us all. This idea that fulfillment is to some extent independent of individual circumstance is certainly one of the easiest, most obvious strategies for reducing suffering. We acknowledge that circumstances place many at an incredible disadvantage, but we cannot control that and to paraphrase Shakespeare, "Things are not as they appear". Most who enter into The Process discover that much of what they thought was a disadvantage can relatively easily become an asset. What we can do is work with all our might to understand and propagate that which is most likely to enable those at terrible disadvantage to escape the prison of their circumstances. That said, what greater adventure is there to engage in than this? It is natural to make a best effort to explore and pass on what we are learning, what is rewarding us so much. But even more to the point, the process of teaching forces us to learn more. We teach those things we need to learn and we teach them until we learn them.

In looking for words to describe what The Process Project is about, I find language limited. Words that seem to point in the right directions include: self-actualization, self-knowledge, transformation, personal growth, performance and life enhancement, etc. They are all useful, yet none of them is really adequate. But then dealing with the limitations of language is part of the challenge. Peak performance and functional transformation are examples of terms that seem to be rising from the collective mind.

*Heuristic, the method in which the learners discover for themselves while reducing dependence on past experiences and outside authority to the minimum (wisdom deems appropriate).*

However, we intend to push the envelope of what peak performance can mean. For example, traditional peak performance usually implies winning first place, achieving goals (regardless of the quality of those goals), competition, having better sex, making more money, gaining more respect, pleasure, etc. These are all understandable goals of personal fulfillment. We intend to address those issues and push beyond towards the application of principles which can deliver a richer, more balanced, wiser, more profound life; a life which enfolds those 'lower' orders of achievement like quantum physics enfolds valid aspects of Newtonian physics.

To me, self-actualization, real learning, the process of transformation, is a practical, learnable art and science. In fact, can there be any doubt that it is the most practical use of one's mind and body there is? And yet it is loaded (like all art and science) with mystery and paradox. Tangible progress in these areas often seems inaccessible, even to energetic minds. Our tendency is to expend huge amounts of energy, our life force, avoiding dealing with these issues because we are afraid and the distractions are many.

I have been teaching some of these concepts, mostly to health care and educational professionals, for more than 29 years and vigorously studying them for much longer than that. For decades I sought to understand and apply the great perennial principles to my own life. I dreamt of a way whereby I might share some of the treasures that had so enriched and infused my life with wonder, meaning, love and, at least so far, the resources to survive the adversity and inner enemies that I continue to encounter. The heuristic learning program dubbed The Process is an outcome of that longing, and at least a partial materialization of the vision and the dream this immense journey is borning. Designed to bring this work directly to the general public (as well as mental health and educational professionals) in the most practical, effective way our team can, The Process has the quality of a living being in its own right, as it is constantly changing, experimenting, adapting as if it is Learning Itself. Learning how to raise learning to the highest orders imaginable and even beyond what we have so far imagined, this program provides an excellent environment for discovering what works, what doesn't work…what to keep and what to throw away. This book includes a condensed version of The Process seminar training in chapter five.

**Quality of consciousness is everything!?**

The Process may seem difficult to some because these mind maps fly in the face of much of our cultural conditioning. Also, even the best of maps are not the territory, and the real royal roads to the coherent, inspired life are constantly changing like everything else in creation. Most of us are aware of how our general conditioning has a dampening effect on our creativity, our humanity, and the actualization of our potential. Also, we know, sense in our heart of hearts, there is a better way, a high road that fits our feet, and welcomes us. We, as a culture, have been finding more than enough clues for a long time.

Besides, from time to time we have all found ourselves on this high road, but usually not often enough to satisfy the longing. So we are going to improve our maps; and even more important walk together on the actual road, get into the terrain and discover the differences together between the maps and the actual roads. We are all doers. We just want to make sure we are doing those things that work and which are truly in our own best interests; the best interests of those we love, of our families and our extended families—the Tribe—with a big T.

What are those principles, that Process where the rubber meets the road—whereby our highest orders of intelligence are activated—are heuristically brought to the fore—our emotional intelligence (EQ) and our wisdom emerge? Is it possible to become clear about those principles which really work and apply them? Perhaps we don't have to understand them completely in order to use them any more than we have to understand gravity or electricity or the wind in order to apply those powers.

**A Hypothesis**

This book is about a simple concept, but a concept that may be difficult to accept at first. Therefore, lets present it as a hypothesis to be tested. Spengler, the German philosopher, points out that a hypothesis does not have to be absolutely true to be valuable. It merely needs to be useful.

Actually, this hypothetical concept, principle, or set of principles is already being tested; and from a cultural point of view is probably the greatest experiment of our time. Many believe these perilous times are propelling us toward some preordained and specific final outcome. This hypothesis assumes that there is more than one possible outcome for humanity (the collective and the individual). Accepting the notion that there is only one outcome (predestination) implies the principle of faith (as belief). Faith and belief are immeasurably powerful forces in their own right; however, we intend to extend our powers into the realm of action further than many, and in so doing accept a kind of ultimate sense of responsibility.

This hypothesis assumes that it is possible for humankind to destroy itself. But it is also possible we can transform ourselves into some kind of society that cannot from this vantage point be defined or adequately described, but which can be sensed, felt, intuited. The potential for an incredible future can be found in the present. This possible future can be a source and a kind of guide if we can find a way to have right relationship with it. Things as they are can begin to work in concert and assemble themselves, if we can be aware of and open to this possibility. Fred Allen Wolf and other scientists believe the future can affect the present, and our intentions and beliefs in the present are co-creating the future.

Teilhard de Chardin describes the notion of Cosmogenisis as a kind of spiritual evolution or healthy mutation. This transformation must first occur individually and then extend to the group, and it is an expression of the deepest, most profound longings and aspirations of the human heart-mind. A leap of learning takes place, according to many traditions as well as our own (authors) experience. This leap is in some direct relationship to the degree and ability of the mind to contact 'what is' directly. Therefore, the action required for this leap is in great part simply a deepening exercise of the principle of attention. Application of this principle results in a higher level of organization of the brain/mind, greater insight, and a vital, penetrating enhancement of awareness.

The simplicity and beauty of this principle holds astonishing implications for all of science while delivering the possibility of virtually unlimited benefits to even the humblest, least educated person hungering for the fullness of life. The very act of becoming aware of this allows a rapid actualization of latent intelligence to unfold. This hypothesis holds that high quality attention itself is a way of being which produces individual and societal evolution and transformation. Many actions spring from this attention and manifest as intelligent decisions made and actions undertaken or avoided. Individuals who yearn to awaken themselves are the ultimate expression of the maxim 'all politics are local'. These powerful, creative, holistic, renewing actions flow from simple attention to 'what is'. A metaphor which may serve is that attention is like the sun shining and radiating energy and causing an infinite amount of incredibly complex creative phenomena. Most of us are strangely unable to see that our inner teacher is pointing to this sun but we are entranced by the finger and missing the insight that we must become aware of the sun. We predict that quality attention to 'what is' by some as yet undetermined but probably relatively small number of human beings has the potential for producing a spontaneous explosion of infinitely complex creative action resulting in the transformation of Living Spaceship Earth. We believe this process has been underway for many millennia and is accelerating.

The action we speak of is also in the form of emerging qualities of consciousness. Emerging in the sense that some percentage of the population is learning how to bring these qualities of mind about. These concepts/principles have been known, practiced, articulated, and taught for at least the entire recorded history of humankind. Perhaps, the first thing to learn is 'Trust yourself! You know more than you think you do' (interestingly enough these are the opening words to one of the best selling books of all time, **Baby And Child Care**, by Benjamin Spock). Trusting in your own ability to teach yourself what you need to know in order to live healthily and to thrive on your challenges is a key to self-knowledge. Self-knowledge is the soul of The Process.

In honoring the principle of heuristic learning we have done our best to explain most of the concepts in a practical, relatively easy 'nuts and bolts' method; although, there is often a much deeper aspect requiring more subtlety to grasp and apply.

## The Effort To Change

The idea that most of us have some power to modify our perceptions and our states of consciousness is very old. In fact almost everything we do, whether enlightened or misguided, is an attempt to make ourselves feel better. Even reaching out relatively selflessly to another we do because we want the state of mind and the feeling it can engender. The problem is that many, perhaps most efforts to improve the quality of our mind and our consciousness seems to go awry. Change is very hard to implement. There is a subtle art to this path which seems to elude most of us. Perhaps the solution lies in simplicity. The complexity of our world tends to confuse and overwhelm us. We often seek equally complex explanations of how to make our lives work better. The Zen masters (and many other teachers) say, "ATTENTION, ATTENTION, ATTENTION!" The answer comes when there is a profound form of attention. Great minds of the past have relied on Occam's Razor to deal with many problems. The simplest explanation is often the closest to the truth as Einstein noted.

Some seem to be very good at this profound attention. And characteristic of those who have learned a little or a lot, is the desire to help someone else have some of what they have. This means teaching even if only by example. One of 'our' greatest teachers has been Einstein. Of course, his scientific discoveries have changed all of our lives; but to us he is one of many inspired philosophers as well. He was eager to acknowledge that whatever he had accomplished had been built upon the shoulders of countless others who have gone before.

Humility naturally flows in overwhelming waves as any of us even glimpse the reality, the interconnectedness, the interdependence, the clouds of glory pouring forth from trees, the eyes of living creatures, stones in the earth, galactic clusters. It is with such a sense that we undertake to write about these principles which so permeate our waking/sleeping consciousness, unconsciousness and 'trans—consciousness'.

## Dilemmas of Language

We intend to ambitiously push the envelope of language and communication in general. One aspect of that is recognizing that we have to be very careful with words as we penetrate those concepts, principles, and strategies that are most effective in enhancement of mind, consciousness, and normal human performance. Words are often confusing even when describing everyday, common objects, situations, and events. The danger of semantically misunderstanding increases as we grapple with the challenge of The Process. Ultimately we will be forced to go beyond the domain of words and into the unknown so that we can see ourselves and our lives as though for the first time ever. We must go beyond the realm of social dialogue from which our present identity issues and attend directly and profoundly. We must do all we can to allow our natural capacity for breakthrough thinking to break through.

One of the first obstacles we must break through is this concept of teacher and student; because the much less traveled high road demands that those who crawl it, walk it, run it or fly over it be both teachers and students, lights to themselves. Each life is unique and if there were only one way there would probably be only one human being. Each seedling must find its own path to the sun through the chaos of undergrowth.

## Escapism, Wishful Thinking or Transformation?

*To transform, to change in form, appearance, metamorphose, to change into another substance, to transmute, to transfigure, to change one thing into another, changing the characteristics, to convert, to change the electrical characteristics (i.e. increasing voltage) of an electrical current, to change one form of energy into another form of energy, a mathematical quantity obtained from a given quantity by an algebraic, geometric, or functional transformation.*

Perhaps, the word means too many things to too many people like those 'tools (principles) of transformation' meditation and love. We are keeping in mind that making a serious effort requires carefulness with language. After all, we want to get clearer, not confuse ourselves. We must be patient with one another.

So, what are we talking about? It is change isn't it? Just change. Change means stress, doesn't it? Implied in this is healthy change—healthy stress. And we are not talking about small change but rather large change aren't we? We don't really think about children transforming do we? In fact, when adults transform in a healthy way they become more childlike don't we? There is this sense of finding one's way back to what one has lost. There is a quality of fixing something that is broken, a kind of mending, a healing, even more, a profound renewal. Is transformation too hot, too unpleasant a word? Is it easier to think in terms of unfolding, becoming who we really are, breaking through our barriers, our conditioning, our inner enemies? Could we simplify it by just referring to achievement of an original, beautiful and 'true' life?

Is there a practical science, an art as the traditionalists would say, a Way, a Path that leads to an enchanted land? I say there is but when we try to discuss it with one another we tend to fall apart. Our efforts to describe it break down because language seems inadequate. The essence of what we care about so much and want to magically produce personally and collectively is beyond language, beyond thought. Or is it? Is the problem really language and thought or is it the quality of consciousness of the thinker and speaker at the time (s)he is thinking and speaking? Ahhhh, now there is a real rub. Perhaps we are getting somewhere.

I say that for all of us who see the *possibility* of functional, healthy transformation or change, the attempt to bring that change about is choiceless. Without this sense of continuous renewal there is the fear of being stuck, the sense of loss of freedom. Conversely, even small movement in the direction of healthy change is usually accompanied by an increased sense of freedom, a kind of exhilarating peace, a sense of coming home, a sense of completeness, a feeling that in one's essence one is an archetypal, even heroic creature—a sense that you and I are far less limited and far more valuable creatures than we have been conditioned to believe. This amounts to a revolution in our belief structures.

So, then what is the most effective practical way to approach this journey, this adventure? We can start by trying to call things by their right names. Or at least to reach for more efficient ways to communicate about what works.

That is why I have come to conceptualize transformation as MindFitness—The Process. Transformation has such a wonderful, magical, poetic ring to it. It really is a beautiful word. But, in a sense it conjures up the unachievable, images of something that happens to other people. It seems ludicrous to say, even if we just say it to ourselves, 'My God, my God I'm actually transforming myself! I, the worm, am becoming a butterfly! I, the loser am becoming the wise, incredibly competent, compassionate, wonderful winner.' Yet is it not one of the deepest longings of the human heart? It is hard to say that. We fear there may be something counterproductive about that kind of thinking; although, it does have a certain appeal doesn't it? Wise, competent, compassionate winner. Oh, those delicious sounds, those attributes pouring over me and permeating every molecule of me, like a magical perfume that makes princes and princesses out of frogs, angels out of sinners, ecstasy out of agony. Interestingly enough, both Plato and Maslow taught that the natural condition, the birthright of the human being is to become fully actualized, a flower in full blossom; but most of us get stuck in the bud stage. Breaking those threads of unhealthy conditioning that are preventing the bud from flowering is another way to conceptualize The Process.

MindFitness implies that we can do some things and then we will be better. Fitness carries with it the notion that we can meet the challenges of life better by being more fit. There is a sense of process about it, a feeling that we can start from where we are at and take one step, then another, and soon find ourselves immersed in an odyssey, a great story, our story—our own true story—The Story of how we become who we really are!

When it comes to MindFitness we are in the main dealing with people who are already rather functional. In fact, if you look at the kind of people who have the energy, curiosity, resources, etc. to show up for this type of training or read this kind of book, you might say that they (you) are already more functional than most. They (you) already know to some degree how your particular mind works. Our intention is to assist in the achievement of the next level of functionality including learning more about the way the mind works than we already know.

### Subclinical Symptoms

The NY Times Science section reports that subclinical symptoms (conforming to DSM IV criteria) afflict most of the population and are the next big opportunity for mental health practitioners. Lives can be ruined by subclinical symptoms. It seems obvious that effectively dealing with subclinical symptoms before they become clinical will reduce the nations health cost burden more than any other strategy we are aware of. But even more to the point of our focus here, subclinical symptoms dramatically reduce performance and quality of life. Therefore, reducing subclinical symptoms, like stress management, is fundamental to any Performance/Life Enhancement Program.

MindFitness implies the art and science of bringing about those conditions which produce the highest quality of consciousness for the longest periods of time. Part of the challenge is improving the capability to recognize when the consciousness is deteriorating and to reverse that trend at the earliest moment. The late, great mind/body physicist David Bohm was intrigued by Electro Dermal Response (EDR—a measure of skin conductance and emotional arousal) because it showed the approximately three second interval between stimulus and emotion (for example, the insult and the anger flash). Once the time is used up anger can become uncontrollable. He was also interested in EDR because he believed (as

Jung did) that true insight and creative imagery, is also felt. In fact, Bohm believed we need a word for feeling kinds of thoughts and invented the term 'felts'.

The work of Antonio Demasio, a leading neurophysiological researcher, also appears to support the idea that emotion plays an important role in cognition and consciousness. He reports that neurophysiological research is presently documenting that there is an emotional charge or valence to all ideas, thoughts and concepts even though most of us are not consciously aware of it. His work indicates that we think with our entire bodies, and that thought without emotion is not really possible. Paying close attention to what we are feeling and why is crucial to bringing our lives into balance. By the way, EDR is a type of biofeedback instrumentation that can help increase awareness of how we use thought and emotion to shift consciousness and how we can improve our abilities in this area.

For us peak performance refers to the specific ability of some athletes, business people, artists etc. to deliver their best when it really counts. It is a sometimes mysterious and astonishing timing and strategic capacity. For example, it is generally agreed that most elite athletes are fairly close in physical capability. Therefore, winning is a mind game requiring the ability to peak at the right moment when the competition is greatest. This specific peak performance phenomenon is a subset of the more comprehensive concept of performance enhancement. And performance enhancement is a subset of the even greater concept of Life Enhancement—Life Long Life Enhancement. Performance enhancement is only a part of what attracts us to the greater adventure of Life Enhancement. Doesn't it make sense to first enhance the quality of living and let performing flow naturally from that? Of course, practically, we have to do both simultaneously. Personally, I believe that the shortest path to improving even the special case of peak performance also lies in the development of what we prefer to call profound attention.

There are those who say that science, art and religion are separate things, but I say they only appear separate in relatively dysfunctional, conditioned states of consciousness. However, the word religion is such a huge problem for many that I struggle to find a better word for that quality of mind that feels a sense of sacredness about truth, beauty, the earth, at least some other beings. May we suggest that there is a science and an art of living life to the fullest and where they intersect is, for many of us, the Highest Value? It is like climbing Mt. Everest. Some describe it as a religious experience and some as a scientific one, but descriptions are just words. What is important is the actual climbing. That is what The Process project aspires to, the actual climbing.

## Consciousness and brainwaves

We have been throwing around the word consciousness quite freely here and I wish to clarify this most important term in keeping with our concern for using language more effectively. Consciousness has had many subtle meanings over the millennia. For us consciousness includes levels, qualities, dimensions of awareness of phenomena and involves a sense of self in that awareness process. It is this sense of self which becomes transformed as consciousness grows in intensity and quality. One of the rudimentary ways modern psychology measures consciousness incorporates electroencephalograph devices. We have categorized brainwave activities using these devices and divided consciousness into realms of activities crudely correlated with brainwave activity. For example, sleep and unconscious activity is in the category of slow waves, and processing information in standard, heavily conditioned waking consciousness tends to involve faster waves.

Julian Janes, a Harvard psychologist, suggests that we do not need to be conscious to do most of our human activities, and cognitive psychologists have supported that idea with their research. Wolinsky has presented a strong case implying that most of us most of the time are usually in a 'trance' state lacking a robust quality of consciousness. The implication is that we are living far below our potential because we go through much of our day to day activities in a kind of semiconscious twilight zone, and tragically we are not aware it is happening. Modern thinkers and ancient sages alike believe this trance-like, delusional condition is the source of most if not all human suffering. However, we will discuss how some fast wave activity is associated with trance like, dissociated 'waking sleep' states, while some slow wave activity is associated with highly awake, aware functional states.

## Risk vs Security

As we move deeper into the how of self-regulation, self-transformation, we have to confront the problem of risk and security. It would be nice if I could explain The Process in such a way as to always be comfortable and exciting, but that probably won't happen. Healthy change is often difficult, uncomfortable, entails risk, and may at times seem boring. Healthy change demands that we confront boredom and other unpleasant internal states we have been avoiding. How many are willing to risk breaking through the illusion of their current self-image and opening up to the unknown? Many say they do, but when the going gets tough the ranks thin out quickly.

For most, the search for freedom is just an escape from discomfort. As philosophers and psychologists have noted over the centuries, people seek pleasure and avoid pain. The path to real growth and insight; however, requires us to see discomfort and pain as a signal system and ally. Without pain receptors we could not even use our joints and muscles properly. As Buddha noted, pain and pleasure are just two aspects of the same process. We need this feedback system to navigate reality. We need to honor and accept both pleasure and pain as part of the process of growth. When we focus our intent on growth, pleasure and pain become our servants and not our masters. There can be no growth without change and change often involves an uncomfortable effort and expenditure of energy. Peak performers learn to incorporate appropriate discomfort into their regimen.

One of the hurdles we have to get over here, one of the heuristics we have to grasp, is the problem of paradox. If we are to play together at the highest levels we must realize that the best way to deal with the problem of insecurity is to realize that there is no actual security. Life itself may end next heartbeat. (S)he who lives each day as though it is the last tends to be aware in the moment and this quality of awareness breeds enthusiasm for life today, one day at a time. Paradoxically, people who live this way also tend to be the best planners. It is the beginning of a transformational perspective. The Process is not an escape to freedom, it is a rigorous expedition into the unknown that results in freedom.

## Finally

For twenty nine years I have been learning and teaching a watered down version of the principles discussed in this book to health care and educational professionals. I say a diluted version because that is usually what works with patients on the clinical, dysfunctional end of the human potential spectrum. Also, my work in applied psychophysiology, self-regulation/self-knowledge technology has had to fit into the economic realities of the medical/industrial establishment. So, in a real sense this book and the development of The Process is a kind of coming out of the closet. I have finally arrived at a place in life where circumstances permit- no, compel me to bring the less diluted version of this life work into practical reach of those who might find it useful. I expect this to be people who are at relatively functional stages of their lives and want to maximize their human potential and realize that stardom within the firmament of ones own mind/spirit is a natural birthright and breeds humility, fulfillment, unfoldment and compassion. There are both scientists and mystics who say, 'we are in every sense star stuff...and love is the wind beneath our wings.'

# Chapter 1

# Mindfitness and Self-Regulation of Brain Waves

We begin our story about The Process with several chapters on neurofeedback because the present form of The Process took shape in conjunction with the emergence of this new technology and has been heavily influenced by it. This book, however, is not primarily about the virtues of EEG Biofeedback. It is about The Process we are all going through as we strive to reach as much as we can of our human potential before death catches us. However, EEG (neurofeedback) has and is playing an important role in The Process at the present, as it inspires our own and thousands of other journeys of self-discovery. There are many criticisms of this phenomenon, as there have been of all technological breakthroughs. We believe, however, that the power of this technology is far greater than most realize, and a peculiar confluence of events has prevented most people from becoming aware of the potential and accessibility of this amazing self-knowledge tool (especially in so much as it relates to performance and life enhancement, since clinical applications are already receiving considerable attention).

It is time that we make an effort to unfold the incredible story of at least some of those who are providing and receiving benefits from neurofeedback training. Psychology Today printed an article on neurofeedback entitled 'Wired For Miracles?' because sometimes 'miracles' seem to accompany the use of NFB. In fact one of the early, and most successful clinics has a sign on the wall that says 'expect miracles.' Practitioners report that clients are giving up addictions, overcoming chronic depression and anxiety, rediscovering the depth of their relationships, losing weight, taking up healthier habits, and experiencing a kind of 'non—specific' happiness in the same way that they used to experience non—specific anxiety.

## A Dangerous Obsession

He had reached an advanced stage of anorexia. As a 54 year old construction worker, he was normally 6' and a well muscled 155 lbs. At the beginning of therapy he was 118 lbs., eyes sunken, somewhat manic, claiming his diet of mostly lettuce was making him high and filling him with energy. He was almost completely isolated as his behavior had destroyed his marriage and alienated him from his friends. He had not worked for five years at his trade as he was on disability. He was almost broke even though he earned between sixty and one hundred thousand per year when he was working. He was obsessed with a well known cult which had counseled him to distance himself from his family, and against seeking therapeutic help. He had invested over $200,000.00, virtually his life savings, in the cults system of 'therapy and enlightenment.'

He discussed the possibility of suicide on several occasions in the beginning and was experiencing many stress related disorders including sleeplessness, irritability, hyperactivity, intense loneliness, and much obsessive/compulsive symptomology including going over and over often unimportant details. He fluctuated between overtly aggressive, hyper behavior as he tried to convert people to his ideas, and passively aggressive behavior when individuals attempted to establish relationship with him. A strong concern at the beginning of therapy was that irreversible organ damage might have already occurred because of his complexion, gaunt, haunted appearance and the obviously massive loss of muscle tissue, even though he continued to exercise vigorously (as is the case with many anorexics). Biofeedback therapy was for him a desperate last resort.

Within three weeks of beginning neurofeedback training (adjunctive to counseling) his demeanor had changed remarkably, he had begun to gain weight and he entered enthusiastically into the life rebuilding process. He began sleeping better, felt much calmer and more optimistic, less lonely and isolated. He began to form new relationships and he was opening up and talking to people in ways that were impossible before. He wanted to report on his 'Love Stories'. An interesting example follows: He would go to playgrounds and sit and watch children play. This made him feel so happy at times that he would weep. This appears to be healthy abreactive phenomena happening hours or days after actual neurofeedback training. People he met or had known before seemed to be easier to be with. He saw that he had changed and was giving others the chance to be affectionate and not blocking them with his rigidity, restlessness and passive aggression. He began to eat a more balanced diet and gained weight reaching 150 lbs. within the first year.

Although he had studied 'meditation' extensively, he almost never did it because he felt it was boring and a waste of time. It was suggested that he forget about meditation as he knew it and just do the EEG work. After the first week he had learned enough to do his version of the 'EEG work' without hooking up. He said that now instead of forcing himself to meditate he looks for opportunities to sit and simply make his alpha. He reports surprising benefits like those he had hoped to receive from meditation are flowing from these alpha sessions. He realizes now that what he had thought was meditation was not, because he was merely sitting still and straining to concentrate, which is why it was boring, unpleasant and flat.

He has since obtained his own EEG home trainer and continues a remarkable transformation of life style. Interestingly, at first he didn't realize how important the EEG work was. Like many clients he discounted the neurotherapy and looked for other things to attribute his improvement to. This is common and frustrating for NFB practitioners. During the neurofeedback training he constantly wanted to talk.

Instead, he was encouraged to train first and discuss later. The results spoke for themselves.

About nineteen months after he began neurofeedback therapy, he looked quite fit for his 56 years, his complexion was good and his personality, even his voice seemed remarkably changed. He was working full time and furthering his education pursuant to changing his profession. A follow up revealed that at age 60 he was continuing to work (maybe too hard) and he reports that he has solved his economic problems; and the combination of his working and investing will generate a considerable net worth within a relatively short time. He is engaged and intends to marry this year. He continues in the construction business and is unusually fit for his age. He believes neurofeedback and the counseling that accompanied it is responsible for saving and assisting him in transforming the quality of his life.

## Success Stories Stimulate Research Interests

It all seems too good to be true, that just sitting in front of a computer screen and training brainwaves can have a powerful effect on some lives. Many are properly skeptical when they first hear about it. And, indeed, after doing brain wave training with thousands of people over almost thirty years, it seems clear that NFB is adjunctive to a quality learning program when applied to Performance, Life Enhancement, and subclinical symptoms. NFB is definitely adjunctive to quality therapy when applied to clinical symptoms. An issue that research is struggling to determine is what is the magnitude of synergism when quality learning or therapy and NFB are combined? And is it possible that the combination is so powerful that it cannot even be measured using traditional measurement strategies? Furthermore, is this concept of self-regulation of the brain really any more amazing or less natural than taking a pill in order to feel better?

Our conditioning tends to make us accepting of older, established technologies and fearful of emerging technologies. After all, the unknown is scary, our hopes have often turned out to be ill founded. Our educational system has not prepared us well for weeding out the true from the false. The medical/industrial establishment is economically addicted to the disease model, and the scientific system presently in place seems tragically slow when it comes to demonstrating the value of the wellness model and non-patentable, cost saving alternative health care strategies and therapies.

At this point in time a lot of the healing attributed to neurofeedback is only documented at the clinical level. There has been quite a bit of research at the institutional level, but far less than the results of the existing research indicates there should be. The funding is not there yet, but the pressure is mounting as new research comes in and clinical evidence continues to mount. For example, a school in a Yonkers ghetto neighborhood, the Enrico Fermi Center for the Performing Arts, has just finished a three year experimental program developed and implemented by Dr. Mary Jo Sabo and Linda Vargara with sixty hyperactive LD/ADD 'problem' students. The program is reported to have saved $500,000 in special education services. It is expected that as many as twenty-two schools in the district will eventually be offering neurofeedback services. This kind of institutional movement is harder to ignore than individual case studies coming mostly from middle class families. Although, laboratory science and technology are inextricably related, technology tends to develop largely in the market place 'where the rubber meets the road' ( in this case by clinicians and educators). Technology developed in the field often precedes technology developed in the lab.

It seems to us that the responsible thing to do is to see to it that at least a few of the thousands of neurofeedback success stories be told. There is resistance on the part of the medical/industrial establishment to provide reasonable support for self-regulation research. Perhaps the professional community and the public require more education before the electorate will demand correction of this tragic blindness. The lack of research funding for biofeedback, alternative medicine and the wellness-prevention model has forced clinicians to develop the field well ahead of the traditional research establishment. More than thirty years ago studies were done indicating that delivery of appropriate, timely mental health services reduces long term health costs more than practically any other intervention.

We assert the evidence suggests that adding quality biofeedback to those therapies for which it is indicated makes most of those same therapies at least twice as efficient, cutting health care costs by an estimated additional fifty percent. In fact, some biofeedback practitioners (by measuring the decrease of frequency and amplitude of symptoms against time elapsed) report that appropriately delivered biofeedback services have improved the effectiveness of some therapies by as much as ten times...1000%! So, why does this resistance to such a promising new science prevail? Where does it come from?

We have found that the majority of biofeedback clinicians and researchers are among the most responsible professionals in the entire healthcare system. Although the pressure to turn out more research is unrelenting, most newcomers are surprised to find out that there have already been thousands of studies (largely funded out of the pockets of the clinicians themselves). Yet the establishment continues to call for multi-million dollar, large scale, double-blind studies. In a medical environment as litigious as ours, even Bill Gates would be bankrupted by the kinds of law suits engendered by giving false feedback to patients over a prolonged period. In addition, new human subject ethical and legal research standards forbid it.

In fact, double-blind studies might be impossible because the nature of the biofeedback instruments would probably cause all but the dumbest of patients to realize that something was amiss. Imagine flying an airplane (your body) upside down and straight towards a mountain with all of your senses intact but your instruments say you are right side up and there is no mountain there. Imagine sitting in front of an EMG (muscle feedback instrument) and tensing and relaxing your muscles and the instrument shows the opposite of your senses or no change at all. Isn't that idea ridiculous?

That's what trying to give false feedback is like. That's part of the reason why traditional double-blind drug research models are inappropriate, probably impossible, for testing the effectiveness of instrument assisted self-regulation techniques. That said, there has been at least one quality false feedback study (Lubar, et al) and it indicates that biofeedback is certainly not a placebo. And of course, scientists can be extremely clever at coming up with ways to establish control groups and prove effectiveness or lack of it. We just have to give them reasonable support.

Furthermore, established medicine commonly supports the development and practice of techniques and therapies in the clinic and operating room etc., long before acceptable studies have been done. Often what works for one doctor is quickly absorbed and practiced by others. Why this double standard? The age of large scale institutional medicine, with its requirements for extensive controlled studies on all emerging treatments, is relatively new and does not always provide the most efficient, nor effective healthcare delivery system. Demographics show that our current system is vastly more expensive than other systems that deliver the same or better national health results. We can do much better. And biofeedback assisted self-regulation training is one of the greatest imaginable opportunities, perhaps even the key to a sea change in our system.

The research (often animal experimentation) required to qualify the average drug for release into the marketplace costs over 100 million dollars; and yet the list of devastating, sometimes fatal side effects of many of these drugs grows longer every day. Yet we in biofeedback have helped hundreds of thousands of people, often with no other place to turn, and there are few if any documented cases of harm done. Although neurofeedback is considered relatively new by most (it is actually old by biofeedback standards) and is believed by some to be the most powerful of all forms of biofeedback, the documented, harmful side effects of services delivered by well trained practitioners are to our knowledge also minimal.

As of this writing, we are not aware of a single dollar ever paid out in a malpractice judgment because of damage caused from biofeedback training.

Think about that! Hundreds of millions of dollars of biofeedback services of one kind or another have been delivered since at least 1948, and not a dollar paid out in a malpractice judgment! Hello??? Is any body listening? What more do we have to do? Is there anything else in healthcare that has a cost benefit ratio that is better? We would be so delighted to find out what it is so we could celebrate and demonstrate how integrating biofeedback would improve its cost/benefit even further, probably much further. By the way, it is inevitable that there will be some kind of a malpractice settlement some time, maybe soon; but we believe biofeedback will continue to have one of the greatest cost/benefit and injury/benefit ratios of any healthcare/educational strategy ever.

Most are not aware of the quality of the research and researchers that have pioneered the development of neurofeedback. A representative list of highly credentialed and talented researchers would include but not be limited to: Margaret Ayers, Tom Budzynski, Steve Fahrion, Les Fehmi, Elmer Green, Joe Kamiya, Paul Kulkosky, Michael Linden, Joel and Judith Lubar, Thom Mulholland, Pat Norris, Sigfried and Sue Othmer, Eugene Peniston, Ferdinand Poirer, Barry Sterman, Charles Stroebel, Paul Swingle, Michael Tansey, Dale Walters and many other well established scientists who have been actively researching the field, some of them for over thirty years.

Their findings are empirical. These are not dreamers and schemers on the fringe of modern alternative medicine. For example, Lubar has already done several substantial controlled studies, and some of Peniston's studies have been published in the most refereed journals in their respective fields. Similar claims could be made for all of the others mentioned and many others not mentioned.

In the early seventies I was invited to address a group of about 125 Army psychologists on the subject of brainwave biofeedback in Washington DC. I had already worked out a hypothetical neurofeedback model which was getting some attention. Since I had been told these psychologists knew almost nothing about this exciting new area, I enthusiastically expounded for over an hour. After the talk, a group of about a dozen came up to the podium and continued asking questions. I remarked that the surprising depth of the questions indicated that some of them knew a lot more than I had expected. One of the officers then volunteered that there had already been about a hundred and twenty government studies of brain wave biofeedback and around sixty were still top secret. The Soviet Union had also done a number of military neurofeedback studies. One of the astronauts who went to the moon told me that neurofeedback training was part of the NASA program. There is ongoing research in the use of neurofeedback to enhance pilot performance, and even research, into the use of self-regulation of brainwaves and other physical parameters to control equipment such as airplanes, boats, musical instruments etc.

The dynamics of the marketplace frequently works against innovation if it is perceived as threatening the bottom line. A recent release by the FDA indicates that a major drug company had been giving money to one of the most important national parental support groups for parents with ADD children. That same support group has been discouraging their members from trying neurofeedback therapy with their children.` We visited a well known biofeedback clinic in Los Angeles and had a discussion with a mother who was a former head of the Los Angeles Chapter of this national group. Both she and her son had been receiving neurofeedback training for ADHD and had experienced outstanding results. She humbly acknowledged her previous activities involving the discouragement of neurofeedback among fellow members and related that she was sorry she had not investigated more carefully. She could have saved herself and her son years of misery.

It seems too cynical to contemplate, but the question should at least be asked. Is it possible that some drug company executives are afraid that neurofeedback could cut into their enormous profits? Having taught a course in the social-psychology of White Collar Crime at the University of Arizona, I am only too well aware of how some drug companies have engaged in illegal activities to manipulate the marketplace and willfully mislead the FDA in the past. All scientists that we know agree that the drug companies are destined to continue to be some of the most successful businesses on earth indefinitely into the future. It would be good for the companies and society if they would support self- regulation technologies, especially so since most scientists believe these technologies enhance the effectiveness of drugs, as well as the health and longevity of the patient (the very people who are likely to buy more and more drugs as they grow older no matter how healthy they are).

There are many forces at work in the marketplace of ideas and medical technologies. Although neurofeedback cannot be easily pigeonholed as a medical technology, it overlaps much of what takes place in that arena. Neurofeedback is difficult to categorize because it brings together mind and body in its approach to recovery and healing, and crosses many fields in the process. It stands for a new way of seeing the world and it is amazingly compatible with the 'new science' and the perspective growing out of psychology, quantum physics, chaos theory, microbiology, and neuroscience over the last century. It is no mistake that many prominent contributors to the field including but not limited to Green, Stroebel, Fehmi, Othmer, etc. have a strong physics background.

## A Cancer Case

She was a seventy seven year old woman with a diagnosis of multiple myeloma (bone cancer) and intestinal cancer. Her oncologist estimated that she would live between four months to one year. She was being treated by first rate doctors at Swedish hospital in Seattle, which is probably one of the best hospitals in the US. Doctors developed a treatment plan including a resection, a relatively small amount of radiation, and a mild form of chemotherapy in order to make her more comfortable.

She was trained in neurofeedback on a CapScan for two 1-hour alpha-theta sessions per day for ten days and after that she continued on her own using her 'internal instrumentation'. Approximately three months later we checked her 'calibration' to see if the two hour per day practice of her

'Alpha Meditation' without equipment was delivering the same amplitude and per cent time of alpha and theta as when she was working with the equipment. She was right on the money, producing about 35 uV of alpha approximately 80% of the time. She then received six to ten 1-hour booster sessions per year for several years. She has been retested several times and clearly demonstrates that she is maintaining, even increasing her ability to produce alpha without the feedback equipment. She also loves the attention and the assurance that she is on track.

Frankly, when we began the neurotherapy it was not because we thought it might have a beneficial effect on her immune system. Actually, it was in order to deeply relax her central nervous system and to assist her in getting a handle on mind states that would enable her to deal with the distress of dying. We hoped she would develop her meditation skills to a level which would help her reduce her pain and her need for mind numbing medications, thereby allowing her to enjoy her large family more and to enter the final stage of life with as much mindfulness as possible. One of the inspirations that led to this strategy is the work of John Cabot—Zinn with end stage cancer and chronic pain patients in Boston.

She says the training has helped her handle the drugs and the pain better, and indeed her children have been comforted and inspired by her amazingly cheerful, wise, clear headed and compassionate behavior in the face of her illness. In fact, they report that she seems happier and more mentally alert than she has been in some years. However, as of this writing this case has taken an exceptional turn. She was able to make a trip to the East Coast fifteen months after the diagnosis. Twenty four months after her diagnosis her oncologist stated that he had never seen this type of cancer become so inactive and relatively pain free in a patient who was by that time 79 years old. He avoided using the term remission.

At the time of the diagnosis the patient was mostly confined to a wheel chair. Four years later she was walking up and down stairs and using a cane. She is cheerful and seems remarkably grateful for her relatively good health and active life. She makes at least two air trips a year to stay with her children and her oncologist officially declared her cancer in remission. He said he had not seen this happen before in a patient of her age (at that time almost 81). A follow up indicates she is still in remission (at 85 years old). I have read that there have been less than fifty documented cases of remission of multiple myeloma in the United States in this century.

Stories like these abound. These stories in particular are a consequence of what we call alpha/theta (low frequency) neurofeedback training as differentiated from SMR/beta (high frequency) training. The enhancement of beta and reduction of theta frequencies is often adjunctively utilized with ADHD, Learning Disabilities, Traumatic Brain Injury, Epilepsy, and a growing list of clinical applications. The work of Joel Lubar documents a 60%-70% success rate in the reduction or remission of symptoms associated with ADHD. Henry Catarazzo has reported similar findings. Michael Linden has two studies which indicate the use of neurofeedback increases IQ (we think they score better on IQ tests because they can take a test better). Much more research is underway and if this is the incredible new frontier we believe it to be, will continue through the 21st century and beyond. Most traditional scientists continue to consider clinical neurofeedback experimental (except for relaxation and educational applications). Its use for 'relaxation and education' has grown enormously in the last ten years.

There has been a great deal of work with alpha-theta frequencies especially in the field of Alcoholism and Post Traumatic Stress Disorder. Eugene Peniston and Paul Kulkosky reviewed the work of Elmer Green on States of Consciousness and EEG and experimented on a protocol for alcoholics. The results of their study were astonishing and were published in the most refereed journal in the field, the Journal of Alcoholism, Clinical and Experimental Research. Seventy percent of the subjects who went through the experimental protocol were still sober four years later. By training certain brainwave frequencies they were able to help hard-core alcoholics overcome their addictions. A ten year follow up indicated that all but two were still not using alcohol (one died and one could not be found). With prisons full of addicted individuals and a society staggering under the overwhelming toll that addictive behavior is taking, their break-through study holds great promise for the field of addictions. Several follow up studies have been done including one replication. We have heard that a large replication is planned.

Peniston and Kulkosky have also used this protocol successfully in controlled studies with Vietnam Vets suffering with Post Traumatic Stress Disorder (PTSD). Some of the disorders for which this kind of training has been used adjunctively include, but are not limited to: Multiple Personality Disorder, Depression, General Anxiety Disorder, Pain Management, Fibromyalgia, and Chronic Fatigue Syndrome. The success of neurofeedback continues to confirm the growing perspective that central nervous system therapies may play as the mind-body connection emerges as a central issue in the future of healthcare. This wellness, 'sea change' model is perceived, we think erroneously so, as threatening to some aspects of the medical/industrial establishment, because they're thinking has not yet shifted from the outmoded Cartesian model of healthcare. In actuality, there are incredible opportunities for those innovative, coherently managed corporations that already have the resources and delivery systems in place. Getting on board with self-regulation techniques and technology will be a win-win for those organizations able to meet the challenge.

## Another neuro-immune anomaly?

Following is another case history from one of the biggest rehabilitation hospitals in the US. A female meningenoma patient developed a pea-sized tumor which gradually grew to the size of a grape and then a plum. She underwent brain surgery and began rehabilitation because of neurological problems caused by the surgery. After several years the tumor reappeared and progressed to about the size of a plum again. She underwent another surgery. A number of years later the process repeated itself. The period of the three operations covered about fifteen years.

Sadly, the tumor reappeared for the fourth time and grew again to about the size of a grape and the patient was sent to the neurofeedback therapists at the hospital so that they could do the standard Traumatic Brain Injury protocol with her. They were hoping to improve her social skills and ability to initiate an action. The NFB therapists primarily employed a high frequency (beta) strategy with theta inhibit over the frontal lobes. They also did about three months of beta training over the site of the tumor. When they sent her for her pre op exam the neurologist was amazed to see that the tumor growth had apparently stopped.

This brought great relief because both the neurologist and the surgeon did not believe she would survive another operation; and if she did survive it they were sure she would be severely neurologically impaired. The neurologist said that they would look at her again in a year. Her family was euphoric because they had feared the worst. As of this writing she is stable and her next exam should be in about six months. So far, so good.

The trouble started when her mother began inquiring into what had been done this time that might have caused a better outcome. When she found out that the only thing different was the NFB she speculated that the NFB might be causing changes that had slowed the tumor growth and that continued NFB might even reduce tumor size. Naturally, she petitioned the neurologist and neurosurgeon to continue NFB with the patient. The neurologist asked the NFB therapist to do a literature search to see if anything like this had been reported and when it was clear that it had not he said that the whole idea was too absurd and in any case it was too experimental so he ordered NFB therapy terminated.

The mother was furious but unable to persuade them to change their minds. The neuro surgeon would not even return the therapist's phone calls. There was so much resistance by the administration (neurologist and neurosurgeon) that the NFB therapists felt their jobs were in jeopardy. In fact, because of this episode and other similar conflicts, the neuropsychologist who set up and ran the entire NFB operation (at considerable profit to the hospital) has left and established a private practice nearby. There was apparently tremendous anger over the idea that the NFB therapists had suggested that NFB might have contributed to the stabilization of (or in any way effected) the tumor growth. To emphasize their point all tumor patients at the hospital are prohibited from NFB regardless of the reason (i.e., relaxation, education, rehabilitation, cognitive dysfunction, stroke, etc.). The mother is trying to find a way to continue NFB. It will be interesting to see what happens to the tumor and the patient from here on out.

## Ray's Story

"As a concerned parent, I have spent 33 years trying many kinds of therapy for my brain damaged daughter, Laura. I seem to have finally found something that's helping her mental development. For the first time, I'm seeing real progress. A process called EEG Biofeedback Training seems to be normalizing her brainwaves to the point where she's becoming teachable. This process appears to be a major breakthrough and it could portend a whole new ball game in educating certain types of mentally handicapped individuals. While I'm still not a total believer, it looks very promising.

Shortly after Laura's birth, she was diagnosed as having cerebral palsy and brain damage. Physical rehabilitation specialists helped her learn to walk. She learned to run by herself. Speech therapists helped her learn to talk. Now she talks too well, or rather too much. With lots of help from some marvelous doctors and therapists plus her great spirit, she gradually overcame many of her physical disabilities. Today her physical development is far ahead of her mental development. Since modern medicine hasn't yet learned how to stimulate brain growth or jump-start neurons, I looked for an alternative.

I found EEG Biofeedback Training. It's fairly new, hence its use is relatively uncommon. NASA uses it to train pilots and astronauts. Psychologists are beginning to use it to treat ADHD. Within the past several months it has enabled her to reduce her distractibility about 80%. It seems to have jump-started her cognitive processes, perhaps her neurons. I think 'jump-start' is an appropriate metaphor since it implies a threshold.

Now Laura is planning and organizing her time, reading more and more each day and even reading script. She understands years and months fairly well, weeks and days not as well. She is beginning to understand the hour hand of a clock. The minute hand and the concept of minute is still too abstract for her. Several people have remarked that her self-esteem and self-confidence appear to have improved this past year. Although her distractibility is way down, her ability to concentrate is still poor in many areas. It's premature to go into detail, but it appears that certain of the scores on the neuropsychological tests that comprise what's known as IQ may well have improved. Naturally, my own bias must be considered.

One Year Later: Today, her clinician and I looked with amazement at the graphical performance summary of one of her recent sessions. He said to me, "These brainwave characteristics are no longer any different from yours or mine." More important to me is the fact that her ADHD symptoms are gone! And without the use of any medication! Her EEG Biofeedback Training worked!

Laura's distractibility is no longer a problem. Her attention span is now normal and she can concentrate quite adequately. She has become more composed, responsible, and self-reliant. She prepares her lunch before going to bed, awakens between five and six a.m. and goes to work eagerly and happily each day.

Laura is no longer "caught up in herself'" but is increasingly aware and thoughtful of others, more comfortable in social situations, and more at ease with strangers. Her delightful personality promises to serve her well in her continuing social/behavioral development. Although she is still exuberant and enthusiastic much of the time, significantly, her hyperactivity is gone. With ADD/ADHD no longer a limiting factor, it has become possible for me to observe other neurological factors taking on more prominent roles. These were previously not apparent, having been masked by her hyperactivity. While she still has a long way to go, Laura now behaves more like a 33 year old than she did several months ago."

Last month Ray called me and told me that Laura's therapists had decided that she could now live on her own. Laura now works for two companies and is considered a well-liked and valuable employee.

## The Inner Game

Although stories such as this are common, neurofeedback has more to offer than just remediation of existing disorders. Utilizing this technology to improve healthy people is another possibility that neurofeedback has opened us to. The following account offers insight into changes that are occurring as we attempt to improve the performance of a PGA golf professional utilizing this technology. Only in this instance we are using alpha training in conjunction with methods employed in The Process.

"I cannot begin to explain to others how much better my lifestyle has become. Not only has it tremendously improved my mental skills and outlook relative to my golf, but also my everyday dealings with business and personal family life as well. As you know, but others may not, I am a golf professional with a very strong entrepreneurial and corporate background. My initial intentions were to enhance my focus and concentration during tournament golf. In a very short period of time not only did we accomplish this, but also improved other areas necessary to achieve and maintain peak performance. My scores have dropped considerably and my overall demeanor has improved tremendously.

We were able to enhance my ability to utilize my intuitive skills more instinctively and to be able to control my EMG during the most crucial moments. This not only allowed me to be calm during anxious moments but also to recover from trouble in a quick and calm fashion. It has taught me to understand more about my ability and myself, and at the same time how not to get in the way of myself.

As well, my personal life has always been good, but now it's even better. It's opened my eyes to things that we take for granted and has brought my family even closer together by better communication. We were able to increase my stamina along with greater mental and physical conditioning.

My overall experience has been phenomenal and I continue to look forward as we progress further into the future."

Another golf professional writes: "I am writing to thank you for your help when I came to you seeking advice regarding what could be done to reduce levels of anger and stress surrounding my golf game. As a professional golfer I subject myself to a great deal of performance pressure. My standards are very high and I can anger easily when I feel I am not achieving those high standards.

Your program of neurofeedback training has been instrumental in reducing the levels of anxiety and frustration I experience on the golf course. The neurofeedback work is especially effective in helping me find a calm state of mind where I can relax and focus my energies more efficiently. It has been a revelation to discover just how much a state of relaxation can enhance one's overall enjoyment and consequently, one's levels of performance."

**Life Long Life Enhancement Learning**

Applications of neurofeedback in the areas of performance enhancement, subclinical symptoms, education and meditation may offer even greater possibilities than clinical therapies, because the numbers of potential beneficiaries are higher, and assisting functional people in becoming more capable may produce more overall benefits to society. Some of the researchers and practitioners who have made or are making contributions in the area of EEG and performance enhancement include but are not limited to: Tom Budzynski, Adam Crane, Les Fehmi, Steve Frederico, Elmer Green, Jim Hardt, Joe Kamiya, Joel and Judith Lubar, Richard Patton, Sigfried and Sue Othmer, Mary Jo Sabo, Richard Soutar, Barry Sterman, Charles, Stroebel, Sue Wilson, Anna Wise and dozens of others.

As we mentioned previously, Elmer Green, a former NASA scientist became interested in the relationships between EEG biofeedback, altered states of consciousness, and quantum physics. Dr. Green discovered extraordinary correlation's with the work of many meditation 'masters' including the Indian yogi Patanjali who wrote at length 2500 years ago on the states and potentials of human consciousness, and how to enhance them. Attending training programs developed by Elmer Green and his team at the Menninger Foundation inspired many of the most creative people in neurofeedback. Eugene Peniston reported that while doing alpha/theta training during a Menninger program supervised by Dale Walters, he had a 'theta image' of an egg with a brain wave pattern flowing through it. From this archetypal flash he began to design his now famous research on neurofeedback and alcohol addiction.

One of the most interesting and some believe beneficial phenomena reported by those integrating meditation (and usually many hours of alpha/theta training) are insights into the nature and fear of dying. Some have reported archetypal 'near death' imagery similar to those described in clinical near death consciousness research. We have personally experienced, and many of our clients have reported, these extremely difficult to describe visions or 'mind journeys'. Research documents that those who genuinely go through these kinds of experiences usually find their lives changing for the better in the sense that their attitude and energy seems to be much more upbeat, and strangely their fear of death seems to be decreased. Other NFB clinicians who have reported similar phenomena also usually believe alpha/theta training plays a key role.

From the early seventies on there were at least a handful of EEG biofeedback practitioners who believed that NFB and particularly alpha/theta training could be used to enhance traditional psychological, transpersonal psychological, and creative development in a large percentage of the population. Some of those included Adam Crane, Joe Kamiya, Les Fehmi, Elmer Green, Jim Hart, Charles Stroebel, Dale Walters, and others. The application of neurofeedback to Performance and Life Enhancement is gaining wide acceptance, especially by scientists and practitioners who have lots of NFB experience.

From the beginning the biofeedback community took a direct approach to investigating the relationships of brainwaves and performance enhancement. Researchers simply sought out as many gifted individuals as they could and measured their EEG patterns. Some of those studied included Zen, Yoga and Martial Arts Masters, and high achievers in various fields including scientists, musicians, writers, athletes, doctors, business people, healers, shamans and others. For example, Kasamatsu et al in the late 50's and early 60's found extremely high amplitudes of alpha and theta waves in Zen monks during meditation. Maxwell Cade traveled the world measuring the EEG patterns of people reputed to be self-actualized or 'enlightened'. He believed he found a common pattern rich in alpha and healthy or creative theta. Anna Wise has continued his work. She emphasizes as we do that EEG work is best thought of as adjunctive to the psycho-spiritual growth process leading to what Maslow termed actualization.

One of the reasons this way of working is so appealing is that it is a modern 'Relationship Technology' and a relatively western approach to classic, time honored consciousness enhancing strategies. Neurofeedback seems to many of us an efficient and compassionate strategy for discovering ones own unique way to meditation. To us NFB is a wonderful adjunctive assist for heuristically growing through those natural stages of unfoldment we call The Process.

One of the most difficult, yet critically important aspects of The Process and NFB relates to the problem of conditioning. Krishnamurti, Bohm, Jung, Campbell and literally hundreds of master class 'artists of living' and teachers, both ancient and modern, have pointed out that wrong cultural conditioning causes thinking to run untrue, to become incoherent. It is as though a computer with a faulty program is using that program to continuously create more flawed programs as well as distorting the senses. Insight and much enhanced perception can begin to fix the bugs in the program. One of the effects of NFB is that it seems to reduce at least the influence of much of this wrong conditioning (personal and cultural programming). This allows thinking to begin to run truer, more coherently. An important goal of this kind of work is to assist people in having their own original insights. Therefore, describing the experiences that others have gone through can be counterproductive, because the learner may project this imagery, effectively blocking his own original experiences. However, we feel obliged to go ahead with some descriptions so that the reader can get a feel for the potential in this technology and this way of learning.

For instance, it is common for clients to smile as they do alpha training. They often describe the experience as relaxing and happy. After several sessions some find themselves opening up to strangers and losing their performance anxiety so they can speak before groups more effectively. Just as nonspecific (no known reason) anxiety is a common symptom, so many of our alpha NFB clients report nonspecific happiness. Others experience a 'windshield wiper effect' in which things look clearer and colors seem brighter. Enhanced sensory acuity (especially hearing) is common. As one client said, 'Its as if I have found the color control on the black and white TV of my life.' We and others have begun referring to these kinds of effects as 'increased dimensionality.' Although, we need to find a way to nail this down with quality research, it seems clear to us that there is an increase of what Daniel Goleman and others are calling 'Emotional Intelligence' (EQ). Some clients will actually say they feel their 'heart opening up'. For many, brain and heart seem to integrate in a more healthful manner. Some researchers are presenting evidence that there are physiological correlates of this enhanced brain/heart relationship as well.

It's not all fun. True growth usually requires changes that are difficult. As Joseph Campbell discovered in his studies of mythical heroic journeys, we all have 'dark nights of the soul.' Probably, all of us have repressed fear material buried in the unconscious or subconscious. Research psychologists like Joseph LeDoux suggest physiological mechanisms by which we condition ourselves to experience fear without realizing we have done it, and then walk around trying to subconsciously cope with it. We often have more in the closet then we initially realize. For healthy growth to happen we must effectively deal with these fears. If we do not, they will continue to corrupt the quality of our moment to moment consciousness and sabotage attempts to improve our lives. In order for most of us to enhance the creativity and dimensionality of our lives without using drugs or working to exhaustion, or taking irrational risks, we must learn to relax and quiet the mind, including the emotions.

It is common for individuals who are going through the process of learning quality meditation to experience what we call 'the unstressing phenomenon'. They will often need to sleep more for awhile. We view this as healthy because the average American is chronically sleep deprived, and because sleep is an efficient way to enhance both mental and physical healing. Dream life, including nightmares, may become more vivid. Nervous or 'psychic' energy may build, producing a restless hunger to make things happen. All of these phenomena are characteristic of the creative process.

As peace, awareness, and gratitude for whom one is and what one has increases, so does the insight that improving the status quo is possible. This awareness breeds the hunger, skill, and resources necessary to make that change happen. This aspect of The Process (with or without NFB) may be experienced as a kind of 'dying' to the old, allowing the new to be born. Fear of this part of the Process holds many back. We want change to be easy and pain free. Letting go is an arduous aspect of self-development and transformation. It requires work, patience, perseverance, and strong intent. Goals must be clear and motives as pure as we can make them. A good trainer or coach can provide timely assurance and guidance. However, it is necessary for the one teaching The Process to be living it as well. 'Intellectual understanding' of these principles is possible by those who are unable to do a good job of applying them within their own lives. We find the challenge of learning to walk the talk to be both exhilarating and humbling.

This is not to say, however, that The Process absolutely requires a guide or coach. The Process has an archetypal pattern of its own. Application of the principles inherent in The Process must produce a substantial increase in self-knowledge. After all, learning to learn for oneself is of the essence. The vision we hold is that it is possible for mistakes to be reduced and the learning curve steepened by timely, competent assistance. Indeed, most of us immersed in The Process cannot resist trying to reach out to others who are interested and motivated. Why not? It is such a fun way to live.

# Chapter 2

# What Is Neurofeedback?

It is amusing how often clients will ask this question even while they are manipulating their own brain waves through NFB. Saying precisely and completely what NFB is challenges even those of us who are expert. Taking a crack at it, we could say that using NFB equipment can immensely increase a client's awareness of certain brain wave activity in real time, giving him the information he needs to 'control' those brain waves. This process happens as he becomes sensitive to internal signals which had hitherto been below the threshold of his awareness. When the client becomes sensitive enough to these internal signals, (s)he no longer needs the neurofeedback instrumentation in order to control these same brain waves. Having said that much, we realize that most readers will need a bit more assistance in understanding the way this extraordinary self-knowledge technology works, because neurofeedback (NFB) is so new that many of the ideas it rests upon are not yet commonly understood. There is little street vocabulary for super learning and performance enhancement, much less neurofeedback and the emerging field of sub-clinical symptoms. Those of us immersed in this field find ourselves inventing new words, and using old ones in new ways, in order to more effectively communicate the nuances and concepts that we are continuously grappling with.

Exploring the brain together should make things clearer. Scientific knowledge of how the brain works is growing all the time, and research into the nature of consciousness has become one of the most important scientific frontiers. Sections of the brain have been categorized according to location and function, but far more is unknown than is known. We know that memory is a function of several systems working together, but just how the phenomenon of memory is produced is quite mysterious. We know where the basic speech centers are as well as the location of vision processing, but we are still unraveling the mystery of how attention works.

In order to achieve the goals of this book it is probably necessary to briefly discuss the cortex and the limbic system. The cerebral cortex is the outermost layer of the brain and from an evolutionary point of view the most recent development. It is the area where most of our conscious thinking takes place. Many believe that the evolutionary youth of the cerebral cortex may account for its imperfections and many of the problems (as well as the triumphs) of humanity. The limbic system is much older and located near the center of the brain. It seems to be important in dealing with feelings, emotions, moods and memory. It also influences the rest of the body through a network of glands known as the endocrine system. One of the functions of the endocrine system is to trigger the fight or flight response when we perceive danger or sometimes just a change. The Thalamus sits at the top of the spinal column sorting information to different parts of the brain as it arrives, and it appears to be instrumental in generating electrical oscillations or brain waves which in turn influence cortical function. It is central to attention processes and the overall coordination of the brain.

Brainwaves are electrical patterns generated by brain cells (neurons) and other structures in the brain. Electrochemical processes in each neuron produce a tiny electrical charge. As more of these neurons produce these minute electrical charges there is an increase in electrical power (amplitude). Some neuroscientists say that it's as though each of these neurons is a tiny battery, and as they fire it is similar to linking batteries together in series. You get a summing of the power. Some of the chemicals produced by the brain are called neurotransmitters and they have critically important effects on the health of the mind/body and the quality of consciousness. Many psychotropic drugs which alter our moods, like antidepressants, also effect these neurotransmitters.

Another important aspect of brainwaves is their rate of vibration (frequency) which is measured in cycles per second called hertz and abbreviated Hz. Fast brain waves are associated with thinking, concentration (as a form of exclusionary thinking and differentiated from focused attention), and some types of information processing. These relatively fast brain waves (14—40 Hz) are called beta waves. There are different categories of beta brain waves (SMR, Gamma, The Sheare frequency, etc.) and they are associated with yet more CNS functional differences. Theta (4 -7Hz) is a slower brain wave associated with memory searches, imagination, daydreaming, dreaming, trance states, insight etc. Theta is also associated with some pathological phenomena such as disassociation, epilepsy, and brain injury. Alpha waves (8-13 Hz) are associated with quiet, open focused attention, meditation, some kinds of visualization, dreaming, relaxation, awareness, etc. Delta (.5 -3Hz) is associated with deep sleep (beyond dream) and some kinds of pathology, especially if present in waking consciousness. It is important to remember that these descriptions are extremely superficial and are intended to convey a rough, preliminary, and general sense of what brain waves represent and how they are used.

Neurofeedback equipment has amplifiers which can pick up these brainwaves at the surface of the scalp and amplify them so they can be monitored. Since the amount of electrical activity is measured in millionths of a volt (microvolts abbreviated uV), they must be extremely sensitive, high quality amplifiers. However, once a clean signal is received it can 'tune in' to the desired brain waves using either analog or digital filters. Computerized systems allow us to break up and analyze these waveforms in all sorts of ways which can reveal fascinating patterns.

These brain wave patterns can often be correlated with what we are doing, thinking, and feeling. In other words they are profoundly related to the states, qualities, flexibility, and dimensionality of our moment to moment consciousness. In the last five decades neuroscience has been exploring relationships between some of these brainwave patterns and many disorders including alcoholism, Alzheimer's, bipolar disorder, and depression. E. Roy John, Duffy and others have developed techniques for mapping the entire brain, and they believe there are specific configurations or brain wave signatures for many disorders.

Amazingly, when we can watch this brain wave activity on a computer screen and/or listen to signals indicating their presence, we can then learn to manipulate them relatively easily. This was considered impossible only a few decades ago. Scientists generally believed that there was a whole group of systems in the human body which could not be controlled. However, experiments on yogis, athletes, artists and other mind/body 'prodigies' proved that the ability of human beings to self-regulate their psychophysiology was far greater than mainstream science realized. The emergence of biofeedback dramatically demonstrated the power of self-regulation even to those who were not scientifically trained. For example, by the early seventies, thousands of clients were learning to control blood flow, heart rate and other aspects of the autonomic (ANS) (formerly known as the involuntary) nervous system.

It appears that when brain waves change amazing things can happen. In general clients report feeling better and believe they can do a better job of healing themselves. It is perhaps not so surprising that the list of applications is as long as it is and that it keeps growing, because changes in the CNS must influence in some way the rest of the organism. Although some of this research is only based on clinical case studies, it is still impressive and beyond being merely anecdotal. Unfortunately, the majority of the scientific and medical community is not well informed about biofeedback progress in general, much less EEG biofeedback.

Most of the clinicians we encounter have told us that clients usually require at least 6 or 7 sessions at the minimum to see some improvement. However, the consensus is growing that considerably more sessions are required most of the time. In addition, the proximity of the sessions to one another seems to be of considerable importance. A balance must be struck for each client between neuronal growth and intensity of intervention. Obviously, NFB is not right for everyone and people vary in their sensitivity to EEG training.

**Head gear pinache.**

Some people resist doing EEG training because they feel silly sitting there with electrodes on their head in order to develop a deeper understanding of themselves and better control of brain electrical activity (and all that that implies). Yet the same people would think nothing of putting mud or oatmeal or whatever on their face or walking around with rollers in their hair or painting their face red, white and blue for a football game, or shaving their head or even wearing a safety pin in their cheek or navel, etc. in order to be 'cool'. We are working hard to make it easier for folk. For example, we have developed virtually 'dry' forehead electrodes which mean simply putting on a cool looking headband. However, sooner or later, folks need to get the sensor around to the occipital region in the back of the head. This back of the head placement is already developing its own pinache because it is thought to be so effective for improving performance and quality of life. And in the end anything that does that is very cool indeed.

**Brainwaves and Health**

How is it that this self-knowledge, self-regulation brainwave technology can alter health? If you consider that the brain connects with and regulates virtually all aspects of the physiology, we can begin to see the mechanisms whereby our thoughts and feelings can affect our entire body all the time. The new field known as Health Psychology has grown up around decades of research. Research that forces us to realize the critical importance of the mind/body connection and self-regulation.

The AMA's own statistics reveal that at least 60% of all doctor visits are for undiagnosed ailments (that is ailments which have no obvious physical basis such as a virus or tissue degeneration). We know of conversion disorders where people lose their sight after seeing traumatic events, even though their visual system still has the capacity to process optical information. This same disorder can lead to the loss of use of an arm or other limb. Research has shown that highly stressed individuals experience a reduced function in the immune system which makes them more susceptible to disease. Studies of twins have demonstrated the power of stress to bring out genetic weaknesses in individuals such as schizophrenia. The relationship between stress and heart disease is well established but frequently down played by health care professionals. In fact, international studies of hypertension have demonstrated that it is a disease suffered primarily by highly stressed industrial cultures.

The keyword here is stress. The famous researcher Hans Selye preferred the term distress because stress actually means change and not all change is unhealthy. In The Process, we use the terms 'unhealthy stress' and 'healthy stress'. Psychological distress can kill. The research of Canon, Selye, and more recently Ray Weiss have convincingly supported this perspective. The organ which defines stress for the body is the brain. Our beliefs, ideas, and feelings decide whether an incoming stimulus is a healthy or an unhealthy stressor. A piece of rope can be initially perceived as a snake on the forest floor, and cause the sympathetic side of the ANS to activate the fight or flight response, sending adrenaline pumping through the fearful human body. Next moment, when the piece of rope is recognized as rope, the parasympathetic side of the ANS takes over and restores homeostasis (balance) to the system.

Constant distress can unleash hormones like adrenaline, which if present at high levels over long periods of time, lead to tissue degeneration. Chronic over arousal leads to anxiety disorders and depression, then finally to internal, organic damage which can even lead to death. The progression of essential hypertension will often follow this pattern. Scientists widely believe that distress is the primary cause of overeating, substance abuse, lack of exercise, and the escapist mentality that plagues most societies.

## The Problem of Self-Regulation

We have a crises of self-regulation in modern America. The FDA has asserted recently that there exists no effective weight program besides diet and exercise. We know from studies of dieting that its effect on the hypo-thalamus can be destructive leading to more severe weight problems. At least 40% or more of Americans are overweight. EEG biofeedback is a self-regulation super tool. It teaches individuals to regulate themselves at critical, fundamental levels. Recent research suggests it may do this through disrupting dysfunctional Long Term Potentiation Loops in a part of the brain called the mesolimbic dopamine system. This area of the brain is responsible for attention and motivation processes. Dr. Ronald Ruden has some very interesting theories regarding this in his book **The Craving Brain.**

This self-regulation process leads to increased awareness of disorder in other physical and mental systems, and enhances the natural tendency to seek out order in those systems through diet, exercise, vitamins, medita-tion, prayer and community interaction, etc. As integration increases in the brain we tend to seek more order and balance in our external lives.

There is also a crises of intimacy, and a cloak of shame and denial hides it from our eyes. We are increasingly suffering from progressive isolation as workload and technology separates us. But this is a choice we have made in the pursuit of material wealth in the hope it will bring us happi-ness. We can make other choices. Although, as is the case with most addic-tive disorders, we rarely change until we hit bottom. Many NFB clients have already hit bottom.

Neurofeedback implies more than just changing brainwaves. Since the brain is central to our construction of reality, and since that reality construction is social, interactive, and ongoing, it involves all aspects of culture. When we change the brain we must also change the environment that the brain operates in or wrong conditioning will probably cause it to retreat to its formerly unhealthy condition. We are all connected to each other and the environment. Neurofeedback is fundamentally an ecological process because it changes the brain/mind which is the interactive interface between environmental systems and self-systems. You can take a dysfunctional child, remove it from its family, help it reintegrate to a normal behavioral pattern, and then watch it degrade as it once again encounters its dysfunctional family system. We must and we are changing our environment, the field within which we live when we change our thinking. We change our lives when we change our minds. People undergoing neurofeedback are regaining their congruence as Carl Rodgers would say, and moving toward Maslow's ideal of Self-Actualization.

Neurofeedback as an act of psychophysiological self-regulation must be nurtured into a reorganization and reintegration of the individual life-world. Knowledge stocks must be reinventoried and reevaluated. Mood cycles which have dominated the individual since they were children become painfully obvious. Emotional scripts that have long outlived their usefulness in the formation of the ego must be rewritten.

This inventory can be much like the Twelve Step 'inventory' that many alcoholics find so crucial in their recovery. For some, these kinds of changes can be at times difficult, even painful. Yet meeting the challenge is always rewarding in the long run. We sometimes see clients going through the psychological stages of death, as described by Elizabeth Kubler-Ross, only to emerge on the other side with a new perspective on life. This inventory seems to us to hold much in common with the twelve-step inventory and the 'Dark Night of the Soul' which St. John and St. Teresa took such note of in their own spiritual journeys.

Neurofeedback may be said to have a spiritual quality in that it can lead to healing, reintegration and a sense of wholeness. Fundamental to all human existence is meaning. When we reconnect with that fundamental wholeness at our core we find ourselves. This leap of self-knowledge usually has an 'as though for the first time' quality about it. That's why it is often referred to as a renaissance, a rebirth, or as self-renewal. Rediscovery of our essential self adds a new dimensionality to our lives. Colors seem brighter, food tastes better, feelings seem fuller, thoughts are clearer. The present seems richer. One feels one has options. Life has possibilities. The moment takes on a timeless quality.

Language which some might find useful follows. When NFB works well we reduce the endless series of 'trances' that dominate our lives. The practice of alpha training can allow us to disengage from the constant chatter in our minds. This 'vacation' from mental business as usual leads to relative freedom from the whole engaging pile of mental videos we like to play over and over. As our ability develops to watch the relentless streams of thought and rumination, the brain becomes quieter, less impulsive, and more economical. Neurons are freed up from some of the excessive processing, and as excessive activity is inhibited, the capacity to attend is enhanced.

This increased awareness of thought makes it possible to become less attached to thought as the *only* means of gaining more control of our lives. It is easier to directly experience higher level processing in the form of intuition and spontaneous insight. Increased capacity to attend leads to enhanced awareness of the actuality of our moment to moment existence—to 'what is.' This can lead to an even deeper, more profound quality of attention than the relatively superficial attention usually employed. One researcher described his experience as follows:

"Initially it seemed like I was creating a trance to dispel an aggregate of trance cycles which I passed through from day to day. I focused my entire capacity on one point- the tone of alpha. It seemed I was entering the realm of 'no-mind' as many oriental philosophies call it. I felt as if I was gaining power over time and unifying my capacity more and more. Rather than a fragmented mind, it seemed that I could focus and achieve 'one pointedness'. Strangely, it seemed that I could also open my focus of attention so that I was able to take in everything at once and encounter my field of experience all at once in a unified way. This direct, unified experience made me feel like a mirror of my immediate world. I was filled by this direct experience, like an empty cup."

These rich altered states have physiological correlates. The work of Benson (and Stroebel) on the Relaxation Response has shown that this kind of 'mind control' can have a profoundly healing effect. Research supports this perspective. Body tension reduces, cortisol levels drop, blood pressure and cholesterol decrease, respiration evens out, the endocrine system moves to a finer level of homeostasis, the immune system becomes more robust etc. The ability to learn to attend at these deep levels does not seem to be age specific, and can be exercised even by those who think of themselves as old and have become discouraged about their ability to learn and see things from a new perspective.

## A Brief History of Neurofeedback

The history of neurofeedback (as a sub set of main stream medical and educational biofeedback) could easily be several books. Besides, our primary purpose is to put forward our view of The Process and its relationship to self-knowledge technology. Our sincere apologies to any friends and colleagues who may feel slighted by this extremely incomplete, personal, subjective history of our field. Actually, I have an aversion to hanging out in the past at all since the present demands so much of my limited energy, and the present is so much more interesting and fun. But Dr. Soutar has convinced me that it will help the reader to get an abbreviated overview from my highly subjective perspective. So, here I am trying to think how I can best tell the story of one of the strangest niche/technological art forms ever to develop, and how I came to dedicate so much of my life to it.

I fell in love with a beautiful, mystical actress (whom I later married) and in 1961 she told me about a gifted astrologer she had seen. Since I considered myself much more scientifically trained than she, I felt it my duty to explain to her that astrology was based on superstition and practiced by charlatans. My beautiful friend was not convinced, so I decided to prove it to her by having my chart done and showing her the falseness in the 'reading'.

My first surprise when I arrived for my reading was how different this astrologer was from what I had expected. She was an attractive woman working from her tasteful, immaculate home. Her humility and her kind, comfortable, and innocent personality, immediately charmed me. Thereupon, she sat me down at her kitchen table and proceeded to blow my mind right through my ears…at least so far as the past went. She told me things about my past that no one but me knew, including dates and places. Later I questioned my mother to make sure no one had been asking her questions about my past.

However, the obviously psychic astrologer's view of the future had to be wrong. She told me that my career as an actor would not go well (I was sure I was destined for stardom); however, she said I would be quite successful in a technological field, but not until my thirties. That seemed ridiculous since I expected to be a millionaire within a few years. I asked her if she could give me more detail, and she said she couldn't because this new concept had not been invented yet. Of course, biofeedback had been theoretically invented, but it did not get its name until November 1970 (about ten years later) at an extraordinary gathering of the founders of this field. At that meeting, the conference participants could alternate between listening to often amazing and inspiring presentations or going down to the front of the hotel and watching the New Orleans police beat the hell out of the anti war protesters and haul them away in vans to the notoriously nasty New Orleans jails.

The astrologer's fee was $5.00 and I was so impressed that I slipped an additional fiver under the first (big money for me then). She caught me just before I got into my '49 Caddy and returned the extra five saying it was important (for ethical reasons) that she make only her small fee.

In August of 1968 my wife introduced me to the work of J. Krishnamurti. As America seemed to enter a new cultural dimension advocating creativity, love, and peace, I too encountered a spiritual force in my life which was to propel me into a career quite distant from the entertainment industry. We heard Krishnamurti at Town Hall in New York in October of the same year and were astonished and inspired by his presence and insight. Convinced of the importance of the principles he unfolded through his teachings, I looked for a means to actualize them in my own life while staying true to my sense of a scientific and philosophical revolution unfolding within the world and also within me.

Dagne, my wife, and I frequently spent weekends at a country house in Rhinebeck, New York. At the end of a rather dreamy October day sitting by the lake contemplating The Big Picture, she suggested that I read a magazine article entitled "Alpha, The Wave of the Future". I promptly read it because I had learned that she had an uncanny way of planting good ideas in my mind at just the right time. The article astonished me. In fact, I had a kind of epiphany. I knew right away that it was somehow connected to Krishnamurti's perspective (at least in my mind). I felt an overwhelming hunger to learn all I could about this new integration of technology and the mind/body.

During the next twenty four hours I went through a classic creative experience. Decades of contemplation and thought seemed to converge with a euphoric, laser like intensity. It seemed as though one of the greatest scientific and spiritual stories of all time was unfolding itself before my eyes. And I was being invited to immerse myself in an almost unimaginably beautiful work. I was in a state of wonder, awe, and almost uncontainable excitement. I immediately sold my business and plunged into full time research including attending the 1970 New Orleans Biofeedback Society meeting. I bought an Aquarius Alphaphone, began alpha training, put everything I had into the biofeedback business, and (almost) never looked back. There have been some times when the going got rough and I wondered what my life would have been like had I stayed in the entertainment field, and or continued with my relatively well paying business. Twenty nine years passed by like a summer afternoon.

It seemed that this emerging new field was a perfect fit for my eclectic background. Beginning at age eleven, I had worked at 25 jobs by the time I was 25 (sometimes working two jobs at a time) and had been a member or worked under the auspices of at least 9 different unions. I 'd been an actor (I and some others felt I was at least a reasonably skillful craftsman), I had written poetry, several one act plays and a couple of screenplays. I'd been a chemistry major and premed student at Baylor University, a licensed preacher, a 'roughneck' in the oil fields, a salesman, an entrepreneur, and I read voraciously. I considered myself to have a decent although admittedly unorthodox philosophical and scientific mind.

Several enormous pieces of my life came together at once creating a kind of psychological nuclear explosion and I was aflame with the possibilities. The most important of them all was the relationship between self-regulation, brain wave training, and what I believed was the royal road to both psychological and physical health...meditation (the real thing as opposed to various mind altering techniques which are called meditation but which I considered to be relatively ineffective, often time wasters, and sometimes downright counter productive and superficially mystical.)

The Aquarius Alphaphone was primitive by today's standards and minimally effective at best, consisting of headphones with built in tin electrodes. An alpha craze was developing as people claimed the training was making them high. There was a lot of mixing of brain wave training with grass and other psychotropics, including booze. Many users claimed that a lesser amount of drugs delivered a better effect if they integrated brain wave training (It took a long time for many to see the beneficial implications of this medication potentiation effect). One of the most gifted and charismatic early equipment designers also developed one of the most successful LSD labs on the west coast for which he later served seven years in prison. When he got out he went back into advanced electronics and became a Silicon Valley multimillionaire anyway. So neurofeedback had a pop culture beginning which some of us came to label the 'California-Hippie Effect'.

Many of the old timers believe that the hippie involvement with biofeedback slowed the growth of the field and almost killed NFB until its renaissance about 1990. Personally, I don't think it made much difference one way or the other. I believe the growth of the field has been slowed by the conceptual limitations and near sightedness of the educational and medical/scientific/industrial establishment itself. Additionally, the concept has been slowed because it is only a part of an immense paradigm shift in psychology and physiology, and such historical movements seem to have their own inexorable timing. It is like a freight train. One can push or pull with all ones might but the puny human body cannot make the train go faster or slower. Its mass and power are too great, and it moves according to forces outside the range of human physical strength. So biofeedback and NFB are developing according to forces outside the ken of most observers.

Biofeedback and the implications of instrument assisted self-regulation simply blow through the drug oriented, double blind research models that are respectable and fundable in our time. So researchers had to improve the way science is done in order for the field to grow. Sort of like having to show your parents a better way to hunt so you would not starve to death. Many venerable colleagues in scientifically powerful positions simply do not get the implications of a technology of self-knowledge. "You cannot put this wine into old wine skins." I see a clear relationship between the growth of biofeedback in general and neurofeedback in particular and the replacing of older scientists with younger ones.

It would be irresponsible not to mention that this whole drama is unfolding as described in spite of the fact that this field also owes much to academic and government funded research and many of the most productive scientists have aged along with me. Anyway, I could see from the beginning that a career in this field was going to be both exhilarating and challenging. I was innocently hanging on to the tail of a seven hundred pound Siberian tiger that was about to kill me unless I could instantly overcome my fear and outlove it. Miraculously that must have happened. Or maybe the tiger recognized me as a reincarnation of one of her cubs and decided to protect me. I have often sensed a kind of protective influence from some of the traditional (tiger like) scientists in this field, even though I know they disagreed with some of my hypotheses.

Of course, like any reasonable person who must see to his own economic order, I expected my new small business to become profitable quickly so I could afford to delegate all of the day to day aspects of running the business to others and immerse myself in research and development. I felt I knew then and know even better now how to push this art and science out, way out towards the highest potential possible in our lifetimes…a moonlit ride over the Himalayas on a Magic Horse! But building a viable biofeedback business proved far more challenging, time consuming, and brutally humbling than any of the original equipment producers expected. I know, because most of the survivors are my friends, and I have watched the astonishingly dedicated, often sacrificial odysseys they have gone through so far in order to bring this field to its current considerable strength.

In the 60's researchers had to jury-rig their own equipment in their labs. By 1968 Buryl Paine, a Boston professor and psychologist established PsychoPhysics Labs, the first biofeedback instrument company. I proposed a partnership and he suggested we discuss it while vacationing on the island of Eleuthra. I knew this was not going to be business as usual when Buryl met my wife and me for a meeting on a beautiful, remote beach, and he was completely naked. He was very well built. Later we ran on the beach together and went snorkeling out on the reef whereupon I had my first and only underwater encounter with a large shark. Up to that time I believed that large sharks do not come past the outer reefs. We both scared the hell out of each other and I high tailed it to the beach and continued writing out our historic agreement on a legal pad. Buryl finally signed it and we began our partnership which was destined to last about three months. I would like to blame the failure of our venture all on him, but in retrospect I take responsibility for being a tad aggressive and a bit too confident in the correctness of some of my opinions.

By March of '71 I had become friends with Marjorie and Herschel Toomim. They had developed the Toomim Alpha Pacer which was an excellent, pocket sized brain wave trainer for the time. I experienced remarkable benefits while training on it and began distributing it on the East Coast. I decided to join forces with the Toomims. We founded the Biofeedback Research Institute and Herschel developed a line of solid biofeedback instruments. I persuaded an excellent legal firm to put together a public offering. Strangely, whatever we attempted to do met with endless roadblocks, and three underwriters withdrew from the venture. Eventually I found myself in the back room of a restaurant being told by a compassionate government insider that the underwriting was doomed because of "political pressure being applied by one or more special interest groups with substantial influence in Washington". He told me there was no choice but to cut my losses and quit. I tried to find another way to fund the company but failed. By that time I was broke myself. The stress on all of us was too great so I resigned from BFRI, voluntarily surrendered my stock, and count the Toomims as much respected friends to this day.

I supported myself in New York through a combination of training healthcare professionals, patients, and performance enhancement clients as well as producing and distributing biofeedback instrumentation. In fact, there was a substantial period when I barely had enough to pay the rent and feed myself and so I spent a great deal of time meditating and training on the instrumentation. This activity (or lack of traditional marketing activity) actually became a way of sort of magically earning a living. It became a kind of game. I would become as quiet and go as deeply as I could into meditation, and by and by the phone would ring with a new client or I would get an insight into the next steps which needed to be taken in order to survive. In a way it was very mysterious and romantic. And above all I felt deeply encouraged, sort of protected. I felt more than ever that there was some larger purpose (maybe the universal mind or something) some intelligence that wanted me to continue and prevail and do this work. And, of course, it was and still is great fun.

Since a substantial number of my clients were interested in peak performance training, I wound up working with actors, writers, musicians as well as business people. Some of them were famous. One of the companies I cofounded, Qtran, developed the Mood Ring and we were successful for awhile. The original rings were actually quite attractive and worked well as personal temperature trainers. But the costume jewelry people circumnavigated our patent and ruined the business by making junk rings that did not work. However, they sold over $500,000,000 worth of rings before the fad died.

Clinging to solvency by the skin of my teeth, I financed my new business, the American Biofeedback Corporation (several years later we changed the name to the American BioTec Corporation), mostly with credit cards and investments from several clients, put together a line of low cost, clinical grade instruments, developed formal certification training programs, and started over. Later, we developed the concept of distributing all of the quality systems in the field so that we could offer unbiased turnkey packages, including consulting to professionals. We were a full service company and are to this day.

The story of the computerization of biofeedback would take a book in itself and the pace of the action is accelerating, swept along by the super exponential digital explosion, and the awakening of scientific and secular interest in the mind. The Toomim's BioComp 2001 was one of the first, and best of the early computerized systems. It ran on an Apple 2+ and we sold a lot of them. ASI and Cyborg developed computerized systems, but they encountered economic distress and sold out to Stoelting which parlayed their instrument lines into a strong contemporary presence. I met Sam Caldwell (Expanded Technologies Incorporated) about 1981, and was impressed by a universal interface he had developed, his ingenuity, personal integrity and love of animals. The universal interface really appealed to me since it could run on either Apples, IBM's, or Commodores, and you could connect any combination of whatever instruments a clinician or researcher happened to have.

This concept solved a lot of the kinds of problems that existed in the field at that time. We developed (with the help of John Picciotino) the UniComp and CapScan systems over the years, created many innovations and are enthusiastic about the projects we are currently developing together. Sam is a brilliant computer scientist and psychologist. He is a modest man who takes great pride in his work and would much rather do than talk about it. He tends to stay hunkered down and focused on his goal of constantly improving the quality of the technology in this field. The biofeedback community is largely unaware of the magnitude of his contribution, and his ability to persevere over the last twenty plus years. Hopefully, that will get corrected in the near future.

By the late 1970's a shake out had produced a biofeedback 'Boot Hill'. Strong companies disappeared, others emerged and the churning continues into the present. Thought Technology, under the brilliant leadership of its founders, Hal Meyers and Larry Klein is probably the current economic leader. Unlike the US government, the Canadian government has had the vision to substantially support Thought Technology R&D. American BioTec, J&J, Spectrum, BFRI, ASI, BFS, Aquathought and Lexicor are some of the companies that continue to make contributions to neurofeedback.

In the mid eighties Chuck Stroebel inspired me to take on the development of the ultimate computerized EEG biofeedback system dubbed The CapScan. We believed that the capacity to deliver quality multi-site flexible montage and synchrony NFB would be a major contribution, and that vision has proven true. However, it meant doing FFT's on four amplifiers simultaneously and feeding the updated information back every second. Most engineers thought that was not possible because of the time required to do FFT's on slow brain waves. Using an averaging algorithm, we had done it by fall '89 and are updating so fast now that we expect to reach flicker fusion soon.

The flow of neurofeedback research has been intense and it will be necessary to leave out many of the contributors in this brief review. But the following should at least give the reader a sense of the evolution. As we have mentioned, Joe Kamiya's original studies at the University of Chicago showing the relative ease of learning to self-regulate the alpha brain wave started it all, and some consider Kamiya to be 'the father of biofeedback'. However, Dr. Kamiya would be the first to acknowledge that George Whatmore's work at University of Washington integrating EMG (muscle feedback) and progressive relaxation preceded Kamiya's discoveries by over ten years. By the late sixties, Elmer Green at the Menninger Foundation was showing relationships with meditation, reverie, and even the ancient writings on states of consciousness by the Indian sage Patanjali. Thom Budzynski and John Picciotino at University of Colorado did work on twilight learning; and Les Fehmi at Stonybrook and Princeton developed his views on attention (perhaps the closest to my own) and his widely respected Open Focus imagery techniques. Others had produced work indicating that alpha and theta training could have extraordinary effects on consciousness including qualities of attention, reverie, meditation, dreaming, accessing memories, and unconscious material, etc.

Peniston and Kulkosky's stunning work with alcoholics and PTSD is widely credited with triggering the explosion in NFB that has unfolded since 1990. Building on the work of Sterman, Joel Lubar produced well designed studies, beginning in the mid seventies, on the use of SMR and beta (theta inhibit) to reduce the symptoms of ADHD in children. He has documented a success rate of 60-80% with 10-14 year follow-ups, showing the treatments continuing effectiveness. Many of his patients were able to reduce or eliminate the need for medications. Margaret Ayers is widely acclaimed for her groundbreaking work using NFB with brain injured patients. Maxwell Cade built an EEG device called The Mind Mirror and

identified learnable patterns which he believed assisted in Performance
Enhancement. A multitude of other approaches have been explored by clinicians such as Michael Tansey's application of single hertz training.

Quantitative EEG (QEEG) techniques allow measurements of multiple sites (brain mapping) over the entire head. Both Thatcher and
Sterman are developing databases of normed scores which are being used
to assist in diagnosis, research, and treatment planning. Some patterns are
emerging which are believed to correlate with a variety of disordered states
of mind such as depression, substance abuse, head injury, as well as
enhanced mind/body performance. Some researchers are even speculating
that EEG training may stimulate brain cell growth. Obviously, much
research will have to be done before these hopeful findings are fully
accepted by the scientific establishment.

**Entrainment**

Brainwave entrainment is believed by many to be closely related to EEG
biofeedback; however, there are even more of us who feel that entrainment
is a vastly different technology and produces vastly different results. We
were using, so far as I am aware, the first of the light/sound stimulation
and entrainment devices as early as 1971. It was the Isis developed by Jack
Schwarz. Research is underway which will eventually settle the issue of
what is its proper role, if any, in a neurofeedback self-regulation learning
program. Meanwhile my interpretation of the extremely ambiguous
research that has surfaced so far, including our own experimentation, continues to reinforce our current viewpoint. Using technology to assist in the
learning of voluntary control of brain waves is, in our opinion, one of the
most important breakthroughs of our time. We do not consider entrainment (flashing lights and sounds used to 'drive' brain wave changes) to be
in the same league as neurofeedback. However, I believe there are times
when entrainment can be used as an adjunct to EEG biofeedback.

There are presently a number of respected researchers including Len Ochs
and Harold Russell developing applications for complex entrainment

devices. Although entrainment devices are regulated as is biofeedback by the FDA, there have been thousands of these devices sold to the general public in violation of federal law (not by Ochs, et al). Since advertising has led many to believe that entrainment is the same as EEG self-regulation training, we feel many who might have received benefits from true NFB did not because they were confused by the much different results they would have gotten from entrainment devices. We continue to keep an open mind about entrainment and look forward to additional studies.

**In Summation**

The history of EEG biofeedback is much richer and more complex than this brief accounting. Clinical use of this method has grown consistently, yet most of us feel the field is in its infancy. As quantum physics continues to transform old Newtonian perspectives of time, space, causality and mind, the notion that consciousness, mind, and matter are separate is also dying. The visionary physics of David Bohm have become acceptable to many scientists and academics and the consequences have begun to be felt in the public forum. The medical community is responding to a growing public awareness that mind and body are intimately connected, that the wellness model has been much too neglected, and drugs and traditional medical techniques are not the only way to deal with health problems.

Biofeedback lends tremendous power to the growing movement to make self-regulation for the prevention of disease and enhancement of life a major goal for both individuals and society as a whole. With better education most people can improve their ability to heal themselves and contribute to the success of traditional therapies. We expect biofeedback, the technology of self-knowledge, to grow dramatically in the 21st century. As far as we know, The Process is the first comprehensive effort to condense the best of what is known about classic and contemporary heuristic learning into a life-enhancement program with the *optional* integration of NFB as an adjunctive assist to the self-knowledge learning process. Furthermore, since The Process is designed to aid relatively functional people in becoming even healthier and more self-actualized, we believe it will make an important social contribution. Our vision is that as the healthy get healthier, so will the unhealthy be pulled up to a higher level. We believe The Process is contributing to the raising of the bar for everyone (including yours truly, the authors).

To us it is self-evident that as most people become healthier, they (we) have a natural tendency to reach out to help others profit from what has been learned. Goals change because we feel relatively fulfilled. Eating habits change, thinking habits change, mood cycles shift, our bodies respond differently to food and drugs. Changes in brain chemistry must affect changes in overall body chemistry. For some people that change can be profound.

Being part of the early stages of this great technology and its accompanying educational strategies has been for me an honor and an adventure of the highest order. I took big risks because I wanted to live the most creative life possible. I gambled that the highest, best orders of creativity, responsibility, personal growth (including understanding the mysteries of love and compassion better) would come by investing in the art and science of meditation rather than more recognized (and economically rewarded) art and science forms...respectable as many of them are. So, I invested countless hours, days, weeks, months, years, even decades in learning and trying to learn (and assist others in learning) this principle of meditation, this righting of the mind and soul, this unfolding to the best of one's ability what latent intelligence, wisdom may live within.

It appears that I can, probably will, stay the course; although, like many artists and scientists, I cannot say that I am doing this because of virtue, or strength, or courage...but because I really have no choice. It seems to me that if one thinks one has a choice about such things, one is confused. Or put another way, when one is seeing clearly the high road, the best way is relatively, maybe absolutely choiceless. Whether my long odyssey, my struggle with the understanding of the way the mind works, was (is) the best use of all this time or not is not always clear. Nonetheless, the gamble has been and is being made…the risk taken. I have spent, and I am spending vast amounts of my life energy in this way. May grace teach me and love enfold and unfold me. As I go deeper into the silence…I 'know' less and less, yet life seems to work better and better. I take that as a sign I'm finding the way home. As I get closer and closer my heart leaps up as I recognize more and more of my long 'lost' and sorely missed family along the way.

# Chapter 3

# Science, Politics, and Health

It is useful to consider the social and scientific context within which EEG biofeedback is emerging. Neurofeedback represents a new level of interface between man and his technology…a kind of marriage of technology and consciousness. Mind and computer merged long ago for better *and* for worse. But one of the better manifestations is the magnifying mirror that NFB technology, especially computerized NFB represents. It is a technology which extends our vision beyond the everyday much in the same way as Galileo's telescope. Like Galileo, when we invite others to look we often find that an older way of seeing things prevents their participation at the level which the instrument requires. The technology of self-knowledge belongs to a new era of thinking which requires a 'sea shift' in perspective to appreciate. Thomas Kuhn, the great epistemologist of modern science, would call this a paradigm shift. Kuhn notes that these come rarely within science and unfortunately often not until most of the old guard dies out. (Some of the old guard can and do embrace the new and true even if it is difficult..and costly.) We have to let go of the old before the new can be embraced. Unfortunately, it is all too human, as Piaget noted, for people to rationalize away new information rather than renegotiate their entire perspective. The Process is a perspective grounded in quantum mechanics more than Newtonian physics. We believe neurofeedback is best understood from this vantage point as well.

When revolutions in scientific thought arise, they emerge slowly, at least from the perspective of those who are ushering them in. It took fifty years for Newton's theories to penetrate the academic/intellectual world of 17th century Europe. It has been almost a century since Einstein, Heisenberg, Bohr and others transformed physics, and still a huge majority of our intelligencia do not understand the deeper implications. Too many of our honorable colleagues continue to cling tenaciously to the confining, outmoded worldview implied by Newtonian mechanics and supported by the Cartesian perspective. Such minds are caught in the illusion of a smaller, safer, more controllable and definable world.

It is a dangerous fact that large numbers of the scientific community still cling to ideas such as causality, absolute (linear) time, absolute space, mind/matter dichotomies, and a host of other intellectual bricks that constitute the bastion of the 19th century worldview. Too many of us believe we grasp modern physics, yet are personally trapped in the trance of Cartesian dualism and atomic materialism. This notion is founded on the conviction that mind and all it entails is an epiphenomenon of matter. Physicists like David Bohm, Fritz Capra, Fred Allen Wolf, and others have challenged the idea that there can be any separation between mind, meaning and matter, founding their convictions on 20th century theoretical physics. Wolfgang Pauli (developed the exclusion principle) collaborated with the renowned psychologist Carl Jung early in the century to address the mind/matter problem. Although their work was left unfinished, modern physicists are evolving breathtaking new ideas regarding mind and consciousness. Some progressive psychologists are attacking the problem but general awareness of the implications of the new physics is poorly represented in contemporary psychological or sociological scientific journals. Over the centuries this Newtonian/Cartesian worldview has produced systems of thinking and research including standards of scientific 'proof' which tends to support itself. Some of the best of contemporary thinkers find these self-propagating systems delusional and dangerous. The disconnect and lack of communication between science and society is devastatingly costly.

Most of the healthcare and educational research establishment continues to believe these research strategies represent the scientific gold standard for determining what is valuable and what is not. For a stunning insight into the kind of thinking that we believe will shape a more enlightened research establishment in the future see: Cassidy, Claire, H. Unraveling the Ball of String: Reality, Paradigms, and the Study of Alternative Medicine. Advances: The Journal of Mind-Body Health. Vol.10, No. 1, Winter 1994.

In our opinion the current research standard is more like the tin coating on the real gold standard which is beginning to shine through here and there. There are too many holding outmoded perspectives in control of scientific journals and the system whereby research is funded. We know it has ever been thus and we think it is fun to try and clean off the unnecessary tin anyway. The real gold underneath is worth the work and so energizing.

It is increasingly important for the general electorate to understand how this system works so it can be improved. The medical/industrial establishment controls to a large extent what is legitimized in the scientific domain. As a consequence, those in the clinical setting are licensed and allowed to use equipment approved by the same monolith. This means the status quo controls the market. The public is at the mercy of this process because we tend to work primarily with official information when constructing our realities and options. Naturally, we tend to turn first to officially sanctioned healthcare providers. When that fails to solve our problems, which it does in over fifty percent of the cases, we reach out for other solutions. However, finding out what the many excellent alternative options are is extremely difficult and expensive because money talks and the bureaucracy has vast funding to promote those strategies it deems most profitable. Slowly, however, the public is becoming aware of the complex nature of the problem and starting to demand access to alternative health resources and a huge improvement in the way healthcare science is financed and conducted.

In sharp contrast, many of the most important breakthroughs in health science are being achieved by a loosely knit group of independents doing research according to new paradigms and mostly funded out of their own pockets. One wonders if history will show that in the end the greatest discoveries tend to come from personally funded obsessions rather then from monolithic organizations. I'm thinking of Einstein and his job in a patent office essentially funding the development of the theory of relativity, Bohm and his work on thought and dialogue and his work with Krishnamurti being funded by his meager professor' salary; and Krishnamurti putting together what many believe are some of the most valuable mind/body insights of our time while working alone and living off his modest inheritance. (He eventually turned everything over to a foundation including royalties from his many books.) I don't know. It may be that those things that are reinventing the order of things cannot always depend on the order they are replacing for support. I wonder.

We think one of the most promising dynamics emerging from this research is the relationship between quantum physics and neurofeedback. A growing number of us believe that this relationship is helping to open a doorway, leading to a dramatic increase in opportunity for normal people to enhance the quality of their own moment to moment consciousness. We and others are doing our best to make a case in support of this concept grounded in research in both psychology and physics. As Einstein and Bohm demonstrated so brilliantly, it is natural and beautiful to build the new on the shoulders of what has gone before.

## The Alternative Providers and the Monolith

The presently accepted models of medicine are mostly based on the Newtonian/Cartesian scientific paradigm as we have mentioned. The body, according to this perspective, is a machine which occasionally breaks down, and can be repaired if the mechanic has the right tools and knows enough about the machine. Further this flawed model holds that thoughts and feelings are products of the machine and not intrinsic to its function. This model has also been extended into the mental health field and disorders of the brain can be fixed by manipulation of the chemical machinery or reprogramming the brain as though it were a kind of organic computer.

One researcher in a PBS special on psychology explained that the success of drugs which regulate neurotransmitters clearly indicates that disordered mental processes are not due to cognitive and experiential factors. This implies that they can not be resolved or even significantly influenced by cognitive therapy, self-regulation, or Profound Attention. Might we mention that such a viewpoint nullifies the Heisenberg Principle? This kind of callous disregard for even universally accepted scientific principles is characteristic of Newtonian/Cartesian paradigmatic thinking which still dominates bureaucratic scientific research. It disregards the connectedness of events as interactive systems and the holistic nature of these events. Doesn't this mean then, that this kind of science is really pseudo science, or worse, 'junk science'? The researcher in the PBS special overlooked the possibility that the chemical processes of the brain were mediating in nature and that intervention at any level in the system, i.e. behavioral, cognitive, or environmental could effect a change. Research strongly supporting this perspective is abundant but overlooked because of the tinted glasses worn by much of the scientific establishment.

Not only does neurofeedback have to confront a dominating outdated paradigm, but also the political and economic biases the existing medical model produces in the intellectual and economic marketplaces. This difficulty is understandable because the medical/industrial establishment is a powerful monolith, a huge business bureaucracy which quite naturally does all it can to survive and propagate itself. Most of us would consider ourselves fortunate to have one of those high paying jobs that exists because of the status quo, and which will have to disappear or be radically changed if the status quo changes significantly. Therefore, we who believe we are part of the emerging new medical and business model serve our own best interests by reaching out to our counterparts in the existing system and by building bridges. If holistic medicine is the future, then surely thinking and behaving holistically now is the best way to get there.

Neurofeedback is difficult to pigeonhole. Most doctors see it as a behavioral intervention, and most psychologists see it as a medical intervention. We assert it is an educational intervention which contains but is not limited to both mental health and medical models. It is in between disciplines because it is a product of a new, holistic mind/body paradigm. It is growing out of a synthesis of the best technology of the present and of the past. Unfortunately the dominant body of psychological thought is still grounded in the old paradigm and the full utility of the technology is not understood. There is a national epidemic of stress related mind/body disorders. Neurofeedback (and other forms of biofeedback as well) is a powerful adjunctive remedy which few can use because outdated scientific perspectives, bureaucratic scientific research, and powerful financial and political interests at the institutional level lead to a way of thinking which, has in general, ignored or discounted it.

## Quick Fixes and Something for Nothing?

We must acknowledge however, that we the public are not without blame. In fact, we have the ultimate responsibility because we are the field that governs the particles. Virtually everyone agrees that we have a crisis in self-regulation in our society. The nine leading causes of death in the United States are the result of dysfunctional behaviors for which the most viable remedy is improved self-regulation. The top three are tobacco, diet/inactivity and alcohol. Others include toxic agents, firearms, motor vehicles and illicit drug use. With 40% of the American Public suffering from overweight and seeking diet pills as a quick fix in place of a proper diet and exercise, it is clear that people are having a problem with self-discipline. The FDA with AMA support has clearly stated that most programs to lose weight other than diet and exercise do not work.

Millions still demand diet drugs, some of which are believed to be dangerous to health. The Quick Fix and Something for Nothing syndrome is sadly alive and well in the American psyche.

Most experts on ADHD stress that regardless of the intervention, whether biofeedback or drugs, parents need to utilize behavior management techniques to help alter cognitive and behavioral patterns entrenched as a consequence of the etiology of the disorder. Treatment usually amounts to a brochure for the parent and a pill for the child. The pill goes in the mouth and the brochure gets lost among the old phone memos and grocery lists. The child improves dramatically and the parents are so pleased that they skip the rest of the necessary intervention. Meanwhile their child still suffers from sometimes severe side effects, problems with peer relations, depression and an idea that drugs are required to feel normal. In fact the child *is **dependent*** on the drug for generating acceptable behavior. Worse yet, some researchers believe that at least half the children diagnosed as ADHD really have another disorder which is not being dealt with, and the drug is masking it. Drug addiction is probably an unadvertised consequence of 'fixing' ADHD and other disorders with drugs. A decrease in some of the more distressing symptoms is mistaken for normal or optimal functioning. Make no mistake, we are not anti-drug; but we do believe there are critically important questions to be asked if we are to find the right balance and the most effective, holistic, long term remedies.

What becomes clear to parents who do attempt to employ behavioral and cognitive interventions is that they must change their own habitual behavior patterns as well. This challenge to identity is not well received by the entrenched adult ego. With little outside support the efforts quickly fail. Such parents announce, "It doesn't work for me," and of course it doesn't. Since the intervention is non-material in nature (no surgery, leeches or pills) it has little legitimacy in their minds to begin with. Their failure just reinforces their personal version of the Newtonian, mechanistic paradigm. Our problems may have taken years or even decades to

develop but we expect a quick fix for 'man the machine' (as Rene'
Descartes defines us). We want change but we don't want to go through
the work of changing.

## Mind Matter Dilemmas

As we have mentioned, the concept of man the machine is derived
largely from the same 17th and 18th century thinking which has also
permeated modern science. The French philosopher Descartes popular-
ized the idea at the same time he supported the use of mathematics as a
final solution to all problems. As one of the founders of the new philosophy of science he supported the division of the world into the two
realms of mind and matter. This was somewhat of a novel approach but
was easy to grasp because it paralleled the Church's division of the universe into spirit and flesh. Galileo had already empowered the concept
of dividing up the world into the realm of the measurable and the
unmeasurable. He had further demonstrated that he could predict the
movement of a pendulum based on mathematics and measurement
which led to the development of the pendulum clock. Newton drew
upon the works of Galileo, Tycho Brahe, and Kepler and further defined
this new way of seeing the world, the philosophy of science. The world
became a place of absolute time, space and causality. Mind and matter
were eternally divided, disconnected by the act of measurement. Once
the division was made it took about fifty years to filter into the public
intelligence. It resulted in one of the most powerful, world changing
forces of all time...the convergence of calculus and cannonballs. The
new math of science devised by Newton, Descartes and Leibniz gave
European armies an ability to fire their cannons with deadly accuracy,
and supplied them with added advantage in warfare and hence politics.
Science continued as a fundamental tool of politics.

Over time the Newtonian perspective invaded almost all spheres of
thinking and disconnected us from the world of our ancestors. It soon
dominated the 'medical arts,' as they were once referred to, and they

became the 'medical sciences'. The disease model based on the hypothesis of absolute causality virtually crushed the ancient wellness model because we, the people, had been lulled into a trance by the illusion that an easily understandable science would create utopia. If there was something wrong with the machine, it was only congenital in nature, or it was a consequence of mechanisms from the environment assaulting the otherwise immutable body object. All disease was believed due to organic causes.

At the turn of the century Einstein, Heisenberg, Bohr and many others, introduced a perspective which turned science upside down and inside out. This perspective rapidly dominated physics, but not the other sciences even though they rest upon those physics. Most of the other sciences are only now starting to catch up. Immeasurably powerful electronic technologies created by the new multidimensional, holistic paradigm are being forced to serve an obsolete, dangerously fragmented worldview. It is like strapping a rocket engine to a Conostoga wagon. For a short time you have a thrilling ride on the fastest Conostoga wagon in history…then annihilation. Of course, harmonizing our healthcare and educational system with the wellness model and coherent, holistic thinking is already well underway. No one can predict where this combination is leading, but we believe the potential benefits are breathtaking from an evolutionary perspective. To that wondrous adventure this book is dedicated.

## Mounting Evidence

The division between the old and new paradigm is reflected within biofeedback itself. Powerful evidence mounts to support the evolution of the new paradigm, the quantum perspective within biofeedback. Indeed the electronics and theory behind biofeedback at this point is quantum, yet it is being employed by many professionals who use it with the eyeglasses of Newton. We have already described the political and economic forces which have shaped this situation. The competing theories and techniques of biofeedback emerge from this conflict of paradigms and represent somewhat divergent camps of thought. We assert the evidence is growing in favor of those who wish to employ it within the new paradigm and outside the traditional medical science model, but a comprehensive perspective is only beginning to be elucidated. One of the missions of The Process is to contribute to the establishment of such a comprehensive perspective within which neurofeedback can more freely and fully flourish as a discipline.

Although we see evidence that the differing camps in NFB are coming together, it seems to us that those over emphasizing high frequency training and often unnecessarily complicated and expensive training strategies may be inadvertently enabling what we believe is an older, less relevant scientific model. It seems to us that the most holistic, quantum compatible model must include a relatively heavy emphasis on lower frequency, simplified training integrated with the concept of Profound Attention and The Process (or something akin to it). The authors are sensitive to their own identification with some of the language used and hence the self-serving impression our perspective may present. However, we must do our best to get these ideas and questions into the mainstream dialogue. We hope we have made it clear that we think a revolution, a renaissance, a paradigm shift is well underway and we are doing our best to present our view of the elephant. We think Sir John Templeton is right when he asserts that humankind's understanding of 'spiritual' principles will soon increase '100 times' and a new, vastly richer science will play a key role. We consider ourselves two of many legions of players in an unfolding, immensely human drama. We hope you like our work; but whether you do or not we have to show up and do our best anyway.

## Magnifying Consciousness

Elmer Green and others explored in depth the relation of EEG to states of consciousness which had relatively little recognition, culturally or scientifically. The majority of psychologists still view these states as unsubstantiated by research and theory in the same way the medical community (without substantiating their own position through empirical research!) once denied that yogis and others had an ability to manipulate their autonomic nervous systems. The infiltration of the LSD experience into western culture made it apparent to great numbers that traditional scientific views of consciousness were narrow and unsubstantiated themselves. John Lilly's work with flotation tanks and Dolphins inspired yet another technology of consciousness. Empirical research on yogis and other psychophysiological prodigies made it evident that sufficiently dedicated human beings could achieve levels of autonomic, and even central nervous system control, that were far beyond limitations set by establishment science. Much of this was due to the mistaken western assumption that mind and matter were separate.

The realization that autonomic functions could be brought under voluntary control is a breakthrough with immense implications. The work of researchers like Kamiya, Sterman, Stroebel, Budzynsky, Peniston, Green, and theorists like Bohm, Tart, Ornstein, Sheldrake, Wolf and others helped pave the way for modern biofeedback as it relates to consciousness. Not only can physical functions be altered, but also electronic and other energy patterns in the body can be altered. EEG frequencies can be monitored and changed with apparently correlated changes in material physiological functions. These physiological functions are also correlated with changes in mood, arousal level, cognitive processing, and consequently consciousness.

Green began the development of a modern vocabulary of consciousness to more effectively communicate this emerging body of information empirically. The possibility of measuring, or at least evaluating qualities of consciousness, is unfolding before us with literally unimaginable implications. Fritz Capra in **The Tao of Physics** urged his peers to understand how the systems of consciousness developed by the east were experimental technologies like our own, but which had researched the material, the non material and the bridge connecting the two.

Contemporary researchers in neurophysiology such as Antonio Demasio have continued to demonstrate that the mind/body division is dead wrong. David Bohm's assertion that they represent two correlated systems emerging simultaneously from a fundamental implicate order (that appears to us as chaos) is rapidly being substantiated. Anyone

hooked up to even an EMG (muscle measurement instrument) and talking about things that are important to him will see the powerful effects
thought has on the body's physiology. This same thought by extension
has also been altering the earth's environment for at least the past ten
thousand years. Mind and matter appear to science today more and
more as interactive fields. After the philosopher George Herbert Mead
reviewed relativity theory, he put forth the idea that the organism and
the environment were interactive systems unfolding in the extended
(infinite) present, which was the field of fundamental intelligence
(implicate order). The few social psychologists who agree are known as
symbolic interactionists.

Many of us believe that modifying our brainwaves can help us achieve
greater awareness, control and order within our consciousness, and that
includes alteration of 'pathological patterns'. Further, there is the suggestion that skillful use of QEEG (quantifying) technology can reflect some
of these patterns, making it easier to modify them. The present focus in
our field on neurofeedback as a tool for fixing mental disorders through
manipulation of neurotransmitter processes, thalamic function, or neural
blood flow patterns is dramatic and seductive; however, it may also be paradoxically limiting NFB's full potential in so much as that kind of thinking sustains an overly mechanistic brain as a computer model, and ignores
the brain as a mediating organism, part of a biosystem involving the body
and the environment. We suggest that cognition links us to the implicate
order in ways contemporary science does not see, cannot yet measure,
prove or disprove.

This interactive integration with the implicate order is not fanciful
thinking, but has a sound theoretical basis in experimental physics and
experimental psychology. Neurofeedback presents us with dilemmas
which staunchly resist our efforts to confine it to a reductionist
perspective—and why shouldn't it? The brain is probably the most
complex structure in the known universe. Neurofeedback is an invaluable
tool for exploring dimensions of consciousness and how cognition and

consciousness directly impact all levels of health. The growing field of psychoneuroimmunology supports this perspective.

Relaxing the mind is not as easy as it first sounds (except when it is), and yet success at mental relaxation has critically important ramifications at all levels of experience. Meditation is not as simple as it first appears to be either (except when it is). Older systems of eastern psychology present us with extremely sophisticated maps of consciousness that we are only beginning to understand. Alpha training also has consequences which are easily overlooked if one is using a limited scientific perspective. To exclude, delegitimate or minimize this avenue of investigation (meditation and brain wave training) because it does not always agree with current, clearly questionable scientific models is less than sanguine and unscientific in itself. Such fearful delegitimation attacks have been aimed at many high caliber scientific thinkers including Carl Jung, Wolfgang Pauli, Abraham Maslow, Carl Rodgers, David Bohm, Milton Erikson, etc. For us alpha/theta neurofeedback can be an important adjunct to self-actualization, and accelerate the process of self-knowledge. For western man in the postindustrial era it may be one of the most effective ways to reintroduce important potentials and qualities of consciousness which modern life has tragically attenuated. The Process makes use of the best of traditional heuristic learning strategies, yet goes beyond cognitive psychology in its (optional) utilization of neurofeedback as a means to assist human beings in regaining access to latent potentials of the mind/body.

## The Process as New Technology

Just as science owes as much to early English coffeehouses and clubs as it does to universities, so wonderful, alternative mind/body models owe much of their vitality, and maybe their existence, to companies that have put their money where their mouths are, and practitioners who have gone deeply inside themselves and found ways to be effective with (and without) this technology. Furthermore, they have usually had to do this far ahead of academic laboratories. The Process is just a term implying that it is possible to understand how the mind/body works and to raise the level of functioning of one's own mind to much higher levels in much shorter times. Therefore, The Process uses whatever technology serves its mission. Many of us are now asserting that EEG biofeedback, especially in conjunction with other forms of biofeedback, can be an adjunctive bridge connecting material and nonmaterial aspects of consciousness. We continue to suggest that this notion has credence precisely because it is, like the mirror, a technology of self-knowledge.

One of the hypotheses of the new paradigm is that what we have in the past called 'spirit' is an aspect of the implicate order to which we can have direct cognitive links. Through this link we can actually alter the course of the so-called physical world when we engage it in the right way. If we reach out to those who believe use of concepts like spirit are unsound and too fuzzy, then we might see if substituting creative thought for spirit helps. Many outstanding thinkers are now suggesting that our thinking *is* our reality and it is changeable if we understand enough about how the mind, including thinking function, works. There is the further electrifying implication that practically anyone can learn enough about how the mind works to bring about astonishing quality of life changes.

Traditional science reflects a world view, which through the mind-matter division, prevents us from seriously considering such possibilities. A tragically limited mind/body model prevents the discovery of life changing mental tools laying in plain view, and relatively easy for almost all of us to learn to use. The Process builds bridges to that new model and assists in the leap from a life drowning, or at least treading water, in a sea of abstractions, to a life firmly rooted in the ground of actuality, the ground of being, contact with 'what is'. The Process implies access to the implicate order (collective unconscious if you like) and directly affecting change in the collective cultural reality.

The consequences for the individual are profound transformation and a direct experience of reality reserved in the past for a talented and privileged few. The avenue through which we access this is Profound

Attention, the combination of focused and unfocused attention. This concept is strikingly similar to those techniques used in several Buddhist systems of self-transformation as described by the psychologist Daniel Goleman in his review of the technical aspects of the Visuddhimagga. In fact, our research indicates that this concept is imbedded in many of the ancient traditions and was vigorously explored by Aldous Huxley in his work on the Perennial Philosophy.

The work of Krishnamurti, Bohm, and others is unfolding these principles directly out of the ground of our current culture, our being as we are now. In the same way this wondrous mind field of mental and emotional possibilities has emerged from the ground of being of past cultures, it is exploding now in our time. And as happened in the past, this human awakening carries with it the fourth dimensional quality of being born, as though for the first time ever. Like the dawn, like chaotic attractors, there has never been a day like this and there will never be again.

Our thesis implies that without awareness of our link to the implicate order we are like teenagers driving around in Dad's new sports car on a drunken Saturday night rampage. We haven't got full control of our human equipment and we are doing ourselves and others considerable damage as a consequence. If psychology is progressively proving a major portion of medical disorders are psychologically based, it is also confronting the problem that it must include what has been traditionally called a spiritual component to be maximally effective at the clinical level. The Process defines this enigma in modern technological terms and in a way that can be accessed by at least some of the general public directly and by most of the public with appropriate education and coaching. Of course, there is always the risk of classic pitfalls such as ritualism, dogmatism, and the commercial priesthood. If approached properly, however, these need not become impediments. May these words travel from our mouths to God's ears. May heaven protect us from those counter productive forces that often accompany success and organizational activity even as The Process becomes more successful and organized.

If we teach ourselves and our young to more fully use our capabilities, we can vastly reduce medical and psychological suffering. Surely, this will transform the world in an unimaginable way. Humans cause most suffering. We have a legacy of conditioning which blinds us to the urgency and the possibilities of fulfillment and healthy, life affirming change. We now have a new order of self-knowledge technology, a human technology which can help us overcome impediments to our fulfillment. By starting with subclinical symptoms and the professional/managerial class, we assert that the applied principles addressed by The Process ought to produce spontaneous improvements in the general population.

We base this assumption on the fact that the professional/managerial class is largely made up of the Actualizer segment of the Value Added Lifestyle Survey* and they are trendsetters, predicting with considerable accuracy the direction of the future. For example, in order for most people to implement The Process in their actual day to day lives, personal consumption patterns must change in a way which we believe takes pressure off the environment while leading to greater real productivity and quality of life. Cultural wisdom has lagged technology in a catastrophic fashion in this last century. NFB, as a 21st century human technology of consciousness, may exponentially increase our ability to adjust technological imbalances and atone for scientific sins of the past.

*The Value Added Lifestyle Survey is arguably the most important tool for understanding the market place developed to date. Based on Maslow's hierarchy of needs, it divides the market into nine segments, from highly conditionable, relatively unaware, easily exploitable 'consuming machines' to relatively aware, well educated, affluent, sophisticated consumers who also tend to be trend setters and who are relatively discriminating buyers. 'Actualizers' are the ninth and highest level in the VALS. They tend to be buying the things the majority will be buying in the future.

## Alpha Training and Focused Attention

Joe Kamiya discovered that alpha training seemed to result in a reduction in anxiety. Maxwell Cade and other experimenters found states of high alpha present in Zen masters and other adepts. Tom Budzynski experimented with alpha and theta states in conjunction with systematic desensitization techniques. He suggested that these alpha/theta 'Twilight States' might be useful for uncovering repressed material and reducing symptoms of many psychological disorders. Peniston and Kulkosky successfully used similar techniques in conjunction with visualization to assist alcoholics in their recovery process and to reduce PTSD symptoms. They had observed that alcoholics were generally low in alpha production compared with nonalcoholics.

Remember, the majority of the population are 'Alpha Responsives', meaning they can be trained to increase alpha fairly easily. Brain wave training for the minority of the population, 'Alpha Persistents and 'Alpha Minuses' may require modified brain wave training protocols. We believe training 'Alpha P's and M's is a valuable application of synchrony neurofeedback. Although alpha training alone has not produced any Zen masters to date, the correlation of the absence of alpha (in Alpha R's) with conditions of psychological suffering and the presence of alpha with peacefulness and serenity suggests that enhanced alpha is at least a potential indicator of psychological well being. Clinical work demonstrates that alpha increases can catalyze therapeutic processes, and a growing number of practitioners interested in performance enhancement and self-actualizing models claim it can be a tool for transformation.

Progress is being made in the struggle to understand brain wave training according to traditional neuroscience, relatively mechanistic, and organic models; however, such progress is frustratingly slow and fraught with many dead end, wild goose chases. We believe much greater progress will be made as we change the paradigm which we are using to understand NFB. We have only isolated some 100 or so neurotransmitters out of a

possible 500 and barely understand how they function. Some theorists
have suggested that brain wave training (especially alpha) affects the thalamus in some manner that restores neurotransmitters to healthy balances.
We believe that concept may well be true and if so the implications are
stunning; however, from a hard science point of view it does not seem
much better than just saying it works. It would perhaps be more fruitful
to widen and deepen our approach in order to improve this exciting,
emerging paradigm. Shedding light on what that paradigm might be is
one of the missions of The Process.

Les Fehmi has found that alpha (especially when it is relatively synchronous) is correlated with a condition he refers to as 'Open Focus' attention. His description of this state seems amazingly close to mind states
attributed to the 'right practice' of Buddhist meditation. Fehmi reports
that this 'Open Focus' attention reduces pain, psychological tension, sleep
disorders, allergies, asthma, etc. Further, he reports that vigorous practice
of 'Open Focus' attention produces renewed energy, productivity,
enhanced intimacy and self-disclosure experiences as well as an improved
self-image. In sum, application of this way of working with the mind
seems to be encouraging the organism to heal itself through some kind of
direct intervention at the CNS level.

Biofeedback as a discipline has made it clear that thinking has an
immediate effect on physiology. Mind and body are not in any way separate except as a superstition we have conditioned ourselves to believe.
Open Focus puts us in a new relationship with thought. We are less
entranced by the stream of automatic thinking which makes up our illusory social self. We are more fully awake to psychological, physiological,
and environmental processes unfolding in an expanded present. In The
Process we refer to this new relationship with the actual and thought as
'Profound Attention.'

Profound Attention, according to clinical experience, allows and
invites healing. We are better able to relinquish the cumulative effects
of unhealthy stress and reap the benefits of healthy stress. It is well

documented that the relaxation response physiologically reverses the effects of maladaptive stress (distress). If a majority of doctor visits are due to psychogenic problems, doesn't that imply that there must be psychological states that lead to optimum physiological functioning? We assert that Profound Attention *is* this state. Profound Attention has other attributes which have astonishing implications and we shall cover these more fully in chapters four and five. Evidence is overwhelmingly in favor of deep levels of attention (awareness) as being critical to optimal functioning. Those medical and psychological approaches that are effective in producing holistic healing, and a true transformation of life style usually, one way or the other bring the individual to this end point, this bed rock foundation which is built out of a deeper, higher quality attention/awareness. Some who are enthusiastic about the application of Chaos Theory to psychology believe Profound Attention qualifies as a kind of 'basin' which allows the materialization of benevolent 'strange attractors'. Beyond is the realm of spirituality.

## Conflicting Paradigms

Bohm's theories demonstrate that mind and matter are two aspects in reciprocal relationship which emerge from the implicate order. Actually, thought is a form of material reality. The human species is having an undeniable effect on the evolution of the universe in this corner of the galaxy. Profound Attention appears to be a bridge between mind and matter. Its full value is only beginning to be appreciated by western paradigms of reality. Even if we look at Profound Attention from a conservative material, Newtonian, mechanistic bias, this quality of mind holds considerable value for the field of human health.

There are, of course, important applications for QEEG technology and the training of beta and SMR frequencies. For example, QEEG can be helpful in determining best training sites in the case of brain injury. However, some of our esteemed colleagues seem to feel that QEEG (brain mapping) is necessary for every client regardless of the expense and inconvenience.

Many of these same practitioners seem to us to be over emphasizing high frequency training. We think this may be happening because QEEG and high frequency training is more easily correlated with what we see as a more comfortable, more generally acceptable yet outmoded and declining scientific paradigm. It is awkward and painful for us to say this because we so respect and value the enormous work and contributions many of our colleagues holding this bias are making. And we hasten to add that we feel their work is absolutely critical to the evolution of the field and to the effective treatment of many disorders. Furthermore, whereas we consider alpha to be low frequency training, many of the NFB establishment are beginning to include alpha in the high frequency category. They make some strong points. We are working it out.

Just as they are doing their jobs when they assert we have an alpha bias, we believe our job is to suggest that this beta bias rests on the belief that stimulating thinking and reconditioning sits at the pinnacle of psychological value. We assert this notion has merit and can produce results. To us stimulating thinking is like stimulating sex. It usually is unnecessary. The far greater problem is reducing the over activity of thought in order for something else which is more critical to the functioning of intelligence to emerge. We suggest that superior results can be attained by applying the principle of attention, and that is best done for most people through relatively low frequency training. We assert that in order for thought to function sanely, coherently it must 'rest' or take place within the field of attention/awareness, and further, that this paradigm moves us substantially closer towards something **else** which *is* at the pinnacle of psychological value. We see beta training as thinking training and its value is that, especially in the cases of ADD and some other disorders where it can cause a shift from dysfunctional thinking to a more functional variety of thinking. The model which makes most sense to us suggests that Profound Attention includes that 'beta thinking upgrade', and goes beyond thinking into realms of higher orders of intelligence. A kind of 'silent awareness' which brings a discipline and order to thought, and which leads to emotional intelligence and beyond.

The quantum alpha perspective seeks to wake up from all trance states including relatively functional ones. Symbolic thinking systems are illusory, virtual reality abstractions. They exist and we have no choice but to improve them as best we can. However, we also assert that it is possible for many self-knowledge devotees to leap into a mind field relatively free of abstract representations of creation. The result of this leap is a much greater grasp of and contact with actuality (what is), and the enhancement of moment to moment living this contact delivers. Krishnamurti and Bohm press this perspective in what some of us feel are three of the most important (visionary, revolutionary) pieces of literature of our century, **The Awakening of Intelligence, The Ending of Time,** and **The Limits of Thought.**

*"I agree, Adam, that the combination of Virtual Reality and Biofeedback will create some of the most powerful learning technology ever. However, if our perception of reality is determined and distorted by our thinking and conditioning then all of us are already living in a kind of virtual reality aren't we?"* Eric Peper

The relationship of thinking to profound attention/awareness seems to correlate eerily with the relationship of Relativity to Newtonian physics. They are both true but Newtonian physics exists as a subset within the vastly greater field of Relativity *"When pointing at the sun do not confuse the pointing finger for the sun itself."* Confusing the symbol for the actuality is a dangerous trap and a source of endless suffering.

## Self-Regulation

The concept of self-regulation is by itself enormously appealing. However, there is a deeper current which some may not be aware of, and which adds greatly to the beauty and social benefit of biofeedback. Simply stated, it is that reduction of the maladaptive stress response sets the mind/body on a path which if followed to the end leads to a strengthening of the highest personal and social values and insight. This kind of strengthening and insight leads to actualization, and actualizing one's potential seems to be the essence of living. Of course, there are many such 'paths' but there is something particularly beautiful, mysterious, and useful about technology that serves this purpose; technology which is itself rapidly evolving as though it also is somehow quickened by the lives it is benefiting.

For us this pattern or process unfolds in the following way. Reduction of the maladaptive stress response also reduces dysponesis (energy wastage) in the voluntary, autonomic and central nervous systems. A normal human being is a kind of energy generator, taking in nutrients including subtle mental and emotional foods, and transforming all of this into energy (which in turn is radiated back into the environment). Energy which is not wasted and is not needed for survival accumulates. If energy accumulates in a finite container (the human being) then it eventually explodes. This explosion *is* the creative process. Living creatively is one of those highest values both for the individual and the tribe.

Another deep current implied in the application of self-regulation/self-knowledge technology revolves around the problems of conditioning and fear. If we look at those things which cause greatest suffering and which are causing greatest damage to society and the environment we see that unhealthy conditioning as manifested in over consumption, ridiculously aggressive and counterproductive competitiveness, and fear are at the root of almost everything that is wrong with both the individual and the collective—the global village. We hasten to add that competitiveness has its place. The issue is that too much, way too much of a good thing can become too much, way too much of a bad thing.

There are a growing number of individuals who realize that something can be done about this unhealthy conditioning, suffering and fear. Those who are really good at it often become teachers, and these teachers are by and large teaching the same basic principles in different ways.

By the way, we feel that there is a huge problem with those who are themselves relatively dysfunctional teaching others how to be more functional than they. It is like allowing incompetent pilots to not only fly but teach others to fly. The cost is extremely high. It is a lot easier to determine what a competent pilot is than a competent therapist— teacher. For now, in our free market democracy all we have is caveat emptor. But then the essence of caveat emptor is awareness/Profound Attention isn't it? So we come full circle.

Fear is both physical and mental. Great progress can be made with most fear by working with the body. This manipulation, or self-regulation of the body requires attention, and attention itself reduces fear. Scientists and philosophers alike tell us that thought is matter and fear is a form of thought. Therefore, in so much as biofeedback learning can modify thought and fear, its value as technology can stretch toward infinity. The same technology can also be used to demonstrate the material nature of thought and fear. Energy pumped into thought makes thought 'thicker'; therefore, we are literally materializing what we think for better or for worse. We are also, to a substantial degree, materializing our fears and becoming what we think about.

As these principles are realized individually and collectively the science and art of enhancement of attentional processes, and reduction of unhealthy conditioning and fear will take on even greater importance because it will become increasingly clear that these mental vulnerabilities are the source of most if not all that has gone wrong. Have things gone wrong? Or is Universe unfolding as it ought? Either way, the good news is that these processes and misuses of the mind/body can be changed in a substantial part of the population…a large enough part to make a staggering difference worldwide.

*"Never doubt that a small group of thoughtful, committed citizens can change the world. Indeed, it's the only thing that ever has." Margaret Mead.*

# Chapter 4

# Details and Underpinnings of the Process

**Roots of The Process in Research and Clinical Experience**

In the last chapter we looked at the big picture...the social and philosophical dilemmas that surround neurofeedback and The Process. In this chapter we discuss some of the sources of The Process in research, where the ideas for it come from, and how we think these things explain neurofeedback and The Process. We are explaining the underpinnings of The Process and offering support for our approach in a more specific manner.

To us The Process is the convergence of many streams of thought and insight flowing from physics, psychology and metaphysics. Like Aldous Huxley, we see a perennial philosophy of spirit that is congruent with a common philosophy of mind emerging from different branches of psychology. Wolfgang Pauli, Fritz Capra, David Bohm, Fred Alan Wolf and a host of others inspire us by revealing beautiful interrelated patterns marrying physics, neuroscience, psychology, education and metaphysics. This convergence of the ancient and modern, of east and west, of mind and body, make up a kind of Process-Field, a benevolent environment, and a playground where (for some) the mastery of neurofeedback is just part of the fun.

The experiences of our clients have compelled us to seek maps and models to interpret those experiences outside of traditional science, because science is only just beginning to address the issues we encounter.

In some cases science is not sufficient to the task at all. Therefore, we must also acknowledge that our investigations and clinical experience have forced us to take into account the work of both spiritual and psychological traditions. Much of early psychology was embedded in religion.

It is also fair to call us dreamers for we do have a dream, but remember, we are also scientists and practitioners. These concepts are emerging from practices and laboratories, and we are applying them with all our strength *where the rubber meets the road* in the super school of our own day to day lives. The difference between our present approach and traditional perspectives is that this one is growing out of a western scientific tradition which is being forced to confront many questions it was not originally intended to deal with. Our science has matured. And yet our discoveries parallel our intuitive ancestors. We dream with lab equipment, equations and scientific methodology in hand. We find the dream an important part of reality.

We do not intend to just argue and conclude, but rather to explore and discover. We must move carefully, tentatively, always keeping in mind that The Process is nothing unless it is a living, growing, changing manifestation of the natural intelligence/wisdom enfolded in most, if not all of us. We assert that the sources of these ideas are impeccably pedigreed; however, space and the challenge of making this work as readable as we can for a wide audience precludes listing all citations. However, we intend to continue adding flesh to these bones in future works.

Up to this point we have done our best to present a coherent introduction to neurofeedback and provide a background of history, themes and ideas which can serve as a foundation for dialogue and deeper understanding. Now, we would like to explore further the basic concepts which make up The Process. We intend to lay out a rich history of ideas and research which support the concept of The Process—a Process that can be enhanced through application of heuristic learning and the principle of deep, heart-brain attention. Telling this story will, we hope, reveal the urgency of implementation of these principles as well as demonstrate the ripeness of this evolution at this liminal moment in time. We hope these concepts are as valid, as robust, and the implications as tantalizing for you as they are for us. In your personal pursuit of greater freedom, meaning and quality of life, we hope you will join us in the work and fun of this bountiful harvest.

## The Technology of Self-knowledge: Defining the Tools of the Trade Neurofeedback as just another step forward

Perhaps the best way to begin is to remind ourselves that gaining deep insight into who and what we are and what the mind is and how it works is of the highest order of human intelligence and aspiration. When we ponder what role technology plays in the gaining of true self-knowledge we come to an incredibly explosive place. We must go carefully here.

In the first place there is a rapidly growing consensus that there is an emerging technology of self-knowledge generally called biofeedback; although, that term will probably grow into something else in the future. We refer to it as 'self-knowledge technology' every chance we get. Biofeedback is essentially electronic mirrors which reflect back certain facts and details about the physical body. Once given this information it becomes possible, sometimes relatively easy, for the person using this equipment to make extremely subtle changes in the body which may be much more difficult, or virtually impossible, without this information or 'feedback'. These subtle changes in the body, especially over time, can produce large changes in thinking, feeling, creativity, intelligence, and perhaps more importantly, emotional intelligence. Understanding the value of this information and using it to improve the quality of life is an emerging scientific art form.

Let us again take this opportunity to make sure there is no misunderstanding about a critically important, an immense actuality. In our opinion everything that can be learned using biofeedback instruments can be learned without them…if the individual is sensitive (intelligent) enough. The issue really is, what is the most productive, common sense, healthy thing to do? Les Fehmi once told me that he had counted 2500 or more 'biofeedback instruments' within the human body. It is possible then to go directly to those inbuilt 'instruments' and countless numbers of inspired and gifted people have done this before us. In fact, they were the inspiration for the invention of the technology of self-knowledge. The question becomes, what is the appropriate use of technology in accelerating this kind of natural, heuristic learning Process? We can walk to San Fransisco from New York in about three months and such a walk would probably change the walker's life. But we can drive it in three or four days and fly in five hours and both of those modes seem to be more appropriate most of the time. What then is wrong with accelerating the acquisition of self-knowledge through the wise use of technology?

If we go deeper into the question of the technology of self-knowledge we see that there are many forms of technology which can reflect the truth of ourselves back to the mirror of our own minds. Examples of other self-knowledge technologies include mirrors (without the smoke), audio and videotape, photographs, microscopes and diagnostic instruments of all kinds. Going further we see that writing itself is technology, and that certain kinds of writing, from a training journal to poetry, can deepen our understanding of who and what we are; and that deepening can mean everything in terms of true growth and life enhancement. Journaling is also an important aspect of the Process and one we employ extensively.

To date we, as a society, have progressively employed all these technologies in the service of self-knowledge. In fact, if we consider the abundance of excellent teachers of the concept and practice of self-knowledge, we see that they use many forms of technology to spread their work, from transportation to communication and media, including the full gamut of the digital revolution, 'R Tech' (Relationship Technology) and the Internet. Going even further, we see that wise and subtle minds are pointing out that all tools are technology and that the first tool was probably the first word…"In the beginning was the word". Anthropologists might say that the first tool was probably a stick, a rock, or fire, but we prefer to push the envelope by suggesting that it was the first word, the first thought. And any tool's greatest purpose is to teach us who and what we are. To bring us ever closer to the greatest of all teachers…The Mirror of Relationship. Within relationship is found some of the most enriching forms of feedback and a reconnection with what is. This is a pathway to integration, transcendence, and unity; perhaps completion of a cycle. In a very wide sense all technology is a reflection of the Mind and therefore, an opportunity to learn the truth about ourselves. To paraphrase John Lilly: A human being is an assembly of trillions of cells that the Universe has put together as a means of being aware of Itself. Many call it the 'anthropic principle'. So those that say that there is the spiritual and there is technology may be making the understandable but tragic mistake of dualistic thinking. Music was once only a 'spiritual' technology, as was writing. Visualization has been harnessed as a tool from the earliest of times. Neurofeedback is just another step, another refinement in the application of technology to the all-important mission of self-knowledge. We have unfolded out of the Great Mind, and technology has unfolded out of our mind. It is critically important that we are aware of and profoundly attend to That Source.

*"What makes the anthropic principle and the Gaia hypothesis so inspiring? One simple thing: both remind us of what we have long suspected, of what we have long projected into our forgotten myths and what perhaps has always lain dormant within us as archetypes. That is, the awareness of our being anchored in the earth and the universe, the awareness that we are not here alone, nor for ourselves alone but that we are an integral part of higher, mysterious entities against whom it is not advisable to blaspheme." Vaclav Havel*

### More on other forms of feedback

This morning the wind is rolling in like waves on the sea…steady regular surges making the trees whisper…calling the wind along a path, a faint trail of listening. Suddenly, the wind is quiet for a bit and in the silence there is a subtle sense of anticipation. The cicadas and crickets have become much less noisy now, just a small, background whirring sound. Sound is so basic. "In the beginning was the word." If the Big Bang is right what a word it was!

Can we be just friends, pilgrims, an invisible extension, parts of us, our own minds reflecting back and sharing the fun, the delight, the difficulties, the dangers of our journey together? Movies, theater, TV, and novels reflect our mind(s) back to us. These are forms of visualization. Mostly it is appalling, beating our consciousness down into a numbed, discouraged insensibility. Books and radio guide our visualization in a general way, but TV and movies are more specific. One could argue that movies are modern yantras of Shakespeare's basic plots, or that they are the cultural daydream of an adolescent civilization. They reflect back to us how we might explore life if we were immortal like the actors who return to life in different movie incarnations. Once in awhile these stories inspire us to reach....to reach for what? What are these movies reaching for? Safety, love, self-esteem, potential self-actualizations? Aren't these images the things that guide us to our goals? Part of The Process is understanding that visualization can be used more effectively if we can only understand it better.

It has been suggested that the older brain structures utilize images, while the newer cortex employs symbols and finally words. But the words and images are bound together in human experience as much as the new cortex and the older brain structures are bound in function. Many clinicians have found that you often get better results when you talk to yourself in images rather than words. They observe that we usually dream in images, although, it is clear that there is considerable dreaming in words as well. The language of the automatic subconscious processing systems of the brain is believed to be primarily imagery. Of course, Carl Jung based much of his life work on this idea. The anology in modern computers might be how Windows uses DOS. So master clinicians like Milton

Erikson devised a whole vocabulary of visualizations to help individuals profoundly alter their story and discover doorways out of their dilemmas.

Today there are hundreds of books on how to employ visualization to transform yourself and profoundly change your life. Many of these books tell us we can have whatever we want if we can only visualize it. Famous pro golfers and other athletes tell us you can't win without it. Quantum mechanics tells us we can influence reality with our minds, but they don't have a calculus to describe this kind of grand influence. Nevertheless, amazing changes occur when we engage in these activities appropriately. The question is, what is appropriately? We can learn a lot from Milton Erikson's methods as well as many forms of meditation. Visualization is also a powerful tool in what we call alpha-theta training in neurofeedback. In every case, we seem to need a vision which connects with our own story.

Tellers of stories sometimes say there are only a few stories, but because these stories are classical, true archetypes, there are unlimited ways to tell them. Who will tell your story? Will you, will I? Like a chorus will we sing it together? Stories are often told according to a formula which rewards the storytellers with lots of money. This equation has evolved over a long time and it is successful because in the main it brings pleasure and excitement to human beings who are trapped in what may be termed 2nd or 3rd dimensional consciousness. When we are in this mode we want to identify with someone else, a movie star, a sports figure, a business tycoon, an artist, someone who seems to have a better life than we, because too much of the time we feel trapped by a kind of second hand consciousness.

*"Mankind is ruled by tall tales." Einstein*

Stories can, however, guide and liberate us as they do in the best of literature, ancient and modern. Stories are rich mirrors of information which reflect back to us what we know or what others know. In the telling both the storyteller and the listener grow as they integrate their new understanding. The parable is a powerfully concentrated story form used in western spiritual traditions. Learning to use stories and telling your own powerfully and consciously is central to growth, relationship and life enhancement.

So let us ask ourselves, are there really only a few old stories? Or is there something always altogether new in the seemingly old? Dare we think that we, conditioned and brutalized, overstimulated by the way society is, by some of our storytellers…dare we seek a new story? What is your story? Do you have the big picture or only fragments of a jumbled novel? What kind of power can a disjointed story have? Will you continue reading if it is not well told?

Dare we seek a new cultural story? As Joseph Campbell, Steve Larson, Jean Houston, and many others have said…a new mythology? But is myth a misleading word? For these 'myths' are matter already, and they are Creation Itself materializing our reality, our society, our world, our Actuality. Do stories manifest civilizations (and if they can) what can they manifest for you? Can you liberate yourself from the cultural myths to discover new lands? Perhaps a hidden civilization? It could be right under your nose. But that journey is for heroes and, who are you anyway? Just who do you think you are!?

We romanticize ancient times and think, if only we had been born at some ideal time in the past; say, 50, 100, 1000 or 5000 years ago, we would have been able to have a better life…our story would be an Original One, a heroic one. We would not find ourselves in a life that feels somehow tired, mundane, over conditioned. Surely, the belief that another time would have been better is illusion. Perhaps we can find a way to live originally as easily now as we would if we had been born in those imagined simpler times. By my reckoning we have it far easier than our forbearers had it if we are at all serious about seizing the moment and living life fully. In any case, what choice have we? Is continuing in a conditioned, secondhand life a viable option? There is no other game in town but to reach for the original life…to 'remember' how to be who we really are. And we must begin from where we are. We must bloom where we are planted.

## Trances and Consciousness

Our culture, the stories we are told, and the beliefs we hold for the most part have the effect of dulling awareness and luring us into trancy states of consciousness. We conceptualize these states as first, second or third dimensional consciousness. The word trance, like the words meditation, attention, hypnosis, is problematical. We and others are pressing for much more careful definitions of these concepts. We suggest StephenWolinsky in his book, **Trances People Live,** makes a major contribution to understanding about trance. Our perspective views trances as essentially *dissociative* in nature, and even in the best cases far below the quality of high order (fourth dimensional) super-functional, associative, actuality-oriented, creative states of consciousness and thinking. They are by definition a form of virtual reality which reduce the level of awareness in the present, and our ability to connect with what is actually taking place. We recognize that many of our colleagues believe these trance like states may actually play a kind of protective role, sort of like a circuit breaker when the power of the perceptions coming in is too much for the system to handle. We respect their points of view; however, we assert that the time has come to focus on increasing the ability of the circuitry to handle the truth, and further that this is the most efficient way to improve the quality of life for the greatest percentage of the population.

Many of us recall how bright and alive the world looked through the eyes of childhood. Jesus and other spiritual leaders told us it is wise to look upon the world with the eyes of a child. Yet the emergence of the image of the self or ego seems inevitable and this image or set of images is both a product and a propagator of conditioning, especially conditioning which limits consciousness and emotional intelligence. We develop habits and subroutines to manage our complex lives. We habituate to our environment until we see our seeing instead of what is there.

Research on perception tells us that we select out of our memory the images we need to construct the world we expect and are conditioned to see. Our present perception of reality is powerfully shaped by our past, by our beliefs, by our hopes, by our fears. So habit, this "great fly wheel of society", as William James referred to it, seems to be both essential to survival and yet destructive to our ability to fully experience the wonder and mystery of life.

*"If we could but cleanse the doors of perception we would find a world of astounding beauty that is miraculous in nature." Aldous Huxley*

These subroutines of habit constantly draw us into trances as Stephen Wolinsky notes. They cloud our perception of the moment and distract us. The remarkable Vedic teacher Vivekenanda likened these heavily conditioned mind states to a wild monkey sitting on our shoulder and screaming into our ear all day long (no disrespect meant to wild monkeys). We respond much too mechanically to the cues of our environment based on our past programming. The ego, guiding us with shields up and defense mechanisms in place, makes us slaves, asleep at the wheel. Meantime nature celebrates her miraculous party of life while many of our own, our brothers and sisters unnecessarily waste away, plodding down the road of life in a mostly sad and lonely, disconnected, dreamy trance.

*"Life is a banquet and most poor s.o.b.'s are crawling around under the table looking for crumbs." Auntie Mame*

Can we wash away these clouds of the past and shine our mind mirror until we can see our true self, and experience the joy of being? Many great teachers tell us yes, but it is arduous. We usually prefer a quick pill in western culture. We do have several such pills. Serotonin agonists such as LSD and Psilocybin can wash away this conditioned mind, but only for a few hours. Research by Masters and Houston as well as Stanlislov Grof suggests that less than 5% of the population can derive any lasting profound insights from the pill (psychedelics). Most of those who do, are usually older and have laid a lot of the groundwork for these experiences through years of efforts at self-knowledge. Those who don't, just experience a sensory roller coaster ride or worse, temporary psychosis. This reminds us that The Process involves much more than implementation of technology, whether it be drugs, neurofeedback or whatever.

The path of sudden insight is also fraught with sudden peril. Those who wish for instant Nirvana must contend with this peril. It would appear that the Zen masters have pushed the envelope as far as one can at this point in history with regard to the techniques of sudden insight. Their pioneering work in this area suggests that there are ways to accelerate the process of self-knowledge, but that a certain investment in time and effort is usually required. Certain highly specialized environments are required which are not accessible to the average postmodern postindustrial man. Renunciation of mainstream social life and the monastic retreat are essential to this ancient mode of transformation. We suggest that the kind of leaps of mind and spirit required for this massive increase in quality of life can be achieved by ordinary people living ordinary lives. Assisting in that achievement is the mission of The Process.

### Are we going too fast?

Spiritual greed does not work either. The Dalai Lama in a recent lecture on the Tibetan spiritual technology laughed about how westerners always ask him what is the fastest, most efficient, most productive method to enlightenment. To him this is funny because he looks at the process in terms of lifetimes. Perhaps our technology will allow us to accelerate the process at this point. But there are questions which should be asked. If we monkey with the monkey too much, could we end up with psychosis instead of self-actualization and transcendence? Might we push the biology too hard? Traditional literature is full of stories of those who have gone mad in their search for the 'Holy Grail'. Indeed madness was a concern for the Desert Fathers as well as Tibetan masters such as Milarepa. It concerned Carl Jung, Krishnamurti, David Bohm, Tim Leary, Richard Alpert, John Lilly, Carlos Castenada and a host of others in search of truth that better enables us to meet the challenges we face in the modern world.

That said, we assert The Process strives to be as safe as possible. We have studied the conditions of this madness and we believe we have found methods to circumvent it. Many feel neurofeedback can have a 'mind balancing', healing and integrating effect. As the mind becomes more integrated it is transformed into a new vehicle of higher level processing—intuition and insight as different from linear plodding. Confusion tends to disperse and solutions tend to emerge. Suffering becomes more transparent. Besides, what is more dangerous, striving to wake up or trudging along as a sleepwalker? And for those who are ready, who can stand the heat, the incredible good news is that the most important orders of learning do not take time as we normally understand time. Real learning can happen extremely fast if we approach it properly. Of course, that sounds like gospel, but we shall do our best to provide the conditions which will allow you to discover this astonishing truth for yourself in your own way. The essence of NFB, Raja Yoga, many other forms of 'teachings' and The Process is DO IT NOW! THE FUTURE IS NOW! Take heaven by storm if you can. Why not?

Utilizing the principles upon which The Process is founded can help rouse the entranced and automatic mind and make it more aware of its subroutines. This increase of self-awareness breeds greater sensitivity to conditioning. We refer to this new level of awareness as Fourth Dimensional Consciousness–a neo(new) stasis (state). Individuals can make conscious changes in their conditioning, as when Aron Beck taught depressed individuals to alter their negative automatic thoughts. The experience of enhanced self-awareness is transformative and healing. According to Wolinsky, it is a tool which is widely used in psychotherapy, but is used in a manner which is usually not acknowledged. Our experience is that neurofeedback can accelerate this emergence of a new level of awareness, a neostasis, when used in conjunction with the concepts and techniques employed in The Process. Neurofeedback appears to accelerate the development of skills that usually take years longer to develop through most types of meditative techniques and/or years of psychotherapy.

### Considering its power is neurofeedback safe?

Back in 1971 I was consulting with Gay Gaer Luce (author of the highly acclaimed book, **Body Time**) and Erik Peper (a leading biofeedback researcher, practitioner, educator and author). I was worried about the power of biofeedback as it related to abreactions. Janov had developed a controversial form of therapy called Primal Scream, and there had been a number of law suits relating to the problems that seemed to occur as the patients went through apparently abreactive experiences. I recognized that biofeedback could accelerate the learning of deep relaxation and mind quieting, and that could in turn produce powerful abreactions. I was especially concerned about EEG biofeedback, and when I asked Gay for her thinking on this matter she responded in a way that was both surprising and comforting.

If my memory serves me right, I can paraphrase her thinking as follows: In the first place she implied that we cannot be sure of what will happen because the whole field is just beginning and the research is yet to be done. However, she believed that there was probably going to be a vast difference in the kind of abreactive experiences that many 'primal scream' patients were having and those produced by skillful biofeedback training. Her reasoning was that essentially biofeedback training was a manifestation of a self-knowledge, meditation model, and that such a method of self-regulation was likely to have a 'built in governor'.

Gay's meaning as I interpreted it was that if biofeedback is applied using a classic stress management meditation strategy, repressed psychological material would more than likely tend to emerge in a timely, healthy way. In that case, the practitioner would need to provide 'arms,' that is a safe, comfortable environment so the client could go through the experience and receive the therapeutic and educational benefits healthy abreactions are supposed to deliver. Almost thirty years later, I cannot think of a single heavily experienced biofeedback practitioner (including Dr. Soutar and myself) who would not agree with her point of view. In fact, most of us are amazed that there have not been more problems reported. And, of course, all of us realize we must continue to be careful and take nothing for granted.

## Neurofeedback and Neuromodulators:
## Looking closer at the neural mechanisms

Neuropsychiatry suspects psychosis may involve the malfunction of several neuromodulator circuits in the brain stem and mesolimbic dopamine system. Most of the drugs used to control schizophrenia seem to target the dopamine circuit in the brain which emerges from a subcortical area known as the Basal Ganglia and Substantial Nigra. Too much Dopamine is highly correlated with schizophrenia. Too little dopamine is correlated with ADD as well as Alcoholism. The drugs that affect these disorders such as Ritalin, methadrine, alcohol, cocaine, etc. all influence the level of dopamine in the synapse. Dopamine levels also become raised during habituation cycles of the attentional process in which brain stem activities in the reticular formation influence frontal lobe activities. Paul Wender injected L-dopa into patients with ADD, the same product used to manage dopamine deficiencies in Parkinson's disease, and found significant improvements in attention. It is interesting to note that the clinical areas which neurofeedback has initially had the most impact on are ADD and alcoholism. Kulkosky told me that he had noted the relationship between low dopamine levels and low alpha production in alcoholics and this encouraged him in his hypothesis that alpha training might impact this deficiency.

The details are still unclear and much research is needed, but interesting patterns are emerging. Research on the mesolimbic dopamine system indicates that attention, memory, motivation and pleasure are all interconnected circuits running off the neurons which produce dopamine.

When something challenges our thinking we tend to drop out of alpha and gear up our brain for processing in beta. Dopamine levels increase and local cortical circuits start working. GABA decreases and Ron Ruden suggests serotonin levels decrease. Nunez reports that theta levels drop with serotonin increases as well. If we do not find the solution to the event or problem that has triggered our concern, then eventually this system becomes exhausted and serotonin levels drop (presumably for protection). If we find ourselves in a 'double-bind' and learned helplessness sets in, we move into depression and a serotonin level that biases our dopamine system so low that we find little pleasure in anything. That's when we begin to rely on intense stimuli to enhance our dopamine levels and stimulate our pleasure center in the nucleus accumbens. We become reliant upon these intense stimuli and addiction sets in.

Pet scans show us a frontal region which is hypofused with blood, where metabolism is low in both ADD and Schizophrenia. The QEEG maps of E. Roy John printed in the journal *Science* also show high levels of theta activity in an underaroused frontal cortex in schizophrenics. Too little dopamine and low serotonin seems correlated with the shutting down of the frontal cortex. Neurophysiologists tell us the frontal cortex has an inhibitory function on all other brain processes. When the frontal area is not operating at the right level of arousal, as regulated by our brain stem, the rest of the brain's systems seem to malfunction. Global slow waves dominate the brain and it becomes hypo-coupled. Operating systems do not work together enough and there is a lack of integration. People become impulsive and under regulated, moody, irritable, and depressed. Psychosis may emerge.

Nunez reports a theta dominant schizophrenia and a beta dominant schizophrenia. This suggests that dopamine sometimes continues to run too high and GABA levels become too low. Anxiety is overwhelming and the individual may become compulsive and over controlled. Obsessive-compulsive disorder emerges, and if the neurotransmitters get too far out, neural confusion and hyper-coupling of local circuits dominates the individual, possibly in the 23-38hz range. Again psychosis emerges. As James Austin notes, "the brain seems delicately balanced between seizure and coma."

The evidence suggests EEG training seems to be influencing these neuromodulator circuits, especially the dopamine circuit. We also seem to be able to influence the serotonin circuits through bilateral training of alpha in clients with depression. Nunez is currently trying to develop a model correlating neuromodulator changes with EEG changes. Although more research needs to be done, many experts in neurofeedback believe that at least some types of NFB training seem to be restoring, as **The Craving Brain's** author Ron Ruden would say, "bio-balance".

The existing research lends credence to the view that alpha training may be underutilized clinically at this point. It is correlated with increased endorphin and enkephalin production as well as decreased cortisol levels. Sterman's work with pilots indicates the important role it plays in performance with respect to stress and recovery cycles. Early research shows its correlation with healing and meditative states. The medical profession is increasingly advocating the importance of a rested CNS in healing. It has been documented that State and Trait anxiety levels can be reduced with alpha NFB. Norris et al are finding it a key component to attention enhancement. Some of us think that alpha training may lead toward greater integration of the self by overriding the habituation process to all our subroutines through the process of global habituation itself. This is paradoxical, but makes a certain kind of sense from a neurological perspective. It may allow us to disengage from long term potentiation loops that keep us locked into vicious cycles of mental behavior such as negative automatic thoughts.

These trances of the ego, the subroutines of behavior and automatic thoughts of the social conversation, become the streets of the self-construed virtual reality we travel in our daily rounds. The research of social psychologists such as Kelly and Festinger document other generic automatic subliminal programs that ghost write the fundamental scripts and emotional patterns of daily life, and which seem hard wired into our cortex. Joseph LeDoux writes about the cognitive and emotional problems our subconscious processing can create, and outlines the neural circuitry involved in detail-again the mesolimbic system. We become conditioned without even realizing it and then become slaves to our own conditioning.

Alan Schore, grounding his presentation in the latest research in neurophysiology, beautifully describes the etching of templates of emotional response into the prefrontal orbital cortex during the first 24 months of post-natal neural development and which we will use to play out the scenes of our future life. Rarely do we actually emerge from all this conditioning for a moment to experience life with the doors of perception cleansed. Powerful events such as religious conversion, sky diving, childbirth, winning the race, the big check in the mail, romantic love, etc. can sometimes do it for us. But what if being itself offers us a fulfillment that is always present? What if it is our birthright? This is what ancient Judeo-Christian, Buddhist, Islamic, and other spiritual systems teach. Most of us may never truly relax long enough to find out.

Researchers in neurofeedback are discussing the possibility that ADHD and schizophrenia may be related to organizational problems starting in the brainstem and affecting areas of the mesolimbic system and ventral medial prefrontal cortex (of course we need to remember this happens in a context of social stress). It follows that neurofeedback might be able to reduce these kinds of symptoms. Depending on how the research is interpreted, it seems reasonable that we can reduce this problem of frontal cortex disorganization with more balanced dopamine levels in the mesolimbic circuit and/or more alpha production (as well as a better organized life). Many of us think that alpha training may lead toward greater skill in organizing activity in the cortex, further enhancing the sense of order and healing. As we move into quieter mind states more regularly we can begin to jettison our old luggage and unhealthy conditioning without drugs or other dependencies, including neurofeedback itself. We can learn to balance in the moment with our minds, like riding a bike.

**Traditional Concepts of Attention Vs Profound Attention:
Thinking and EEG Biofeedback as a Mind Compass**

Psychology sees the brain as an aggregate of complex systems which have evolved over millions of years. We can see the history of the evolution of all animal nervous systems across the phylogenetic scale reflected in our own brain structure. These systems are coordinated during our attentional process to bring different sensory experiences and internal images together in meaningful patterns to guide our behavior in a manner which insures survival. The parietal cortex is the center for the attentional processes, and lesions to this area clearly show up as decrements in attentional functions. The parietal lobe works in conjunction with the frontal cortex, mesolimbic system, temporal lobe memory circuits and the reticular formation in the brain stem to orchestrate the movement of attention in its fullest sense, involving dimensions or levels of consciousness and information processing utilized as feedback to further guide the system. A detailed discussion requires volumes, and requires a good command of brain anatomy, physiology and histology to understand fully. We are only beginning to understand attention because it implicates and involves the entire brain in its operation.

Psychologists have attempted to categorize attention with regard to function. Selective attention allows us to focus on foreground features of our sensory fields according to a complex input of cues from the various associated centers of the brain. If we sustain this process on one feature of our sensory field long enough we are engaging in focused attention. We can expand the focus of our attention until we have taken in large areas of our sensory field as well as our mental processing, an extremely beneficial quality of mind which Les Fehmi describes as open focus attention. In fact Fehmi's research suggests that narrowing the focus of attention usually does not enhance learning or facilitate the processing of information. This makes sense when we consider the research on divided attention which shows us that men, in particular, are able to listen to two different stories at the same time and recall detail surprisingly accurately.

Subliminally we continue to scan all the information entering our sensory memory from our sensory field and only become conscious of it if it contains important information relevant to our situation as we construe it. People who have taken psychedelic drugs often report the experience of being aware of every movement in their sensory field at the same time. Les Fehmi offers training in this type of skill and suggests our use of narrow attention is culturally inspired. Research by the sociologist Charles Durber supports this idea of the social parceling of attention for purposes of status and hierarchy maintenance. Buckminster Fuller presented extraordinary evidence that natural generalists have been made into specialists by most educational systems over the recent centuries (strong generalists were usually 'not for sale' and perceived as a threat to the status quo.)

When we continually experience a stimulus which is not of importance to us we eventually habituate to it. We may first encounter the strange smell of a new friend's home but find we eventually lose awareness of it as we remain longer in the house. We do this with all our sensations. If we can reduce the natural saccades of our eye movement enough, we can experience the dropping out of visual information. When there is little activity in the outside world, we tend to shift our attention to the relatively greater activity of the inside world.

Psychological evaluation of Buddhist and Zen meditation training methods indicates that the use of attentional training is central to their technique. Hindu, Sufi, and many Christian prayer and meditation techniques utilize this same principle. These learning systems often focus on 'one-pointed' attention. This concept is one of the most misunderstood and difficult mind skills to teach and learn (except in those cases where it apparently spontaneously happens which we believe NFB can make more likely). This technique is often described as requiring the maintenance of a continual focus on one sensory or processing modality to the exclusion of all others. The Process tries to do a much better job of organizing and verbally communicating these kinds of strategies. For example, we think the term 'exclusion of all others' is a misleading effort of third dimensional consciousness to describe a fourth dimensional quality of perception.

Regardless, of how this way of working with the attentional processes is learned, it appears to result in substantial physiological changes, especially in the brain. The thought processes begin to slow down, respiration decreases and the heart rate drops. Carbon dioxide levels increase in the blood and the brain begins to register the consequences of this shift in metabolism. A variety of sensory phenomena can occur including visual and auditory imagery. The visual field can become white or drop out entirely until one experiences a black void in which only awareness remains. Affective experiences of bliss, rapture and joy also may occur, as well as abreactive and archetypal episodes of a disturbing or fearful nature, although the disturbing events are not usually considered bad news when they take place under the circumstances of these kinds of self-exploratory conditions.

The cartographers of consciousness in the east have documented most of these phenomena and have an entire educational technology established around them. James Austin, Professor Emeritus of Neurology at the University of Colorado, claims not only to have experienced many of these altered states first hand, but has also gone into painstaking detail explaining them by drawing on his extensive knowledge of the literature on neurophysiology. All this from the manipulation of attention using the so-called 'one point' strategy. The Process posits that another and perhaps better way to think of this phenomenon is that the real thing takes place within a deep multidimensional field of attention, and that within this field a high degree of focus can take place, but that 'effort' to make it happen is problematical at best. Trying too hard seems to block, yet there must be intention and attention. Somehow the 'heart' must be 'drawn' in the right 'direction.' We have termed this mind quality 'Profound Attention'. We think the term 'one point' may be another poor translation of Sanskrit text.

In terms of EEG the research reports high levels of alpha production (in combination with theta) at various specific frequencies occurs in meditation. These are frequencies indicating a brain which is at rest with respect to local cell column processing, but very active in global cortical loops. Austin and others also report a high frequency beta (gamma) component as well. It is speculated that this gamma component seems to be related to vigilance, and that slightly lower frequencies may be correlated with hyper vigilance and other pathological activities when they are too predominant. Other researchers report high levels of alpha symmetry including synchrony.

The healing properties of these meditative altered states, arising from attentional techniques, have been well documented by medical research, and have been incorporated into the field of Health Psychology. The psychological benefits have also been well documented. Unfortunately our culture continues to under use this technology. Many like us are experimenting with both meditation and various modes of alpha and theta training in an attempt to uncover relationships between the two. Our experience and clinical observations suggest to us that these meditative states (or states similar to them) can be achieved relatively rapidly utilizing neurofeedback to generate brainwave patterns similar to those recorded in advanced meditators. Experiential reports are similar as well. However, as most experts in the meditative technologies can tell you, it is not just a matter of experience, but also how we integrate that experience into the day to day reality of our lives. The Process is designed to integrate these experiences as rapidly as possible. The problem is often not how fast you can attain these levels of experience, but how well can you deal with the changes they bring into your everyday life.

The top ten causes of death are due to failures in self-regulation (alcoholism, overeating, driving too fast, unprotected sex etc.) and most of us are not living very healthy lives. Many of us are not prepared to make the changes these altered states suggest are necessary if we are going to enhance the quality of our daily lives. This is where preparation becomes most important.

## Getting to Profound Attention

None of us actually knows exactly how brain wave biofeedback is working although some of us are talking with greater confidence than is probably justified. Surely, all of our views are hypothetical—including the authors'. We've dubbed our hypothetical spin the Profound Attention model, and we believe it to be consistent with quantum physics and the work of a huge list of philosophical and neuroscience leaders. We hold that thought is already a form of subtle matter and (like movies and computers) thinking is a material process as well as an image making process based on memory. Furthermore, high order 'Profound Attention' is probably the most important mental asset a human being can have. This deep, 'heart felt' level of attention brings coherence (EQ) to thinking while reducing dysfunctional thinking.

Capacity for 'Profound Attention' can in many, if not most, human beings be enhanced. This enhanced 'Profound Attention' carries with it the capability of conscious observation of thought. The implications are that watching oneself think is the healthiest possible way to manage and improve the quality of thought. This observation is a kind of 'field'. Einstein said, "The field is the soul governing agency of the particles". In this case the particles are thought. The implication follows that one of the most effective ways in the history of learning to enhance this 'Profound Attention' and improve the quality of thought may be slow wave, relatively synchronous neurofeedback training.

This hypothesis further asserts that as cartographers of consciousness we must now come to much more precise definitions of intelligence, thinking, imagery which transcends thinking, attention, consciousness, feeling, emotion, felts, and meditation etc. in order to clarify what we really want to reach for, what we want to communicate, teach and actualize.

If the ancient (and many of the modern masters) are correct, the problem is that psychothenia (over thinking, unconscious or unobserved thinking) is the fundamental barrier to the natural intelligence and creativity latent in humans. And if it is true that in most of the population (at least 2/3rds according to the work of Grey Walter, and there are modified brain wave training strategies for the other third) alpha can be relatively easily trained, and if it is also true that slow wave (alpha/theta) but mostly midrange alpha training can enhance the ability to profoundly attend to internal (thought, archetypal imagery, etc.) as well as external phenomena simultaneously, in real time; then indeed alpha/theta neurofeedback (skillfully applied) is one of the most valuable educational tools ever developed. Like a compass it can help the mind find its way through the confusion of too much, and overly conditioned thinking, to Profound Attention, the road less traveled, relative neural silence, the way home, the source of the inspired and inspiring life.

This hypothesis is not prejudiced against fast wave training (SMR/beta); however, it does hold that the type of 'attention' enhanced by SMR/beta training should be redefined as a kind of 'seize and hold' attention...a kind or class of attention highly impregnated by thought and very useful in its own right. This kind of attention is not the 'Profound Attention' enhanced by alpha/theta; it can, however, lead to 'Profound Attention'. And we suggest that should be a goal of advanced neurofeedback training (including many if not most ADHD clients). In fact, I believe that there is a crucial difference between the orders of attention and the orders of thinking. And if we define thinking as image making process based on memory then 'data- capture-and-hold' type of attention (the kind we train for in ADHD therapy) learning is actually thinking training. We assert most SMR/beta training teaches the learner to think in more functional ways. Of course, the Profound Attention model holds that this thinking quality shift is mediated by true attention. We are training the client to change from a less functional type of thinking to a more functional type of thinking. Obviously, I could be mistaken about this;

however, I strongly believe that the evidence indicates the essential validity of this hypothesis.

I once asked Dr. Les Fehmi to work with me teaching Attention Deficit Disorder protocols, and he commented, "Who in the world does not have Attention Deficit Disorder?" He was, of course, referring to the almost universal deficiency in the exercise of what we term 'Profound Attention' (Dr. Fehmi might prefer 'Open Focus Attention') as differentiated from 'data-capture-and-hold' (thinking) type of attention. 'Profound Attention' may be general or focused, and carries with it a quality of depth, or emotional integration as though one is attending with the heart as well as the brain. It is the essence of emotional intelligence.

Consider what type of attention dominates our culture. Dr. Fehmi notes that we cling to this narrow focused attention in our culture as if it were the only legitimate way to attend. We think research supports the notion that relying too much on a narrow, focused 'beta consciousness' may not be the most efficient form of information processing. In fact, as we have said, it may be more a consequence of social forces, politics, and unhealthy conditioning than anything else. A culture that demands strong hierarchy also conditions thinking to place a disproportionate value on personality, physical, economic and other factors leading to inappropriate comparisons, competition etc., and the stimulation of psychothenia (over thinking) and other mental disorders. Attention is status. Our notion is that wrong use of attention leads to personal and cultural isolation and disorder.

Our hypothesis is that what we are calling Profound Attention is a form of awareness that requires skill, maturity and neuronal balance to achieve. If achieved it propels the attender into continuous growth and actualization of latent potential. The kind of maturity required does not relate to age. In fact, these orders of attention spontaneously occur with many children, and when they happen in adults others tend to describe those adults as childlike, and they mean it as a compliment. Although, it may seem difficult for the reader at first, it is important to remember that when we say Profound Attention requires skill and work and maturity, we are referring to the problem of unconditioning heavily conditioned people, usually adults. There are plenty of cases of unusually gifted adults and children achieving these high orders of attention, consciousness, and awareness simply, spontaneously in a natural easy way. In fact, we believe one of the long term goals of this way of working (The Process) is to develop an educational system and cultural milieu which supports and nurtures heuristic education and these much better, less conditioned ways of using the mind.

## (Naughty?)Theta and Trances

One of the problems of definition that exists with regard to trances and attention is the confusion over theta brain waves. As we have suggested, it appears that there is healthy theta and unhealthy theta, which might be dubbed Htheta and Utheta. This model holds that unhealthy theta relates to a kind of trance-like behavior, the result of which is a kind of detachment from 'what is'. We assert that these dissociative phenomena may be broken out of by 'Profound Attention'. Indeed, awareness of one's own dissociation may be a prerequisite for breaking through. Prolonged attention/awareness (Profound Attention ) may be the only way of not falling back into dissociation. Many of us have noticed how alpha training tends to attenuate the unhealthy theta while opening the 'window' for the healthy theta to emerge.

On the other hand, 'Profound Attention' increases sensitivity to subtle internal imagery such as the fast moving archetypal, insight imagery associated with healthy theta. Alpha training prolonged produces the 'window'. This window appears to be a condition in which healthy theta emerges, constructed visualizations have enhanced effect, and consciousness—contaminating repressed psychological material rises up…to be, as it were, burnt up by insight, energy…a kind of fire in the mind. Another hypothesis is that one of the benefits of alpha training is that it can strengthen the ability to sustain awareness as one descends into the healthy theta region. This means one can 'bring back' and apply the treasure that may be discovered 'down there'.

SMR/beta protocols may have greater economic power at this moment largely because the 'Actualizer' mothers have the means and the motivation to acquire neurotherapy for their ADHD children (and often themselves). However, the alpha/theta protocols are basic to our field. Indeed, Dr. Ferdinand Poirer of the Clinique de Epilepsie de Montreal reported that high alpha (10 Hz and above) had been used to achieve excellent results with many of his epileptic patients, and Richard Brunner suggested that he could produce outstanding results using high alpha training with many of his ADHD patients. As we have suggested before, the present trend to focus so much importance on SMR/beta while at times neglecting the slower frequencies (alpha in particular) is probably a reflection of our cultural bias. We value narrow focused attention and linear information processing above other modes because these other modes are more mysterious, ego threatening, and often challenge at least the superficial aspects of our value system, and by extension the status quo. The market place can be hard on those walking the road less traveled.

Solving problems in a way that the culture approves implies doing it the way it has been done before. This means using formulas which make others feel more secure. We teach this form of mental discipline in our school systems. We highly value productivity and believe that thinking harder is the way to get there. SMR/beta training may be a way to get those who have wandered too far from the fold to get with it and start playing the social game again, especially kids with ADHD. We are breaking the trance they are in (for better or for worse) and training them to reenter the social trance. This is fine as long as it does not become a prison from which they cannot escape when the opportunity to break free and live a much more original life finally arrives. We recall R.D. Laing's assertion that the culture considers only those who fit into the culture as normal and well adjusted. But what if the culture is sick (i.e. Nazism, the Inquisition, The Greed is Good Syndrome, Conspicuous

Consumerism, Apartheid, etc.?). If we have created a ravenous worship of consumerism which could devour the earth, can we wake up to this cultural trance before it is too late? Or do we believe that as Americans we could not possibly be that mistaken, that asleep?

Over-thinking, or psychothenia, error prone thinking, and inappropriate conditioning, are barriers to health and creativity. Over-thinking similar to rumination or obsessional processing reflects a mind out of control. It seems to us the brain often gets stuck in a dysfunctional pattern, running too fast or slow, or in a loop which is probably oscillating back and forth from unhealthy beta to unhealthy theta, in and out of unhealthy, illusional trances. The limbic system does not sit idly by while the cortex platonically processes. The hypothalamus integrates this processing with the limbic structures and with our body through the autonomic nervous system and the endocrine system. It results in chronic over arousal and the constant release of high levels of adrenaline and cortisol into our system. One of the undesirable side effects of this response to stress is the release of too much cortisol into the brain and a toxic bathing of our hippocampus in cortisol. This has devastating consequences for memory. Recent research shows that injecting high levels of cortisol into the body causes serious decrements to working memory, although it recovers if cortisol levels drop back to normal after a few days. Over-thinking can lead to chronic over-arousal. This is like driving with the brakes on. It is destructive to neural tissue.

Indeed we can see the disintegration of neural activity in most advanced forms of mental disorders. QEEG normative databases allow us to compare individuals with mental disorders to those who are relatively normal. Their EEG patterns are more disorganized. MRI's reveal structural changes which are correlated with or seem to follow chronic disorganization. Research indicates that clinical depression in mid-life is highly correlated with the later emergence of Alzheimer's. Again, the high levels of stress leading to depression apparently causes considerable destruction to hippocampus tissue through activities of excessive cortisol and other neurochemical processes. Problems with attention, dissociation, and poor problem solving skills are the hallmark of a disordered mind. Alpha training, on the other hand, tends to order the mind if done properly. We have suggested that alpha training can be helpful with some forms of depression and ADHD. The Process subscribes to the notion that most types of neurofeedback training can work as long as it moves the over-conditioned brain out of its 'parking place' and into biobalance.

I call this 'the iron filings and the magnet principle'. Breaking the conditioned patterns apart with neurofeedback is like breaking a hunk of iron into filings. The brain is better able to reorganize itself, like the filings, along the natural lines of force of the 'magnet' or 'attractor', if you will. Alpha appears to be a powerful 'attractor' in a neural system so complex that experts in neocortical dynamics refer to it as a truly chaotic system (as in chaos and turbulence theory). This kind of 'chaos' actually implies 'ordered' patterns emerging out of the apparently unfathomable Mind of Nature. So, more often than not, alpha is probably the safest first move to make (except when contraindicated). This perspective holds that alpha training in many 'mind explorers' goes much further because it teaches the difference between active, memory based image making, and true relative neural silence. This neural quietness is essential for the healthy management of thought.

**The Hypothesis Explodes**

The following hypothetical model has considerable appeal to some: Brain cell columns appear to fire in patterns that generate interference waves which provide the basis for thinking, according to Pribram. Other cells in the brain stem, and especially the thalamus, seem to be devoted to accepting feedback from the cortex and organizing the brain's attention. The shifts in attention from one focus to the next may be reflected in shifts between alpha and beta, as well as shifts in dopamine levels and other neuromodulators.

The brain makes a model of the external world and constantly tests input against it. What we usually experience then is the category (set of memory based images) which is evoked by a stimulus rather than the stimulus itself. We are constantly making 'unconscious inferences' which direct our perceptions and cognition's. According to Ornstein, "Some have gone so far as to maintain that consciousness depends solely upon the output of the brain, regardless of which input keys off a given output". Our beliefs and memories structure the nature of our experience even at the perceptual level. Indeed we all see the world differently metaphorically and perceptually. We are seeing our seeing. This is 'mistaking the finger pointing to the sun for the sun itself,' or mistaking the word for the thing itself. This is why as the poet said; 'a rose is a rose is a rose'. We are each living in at least a slightly different virtual reality.

A goal of meditation is to generate a state which does not habituate to the incoming stimulus because this leads to experiencing 'categories'. Meditation 'the real thing', cleanses the doors of perception and leads to experiencing the experience itself. This direct experience is by definition a much higher order of consciousness. To achieve this we must somehow breakthrough habituation and categorization processes. This is made all the more difficult because the categorical imperative is the basis for the image building process that produces the ego. Furthermore, not only are we conditioned to seeing our own categories, but also the stream of categories has a hypnotic power which keeps us in perpetual trance. We shift from data stream to data stream in a constant waking dream. It is counter productive to panic about this problem, but it is wonderfully effective to be aware of it and to think of it as just a stage of neural development that most of us must grow through.

These trance states, as we have said, are often correlated with the unhealthy, dissociative type of theta waves which we like to call 'Naughty Theta'. Anna Wise suggests that we seem to see saw constantly between theta and beta crossing over alpha as our attention shifts. The center or balance point appears to be alpha because of its relationship to dishabituation and the coordination of attention. Some research on some yogis indicates that when they are meditating they do not respond to external stimuli and appear to be in a state of high theta/low alpha (presumable this theta is of the healthy, associative variety), but when they stop meditating they tend to a high alpha condition and do not habituate to new stimuli as much as other people. This is commonly thought of as an after effect of meditation. However, we believe this is actually an extension of meditation. The goal of the yogi is to learn to live his or her life in the most functional and intelligent state possible and that includes an infinite variety of orders of meditation, some extremely active (i.e. hatha yoga, earning a living, teaching, martial arts etc.) and some extremely passive (i.e. conditions of utter silence and stillness etc.).

There is a renaissance underway in psychology and education (are they really different?). The term 'The Psychology of Awareness' may emerge as the best description of this revolution. We suggest these conceptual changes are great good news and imply that the greater the awareness, the greater the loss of unhealthy conditioning. The more innocent our mind becomes....the more our true self emerges.

As we have mentioned, The Process draws upon some of the traditional modes of psycho-spiritual growth, and neurofeedback adds yet another technological dimension because it can enhance the process of learning to quiet the brain, which we believe is a necessary condition for the emergence of the phenomenon of meditation.* The mandala itself is a form of technological, educational imagery, and we see neurofeedback as taking its proper place near the center of an even greater mandala of self-knowledge technologies.

* We will use the term meditation throughout this book; however, we do so with considerable concern because it means so many things to so many different people. Meditation—the real thing- is to us the maximum actualization of intelligence (including compassion and love) and holds within its sphere of being the fields of reason, contemplation, prayer, a sense of the sacred and any

*other activity or quality of the mind which brings about the flowering of real (EQ) intelligence, wisdom and the unfoldment of the highest potentials within the individual human being, and by extension the world.*

The research of Kasumatsu and Hirai found that Zen masters do not habituate to new stimuli either. The Zen monks practice different forms of meditation, some of which seem to limit some kinds of awareness and others which seem to open all kinds of awareness simultaneously. Too little research has been done on these variations but we might expect a richer alpha mix to appear during the latter. In any event, we suggest the intense amplification of awareness reduces unnecessary processing which increases sensitivity and decreases dependence on illusory—prone conditioning, past experience and outside authority. As previously mentioned, the kind of attention enhanced by SMR/beta training is what some are calling data-capture-and-hold attention; and we believe this kind of attention will eventually be redefined as a subset of thinking.

Therefore, alpha training (perhaps other frequencies under different conditions allowing for individual idiosyncrasies) enables the individual, for reasons which are not yet fully clear, to substantially increase the number of brain cells, or at least expand the number engaged in the process of attending to thinking. Perhaps in the end, we will discover that it is unnecessary to increase the number of brain cells attending, so long as the quality of the attention is increased. Either way the brain is attending to 'what is'. That is, these brain cells are reflecting (like smooth water) subtle signals (vibration). One of the most important things they are attending to or watching is thought.

This model holds that thought is in the form of images being generated by other brain cell columns radiating energy (some of which manifests at the frequency of approximately beta). In short, alpha training can, in at least some people, enhance the ability to watch thought more clearly. The more clearly thought is attended to, the less subject to error it is. We suggest that high order (Profound Attention) can reduce thinking function errors so much that a transformation of life style may occur. In terms of the task of cognitive processing, I believe brain cells (and their field) are engaged in cortical circuits which are either attending or thinking. The interface between these two activities is probably in working memory, as Le Doux has suggested, and it is also probably where self-awareness emerges. This at least partially explains the shifts in awareness that emerge from alpha training as well.

Much of what we have discussed so far are the consequences of alpha training and its impact on the mind/body. It seems incredible, even counter intuitive, that a form of electronics can be helpful in discovering one's own particular way of meditation. But comfortable or not we think it is so. Meditation is probably the best strategy there is for truly living creatively and healthily. But learning how to meditate consistently and well can be discouragingly difficult for most. In fact, most of us attempt to learn meditation out of desperation because we are in deep trouble and there is no where else to turn (La Via Negativa again). When successful, the mind explorer has transformed the curse of despair into a blessing, snatching success from the jaws of failure.

Of course, there are probably those for whom meditation simply unfolds naturally like a blossom in the spring. But for most, that unfolding, that spring comes after a particularly severe winter. 'Dark nights of the soul' traditionally seem to often precede the development of meditation abilities.

The learning of meditation or contemplation or quieting the mind so one can make better contact with truth, 'what is' or whatever one calls it, is apparently fraught with danger and illusion and discouraging setbacks. Are we still together? Are we still all here? Has the way become too scary? Is our confidence shaken? Well, this adventure is for real and what adventure has no crisis, no danger?

We have to come back to this meditation principle time and again. Perhaps attempting to simplify it will be productive. Why is there such a vast body of literature dealing with meditation? Why have so many of the best minds of all time apparently intensely practiced and usually urgently taught it? (They did not always call it that because the word itself can be a barrier to actually learning how to bring it about). They have said that meditation reduces illusion, enhances healthy creativity (could some creativity be unhealthy?) and brings the meditator closer to the truth. In short, when meditation works well it clears and cleanses the mind, and that implies the body as well since it appears that all of the body (including the brain) is within the mind; although all of the mind is not within the body. One of the greatest powers of right meditation is enhancing self-knowledge.

So then, the essence of meditation is attention to 'what is' including the thoughts tumbling through our brains (and bodies?). There is an implication that as these thoughts are watched (as in quality meditation) they tend to slow down and dissipate and subtle more creative imagery emerges. This becomes a kind of guidance system—sort of like a compass. And we need a compass on this journey don't we? Surrounded as we are by a landscape that is sometimes dangerous, sometimes nurturing and always more than we can completely grasp at least in third dimensional consciousness (see session five). Meditation is one of the best ways to set up priorities and determine what to throw away and what to keep…what is necessary and what is unnecessary. By the way, notice how heavy the unnecessary already feels?

Maybe we should consider calling meditation attention/awareness learning. Because the word has so many meanings that it's hard to use it for communication. In any case it is critically important that each of us understand this way of using the mind to think and perceive more clearly as best we possibly can. And then make adequate time to do it! Saying I don't have enough time in order to fix my pathologically dysfunctional relationship with time doesn't make much time—sense does it?

Thank God for Einstein because he made it easier to think in terms of relativity. Now we can say there are many levels of quiet mind or meditation. Some are relatively more effective than others. Perhaps there are steps we can take to become relatively more effective, better at it. What might those steps be?

It is important to keep in mind that this training or meditation is only part of the story. The Process provides important other parts which interact with alpha training. A synergy arises when these different aspects of training come together. In many ancient approaches to human transformation there are similar parallels. Unfortunately many of these systems were oral traditions which have been lost. They weren't grounded in the methodology of modern science. Over time definitions and terms have been lost and confused. We seek to reassemble the essence of these lost traditions in a modern western format. We do not need to import other traditions. Our own is emerging right here and now.

Sitting here in the midst of the flowers and the blue skies of a summer afternoon. Crickets, cars down on the road, planes overhead, wind in the trees, distant voices now and then. Breathing slowly deeply, the air has a fresh, sweet quality here...what a blessing.

In any case, alpha training, from our experience, assists individuals in initially achieving mind conditions that seem conducive to meditation more efficiently than most traditional strategies we are aware of. Alpha training appears to generate awareness outside the training session, making it is easier to observe and influence habitual responses and actions. This quality of awareness increases the capacity to monitor and modify ego-based behavior. In addition, it increases sensitivity and the ability to reduce the excess baggage we bring to each moment. Other phenomena, which we are just beginning to understand, seem to occur as well, such as changes in body chemistry, immune system, and sensitivity to various foods and drugs.

## Regarding alpha and body chemistry

According to our admittedly limited understanding there is a glucocorticoid negative feedback loop to the hippocampus and hypothalamus which suppresses immune system activity during stress, or switches it back on after stress is over. For many of us the stress is never over, but chronic. The immune system continues suppressed and we are afflicted by constant problems. When it does get turned back on, it overreacts because the 'on switch' is too sensitive, or it fails to switch back on properly. This appears to happen because receptor populations in the synapses are reduced to compensate for prolonged suppression. That is, the body attempts to compensate for its condition and allow at least some effective level of immune system to return despite the stress. There may also be some shifts in neurotransmitter levels and neuro peptides that have yet to be docu-mented. Either way, the immune system is under active resulting in con-stant invasion of the body by pathogens, resulting in immunodeficiency disorders—or over active, resulting in autoimmune disorders.

As we have said, alpha training reduces the release of adrenaline and cortisol. This resting activity may also allow receptor populations to recover at those sites that have attempted to compensate from chronic over-activity due to chronic stress. These shifts in endocrine and immune systems would account for profound changes in body chemistry and the clinical reports we get of changes in sensitivity to foods and drugs.

There are fairly direct connections between cognition's and immune response. Disease emerges when pathogen populations outside the body reach certain threshold levels; but this threshold is also determined by immune efficiency, which in turn is responsive to cognitive-emotional states. The immune system and the brain share many neurotransmitters and neuro peptides in common, and Richard Brown suggests in his text on neuroendocrinology that these avenues of communication may exist so that the brain can be sensitive to pathogens and help direct immune system activities. We act consciously to assist in these processes as well. Motivation may emerge from deeper levels of processing. At any rate, shifts in immune responses could easily affect histamine levels and aller-gic responses.

## Back to conditioning

The action of conditioning, usually in the background of consciousness, unfolds in a continual stream producing a sorting process. Behaviorists would tell us that we are entirely products of conditioning. This position is extreme. However it does suggest how important psychology has found the concept of conditioning to be in the evolution of the self. We learn as we grow, and that learning can be a result of classical conditioning or operant conditioning. Either way we are conditioned, and that conditioning becomes subroutinized (perhaps so we can free our attention to do other things). But again and again we return to the problem: How do we deal with the fact that we become the prisoners of our own web of conditions which we weave as we learn from our actions? We can learn even if we are not conscious of it. However, if we can become aware of that conditioning as we process information, then we have a choice. We are no longer dreaming the conditioned trance, but relatively free to change our mind (simply shift our thinking) and make better choices. We observe that neurofeedback enhances this awareness of conditioning, but journaling can also intensify and enhance this process. It is as if we are disconnecting bit by bit (or all at once) from past trauma and conditioning which has been contaminating and dragging down our present mindfulness. This can be a painful process as we mentioned earlier because letting go might involve mourning and some 'ego death'. On the other hand, a sense of release, freedom and euphoria also often unfolds.

Alpha training (at least in alpha R's) seems to rebalance neural processing and thereby enhances *biobalance.* Furthermore, it seems reasonable to speculate that this intervention may be resulting in a restructuring in top down processing, and eventually bottom up processing. Huge shifts in cognition often happen. Every day experiences can take on new meaning, depth, and wholeness from which we have been relatively exiled due to our bonding with a cognitively fragmented awareness. This unexpected phenomenon has traditionally been pigeonholed as religious experience.

To us it is simply *The Process*, and it is a natural consequence of *Profound Attention.* The educational paradigm shift implied by the terms Profound Attention, Psychology of Awareness and Psychology of Mind gives rise to the notion that attention/awareness itself breeds both optimal mental health and enhanced performance. This awareness and Profound Attention are the same or interdependent. There is no question that these high orders of awareness/attention can be learned without neurofeedback.

As mentioned before, the biofeedback field unfolded largely from the study of people who had developed these mind/body skills without technological feedback as we know it. But these most gifted ones are often quick to see the value of neurofeedback when it is demonstrated to them. They are also quick to point out how mind numbing difficult is the treacherous path to discrimination between high order attention and *thinking* one is attending. Herein lies an awesome potential of brain wave biofeedback.

**IF NEUROFEEDBACK CAN BE USED TO HELP AN INDIVIDUAL DISCRIMINATE BETWEEN THOUGHT AND ATTENTION/AWARENESS....THEN IT IS A TECHNOLOGICAL BREAKTHROUGH AS IMPORTANT TO THE EXPLORER OF THE MIND AS THE COMPASS AND SEXTANT COMBINED ARE TO NAVIGATION.**

*"One of the greatest scientific achievements imaginable would be the discovery of an explicit relationship between the waveform alphabets of quantum theory and certain human states of consciousness."* Nick Herbert, author of **Quantum Reality**

We assert that neurofeedback *is* a manifestation of that relationship. *(NFB seems to us to be a virtual miracle. A case of the map actually becoming and creating the road as it goes along.)*

*"The only prayer one needs to learn is Thank You."* Meister Eckhardt
*"We cannot do great things, only small things with great love."* Mother Teresa

**The Process is proactive.**

There is a social aspect to The Process, and it seems to center around growth, maturity and responsibility. There is a feedback between the organism and its social ecology as it becomes more integrated and achieves higher levels of internal organization. It harnesses the stuff of social inter-action to assist in its own transformation. It becomes the medium of the 'artist of living'. Maturity is associated with mastery of the social reality. We have been accustomed to thinking of maturity as arriving with adult-hood. In his natural environment primitive man lived on the average of 35 years according to anthropologists. He had about 15% fat in his diet and got lots of exercise walking miles everyday. The average Roman male died in his 20's and the average person in Lincoln's time died around 35 years of age again. People matured quickly, if we can call it maturity. For most people in the late 1800s, marriage and childbirth occurred in the teens and early 20's. A 50 year old male was considered an old man.

Much of this state of affairs had to do with poor diet, hard labor, and poor sanitation. Marriage relationships often lasted only about 15 years before a spouse died. We live in a time when people can live the equiva-lent of three of those life times; and most people today are changing careers several times in their lives (and sometimes spouses). It is like hav-ing different incarnations without physically dying. There is a greater pos-sibility for profound relationships to emerge, yet paradoxically many of us feel more isolated, and we tend to blame it on technology. This isolation may be stunting our growth in terms of emotional intelligence (EQ).

Maturity is a much longer road for most of us today. Sociologists and developmental psychologists see adulthood as occurring in the late 20's or early 30's. It seems to us that most people do not achieve significant maturity in a lifetime. But what do we mean by maturity? In terms of self-actualization we see it as maturation of the ego, an unfolding of innate potential, a process of being more 'human'. By maturation of the ego we mean the full establishment of a social identity which is functional, no super functional. Mature individuals tend to be adept socially and good at self-disclosure and communication in general. Contributing to the community is a product of seeing oneself as an integrated part of that community. Maturity implies skill at navigating group dynamics and organizing activities.

However, maturity goes beyond this. Maslow asserts that as the individual begins to transcend the limitations of the ego, the sense of social responsibility, compassion and hunger to serve grows stronger. This is not because of a sense of duty, but rather because (s)he sees herself as the society...the tribe. He is not 'helping those other poor slobs'. (S)he is bailing his own fanny out. It is in his or her own best interests to do all he can to relieve suffering and open doors to the wonders of life. *Love is the ultimate profit system.* If we list the traits of a self-actualized person, he or she begins to look very different from the socially developed person with a huge ego.

The mature individual has a different agenda. It is an agenda grounded in freedom and love. The mature individual allows room for others to develop and grow, allows people the freedom to be whatever they are so that they can make their own mistakes and grow through autonomy. Taking advantage of others is no longer acceptable. There is the sense of 'tough love'. 'Never do for someone what they can do for themselves'. With maturity comes the urge to mentor and guide, but in a passive, coach-like sense. There is the feeling that the human drama is somehow divine, and there is a kind of ritual dance in which the old self is 'sacrificed' for the new self.

The self-actualized person is at home in a state of constant transformation and understanding of human suffering. (S)he seeks to convert suffering into insight as to the possibility of change and motivation to make that change happen. Emotional intelligence (EQ) implies wisdom, and is much more important than IQ in this process. A strong sense of humor and intuition are other attributes required to live so economically that one glides through these human dramas with a minimum of suffering.

Harmonizing with the novelty of life in this way requires a balance of vigilance and serenity while the battle of life is raging all around. The successful Samurai (artist) of Living lives with "death just over his left shoulder" as Don Juan says to Carlos Castenada. We believe this kind of a 'warrior' finds moment to moment existence comfortable and interesting. There is a confidence, a kind of faith that life is unfolding as it ought. Service to others becomes ever more fun, fulfilling, and one of the most effective pathways to the 'warrior's' own growth in terms of quality of moment to moment consciousness. This process requires extremely high orders of awareness (Profound Attention.)

One might reason that if, as Maslow says, there is this natural evolution of appetites until the individual hungers to be maximally responsible, what's to worry about? Evolution will get us there. The Universe is unfolding as it ought, so why take action? The problem arises when we ask, will it get us there in time? And is the astounding amount of suffering now prevalent in the world necessary? More importantly, can this incredible agony that so many are undergoing destroy unrealized potentials lying latent in the pathway of a wiser, more compassionate, braver evolution? Most responsible scientists say we cannot take our survival, much less our flowering, for granted. We are in a crisis now and the crisis in some ways appears to be deepening and accelerating.

*"…Human beings strive perpetually towards ultimate humanness, which itself may be a different kind of becoming and growing. It's as if we were doomed forever to try to arrive at a state to which we could never attain. Fortunately…there is another truth which integrates with it. We are again and again rewarded for good Becoming by transient states of absolute Being, by peak experiences. Achieving basic—need gratification's gives us many peak experiences, each of which are absolute delights, perfect in themselves, and needing no more than themselves to validate life. This is like rejecting the*

*notion that heaven lies someplace beyond the end of the path of life. Heaven, so to speak, lies waiting for us through life, ready to step into for a time of striving. And once we have been in it, we can remember it forever and feed ourselves on this memory and be sustained in time of stress.*

*Not only this, but the process of moment—to moment growth is itself intrinsically rewarding and delightful in an absolute sense. If they are not mountain peak experiences, at least they are foothill peak experiences, little glimpses of absolute, self-validative delight, little moments of Being. Being and Becoming are not contradictory or mutually exclusive. Approaching and arriving are both in themselves rewarding." Abraham Maslow*

In fact, the exponential growth of performance enhancement learning and technology (in so much as it feeds and increases the appetite for more things and more power) may be making the crisis more urgent by intensifying over-consumption of certain products and services which are self-destructive individually and globally. That urgency fuels the growth of the realization that heuristic, self-learning is The Process which must emerge ASAP. It is our view that one of the most powerful byproducts of that Process is the realization that La Via Negativa (elimination of the unnecessary) is one of the easiest ways to improve the quality of one's moment to moment consciousness and hence the quality of one's daily life. The growth of this understanding must strengthen the Voluntary Simplicity Movement. Perhaps Voluntary Simplicity can buy us the time and generate the energy necessary to make it all the way home.

### Change, Stress.

In order to grow we must all change. Change is both frightening and emancipating. For many of us the prospect of change is met with resistance and rationalizations which are masking fear. "I'm not afraid, we say, I just don't have time…or…That will never work for me…Or…That's his problem, not my problem…Or…" Beneath these protestations is a fear of the discomfort and work that might be involved. The messy emotional aspects mean difficult considerations and struggling with hard questions. There is much psychological pain (if that is really different from physical pain). This means things might get worse a little before they get better; and we all want the magic pill which will just make us better. Change through neurofeedback may be accelerated, and this may not always be comfortable. So we need to explore change thoroughly in order to understand and become comfortable with it. Peak performers, artists of living thrive on **stress**, change.

Why do we want to change so much? The wisdom teachings seem to be ambiguous on this issue of change. On the one hand they say, "be what you are, be content with what you have, do not compare yourself with another," and on the other hand they say, "seek the highest, take heaven by storm, turn away from your mistakes, bring about (or allow) your own transformation and then do all you can for humanity". Indeed, the wisest, most compassionate, and apparently most enlightened human beings who ever lived seemed utterly obsessed by the process of assisting others in changing themselves. It seems that these apparently highly actualized individuals are experiencing wonderful states of consciousness, profound changes, and they long to assist others in discovering these treasures for themselves. It would be an understatement to say these great teachers, taken as a whole, are proactive.

What do we mean when we say we want to change? From one perspective the idea seems kind of silly since change is every instant everywhere in the known universe. The atoms and materials of our bodies are changing all the time and so is everything we see. Implied in the notion of change then, is healthy change, useful change which means healthy stress as opposed to unhealthy stress.

Obviously, when we think about changing we want to change for the better. Part of the problem and the risk of trying to change is that we can wind up changing for the worse even though we intend (at least consciously) to change for the better. We inadvertently jumped from the frying pan into the fire. Think about all of the adventurers who set out to find gold, wealth, fame and become important, powerful, respected, loved, and in turn lost all they had. Many lost their minds, many their lives.

It seems wise then to recognize that there is great artfulness, perhaps even a science in bringing about healthy change. In fact, this book is an effort to understand in a practical way, at least, the basics of healthy change, and to go beyond to some understanding of those wondrous archetypal mega changes and natural, healthy, holistic transformation. We have addressed elsewhere in this book some of the easier, more tangible aspects of change. Now let's play with some more of the subtle, psychological strategies and principles.

The applications of "The field is the sole governing agency of the particles" seem to go far beyond physics and into the realm of the psychological, and even the metaphysical. For decades I have noticed that my wife decorated wherever we lived in ways that uplifted the spirit, and subtly (at times not so subtly) nudged all those who found themselves within her decorative field toward her sense of highest values (which I believe is not too shabby). In fact, I have had to deal with the relatively small problem of becoming impatient with myself because I really feel that a man who lives in this kind of 'field' (including her nurturing) ought to be able to do a masterful job of almost anything immediately.

Many of us feel when we are young that we can accomplish all of the changes we really want to, and make all of our dreams come true. Some of us sometimes come close to that. Most of us came to be grateful that certain dreams and fantasies we once yearned to materialize did not actually happen. We come again to the principles of healthy change.

It seems that there are things which conscious effort to change does not affect...at least perceptibly. And there are things which conscious effort does change. But we don't know what will change with quality effort and what will not until we try, and it is clear we can't do it all. So, one of the critical considerations becomes setting priorities. What is really the wisest way to invest time, energy and resources? One consideration is that everything seems in flux, and there is a requirement to shift priorities and strategies quickly and effectively as the seething, churning circumstances of life happen around us, changing the field of which we are the particle...changing that field without and within.

It is as though one is before a wall with many doorways—no let's change that to within a great hall, a palace with many magic rooms filled with possibilities. But all of these possibilities are not beneficial. So we are studying these doors and sensing what we can intuit about the rooms they lead to, sort of like the initiation of the students in the legendary Shaolin temples. How to select the best doors? It seems only meditation can help in an active way. The rest is up to something else..."of which it is unwise to blaspheme". I prefer not to call it an outside agency, perhaps the term Dave Bohm often used 'ground of being' will do for now.

For decades I have resisted writing because I wanted to put all of the creative energy I had left after making a contribution in the biofeedback field, into meditation. My logic was that if I could master meditation, I would be in a position to write, and make a contribution in a truly useful way, rather than add more relatively useless 'word baths' to the endless mountains of books we already have. It seemed to me that putting all of my energy into attending to 'what is' could bring about more benefit to the tribe than using up still more trees. But this meditation I now have seems to be saying the time has come for me to take my best shot and write the best I can for better or for worse. In fact, the writing itself seems now like a way of watching the mind...and particularly thoughts...an extension and a seemingly essential part of the meditation itself.

Perhaps this is a good place to point out that this meditation as we see it, is a way of life. It is not something that one does for so many minutes a day, but rather tries to be a way of using the mind all the time, whether sitting quietly alone, or running in the woods, or writing, or teaching, or eating, or discussing problems to be solved with one's business colleagues, or persuading a customer to become happily involved with our products and services, or sparring in the Dojo with some wild eyed, firebrand who is thirty years younger, (lightening fast, bench presses 250 lbs., thinks he is immortal because he has never been really hurt—or even worse because he has and the residual brain damage has made it impossible to calculate the consequences of his actions, making him willing to take chances that you considered ridiculous even when you were his age) or making love, or sleeping, or watching television or children playing…you fill in the blank. Get the idea? We are talking about a manifestation of Profound Attention, Profound Knowledge, The Process, right use of mind/body. The idea is to be as profoundly attentive (aware) as possible all the time, even when sleeping. And to be aware when one's awareness has deteriorated (as mine does all the time) and take steps to restore it.

It has been surprisingly easy to spend the last thirty or so years working on my own attention, my own version of The Process. In fact it has seemed choiceless. Partly because the principle of Profound Attention begins to appear to be the most important agent of healthy change there is. Elsewhere, I have compared my sense of Profound Attention and its relationship to unfolding the possibilities, the potential inherent in reality to the effect sunlight and rain have on a seed planted in good soil. So if this concept is correct and anyone wants to see a healthy transformation manifest in the world then there must be a deep penetration of his or her own thoughts and mind.

This is easier to say than do, but just try it…see what happens. Ask yourself if you have been doing this without realizing it all along. The question is if you do it more consciously will your life improve? In fact, one of the missions of The Process is to assist the mind in becoming clear as to the way this phenomena unfolds. Note, unfolding potential may hurt at times, and accelerating the developments latent in one's life can have disruptive consequences.

Is it possible that I could be sitting here writing in order to transform myself, and you at some distance in chronological time are reading these words for the same reason; and yet this transformation is happening as a quantum unfoldment of infinite grace and passion beyond psychological or chronological time, and deep within the much more powerful field of real—actual—fourth dimensional time? Is it possible that we are playing, working together at the same moment beyond the limitations of psychological, linear time? Could this be the not so mythological, real—world 'Layla', (mythological games of the 'gods')? Of course, in this sense the Greeks were not using the term 'god' in a blasphemous sense, or in the sense of being a 'demigod'; but rather to refer to those seekers who aspired to 'taking heaven by storm', those who believed that it is possible to live a holistic, sane, coherent life, devoted to truth, beauty, love.

"The pen is mightier than the sword" and "in the beginning was the word" are poetic pointers. And they are pointing at principle...transforming principles. But in order for these principles to work on me, on you, we must somehow merge with them. This merging, this union (the Sanskrit word yoga means union) becomes the most wonderful, ecstatic work/play imaginable. No, more...imagination may play a role, even a glorious role, but union with these principles (or principle?) ultimately blows even imagination into stardust...and something utterly indescribable, indefinable takes place, emerging from the ground of being.

Here language becomes increasingly difficult. Yet it plays an astonishing and critical role. Time after time I (and probably many of those reading these words) have been stunned almost into unconsciousness...(no sometimes I have lost consciousness) in fact, there is circumstantial evidence that I have also lost memory of sublime flashes of insight, visions, moments when my mind and heart touched something far too hot to handle and far too bright to see. Yet an enfolding after glow remains, giving meaning to my life which escapes all my attempts at description. And as this afterglow moves towards form there is a quiet, infinitely humbling excitement about what we are all doing together, our relationship(s).

We are Cartographers of Consciousness, map makers who are using language to merge with the indescribable. This is some kind of a miracle. Yet it clearly happens all the time. And somehow we are using language, words like levers to manifest transforming energy, principles in our lives.

Is this "taking heaven by storm"? We must be tough. There is a martial arts sense of being focused on the real challenge, the real enemy (you know the inner ones), what is most practical, what really works.

How does this seem to work? First, silence…a kind of void, meditation, then intimations, indefinable, vague perceptions, then while watching the silence with a sense of 'it's OK, whatever it is', thoughts emerge. Here the process of negation is useful. How do I discover ways to weaken the unnecessary thoughts? Energy pours into thoughts until they 'thicken' into words. From these words action flows. In fact, these thoughts and words are already matter or action shaping matter in a subtle form.

David Bohm taught about the Implicit and Explicit Order…the enfolded and the unfolding. All possibilities are enfolded and are at the many speeds of light unfolding. Yes, speeds of light because from a quantum point of view it probably can be said that all creation is essentially light manifesting at various 'speeds' or 'thickness'.

Everyone must manifest his or her own destiny, and that is done by right (or wrong?) use of mind. See how the energy, the ability to get things done, live creatively moment to moment waxes and wanes as ego, fear, compassion ebbs and flows? Is there a way to do it better? Or is all writ in the stars and predestined? Does the healthy mind, relatively connected with truth, get more and more passive, or does it find out how the system works and work it in a healthier way? Does it do both?

Does the Field of Wisdom and Compassion and the life filled with Spirit wait somewhere alone and slightly behind? Or is it everywhere, all around? And can it be invited, called? Can we visualize, pray for this Implicit Immensity to fill our thoughts, our heart? If It can, if It will then can we live from moment to moment and transform our adversity, our suffering, our mistakes, our sins? And from there can we go beyond and make the righting of our mistakes fuel for the Wondrous Life?

## Synchrony

Synchrony training is of great interest to many neurofeedback practitioners. Research on meditation and peak performance indicates synchrony may have a high correlation with enhanced qualities of consciousness. However, there seems to be a number of opinions about what synchrony means. We hope to add to the confusion by explaining our views. We will also explain why we feel synchrony training is an important part of neurofeedback's present, and an even more important part of its future.

Is there a neurofeedback Tsunami? I think so and its name is Synchrony. We predict that as multiple channel neurofeedback systems come into fashion synchrony strategies will become critically important to this field. However, as Yoggi Berra said, "The problem with predictions is that they are unreliable, especially in so much as they deal with the future". Stroebel, Fehmi, Green and others came to the view that there was a special relationship between EEG Synchrony and quality of some mind states in the early 70's. This insight came as a result of measuring the synchrony present as unusually gifted individuals demonstrated relatively high orders of perception and self-regulation. The implications of this are staggering. Is it possible that there is a correlation between quality of consciousness and EEG synchrony? My own reading of the Nobel Laureate Sir Francis Crick's book, **Astonishing Hypothesis**, interprets that what he is saying (coming as he is from the traditional neuroscience 'Binding' theory of consciousness) is that EEG Synchrony may be a practical and usable signature of consciousness.

To quote **Astonishing Hypothesis**, "Both German groups suggested that these 40hz oscillations might be the Brain's answer to the 'binding problem'. They proposed that the neurons symbolizing all the different attributes of a single object (shape, color, movement etc.) would bind these attributes to each other by firing together in synchrony". Note that Crick is limiting his investigation to the attribute of visual awareness as an expression of 'consciousness' because the visual aspects of consciousness are much easier to measure than are most other aspects of consciousness. His notion, as I understand it, is that synchronous firing is a way different types of neurons 'bind' (or communicate with each other, possibly using the laws of resonance). The integration and information exchange from these incoming different perceptions is what somehow produces the phenomenon of 'consciousness'. Others are signing on to this speculation. I doubt they are as a group aware of the work by early biofeedback researchers that seems to corroborate at least the synchrony aspect of the Binding Theory.

Our considerable experience with synchrony training has convinced us that it has substantial applications with problem patients including alpha P and Minus types. However, we believe that synchrony will play an even greater role in Performance/Life Enhancement training. The value of right/left hemispheric synchrony training is widely recognized but less is known about rear/frontal. It is a reasonable hypothesis that rear/frontal is at least as important, and relates to perception of the principle, the idea, the vision (if you will) and then the bringing of that vision into the real world via the frontal lobes. Our views are based on clinical observations and the research of others. They are hypothetical and much more controlled research needs to be done. As we all know, there is little funding available for such research, therefore we are forced to use our clinical observations as a practical way of arriving at working hypotheses until the value of these hypotheses attracts adequate research funding.

Understanding what synchrony is can be arduous, and even in the NFB field there are only a handful who are relatively clear about it. In order to sustain the flow we will refrain from presenting many technical details of what we mean by synchrony; although, they are available on our website. There are several versions of what synchrony is when it comes to EEG feedback. Let me try to make clear how we are looking at it. Most of you will find the technical jargon daunting as I do. I'm quite dependent on the assistance and interpretation of our technical team (Caldwell, Picchiottino, and the late Chuck Stroebel). I am also indebted to Les

Fehmi for his insights over the decades on the principle of EEG synchrony and its relationship to attention. In 1986 when we first decided to take on the task of creating the first, and hopefully the best computerized NFB synchrony training system in the world, we were told by some well trained technical people that we would never be able to deliver truly effective, low frequency NFB synchrony on four brain quadrants within one second epochs. Others, including Chuck Stroebel and Les Fehmi, said it could be done, and by 1989 we had done it.

We put together a form of synchrony training which from our point of view has been exceptionally successful. Some say we just got lucky, but that luck was founded on John Picchiottino and Sam Caldwell's skillful execution of Chuck Stroebel's brilliant algorithm. Because our philosophy is to try to integrate into our software all ideas that we believe have merit, we wound up with four types of synchrony in the DOS software, and have introduced a fifth algorithm in the Windows version. Our intention has always been to make all valid versions available so practitioners can do their own experimentation and decide for themselves what works best.

There are several ways of looking at synchrony. Obviously, the system which comes closest to matching the kind of synchrony created by the human brain (as different than a signal generator) is most valuable. Some feel that synchrony may be seen as same frequency even if the angle of the sine wave is 180 degrees out of phase. Others add making the amplitude equal as synchrony criteria. This does not seem to me to be intuitive because it is not as close as other techniques to what happens in nature. Still, we provide the option of experimenting with it.

We think the best way includes relative coherence (closeness of the phase angle) of the sine wave. We suggest relative synchrony seems to employ the energy and other potentials yielded by the laws of resonance. We believe this kind of synchrony ('harnessing the power of resonance') is similar to the coherent synchrony that makes AC current travel farther than DC, or a sense of beauty when two notes from different instruments harmonize, or the proverbial bridge to collapse if the

Roman soldiers do not break step. Picchiottino uses the example of two children swinging on swings side by side at the same frequency and holding hands at the same time. They have to be together. Just swinging at the same frequency is not enough.

There have been, (so far) relatively few synchrony studies, but I predict that they will be steadily growing as equipment makes it easier to do, and our community becomes more aware of some of the implications of synchrony. Peniston and Kulkosky published a study in Advances in Medical Psychotherapy 1993, Volume 6. They used a CapScan Prism 5. They reported a significant increase in the percentages of brain channel pair synchrony over 20 sessions in the frontal and parietal/occipital lobes of the cerebral cortex in Vietnam Theater veterans with combat–related PTSD symptoms. A twenty six-month follow up showed that four of the patients had a relapse of PTSD symptoms while 16 showed continued absence of symptoms. Those understanding the high incentive for 'faking bad' that VA PTSD patients have if they *do not get well, and can sustain their PTSD symptoms,* will be even more impressed by these numbers.

The mean amplitudes of alpha and theta brainwaves across the 20 trials of the abreactive imagery BWNT sessions displayed a statistically reliable interaction seen as a 'crossover' pattern, wherein theta waves gradually increased across trials, and alpha waves decreased across trials. The aforementioned pattern is thought to identify a state of consciousness in which the patient is sensitive to hypnogogic imagery which relates symbolically to issues in the patient's own life. We have long referred to this state of consciousness as a 'window of opportunity'. The concept is that you cannot make insight happen anymore than you can force the breeze to come through the window. But you can keep the window open longer and thereby dramatically increase the chances of the breeze (insight-the 'AHA' phenomenon) coming through. This insight often takes the form of hypnogogic imagery.

"It is postulated that the increases in theta amplitude in conjunction with the decreases in alpha during the abreactive sessions seem to be correlated with the strong affective experiences of childhood and/or adulthood—particularly past traumatic anxiety-evoking events (i.e. abreactive imageries). It is hypothesized that the more the synchronicity and amplitude of theta waves increase, the deeper the patient is able to descend into the reverie (theta) state which activates anxiety–evoking imageries…the limbic system and both hemispheres are more synchronized and the increased theta and beta rhythms reflect a brain process which enables the patient to remember and/or relive the traumatic anxiety provoking event. It was as though the patient was capable of integrating past traumatic experiences by coping with previously unresolved conflicts represented in the essentially anxiety-free imageries and memories generated during the theta state of consciousness."

Levine, Herbert, Haynes and Stroebel found that meditators are able to produce high amplitude, synchronous beta, alpha and theta frequencies. The literature has indicated that during deep meditation, alpha, and theta frequencies become synchronous.

Hypnogogic, dreamlike images have been found to occur during the theta and or reverie states. This work was reported by Budzynski and Stoyva, Green, Green and Walters, Folkes and Vogel. The combination of sensory and cognitive perceptions comprises the experiences of hypnogogic imagery. Green, Green and Walters associated this type of imagery with creativity and integrative experiences, and Peniston and Kulkosky associated it with abreactive (i.e. traumatic—anxiety provoking) experiences. In order to experience vivid imaging, the subject should be in an alpha—theta mode for a sustained period of time.

I would point out that Sue Wilson suggests that the first use of EEG feedback in Peak Performance with elite athletes is to deal with subclinical PTSD. We agree with her because the model that makes sense to us holds that these repressed fears are contaminating the 'field of mind'. This is what we mean by 'cleaning up the field of mind.' Classic meditation models hold that quality of consciousness is enhanced in some proportion to the amount of repressed fear material that is pulled up from the unconscious and as we like to put it, 'burned up in the fires of consciousness'.

This is the kind of therapeutic abreaction that was dramatized in the hit movie Good Will Hunting, between Matt Damon and Robin Williams. Following are two examples of how synchrony training apparently produced excellent results with an 'alpha blocked' psychiatrist and an alpha minus psychologist I trained.

### Applied synchrony training

The psychiatrist was actually an old friend who strangely seemed to have a tendency to cut you down suddenly during what you would think is a friendly, innocent conversation—and then turn his back and walk away leaving you smarting. Yet, equally strangely, I was always glad to see him, perhaps sensing that this was some kind of game which leads somewhere worthwhile. I had been trying for about ten years to persuade him to add EEG biofeedback to his existing traditional biofeedback practice. Finally, I got around to hooking him up and discovered that I could not assist him in having a decent alpha feedback experience because his alpha was quite low amplitude (about 3—4 uV P-P) and I assumed he was an alpha P. Also, his theta was quite high and I realized that in a way his behavior was a bit dissociative.

So, I decided to train him in synchrony for about thirty minutes. Then I switched him back to traditional alpha feedback, and was delighted to see that he was now doing 12 -15uV(indicating he was an alpha R). There were witnesses to this event and they agreed that his whole affect had changed. His face had lit up and he smiled much more and seemed to be 'high' in a healthy way. He said he felt much better and could hardly wait to begin offering EEG Biofeedback to his patients. He subsequently developed a successful neurofeedback practice.

Interestingly, upon finding out how much relative theta he had, he commented that he had often felt frustrated when working with patients because he felt he was in a kind of trance, and found it difficult to bring through into the therapy session all of the insights he was actually having. He felt that this kind of training was going to help with this long-term creativity problem. Here the model would be that alpha is serving as a kind of 'bridge' allowing deep, creative, 'healthy theta' imagery and insights to 'travel' up to practical 'beta applications'.

### Near Death in Mexico

Another example was a psychologist I was training at the University of Mexico. She appeared to be an alpha Minus so I immediately put her into a ten-minute synchrony session. At the end of the session I saw that she had gone pretty deep so I gently brought her out and asked if she had enough for today. With some urgency she said that she would like to do more. She described things getting very dark and feeling she was in some kind of large tunnel but she wanted to go back. I could see that we were moving into an abreaction but since the room was filled with mental health professionals I thought it would be a good opportunity to show them something about synchrony training.

When I brought her out of the second session she was tearing but had a peaceful smile on her face. She said that she had come to the end of the tunnel and found herself looking at a magnificent stained glass window. I started to unhook her, recognizing a classic archetypal abreaction shaping up, and felt I did not have enough time to properly deal with it because I was running a comprehensive biofeedback seminar. She pleaded to go back and by now the other psychologists were extremely interested in the demonstration. So, she went back in for another ten minutes of option 3 (Dominant Plus Average Sign on The Prism 5) synchrony. At the end of this session she was freely weeping and had obviously had a profound experience. I gently asked if she wanted to talk about it, and she said that she had crashed though the stained glass window into pure white light and she felt somehow changed in a beautiful way. She knew she had had an archetypal 'near death' experience and felt it was very 'healing'. Here the model is that synchrony training can work with difficult clients such as this alpha Minus. It can allow breakthroughs with those for whom other forms of NFB aren't working.

So the question I continuously get asked is—what is the practical application? Putting it in simple language I would say the following: Synchrony appears to be an effective way to work with alpha P's and Minus', those who have difficulty training alpha. It also seems to 'break through' when working with other kinds of difficult NFB clients. NFB is already a fast learning technique. In fact, amplitude training is at least an indirect measure of synchrony. A good way to think about synchrony training relative to traditional NFB is as you would think about an afterburner being added to a jet engine, or fuel injectors added to an internal combustion engine. Both types of engines were already powerful. You simply make them more powerful. You take an already steep learning curve and make it even steeper. If that is true then clinical implications for synchrony are substantial, and mindfitness applications even greater.

## Consciousness Processing

The 'Consciousness Processing' graph is arguably the most important graph I have ever seen. Furthermore, the insight implied was developed by some British sociologists more than 15 years ago. You can read about this idea in Peter Russell's outstanding book, **Global Brain**. (see illustration on our website: www.MindFitness.com). This is my interpretation of information in Global Brain. I have not consulted with Mr. Russell. I believe this graph to be essentially correct in principle; although, the timing of the Consciousness/Information Processing Crossover is still unclear. From the dawn of history to now, Agricultural Processing has gradually grown. However, about 1900 the growth of Industrial Processing in terms of total human work and economic power (doubling every 17 years) exceeded Agricultural Processing. In 1975, Information Processing (doubling every 8 years) broke through the growth curve of Industrial Processing. But Consciousness Processing including 'R—Tech' (doubling about every 4 years) is expected to exceed Information Processing about the year 2010.

We all understand Information Processing, but what in heaven's name does Consciousness Processing mean? For one thing, if we had understood

Information Processing early in the game and invested accordingly, we would be rich. Maybe if we realize that Self-Knowledge Technology (Biofeedback) is of the very soul of Consciousness Processing, we can invest enough to make a few pesos just in time to offset the collapse of social security. (We hope you are smiling.) A subset of Consciousness Processing Technology (i.e. the Web and Virtual Reality etc.) goes by the cool new label of 'R—Tech' (Relationship Technology).

Trying to think of a metaphor to help people understand Consciousness Processing Technology is difficult because nothing like it has ever happened before—just as Information Processing was hard to understand before it massively changed the world. For about a year I had been grappling with the concept of Consciousness Processing, how to get my arms around it. I had the insight I was looking for while flying back from Seattle after putting on a neurofeedback seminar. I'm not sure whether it was the altitude (flying seems conducive to meditation to me) or the espresso at the airport, but I love the following model that came in a flash.

See if this way of looking at it helps. Consciousness Processing is like an incredible new kind of 'airplane'. It is built out of the material of the Digital Revolution and uses Information Processing as 'fuel'. The creators, engineers, pilots and crew of these 'flying machines' relate to this technology as though it had a kind of life force of its own. The Information Processing 'fuel' produces almost infinite energy through the primeval principle of La Via Negativa (elimination of the unnecessary—in this case, information). Note information is not knowledge. In fact too much information and information of the wrong kind can reduce the acquisition of useful knowledge and wisdom.

The super exponentially growing Web is a manifestation of Consciousness Processing Technology. However, some of us believe there is already another manifestation of Consciousness Processing Technology even greater than the Web, emerging in the background. It is so immense that it will absorb the Web into itself like the Web is absorbing electronics, television, radio and computers, etc. As much as the Web is forcing transformation of the world, breaking through national boundaries (and to some extent privacy) and empowering the individual, so the new as yet unnamed manifestation of Consciousness Processing Technology will explode over the world like a Tsunami of Light. Like all true revolutions some will see it as a curse, others as a blessing.

As for me, I see it as a blessing because I am convinced that it's essence will be self-knowledge, and self-knowledge is an 'end point'. Of course self-knowledge is not always pretty. To paraphrase Betty Davis, self-knowledge (like aging) 'ain't for sissies'. And what we now call biofeedback and applied psychophysiology will be seen as a critically important part of this evolutionary revolution. Now, if that doesn't get your heart started, go ahead and have that double espresso.

## Toward A Theory of Performance and Life Enhancement

The usefulness of neurofeedback extends beyond the clinic. If we assume that the quality of mindfitness, of the consciousness of a relatively small, but relatively more actualized segment of the population, is the greatest hope for humanity (because they-we set the trends and values), then, doesn't it follow that more benefit worldwide can be achieved by applying heuristic, super learning techniques (including biofeedback) in the field of performance and life enhancement to these relatively functional 'leaders', than by working with the relatively dysfunctional? Please don't misunderstand, I have devoted most of the last 29 years to application of biofeedback and applied psychophysiology to those who are at least temporarily dysfunctional or have clinical symptoms. But while doing that I have gradually come to the view that if we take a Deming Profound Knowledge approach, it seems great benefit can be brought to the 'tribe' by working with the strong. Also, clinical biofeedback and neurofeedback are well established now, indeed the companies I founded or co founded together with other fine organizations continue to develop new training strategies and better equipment for clinical, psychological and medical applications.

So one of the most fulfilling challenges for me at this point in my career is to try to raise the bar and see if even greater healing for the greater numbers can be achieved by focusing on The Process of assisting the functional in becoming more (maybe much more) functional. As the functional enhance their lives, are they not forced by the very actualized emotional intelligence that so blesses them to find ways to raise the quality of living for those who are now perceived as an extension of themselves, their greater family? Either that is so, or emotional intelligence is dumb.

If we really want to do more than pay lip service to the suffering masses, where and with whom must we start? Much if not most of the suffering in the world is probably the result of misguided social engineering. Doesn't changing the minds and upgrading the value systems of those that hold the power and economic strings seem like a rational, coherent way to bring orderly, constructive change? Isn't the alternative to this strategy the same old ignorant strategy of letting the suffering build until the sufferers have nothing left to lose by revolution? And of course, focusing only on the so called powerful (though it must be done) can also be the wrong end of the lever. Any change begins with individuals—you and me. If we get our house in order, we individuals, we the so-called 'little' people—the so-called leaders will eventually follow. The problem is solved because we are the field and the field governs the particles. We create our leaders. We find ways to keep ourselves asleep and then we can blame our self-centered misery on outside circumstances including those in power. As people 'get better' the question of 'how much better do you want to be' emerges. How much better can we get, and what does much better look like? If we truly get better, won't that be reflected in our relationships and our attitude towards those (of our extended family) who are in trouble?

When people get to the top, having acquired all their toys, we find they still search for fulfillment in relationship. The wealthy and powerful still come to the clinics looking for better relationships, and often do so because they discover (sometimes late in life) that they never have experienced a really good relationship. They don't even know what it looks like or how to do it. Yet it is through relationship that we discover the depths of our own humanity and the wealth we carry inside. We find it is through this sharing of ourselves that we also discover the potential that exists in all of those around us. Our fear seems to keep us apart. This fear is one of the things that begins to dissolve in alpha training. This is apparently why many begin to lose their fear of speaking to groups after only a few sessions. It is also this fear and anxiety that becomes transformed into the anger which often leads to depression. The physical stress due to constant fear and anger leads to a host of disorders. It also profoundly aggravates existing physical disorders. This is not conjecture. One has only to review the huge body of research on this topic.

At this point we enter into the arena of Health Psychology and the outer limits of Humanistic Psychology and related thinkers. There the ideas of Krishnamurti, David Bohm, Abraham Maslow, Carl Jung, Carl Rogers, Fritz Perls, Joseph Campbell, Martin Seligman, George Pransky and hundreds of others are creating a renaissance—a revolution of psychology. What is the full expression of psychological health? Is it useful to consider it separately from bodily health? According to Health Psychologists it is not. Studies involving the neuro-immune-endocrine connection indicate that prevention begins with the mind. Prevention is increasingly becoming our public goal. Unfortunately, prevention means self-regulation and a change in life style. It is strange how relatively few seem up to this task, considering the utterly awesome rewards these changes bring.

We must conclude at this point that psychological health is the key to physical health. That's why we are introducing the term mindfitness. Remember, all of the body is within the mind, but not all of the mind is within the body. If the mind is right, the body will be right. That concept includes those who have severe diseases, broken necks and all other incredible tragedies that the flesh is heir to. The concept is that if the mind is right, one will make the most of what one has, whatever that may be (there are countless inspiring examples of this such as Stephen Hawking and Christopher Reeve). Many people today are struggling with this issue. In fact, with almost 50% of the population heading for or recovering from a serious mental disorder we must consider that optimal psychological health is a continuous goal for most of the population. And the road to that objective is filled with mind mines. Strategic mistakes can result in self-destruction, even while the confused pilgrim is striving to improve.

Coherent procedures for optimizing health and performance are growing out of this psychological and educational renaissance. Martin Seligman, past President of the American Psychological Association, has embarked on an ambitious plan to focus the APA on a wellness model of psychology. He claims that a relatively few powerful but misguided individuals have discouraged this approach, and that this discouragement is not a consequence of quality research.

## The Demographics Are Auspicious

As we have implied, one of the most promising trends to emerge in mental health is assisting functional people in becoming more functional (sometimes referred to as the subclinical symptom market, as differentiated from treating clinical symptoms in the relatively dysfunctional). The educational specialty popularly known as Performance Enhancement is already a big business, and we believe it will grow exponentially in the near future. EEG biofeedback opens an important new niche in the Performance Enhancement field. Many practitioners long to shift more of their practice into this area and are looking for assistance in getting started. To that end Process seminars for mental health professionals have been developed. Seminar participants learn by going through a modified version of the program that has been developed for the general public.

*Martin Seligman* is doing a magnificent job of awakening educators and mental health professionals to the challenge and opportunity of life enhancement learning. His crusade has become a high profile manifestation of a psychological renaissance. We assert that The Process is another manifestation of this paradigm—shifting renaissance, as is advanced biofeedback (self-regulation techniques and technology).

*Following are edited excerpts from a 1998 New York Times science section article.*

### Seeking a Focus on Joy in Field of Psychology

"...Psychological journals have published 45,000 articles in the last 30 years on depression, but only 400 on joy. Joy is not covered by insurance nor does it lead to tenure."

"When Psychology began developing as a profession it had three goals: To identify genius, to heal the sick, and to help people live better, happier lives. Over the last century; however, it has focused almost entirely on pathology, taking the science of medicine, itself structured around disease, as its model."

"That is an imbalance, says Martin Seligman, Dr. Seligman, a professor at University of Pennsylvania who is known for his work on optimism, pessimism, learned helplessness and motivation, has a strategy for transforming a profession he thinks has gone awry. "I believe America is fed up with the victim model and wants to make life better. I don't want to cut out the disease model. But we need a science that tells us about human strengths. I want to remind psychologists of normal people."

"Not one of the top university psychology departments is primarily engaged in studying the three central aspects of people's lives: love, work and play, or in synthesizing what has been learned so that people can make use of their findings....Psychology has been negative essentially for 100 years." Theories have generally focused on damage as have techniques for intervention. "Social science has believed negative things were authentic and human strengths were coping mechanisms."

"But what he sees in his own children are 'pure unadulterated strengths' that are not compensations for trauma, but intrinsic. I find myself beginning to believe psychology needs to ask, What are the virtues? We need to delineate them, assess them, and ask causal questions. What are the inter-actions? How does it grow? Let's talk about growth and questions of strength." "...He has begun giving speeches...arguing for a new 'positive psychology' that would use rigorous scientific methods to study questions that have not been acceptable, questions that have not had financing. Rather than spending 10 million on, say, phobias and fears, he says study courage. Citing the standing ovations that have greeted his remarks, he says that the time is right for a transformation."

"I was talking about reclaiming our identify, and people were weeping, I think I'm touching a nerve." His intellectual partner in this undertaking is Mihaly Csikszentmihalyi, known for his work on 'flow', which he defines as the peak experiences and the great joys that people experience when they take on tasks that demand skill and commitment."

"Dr. Seligman has begun writing grant requests, hoping to establish a research network that will get positive psychology off the ground. He also expects more money for research from the National Institute of Mental Health, which he said, realizes that the disease model does not offer suffi-cient insights into prevention. It does not seem possible that changes in the field of psychology could occur in such a structured way. But the cur-rent focus of psychology, Dr. Seligman said, is believed to have been deter-mined by just a few people. "It actually happened at a moment in time, he said, referring to a meeting of the Society of Experimental Psychologists 65 years ago."

"The chairmen of the psychology departments at Harvard, Yale and Pennsylvania State University had a conversation then about applied psy-chology and agreed that they would not hire people who specialized in that approach. That was the end of significant work in areas like industrial psychology at universities, a field in which psychologists sought to analyze and change the workplace."

## In Summary

We have explored ideas in more depth relating to the neurophysiological underpinnings of neurofeedback and The Process. The tools of the trade are ancient and proven but we feel we are presenting them in a new package. They are conceptual tools, behavioral tools, and social tools. They include journaling, visualization, attention, self-disclosure, relationship skills, meditation, and (optionally) neurofeedback. The concepts we employ to organize our journey to self-actualization, maturity, and transcendence will be more fully developed in chapter five along with their implementation. We hope we have set the stage for a thorough understanding of The Process, where it comes from, and how we came to conceive of its implementation in the present time in socio-cultural history. We believe there is a history of psychology we are drawing from as well, and which is unfolding along with a spiritual dimension implicate in the universal order. As we have said, much of this perspective emerged from our own interaction with neurofeedback and the higher order of integration and processing that we have personally experienced.

# Chapter 5

# The Process in Seminar form. A Transcript.

*"Try to develop models which are not arbitrary and man-made but organic and natural. The difference is in the intention. Arbitrary man-made models have as their intention manipulation and control. Natural, organic models have as their intention resonance and reverence." Margaret Mead*

The following is a transcript of approximately half of the twenty hour Process seminar so the transcript takes at least ten hours to do live; however, we have edited it to make the reading experience of The Process as effective and as much fun as we can. There is, of course, a major difference between doing a seminar live and reading or even seeing a video of the same thing. Each of these learning strategies has their own strengths and weaknesses. For example, in the live seminar we devote a substantial amount of time to brain wave training, which induces deep relaxation and relative neural silence. Then we follow it up with a 'Bohmian' style Dialogue discussion session. On the other hand, reading can be done whenever it is convenient and there is less need for repetition than when working live.

The issue for me is that I have learned some things…some principles which, when I have been able to competently practice and integrate them into day to day living, have resulted in my life working much better. Naturally, I want to share what I have learned, and when I pondered how best to do that it seemed obvious that I should use the seminar strategies that I had been using for decades in order to teach healthcare and educational professionals about biofeedback. I guessed that a bare introduction to these principles might be done in about 20 hours, and could be delivered in a three-day weekend. It seems reasonable to assume that doing the training in two-hour classes once or twice per week would be rather civilized, and allow plenty of time for integration and reflection between segments. However, logistics have made it necessary to deliver most of The Process training to date in seminars usually over a long weekend. This immersion style seems to have its own dynamics, and I have been gratified and intrigued by the effectiveness of even the early concentrated three-day programs.

As we have said, The Process is designed to stand alone with or without feedback; however, some of you will have access to EEG biofeedback equipment. We suggest that you read one of the ten 'sessions', and then do a half-hour of EEG Biofeedback training. Of course, we remind you that this is above all a heuristic learning program, and we urge you to listen to your intuition about the best way to work. Remember, doing too little EEG training is one of the most common factors limiting the benefits that EEG biofeedback can provide. Certainly, doing too much is also possible; however, I have not seen that happen so far, even with some obsessive/compulsives that I have trained in my almost thirty years of experience.

We have tried to reduce redundancy. However, we have repeated some quotes and statements because it seems appropriate within the context of the actual sessions. Also, your perception and understanding of this material may change as you go through it again. It is reasonable to warn you that Process strategies and the values implied may seem different from most traditional approaches to personal growth. But then we believe The Process represents a leap and works with key problems in a more effective way than most life enhancement learning programs. Without intending disrespect for the many extraordinary programs that exist, a great many who have taken such programs are still hungry to find better ways to bring about healthy change, individually and collectively. To us The Process as a living work in progress addresses that need; and it will undoubtedly have been improved by the time this book is published.

## Session One

### A RENAISSANCE OF PSYCHOLOGY AND LEARNING

**RENAISSANCE, to be born, to be born anew, rebirth, revival.**
**PSYCHOLOGY, the science dealing with the mind and mental processes, feelings, desires etc.**
**LEARNING, the acquiring of knowledge or skill.**

The Process is devoted to the unfoldment of a New Mind in humanity. A mind that is free, relatively unconditioned. Implied is the transformation of those who can, and by extension our society, our science, our technology. This kind of mind sees and listens to the whisperings of nature as the source, and for the inspiration required to develop a sane scientific and technological evolution. This kind of mind considers neither life nor death the enemy, and finds its own way to live and die within the Field of Love.

*"The most invisible creators I know of are those artists whose medium is life itself. The ones who express the inexpressible—without brush, hammer, clay or guitar. They neither paint nor sculpt—their medium is being. Whatsoever their presence touches has increased life. They see and don't have to draw. They are the artists of being alive." J. Stone*

The Process is the understanding, application and integration of those principles which increase insight, allow the mind/body to make a leap, to transform itself, to unfold the potential within. It is the application of those principles which operate like an antidote for the poisons existing in society and life itself. There is a Process whereby we become all we can be…whereby we make the most of what we have..of what we are. The foundation is simply doing the best with what we have, what we are; therefore, The Process is about gaining best quality self-knowledge as quickly as possible. Of course, everyone is unique; therefore, each of us must discover our own individual Process. This Royal Road is founded on heuristic (self) learning and teaching.

The Process means bringing order to the conditioned, 'mechanical', computer-like aspects of the brain so that there is easier access to the higher, 'non-mechanical' orders of intelligence and so those orders of intelligence, can run the 'mechanical' part efficiently (and in line with highest personal values). Although this process of making life work much better seems formidable, perhaps impossible, there is no choice. To me it seems like the only game in town, the greatest adventure imaginable.

"The times, they are a changin" and we must change with them. What can we do or not do to make that change turn out for the best it possibly can? The mission of The Process is to deliver the knowledge and skill that will allow you to bring about a renaissance in your life. To us The Process for reinventing, rediscovering, rebirthing ourselves seems simple in principle. There must be insight, clarity of thinking and understanding of the way the mind works, self-knowledge and healthy, right action. For the next twenty hours or so we are going to do all we can to learn how to learn better, and how to make the learning and the doing one. We are going to make the best maps we can and we are going to step from the map to the Real Royal Road. Those of us who feel particularly strong may even run along that road at times.

Many of us believe there is a renaissance emerging in psychology and education, and the implications go beyond what we can imagine or express, making this opportunity, this adventure of working with you and with ourselves an incredible, astonishing, exquisite, although humbling privilege. To us learning how to learn for oneself is an ultimate art. In order to learn about learning together we must communicate at a much higher level than most people do most of the time. Therefore, we must go carefully, and not assume that we all have the same meanings for words. Indeed, one of the most extraordinary aspects of this renaissance is much more effective use of language, especially in so much as it is used to understand consciousness, attention, awareness, thought, feeling and human creativity.

So, to the best of our ability, let us return to our innocence together. Can we have a child-like spirit of play? If we can, we probably can make great leaps in understanding. Words can be wonderful, but we must go far beyond words if we are to achieve the levels of humanity and the quality of relationships that we all long to have with one another. Since the kind of learning we are doing is self (heuristic) learning, we must all become our own mapmakers, cartographers of consciousness. Although we must go way beyond words, we must also use words to help us on our many journeys. All of my life I have been fascinated with the possibilities of words. If the circumstances and the mind are right, words can have a power for change that is mysterious and stretches into infinity.

Therefore, we have been using words (especially in so much as they relate to our field) in different (and we believe more effective ways) for at least thirty years. The Process is based on the insight that a practical understanding of the principles of mind are not only relatively easy to learn (for those with adequate motivation) but that learning the principles becomes choicelss when we consider the consequences of not learning them. We assert that an explosion, a kind of healthy mutation is already taking place within the mind of humanity, and is leading to unimaginable opportunities for realization of mind/body health and a long overdue uplifting of the beleaguered and battered human spirit.

## PROCESSMISSION

**A mission statement is a living thing and subject to change. However, for now we can say that the mission of The Process *is to assist as many people as possible, including ourselves, in becoming better 'artists of being***

*alive' by providing the best mind/body, heuristic, self-liberating, learning opportunities we can. The implementation of this mission includes assisting in the practical understanding of how the mind works and staying absolutely true to those self-knowledge principles which allow each of us to naturally unfold our unique purpose and potential. What we want to do is to be and to assist others in being artists of living.*

## WHAT IS YOUR MISSION?

This is the beginning of a journey…a remarkable adventure, an effort to bring about the greatest possible healthy, holistic change in ourselves. We believe the principles we are applying are grounded in what some are calling 'the new science'. Part of The Process is learning how to collect and evaluate your own data, and discover for yourself the best methodology for evaluating your own data and bringing about healthy change. In fact, one of the most wonderful aspects of this process is that I must learn with you. We teach those things we most need to learn, and we teach them until we learn them. Holistic definitions of mind hold that all of the body is in the mind but not all of the mind is in the body. So, we are taking a journey of the mind and body.

There are many kinds of peak performance programs—how to perform better at work, be a better athlete, a better husband or wife or parent, a better student, artist, environmentalist, politician, businesswoman, salesman, a more compassionate human being, and we are interested in all of them. There are elegant, underlying principles, a foundation that supports all forms of life enhancement. We call these principles the basics and upon this foundation, we assert, it is possible to bring about the kinds of changes that can substantially (if not incredibly) enhance the quality of our day to day lives.

We have learned and are learning from inspiring teachers all over the world, dead and alive. And the best of them have persuaded us that the Royal Road to Inner Riches is made of self-knowledge and self-education.

It is our privilege to apply what we have learned to ourselves and others who are interested in it this strategy for understanding the way the mind works. Often I will use the term we or ourselves. I don't really mean the royal we, but rather to refer to the fact that in all of this work I am inter-related with other people, constituting both a formal and informal team. The strategies that we teach are the ones that work for us. There are lots of other techniques, some of which we have tried, and some which others feel are excellent, but if they don't work for us then we don't bring them to you.

*"In sport, to be a champion, do simple things well daily", Sue Wilson.*

Whenever we find a better idea we integrate our version of it into the training. All Performance/Life Enhancement programs are fundamen-tally the same in that they primarily focus on improving the quality of consciousness over the average second, minute, hour, day, week, month, year. We think that for most people (especially the kind of people who are attracted to this type of material) major change is possible, and we get to serve as a kind of heuristic, educational catalyst for as many of those as we can.

Whenever any of us can actually apply the concepts and principles embodied in The Process to our own lives an unusually inspiring enhance-ment to our personal life style is likely to ensue. Often the change is so massive that the term transformational, or transformation of life style is not an exaggeration.

We can take nothing for granted. We must go together carefully, humbly, gently. We are going to work with all our hearts to bring about breakthrough thinking. This implies entering into one of the highest adventures of the mind and heart possible. We assert that there are at least two powerful tools for making breakthroughs:

1. La Via Negativa (elimination of the unnecessary, silence, non- action.)

2. La Via Positiva (right use of words, right action, right relationship, two expressions of which are dialogue and the concept of massive action). We hope you can already see the relationship between these two principles. Perhaps you can even see further that they are not the opposite of one another.

One of the most basic of basics is that learning may proceed from the easy to the more difficult, from the gross to the subtle, from the outside in. So, a place to begin with a mind/body adventure is with the body. We mustn't ignore our body because if we do it will go away. So, be good to your body. If you need to stretch, do. If you need to take a nap, do. Above all, breathe. Right breathing is a key to breakthrough thinking, action, and attention enhancement.

A suggestion for those professionals who are interested in applying Process concepts to their own clients: please look at this training as an opportunity to enhance the quality of your own life first. If it works for you, then you can help others make it work for them. If it doesn't, then perhaps you shouldn't be using it with others.

It is our intention in this program to ask the best questions we can and to use the best heuristic strategies we can to come up with some of the most practical answers—answers that work for us as individuals, and by extension, answers that work for us collectively.

Motivational seminars are big business, and for good reason, because as Emerson said, "Nothing of importance can be accomplished without enthusiasm". In fact, the place to start is with the whole issue of motivation (sense of mission) since that will fuel our adventure together more than anything. Of course, pain is also a motivator, but wouldn't you much rather be motivated by hunger to improve rather than fear of pain? Fear is an inferior motivator and a destroyer of enthusiasm. We need the energy and motivation enthusiasm brings to break out of the bind of the status quo.

One of the most important rhythms of the body/mind is approximately a 90-minute brain temperature rhythm. We have designed The

Process along the lines of this rhythm in order to maximize the learning/productivity curve. You may be aware of the 4 cycles that occur during the night. There is a period of dream (alpha/theta brain waves), then a period of deep sleep beyond dream (delta brain waves), then a period of 'deactivation' like a rest period, then another cycle. Actually, the deactivation period adds about 30 minutes to the whole cycle. Four of these make an 8-hour night. Something similar happens during the day. So, each of the learning modules of The Process is two hours long and integrates material presentation, alpha (silence) training and interactive dialogue. We do this in order to conform so much as is possible to what we believe to be maximally efficient learning cycles.

## THE PROCESS TRAINING IN TEN TWO HOUR SESSIONS

When we do the Process in a group seminar format we present about one hour of material in each session, then immediately do a half-hour of 'mind quieting'. Those participants who wish to are given the opportunity to train on personal brain wave biofeedback instruments during this half-hour. After that we do about a half-hour of 'Bohmian' Dialogue. We recommend that those who have access to quality EEG biofeedback equipment follow the same format. Instruments may be bought or rented from Health Training Seminars. Those not wishing to use instrumentation may find sitting in silence or meditating immediately after each session enhances the acquisition of self-knowledge and the application of the strategies learned. Some will find that participating in a dialogue group can further extend the benefits.

SESSION ONE: A RENAISSANCE IN PSYCHOLOGY AND LEARNING.

SESSION TWO: THE SENSE OF MISSION. THE INQUIRING MIND. THE BEST QUESTIONS.

SESSION THREE: THRIVING ON STRESS (CHANGE). THE PHYSICAL EQUATION. HOW THE BODY 'LANDSCAPES' THE MIND.

SESSION FOUR: PRACTICAL, RELATIVELY EASY WAYS TO UNDERSTAND THINKING—ITS POWERS AND LIMITATIONS.

SESSION FIVE: PROFOUND ATTENTION. ENHANCE-MENT OF DIMENSIONALITY/FLEXIBILITY IMPROVES QUALITY OF LIFE.

SESSION SIX: AWAKENING TO SLEEP. THE MAGIC, MYS-TERY AND POWER OF SLEEP.

SESSION SEVEN: ECONOMIC ORDER. FINANCING QUAL-ITY CHANGE. VOLUNTARY SIMPLICITY. WHAT ARE YOUR ACTUAL RESOURCES?

SESSION EIGHT: 'LA VIA NEGATIVA'. ELIMINATING THE UNNECESSARY. INVITING THE LIMINAL MOMENT, INSIGHT, THE CREATIVE—LIFE PROCESS.

SESSION NINE: AWAKENING 'EMOTIONAL INTELLI-GENCE.' LOVE AS PRINCIPLE, CHALLENGE AND A 'FIELD' BEYOND THOUGHT.

*"One of the greatest scientific achievements imaginable would be the discovery of an explicit relationship between the waveform alphabets of quantum theory and certain states of consciousness." Nick Herbert, Quantum Reality.*

*We assert that Brain wave Biofeedback is that relationship.*

For the rest of this first session we are going to briefly introduce you to the basic principles upon which the Process is founded. Throughout the remainder of the training we will be doing everything we can to deepen your understanding of these principles. We intend to use as many metaphors and illustrations as we can think of with the intention of allowing you another way to look at the 'elephant'. Together, let's see if it is possible to easily, naturally step from the map to the 'royal road' of self-knowledge.

## THE PROCESS AND SILENCE

**"If for every time I loved you, words could disappear, then silence, oh yes silence, would be all that you could hear." "Silence" by Emily Matthews**
As Korzybski said, " The word is not the thing and the description is not the described", and yet we must work, go exploring, try to communicate with each other using words, mustn't we? Of course, we also have nonverbal tools as well (in fact 90% of communication appears to be nonverbal). We can be silent. In fact, some gifted communicators have used silence with awesome effectiveness. According to legend, one day while Plato was teaching, his students asked the master if he would talk to them about the nature and mystery of time. Plato silently got up and walked outside into the garden and stood motionless and mute for twenty-four hours. He then resumed the discussion. There are countless examples of the power of silence. Indeed, we integrate the principle of silence in The Process as well as explore how silence works, how to make it work better. Silence creates a field in which words can take on deeper meaning and the mind can embrace that miraculous dimension beyond words and thought.

There were three holy men meditating in silence in the Himalayas. Of course, it has to be the Himalayas! Ten years pass, one of them says. "Oh, what a lovely evening this is"! Another ten years pass and the other man says, "I hope it will rain". Another ten years pass and the third man says: "I wish you two would be quiet".

The Lord of tomorrow is Profound Attention Today. We are beginning with a brief introduction to silence because we must use words so much that it is easy to forget how important it is to deepen the ability to listen. One of the principles of The Process is to understand the power of silence and apply it to healing as well as the enhancement of 'thought recognition' (or the ability to increase awareness of thought as it is taking place). We will be working hard together to understand and practically improve our ability to watch ourselves think and feel with much greater clarity. This sense of clarity means a kind of control, a power to bring about healthy change. A key to this is implementation of the principle La Via Negativa—elimination of the unnecessary. In this case we mean truly quieting the brain so it can deeply listen. In a sense so it can 'hide and watch' from a 'safe place'.

*"The softest of stuff in the world penetrates quickly the hardest; Insubstantial, it enters where no room is. By this I know the benefit of something done by quiet beings; in all the world but few can know accomplishment apart from work, instruction when no word is used."*
*Tao Te Ching*

One of the most powerful and mysterious ways that a human being can change his or her life and discover wonder, beauty, strength, healing, creativity, power problem solving, breakthrough thinking, and light within is to naturally, easily enter into periods of deep quiet. I don't know how many of us have really tried it, but I have and am now 'addicted' in what I believe is a healthy sense. All my life I had been intuitively seeking the opportunity to be alone. Whenever possible I would seek out a spot that was as beautiful as I could find in the out of doors. But if I couldn't do that then my room would do.

However, the power of silence was hammered home to me in a particular way during a trip to the Saanen valley in Switzerland and the coastal mountains of California. In both cases I went to listen to an extraordinary teacher every day and then wandered off alone into the mountains to do my best to absorb what I had heard, and to find out for myself if I could understand my own mind better. During the California event I actually did not speak for ten days. This precipitated a kind of epiphany for me which included the realization that thought and feeling watching got much easier when one is silent. But that wasn't all. While spending all day under great evergreen trees, high on a hill, looking down into one of those golden California valleys, a series of spontaneous visions accompanied by a wide range of powerful feelings which I still only partly understand took place. These experiences were (and still are since they are continuing) as mysterious as they were/are beautiful and they eventually led to many things including the concept of thinking of consciousness from a multi-dimensional perspective.

So, an important part of The Process is assisting you in deepening your already natural ability to quiet the mind and listen…really, actually, carefully listen…listen with the brain and listen with the heart. To that end and because our first session is almost up we must now briefly introduce you to neurofeedback, at least enough so that those who have the capability and want to do an EEG biofeedback session will feel better prepared to do so. Neurofeedback (EEG) training can be a powerful assist in getting the hang of deeply quieting the brain. Of course, there are other ways, and we repeatedly emphasize that neurofeedback is optional in terms of The Process Project. Also, we suggest you consider doing a dialogue session even if the dialogue is with yourself.

*"Can the narrow, conditioned brain break down its conditioning? I'm listening to the question…Am I actually listening or just saying I'm listening? If I'm actually listening, then there is no movement in the brain at all. Of course, there is a nervous response-hearing through the ear, etc. But, apart from the verbal communication, there is no other movement. I'm still listening—this is the breaking down. I don't know if you know what*

*I'm talking about...that very state of listening is the state of ending of a certain thing." Krishnamurti, The Future is Now.*

*"But if one listens a little harder, one comes to hear silence...that silence is an integral part of life...silence is not simply the absence of sounds. Rather it is the presence of the dimension of time. A realization of the instant and the situation. Furthermore, it is an expression of the completeness of the situation. In a very real way, silence is heard as an integral part of existence." Howard Slusher.*

To work at the level we are aspiring to is a daunting challenge and yet, if we are seeing clearly, there is no choice but to take on that challenge. The Process is a symbol/word for indicating a mix of 'perennial' principles, strategies, actions, and non-actions which can assist those of us eager to bring about healthy change. The Process intends to be as light hearted and fun loving as possible about this business of calling as much truth as possible in on one's position, one's life.

Working at this level is not for everyone and at any time. One has to be able and ready. The time needs to be somehow right. Most of those who come to this kind of focus have tried many things in life (including those that give superficial pleasure) and have developed a sense of ennui about it all. 'Been there, done that, bought the T-shirt'. Now, there is a hunger to go deep, to find out what is actually possible. We must be careful, skeptical, yet open, innocent. Innocence is the shortest distance between two points.

**In the 20's the scientific establishment knew that the entire universe was the Milky Way Galaxy. Then Hubble proved there are other galaxies. Now, that is a paradigm shift!**

With the intention of assisting you in bringing about a paradigm shift in your own life, The Process seminar combines three strategies:

1. Presentations (called sessions) designed to bring insights, coherent, practical, usable understanding as to how the mind/body works. What makes it work better? What makes it work worse? How to get the energy needed for breakthrough thinking and creativity.

2. Secondly we do psychophysiological training which teaches participants how to consistently produce relative silence in the mind and body. This includes optional brain wave training which we suggest can dramatically increase the learning curve.

3. Thirdly, we use dialogue for integration and deepening our understandings.

Putting it another way and taking it to a much more advanced level we could say we are learning The Process of unconditioning oneself—seeing oneself truly while gaining insight into the whole. It is as though there are three streams:

1. Knowledge (how to operate in the world, work, etc.), self-knowledge, how the mind/body works.

2. Detailed execution (discipline) go to bed on time, exercise, look neat, etc.

3. Insight into the whole which unfolds another order of knowledge. All these streams come together to make one harmonious river (life). In other words, learn how to live beautifully, harmoniously, happily in this world without being 'of it'. There is a joyful art of learning (at least relatively) to step out of the stream of madness, mindlessness that also exists in society. (Psychologists and neuroscientists express a similar notion when they break human behavior down into the categories of semantic memory (cortex), procedural memory (cerebellum), and working memory (interface of sensory system and memory system—possible seat of self-awareness).

# INTRO TO DIALOGUE (BOHMIAN)

*"...It is proposed that a form of free dialogue may well be one of the most effective ways of investigating the crisis which faces society, and indeed the whole of human nature and consciousness today. Moreover, it may turn out that such a form of free exchange of ideas and information is of fundamental relevance for transforming culture and freeing it of destructive misinformation, so that creativity can be liberated." David Bohm.*

**DIALOGUE, from the Greek dia (through) logos (the word).**

The Process is about individual breakthrough thinking; however, for individual thinking to work well in the world it must integrate synergistically with others. A strategy which can improve breakthrough thinking in relationship with others is a special kind of dialogue which we have dubbed 'Bohmian' in honor of my friend, the late, great physicist David Bohm, from whom we got the idea. Dr Bohm worked with groups in the US, Canada, England and Israel over a period of many years with the goal of creating a better way for people to communicate and be more creative while working and playing together in relatively small groups of fifty or so. For years a group of us met out in the Ojai valley to learn all we could from him.

Integrating Bohm's special sense of dialogue into The Process led to adoption of the term 'Bohmian Dialogue' in order to focus our attention on working together according to our understanding of the principles of dialogue Bohm taught us. This means pushing the envelope of communication, and it seems to require a moderator. Moderating such a gathering is itself extremely challenging, because on the one hand we must create a safe environment so that we can explore, be creative, and learn for ourselves.

## SAFE ENVIRONMENT BUT NOT
## GROUP THERAPY OR FORUM FOR SPEECHES

Yet, it is not group therapy. It is not a forum for delivering speeches. It is an opportunity to go carefully, tentatively into the ways the mind is working with the goal of coming to breakthrough thinking. The moderator must somehow bring the group back on track if the discussion is deteriorating, keep the atmosphere safe for ideas that some or even most in the group might think are inappropriate, and maintain freedom without bringing on a 'free-for-all'. The process of doing this kind of discussion requires deep attention, patience, and affectionate care on the part of everyone. It is necessary for everyone, especially the more intellectually aggressive and articulate players, to see the innocence in the other discussants. So far as I know the only way to learn to do this is by doing it. Mistakes will certainly be made, but if the right kind of environment, the right kind of field, is created, those mistakes will be part of the process of moving in the correct, most productive direction. This becomes part of the process of achieving collective and individual mindfulness, or might we say MindFitness.

Even in dialogue with ourselves we have to create an environment in which it is safe to make a mistake…to consider what may at first seem like ridiculous ideas. When we are working by ourselves we often second guess ourselves; we lose energy and focus because there are so many competing points of view or thought forms. It is important to apply the 'no shame, no blame' principle to ourselves as well as others. This kind of 'virtual tribal' relationship is yet another technique for learning how to align ourselves better with the laws of thinking in more functional, coherent ways. From there we can find out if it is possible to go beyond thinking to touch, to increase the quality of our relationship with that creative Source that is superior, ought to always come before, and give focus and direction to thought. We can call this level of influence by that Source…Insight.

Probably, to all of us such a proposition is an appealing adventure. The term 'edutainment' seems to apply. It ought to be fun to work this way. Yet, heuristic learning (self-teaching) is by its nature venturing into the unknown; and we are conditioned to fear the unknown even while we are called by it. So, like a hard workout, this kind of work will exercise 'unused muscles', bringing its own endorphin high and mind/body benefits.

Resistance to what others are saying is not likely to work well. The key is attention. Remember, you cannot observe anything without changing it (albeit very subtly) by the very act of your observation. The quality of our awareness to what is happening moment to moment has everything to do with the quality of the dialogue that is taking place. Therefore, when dialogue is taking place we have to do all we can to simply watch what is happening; to be as aware as possible, both of what is being said and what our thoughts and 'felts' are about it. And we must do it now, in real time.

I have seen work that has convinced me that there are probably four major thinking styles (preferred modes of thinking) and most of us tend to be strong in two and weak in two. Obviously, this concept is controversial, but I believe it has value as a working hypothesis. For one thing, it helps in the realization of the 'walk-in-the-other-guy's-shoes-principle'. Ned Herrmann has developed the 'preferred modes of thinking' concept over several decades. Many businessmen attest to the benefits Herrmann's consulting and training strategies have brought to their organizations. He calls these four main styles: Right and Left Cerebral and Right and Left Limbic. If you figure that we can theoretically be any combination of the four, you wind up with at least sixteen different potential thinking styles. We go into these styles in more details in advanced Process training. But for now we simply want to make the point that because of these preferred thinking style differences some participants are probably always going to be uncomfortable. Nonetheless, quality Bohmian dialogue must integrate those who are having difficulty and build 'thought bridges' to their minds.

**What Is Dialogue?** (From the Krishnamurti Foundation of America newsletter.)

"During his many talks and dialogues, Krishnamurti described in different ways what he meant by the word dialogue. He talked of awareness and of the art of listening- seeing, learning. He investigated the question of the division between the observer and the observed, and the necessity of being free from attachment for inquiry to take place. Krishnamurti also frequently expressed the need to be 'hungry'—to be passionately interested in understanding the nature of thinking—otherwise only words would be exchanged in talking together with others. And although many of these topics were not discussed in relation to dialogue alone, these areas of consideration are valuable for those interested and involved in understanding the dialogue process. Though we may have seen Krishnamurti either in person or on videotape, listened to cassettes of his talks, or read his books, we are automatically imbued with the complete understanding of everything he was pointing to. We may ask, 'In what manner can we truly talk things over together if we are not free from attachment? How can inquiry take place?'

There may be no easy answer to these questions, yet when we meet in dialogue there are innumerable different opinions and ideas expressed. Although we give verbal assent to the possibility that the knowledge we possess is limited, when we discuss things together, most of us express ourselves as if we have answers to the many fundamental questions being considered. Many of the conflicts that arise in dialogue stem from the different way such statements are perceived. To the listeners the statement appears to be theory. To the person speaking, it appears to be true.

**Dialogue cannot be forced to move away from automatic opinions and ideas to a deeper active and creative consideration of life's problems.** However, if each participant carefully observes the movement of thinking processes, both within themselves and in others, then the dialogue may move to greater depths on its own, without anyone doing something to bring it about. The dialogue process can be going on in our daily life all the time, if we are sufficiently interested, examining those aspects of our being that do not make sense and are creating conflict either within us or in the external world."

## LISTENING

*"I do not know if you have ever examined how you listen. It doesn't matter to what, whether to a bird, to the wind...to the rushing waters...in a dialogue with yourself...If we try to listen we find it extraordinarily difficult, because we are always projecting our opinions and ideas, our prejudices, our background, our inclinations, our impulses; when they dominate we hardly listen to what is being said...one listens and therefore learns, only in a state of attention, a state of silence, in which the whole background is in abeyance, is quiet; then, it seems it is possible to communicate." Krishnamurti*

One effective strategy is 'deep' listening. An excellent way to strengthen these skills is by breaking up into pairs and each pair chooses which one is the talker. The talker then talks for about seven minutes and the listener attends as deeply as possible and says nothing. Then the roles are reversed. After this the whole group discusses what happened and what was learned about the listening process. After an adequate rest this process is repeated, except that now the listener can interrupt in order to ask questions, but must be careful not to take over the talking until it is his or her turn.

Emotional intelligence seems to know how to be discriminating without being critical of others. For example, one of my personal biggest problems has always been being critical of others without realizing what I was doing (usually driving them away or shutting them down). Never mind that I thought I was giving them wonderful, practical advice. I am working hard to change my ways (I believe old dogs can learn new tricks) and even a small amount of progress in this area has brought tremendous benefits.

Anyone interested in this kind of process is already an independent thinker and probably feels smarter than most others and entitled to be critical, even somewhat cynical. It's hard not to be critical. And heaven knows it is critically important to exercise our critical faculties…appropriately. But there is something about being on the front edge, risking, being creative as opposed to standing on the sidelines and being a Monday morning quarterback. Performance and Life Enhancement is probably far more concerned with creativity than criticism. And the very nature of creativity means it tends to violate the status quo and conventional, conditioned thinking. Creativity make mistakes, takes risks. It will be useful to keep that in mind during dialogue even though there must be freedom to constructively criticize. But it must be done ever so carefully.

## The Brainstorm

comes early in the dialogue but like the weather the discussants must be ready for the spirit of insight to blow through the room at any moment, ready to adjust when lightning strikes. The brainstorming part of the process is not the time to reject ideas. The time to eliminate the unnecessary will come soon enough.

The concept of high level dialogue is quite old. This strange, rather mysterious phenomenon, this spontaneous combustion of group intelligence has been recorded countless times over the centuries (for real and in mythology) and obviously there are even more times when no record was kept. Crisis seems to provide a fertile ground for true dialogue. One of the challenges of dialogue during The Process seminars is that there is usually not a feeling of collective crisis, especially right after a deeply relaxing EEG session. Certainly, the sense that there is not a crisis is probably an illusion. If we really focus on the facts we will almost certainly see that there is plenty of interesting danger and opportunity-laden crisis to provide fuel for the dialogue. If we feel that there is not crisis, then we probably don't understand the situation well enough. Need it be said that competently dealing with crisis can be, ought to be great fun?

If we look at our own lives we can see that each day may be our last, and there are powerful forces that are even at this moment trying to shut us down and rob us of our humanity and the sensitivity and power that ought to be our birthright. At the same time there is great opportunity NOW! If we look beyond ourselves we can see a great crisis, nationally, internationally, a crisis in the consciousness of humankind.

I am always smitten by a sense of gratitude to be able to work with people who are deeply focused on Life and Performance Enhancement, the process of Mindfulness. It is a rare and wondrous opportunity, an extraordinary situation to be in. And there is even a greater sense of immediacy in the seminars. It is as though we are a virtual tribe–a kind of family—focusing all our individual and collective energies on learning as much as we can about breakthrough thinking, and the incredible, liberating, uplifting, humanizing, enriching power of Profound Attention!

One of the extraordinary things that sometimes happens when dialogue is successful is that the collective emotional intelligence emerges like a single mind which is in itself more intelligent than any individual…more intelligent than the sum of all the minds involved. I suggest that the reader experiment with applying these dialogue principles in normal, day to day situations. Watch the breath for underbreathing and watch the emotions, especially for fear, anger, and ego-tripping. Watch for the good stuff also. Recognize that the most articulate person is not necessarily 'closest to the bone'. How do you feel when someone has a really good insight? Happy? Jealous or afraid? Is there a temptation to discredit the idea or the person?

## CAM WE INCREASE THE LEARNING CURVE THROUGH BRAIN WAVE BIOFEEDBACK?

As we said, The Process does not require electronic biofeedback. But for those of you who are interested, the following piece may prove helpful. Brain wave training is probably not appropriate for everyone. But it has been very helpful to us and many of the people we have worked with, and it appears that its application to heuristic (self) education and perform-ance enhancement is growing exponentially. In other chapters we have explained why growing numbers of world class scientists and neu-rophilosophers believe that the development of brain wave self-regulation training may be one of the most important technological and educational developments of our time. But for now lets just all understand what it is from a technical viewpoint.

The human body generates a huge number of subtle electrical energies and more are being discovered all the time. But in 1928 Hans Berger developed the EEG which could measure tiny electrical signals coming from the brain cells themselves. This is done by putting electrodes (we prefer to call them sensors) on the head in particular places. These electrical impulses called brain waves radiate from the brain clear through the skull and muscles and skin and into the sensors. The sensors conduct these brain waves through cables to amplifiers where they are magnified and displayed and measured in many ways. There are many types of brain waves but the ones that we feel are most applicable to The Process include alpha, theta, beta, SMR and delta. Brainwave biofeedback or neurofeedback (NFB) can be accomplished using relatively inexpensive and easy to operate instruments. In chapter two we go into additional detail.

One researcher working with the most advanced of the systems we've developed so far (the CapScan Prism 5) documents a 23% increase in cog-nitive functioning as well as substantial increases in situational awareness skills such as vigilance 34%, attention 27%, concentration 27%, and automatic information processing 28%. Much more rigorous research must be done but most skilled neurofeedback practitioners report similar anecdotal findings. Of course the numbers have a limited value because this particular study was uncontrolled. Also, much of the most important phenomena that happen defy measurement (so far). Many practitioners report disappointment because some clients improve their mindfitness and then inexplicably return to their old ways and deteriorate. We think we understand something about why this happens and how it happens. Attempting to reduce this recidivism is an important part of The Process.

Carl Jung, the legendary psychologist, used an electrodermal device (known as Skin Conductance in the biofeedback field) which measures arousal of the autonomic that is the emotional nervous system. He believed his EDR measures proved that archetypal (insight) imagery carries a feeling with it, and that people good at producing and recognizing insight use certain kinds of feelings as a flag. Einstein and David Bohm, as well as countless other recognized geniuses, have reported that they somehow 'feel' solutions coming. Einstein and Bohm claimed they got a certain feeling 'in their muscles' before they got the intellectual insight imagery.

Dr. Bohm asked me to demonstrate various biofeedback instruments to him, and he was extremely interested in the technology. He was intrigued by the Skin Conductance instrument in particular because it seemed to him that there was an almost three second delay between a stimulus and the autonomic nervous system's emotional response, and he saw its application in teaching thought and thought—feeling awareness. If this observation is correct (and many biofeedback practitioners and researchers believe it is) the implications are extraordinary. It seems obvious to me that there is roughly a 2.8-second interval between, for example, an offensive remark and the surge of anger that follows. That means only considerable awareness, watching one's thoughts and felts is fast enough to head off unnecessary and usually counter productive anger. Biofeedback and mind/body training can strengthen this kind of awareness. Dr. Soutar points out that his understanding of LeDoux's research contradicts this hypothesis. However, my own empirical observations compel me to stick to my guns until convinced otherwise. At the very least, I believe 'the 2.8-second delay/awareness notion' is a functional working hypothesis.

Satisfactory EEG feedback occurs when the brain wave we want to train is present in the amounts we want it to be. WARNING. Brain wave power (amplitude) is unique for each individual, and it is particularly important not to compare yourself with another. The temptation to compare can be great. You may not be able to resist it. If so, just watch yourself go through the counter productive exercise of comparison.

Most will probably do best with mid range alpha training. The work of Grey Walter asserts that between 65 and 80% of us are alpha 'Responsives', and training the alpha brainwave for Life Enhancement seems to work best most of the time. The percentage might be higher in the group likely to read this kind of book because such individuals would be self-selecting. The other estimated 20% are alpha P's (persistent) and alpha M's (minus). Alpha R's just close their eyes and relax and alpha increases. P's produce about the same alpha, eyes open or closed, and Minuses make very little alpha eyes open or closed. Alpha P's and Minuses may take more work and experimentation. Don't worry about it. That's part of The Process. All of the fundamental Process principles work for P's and Minuses but we may need to use alternative neurofeedback training strategies.

Learning how to set the right goals and thresholds (as they are called in biofeedback) is an art. Also determining which EEG bandwidths are best for which people takes considerable skill and sometimes trial and error. Remember, it is widely believed that when brainwave training works like it should, it quiets the mind and increases brain flexibility. We believe better language for expressing this mind quality might be to say it increases dimensionality. Asking yourself the best questions you can during this kind of training can be particularly illuminating. Notice if answers come. They may. They may not. Notice if it is easier to watch the 'movies' of your thoughts and feelings. 'Just do it'. See what happens. Jot down insights in your journal, etc.

Expectations may prevent you from seeing the facts. Brainwave training is about increasing ability to be in contact with 'what is'. Watch the breath. Remember the muscles must be relaxed. If they are tense or you are moving about, you can cause an artifact (bogus signal). Go at your own pace.

**WE STRONGLY ENCOURAGE ALL WHO WANT TO TEACH OTHERS HOW TO USE EEG BIOFEEDBACK TO TAKE A PROFESSIONAL EEG BIOFEEDBACK CERTIFICATION TRAINING COURSE.**

## Session Two

## THE SENSE OF MISSION
## (THE INQUIRING MIND—THE BEST QUESTIONS)

*"We detect rather than invent our missions in life. Everyone has his own specific vocation or mission in life…therein he cannot be replaced, nor can his life be repeated. Thus everyone's task is unique as is his specific opportunity to implement it." Victor Frankl*

I have a friend, a classical high achiever who runs one of the most successful, fastest growing political and product development consulting companies in the world, is a tri athlete, and seems to me to exercise his considerable power with an inspiring sense of responsibility. When I asked him to tell me his philosophy, he answered with the following three quotes:

*"I would rather be ashes than dust,*
*I would rather my spark should burn out*

*in a brilliant blaze,*
*than it should be stifled in dry rot.*

*I would rather be a superb meteor,*
*With every atom of me in magnificent glow,*
*Than a sleepy and permanent planet." Jack London*

*Mark paused, and then continued.*
*"Asked to interpret London's credo, Kenny ( The Snake) Stabler, former*
*pro quarterback and carouser said, Throw Deep."*

It was a lovely, balmy afternoon in Connecticut with children playing in the background; our wives were laughing softly. I was turning over the deliciousness of those words in my mind while Mark quietly watched, and with a little smile went on,

*"The only people for me are the mad ones;*
*The ones who are mad to live, mad to talk,*
*Mad to be saved,*
*Desirous of everything at the same time;*
*The ones who never yawn*
*or say a commonplace thing,*
*But burn, burn, burn*
*Like fabulous Roman candles*
*Exploding like spiders across the stars*
*And in the middle*
*You see the blue center light pop*
*And everybody goes, Awwww." Jack Kerouac*

## FEAR

I recently did a contract for a major TV network news program. They wanted me to measure the physiology of a number of people while they watched a horror film. On the average every eleven minutes someone, usually a young woman, was brutally murdered. Of course, everyone showed major fight or flight arousal. As best I remember, there were muscle tension increases of 2000%, heart rates increased by 50 or more beats per minute, blood pressure increases of 50% or so, skin conductance increases of 400% and as much as a 20 degree drop in hand temperature. They wanted me to explain to the audience that this was really good for them...to get this 'adrenaline rush'. Therefore, people should run right out and buy a ticket to a particular horror movie which seemed to have been produced by a company affiliated with the network. They found a psychologist who agreed with their point of view so they got what they wanted anyway.

But to me there is already enough horror in the world, horror of the real kind. And, in fact, it is probably very difficult for real love and fear to coexist. It is not my intention to judge those of us who enjoy horror films. The mind is complex and we all have our formulas for trying to deal with death and life. I simply want to make the point that to break through we must challenge our beliefs and move into the unknown, and that may trigger anxiety, may feel like hurting, may be scary at times, and most certainly will entail giving up some things we are attached to.

## THERE IS A PROCESS...

Whereby some human beings come to an understanding of how the mind works and thereby manifest and implement 'breakthrough thinking', action (and when appropriate) non—action. Furthermore, we assert, this Process is meant to be extended for one's whole life. In some it appears to continue right up to the end of life. In fact, there are many levels of understanding implied in this way of self-knowledge learning, and one of the most difficult (yet most rewarding when it is properly integrated) is the concept of death.

Psychologically, there is a way of living in which one dies to the moment past so that the moment present can be fully alive. This seems to lead to a lessening of the fear of physically dying and a subsequent release of energy because of the reduction of fear. 'Fourth Dimensional Consciousness' tends to lose the belief that life and death are opposites, but tends to see them as an integrated whole, necessary for the process of creation to be. We believe that sustaining this quality of mind and aliveness is what the Game of Life is all about.

How do we encourage break through thinking, how do we sustain it, and how do we restart it when it fails? How do we increase our capability to deal with the nadirs, the 'Dark Nights of the Soul' that so often precede breakthroughs? Is it always necessary to have a breakdown before we can have a breakthrough?

*"I said, living is attachment, pain, fear, pleasure, anxiety, uncertainty, the whole bag, and death is out there, far away. I keep careful distance. I have got property, books, jewels, that is my life. I keep it here and death is there. I say, bring the two together, not tomorrow, but now—which means end all this now. Because that's what death is going to say. Death says you can't take anything with you; so invite death—not suicide—invite death and live with it. Death is now, not tomorrow." Krishnamurti. The Future is Now*

## THE PROCESS AND ECONOMICS

We are not saying that The Process is the way to get as financially rich as possible. But it is a way to become aware of how rich we already are and of the incredible resources that have been locked up within. Resources which can be brought out of the darkness and set free so they can be used. The Process is about ecological order and about how countless people who have allowed the Perennial Principles to work for them have also brought substantial and responsible economic order into their lives and the lives of their loved ones. More about this in session 8.

## THE FOUNDATION

This work is both inspiring and humbling and we do not presume to know the best way for everyone to get the most out of life. However, there are a growing number of people who are already successful through applying some or all of what we shall focus on here. The foundation of The Process is clearing the mind so that thought can become as coherent as possible. Coherent thought can lead in some people (if not everyone) to states of deep attention and awareness which can truly be said to go, that is to perceive beyond thought itself. All of this together can explode the creative process. We call this condition MindFitness. In order to clear the mind (which includes metaphorically and literally the heart) the capacity to relax deeply must be developed. Therefore, stress management as science and art is one of the most fundamental, first steps.

From there the ability to solve problems naturally unfolds. The Greek word problema means to be thrown forward and implies that if the right question is asked one is thrown forward into the solution. Another interpretation of problema is something that is hurled at you. Either way the answer to the question is hiding within the question itself, and the solution to the problem lies within the problem itself. So asking the right question and defining the problem(s) is worth the effort it takes. It is also a critical fundamental. Let's take a look at

## EDWARDS DEMING'S PROFOUND KNOWLEDGE STRATEGY.

Let us assume that the essence of a wonderful life is solving the right problem(s). We can see that it is quite easy to waste all of one's resources solving irrelevant problems. Going a bit more deeply into the way most of our minds are working, we become aware that it is much more difficult, and often uncomfortable, to focus one's mind on those problems, the solution of which, will bring about meaningful change. This brings us to Deming's brilliant Profound Knowledge concept. The late Edwards Deming is one of the most remarkable minds of our time. Deming, a controversial statistician, was considered by General McArthur to be a systems and organizational genius. The General applied Deming's ideas with awesome effectiveness in the Pacific War Theater.

After the Japanese surrender he took Deming into Japan during the occupation, and assembled 28 men who controlled 80% of Japan's investment capital. Essentially, Deming told them that if they followed the principles that he would teach them they could rebuild Japan quickly. Deming convinced them that they could develop their devastated country into one of the greatest economic powers in history, and do it in an incredibly short time. His resulting impact in Japan became legendary. He saw that the salvation of Japan depended on the transformation of their management—so he insisted on teaching their management. The Japanese were desperate, so they listened. Also, Deming's kind spirit attracted their deep attention.

When it became clear to the Japanese that they were going to achieve far more than they could have hoped to accomplish through war by following Deming's strategies, they awarded him the highest medal they give. I believe he is still the only non-Japanese to receive it. Later he assisted many US corporations and organizations, companies like Motorola, Ford, Chrysler, Harley Davidson, etc., in engineering extraordinary turn-arounds. He generated thousands of disciples who are now at the forefront of the new thinking in business. Deming and his business disciples are largely credited with nurturing the kind of creativity that has led America and much of the rest of the world into this period of unprecedented prosperity. He developed a concept he calls Profound Knowledge. Profound Knowledge is applied to systems and we, our lives, our individual organisms, and our very beings are also systems, aren't they? They are systems that are part of and interdependent on larger systems. In order to give you a sense of the revolutionary thinking of this giant of the twentieth century we include Deming's Fourteen Obligations of Management in the Epilogue.

Deming often used the following Profound Knowledge illustration. During the 50's and 60's, carburetor companies were making the best carburetors the world has ever seen, even as the companies themselves were dying. The reason for their predicament is that they were solving the wrong problem, and they were solving the wrong problem because they were asking the wrong question. They were asking, 'How do we make better carburetors and market them more efficiently?' The question they should have been asking is, 'What is the best way to get fuel into the cylinder head?' So, while they were making the best carburetors ever, relatively mediocre fuel injection companies ate their lunch.

The Real Problem is the way we are looking, using the mind, the powers of perception. When I asked my super successful consultant friend what he actually did that made so many companies willing to pay him so much money, he answered, 'Look, we can't hope to know their businesses as well as they do. But what we can do is help them look at their businesses in different ways. You know, we simply turn the coke bottle upside down. Something remarkable usually happens when they look with fresh eyes at old problems.' Looking with 'old eyes' means we are looking through memory, and not truly seeing things as they are now. We are not in adequate contact with the fact…'what is'. This lack of contact, this pulling away (called dissociation in psychology) from contact with 'what is' causes unnecessary internal conflict, resulting in loss of energy and insight. This is the very energy required to be aware; therefore; awareness, the ability to attend, to turn the light on dies, or is too weak, because it simply doesn't have enough power, enough 'juice'.

Duality, either/or's are a sign that the mind is probably looking at the problem in a limited way and is not likely to come up with the right question. One of the most creative people I know used to be a Democratic 'Spin Doctor'. Now he may be doing far more good for the country because he realized that some of the ideas and, more importantly, some of the individuals in both parties were on the right track. So now he focuses on building cooperation between both camps, and he and the politicians he advises are, in my view, the wave of the future, because their focus is on what works rather than partisan politics. A clear mind does not have to choose between the two so-called opposites. It sees the danger of duality and the opportunity, the humility, and the presumption of innocence allowed by, and necessary for cooperation, synthesis and consensus building.

If we can agree that in the area of business, and probably many other areas as well, Deming got it right with his concept of Profound Knowledge, and we apply this principle to our own lives, we will often see that the way we spend much of our energy and time is relatively ineffective. The reason is that we are usually solving relatively unimportant problems instead of gathering all our energy, our intelligence, and using our precious time to solve the problems that really count. Isn't it humorous how fashionable it is to say that Einstein might as well have died at 33 since his greatest contributions were over by then? In fact, from there he spent the rest of his life asking some of the most worthwhile questions that have ever been asked in physics and philosophy. Good Lord, he was trying to perfect the Unified Field Theory. He wanted to 'know the Mind of God'. We are standing on his shoulders. Because he and others have tried and are trying to ask the right questions and solve the most important problems, wings are unfolding from the flesh of man.

So the first thing we must do if we are to define the problem skillfully, is to make contact with the fact of the problem. This is a Process Basic. If we cannot or will not do this, we are probably lost, and are likely to wander around aimlessly solving irrelevant, trivial problems until we die irrelevant, trivial deaths. See how the ego begins to squirm here? Watch the self-image. Watch the thoughts at this point and the 'felts'. There are phenomenal rewards if one can handle this kind of discomfort.

The Great Solution to all our problems may well be to live creatively, and that means staying as close as possible to the truth even if it hurts. If we can see, can define the real problem, then the right question will probably follow. The answer lies within that question. But the correct answer may not be the answer we wanted to hear. In fact, it probably is not the answer we wanted to hear.

When Motorola, Harley Davidson, Ford, Chrysler etc. hired Deming to help them gain profound knowledge and to define their problems, do you think they liked the answers? The real problems were not how to improve sales and inspection strategies, etc. The real problems were that the product was not designed well enough, not manufactured with enough quality. The real problems were that the corporate culture was degrading and stifling. It was robbing employees of their humanity, their creativity, and the joy of doing really good work and being recognized for it. The atmosphere destroyed the employees' sense of mission. All of these companies were in grave crisis, but when they adopted Deming's Fourteen Obligations of Management they went on to undreamed of heights…or should we say dreamed of heights. They materialized their dreams.

So, asking better questions requires intelligence. Intelligence = sensitivity. The Latin Intelligere means to see between the threads finely woven. Sensitivity implies MindFitness, a clean, clear-headed, balanced system, and the foundation of that is Profound Attention. In order to attend profoundly we come back to the necessity of a high level of stress management and the development of great skill at relaxing, quieting the mind and body.

*"Imagination is more important than knowledge." Einstein*

The essence of Deming's Profound Knowledge is creativity. This implies a different kind of knowledge. It is based on insight rather than the same old conditioned way of looking at things—the status quo. It takes imagination. Deming asked outrageous questions. He challenged the way things had always been done. Personally, I almost never eat red meat anymore, but I must admit the saying 'Sacred cows make the best hamburgers' has a ring of truth about it. One of the sacred cows of American business is the concept that the more ferocious the competition, the better. By being unafraid to question assumptions about competition Deming showed management how to reduce the traditional brutally competitive corporate culture, and in so doing produce companies that were paradoxically far more viable and able to compete! If you want to understand the pros and cons of competition from a truly scientific, philosophical, and real-world, practical perspective, we strongly suggest Alfie Kohn's extraordinary book, **No Contest.**

## You Are Already a Hero

If you have come to this book, this place, it is because you long to break through. You hunger to set up, to bring about those circumstances, that field from which you can unfold. Indeed, don't we all long to arise like the Phoenix from our ashes? Who among us has not been devastated by uncontrollable circumstances at some time? Which one of us past 30 or so has not been burnt up by pain and fear? How many of us have seen our dreams consumed in the inferno of madness, of lovelessness, stalking and savaging humanity, our family, you and me? Conversely, what greater adventure, what greater fun is there than to let go that which limits our aliveness, our love, our creativity, and to embrace this endless opportunity to enjoy, to nurture our life, this world, each other?

Events are soul-sized now. It takes everything (courage) to see that change is possible for you now. To see that if our sense of mission, our love is strong enough—change is choiceless. There is mystery here, like the basin that forms attractors from the chaos that is (as in Chaos Theory). There is the Ground of Being from which we emerge and in which we are rooted. It is infinite, and so is our capacity to live in the timeless moment now, the Infinite Present.

Is it possible to live a heroic life—an original life instead of a conditioned, second hand life? If we feel we are not all we can be...is quality change possible? Can this mind, so beaten down by 'the slings and arrows of outrageous fortune' break out of its prison? Can we, together and individually, ask the right questions, and thereby together walk back along the stream of our potential...the stream of consciousness, awakening latent, emotional intelligence so that we are renewed, so that we can at last be at peace with, and fully unfold who and what we really are?

We have all had days when we celebrated our cup being half full, and days when we lamented our cup being half-empty. In 1977 one of my closest friends, his wife and all his employees were murdered by smugglers in Columbia, because he wouldn't let them use his beach to unload drugs. Martin was fond of saying, "You can go down the road feeling sad or you can go down the road feeling glad. But of this you can be sure. You are going down the road". Once, when I was remarking to my wife, Dagne, about how many people in this country completely lose it and go mad, she said, "It's the other way around. The miracle is that more people don't lose their minds and run screaming down the street, considering the pressures that this culture exerts. The way I see it most of us are unrecognized heroes, and when we see that in each other things already get much better."

MindFitness emerges in a direct ratio to self-knowledge. And the most powerful of all self-knowledge learning strategies is to watch thought, and that requires a relaxed body and a quiet mind. Of course, everyone is unique; therefore, each of us must discover our own individual Process.

How best can we approach this Process whereby we become all we can be...whereby we make the most of what we have...of what we are? Surely, the foundation is doing the best with what we have, what we are. A fundamental way to gain best quality self-knowledge as quickly as possible must include watching thoughts and feelings in real time. Now. Try to keep coming back to this concept as the mind wanders and the emotions run up and down the gamut of feelings...and felts. Yet, somehow we must get the hang of 'thought watching' in an easy, natural way. There must be a free-flowing sense to it, a movement which adapts to the changing circumstances of the moment without effort. Flexibility is the key. 'Fight or flight' stress and mechanical, heavily conditioned thinking reduces this flexibility.

We are going to explain why some people feel that brain wave training is exceptionally valuable in carrying on this kind of adventure. But remember, the Perennial Principles of The Process must stand-alone and have for thousands of years without any electronic biofeedback.

We learn almost everything we learn through some kind of feedback. Yet, by what process do I know I am reading my natural, inbuilt feedback 'instruments' correctly? This requires sensitivity. What enhances or reduces the effectiveness and quality of our sensitivity is itself a feedback loop…a kind of mirror. As you read this, are you aware of your breathing? Are the shoulders relaxed? Do you feel alert, attentive, aware, or are you bored, feeling tired, nodding out? Are you watching your feelings, emotions—good, bad, indifferent, happy, frustrated, angry, scared, excited, peaceful?

Are we moving together? Being an authority figure is counterproductive when working with those truly interested in learning. I see myself as a coach, an assist, a guide, and if truly successful, a kind of mirror. Each one of us must somehow become both the teacher and student for ourselves. The quality of our lives depends on it. Again, The Lord of Tomorrow is Profound Attention Today.

## WRITING IS A BRIDGE

Please, cross it! BREAKTHROUGH THINKING AND WRITING GO TOGETHER. SO, IF YOU FEEL AN INNER RESISTANCE TO WRITING, ATTEND TO IT CAREFULLY!

There are, so far as I know, virtually no civilizations that survived intact for a long time, at least not into modern times, who did not have writing.

There were some who developed writing, and then abandoned it or made it punishable by death, and they seem to have disappeared. Furthermore, in general, those civilizations that developed writing to the highest degree have survived the longest and/or given birth to new civilizations that went even further. Writing is a kind of technology that has life. If thought is matter and thinking is a material process then doesn't it logically follow that writing makes thought even denser, 'more materialized...thicker matter'? Doesn't that make writing part of the process of changing our reality? Is not writing a means, a pathway, a road, a channel whereby the implicate order can become explicit, at least relatively?

Most of us probably have difficulty knowing what we think until we write it down. But even more importantly, writing things down goes a long ways towards making them happen. So, if you want to bring about healthy change, write about that change, get a notebook going, or better yet a training/creative journal. It can be exhilarating to watch a sense of mission emerge from that writing, then a set of goals, then a plan of action, then suddenly finding yourself tending the birth of a dream and nurturing its growth. We are doing this together you know? This kind of learning, this book, is a materializing dream to me. We are in this process together. The Process is creating The Process before our very eyes!

## TRAINING JOURNAL—CREATIVE JOURNAL

Notice how you begin collecting newspaper clippings and making notes etc. when you are getting interested in something? You are spontaneously beginning what some call a training/creative journal. This is an important Process strategy. Although there are exceptions to prove the rule, the way you create and use your training/creative journal is probably a predictor of your degree of success. There may be a subconscious resistance to doing this because at some level we don't want to know certain things about ourselves. This scientific process is a kind of tender 'trap' which forces us to learn more about ourselves and helps us see what works and what doesn't.

Since one of the most important goals of this training is to help observe thought/thinking more clearly, the time to start writing is now. Remember, these are scientific journals. Date everything, as some things become clearer when they can be seen in relationship to linear time. It is not necessary for any one else to see this information. It can be as private as you like, so start putting your thoughts and 'felts' down. Overcome the discomfort, if you have it.

The training and creative journals are probably best handled as two books: a diary with one whole page for each day (not your appointment book) and a notebook. We suggest you begin by measuring daily, subjectively on a 0—10 scale several symptoms. An example would be headache. If there were no headache then the rating would be 0. If the headache were the worst it ever gets the rating would be a 10. Begin by rating two or three symptoms (presumably subclinical) and two quality of life measures. We remind you that subclinical means symptoms which are below the level of intensity requiring clinical intervention. Obviously, if the symptoms are clinical, it means that you should probably seek qualified professional help.

Quality of life measures are those things that add to the quality of your life such as sports or other activities you like to do. In the notebook section begin writing about goals and your sense of mission. Symptoms and quality of life ratings should be put down every day (3 days per week minimum). Do the journaling as much or as little as you wish but realize that there may be a relationship between how much you write and how much you achieve. This is part of the art and science of change. Change is inevitable, but bringing about healthy change takes mindfitness, focus, work. The person who can make little, healthy changes over time (even if they are uncomfortable at first) can probably achieve extraordinary things. Please write down as best you can what your sense of mission is. You may have more than one and that is fine. If you cannot identify one, then you may want to try 'clustering'.

## CLUSTERING

Clustering can be a powerful tool for those who are seeking insight as to what their sense of mission is, as well as for those of us who feel we have a sense of mission and are looking for best ways and breakthrough thinking in order to accomplish our mission. So far as I know clustering was developed by a short story writer to help herself and her students enhance their stream of consciousness and free association so they could build stories better. Isn't that what we are doing? Building a story? Or would it be more useful to say we are becoming more aware of a story that is already unfolding? Our story.

There is a tendency to think too much in linear, left-brain, and conditioned ways. We call this Thinking of the Second Kind and some describe it as 'processing' thinking. It is often necessary and certainly has its place. But there is another order of thinking which we call Thinking of the Third Kind while others might use the term 'free- flowing' thinking. Clustering can be a way to gain insight into this much more creative, non-linear way of thinking.

Perhaps the difference between literature, and most of the other endeavors we embark on, is that in literature, once it is written down, it is for all practical intents and purposes finished. Whereas, with most other missions writing down the plan is merely an important first step. A cluster may be done in a few minutes or it may gradually grow over months or even years. The idea is to put your mission or a goal in the middle of the page and circle it. Then begin listing related ideas (circle them) and connect the circled ideas or concepts with a line indicating relationships. Studies show that those who can freely associate, drawing on concepts, thoughts from seemingly unrelated sources, get better, more productive insights. One of the most interesting things about a cluster is that it can help you see the whole picture and this view, in turn, can help you set priorities and realistic goals. Linear thinking has its place. And that place is doing the work, the detail needed to fulfill the mission that has been generated by coherent, holistic, creative, 'free flowing' thinking.

## GRAPHING

THE PRACTICAL TECHNIQUES AND EXERCISES THAT WE ARE GOING OVER WITH YOU ARE THE ONES THAT WE HAVE DONE AND, OR ARE DOING OURSELVES.

I once started graphing the growth of my business. Later, I began to graph our total resources. I had to laugh at myself when I realized how motivating seeing these gross material measures became (After all, my self-image aspires to being beyond being significantly influenced by extrinsic values). But then there really is no separation between the physical and the mental is there? Descartes was wrong in this regard. Bohm is right. How motivating might it be to measure one's progress toward psychological freedom? Is it possible? I think so, and what follows is our spin on assisting you in getting the hang of it.

When we say that we are going to apply scientific strategies to the art of Life Enhancement we mean, among other measures, graphing. If all you do is to discover how to reduce the fight or flight response by about 15—20%, you will probably achieve on the average at least a 25—35% *decrease* in frequency and amplitude of the two or three symptoms you have chosen; and the same kind of *increase* in the two quality of life measures. But remember, there is a strange and perverse inner enemy that does not want to see what we must do to succeed…even worse what we must not do….what we must give up!

The measurement and graphing aspects of this process do not necessarily go on indefinitely. Six months is usually enough to get clear about what's working and what isn't. We need enough time to study those natural rhythms that are occurring all the time. Symptoms (both clinical and sub clinical) wax and wane naturally as do feelings, energies and skill levels that make our lives enjoyable and uplift us. It's important that we get enough data so we can watch our peaks and our nadirs. We want to watch, and when possible measure these trends.

By the way, this strategy applies to clinical symptoms as well; however, we continuously refer to subclinical instead of clinical because (as we have suggested before) symptoms which can be diagnosed as clinical are often more properly handled with the assistance of a well-trained health care professional. Subclinical symptoms refers to problems which can certainly be a drag on the quality of life but are not considered serious enough (yet) to require professional attention. In addition, there are federal laws in the US which require that biofeedback treatment for clinical and diagnosable disorders take place under the supervision of (or upon the order of) the appropriate healthcare professional.

Symptoms are usually easier to identify than quality of life indicators. As suggested, pick your three most difficult (subclinical) stress related problems such as headaches, insomnia, fatigue, anger, anxiety, depression, addictive behaviors, lack of exercise, over-eating, etc. Use minimal code (i.e. H for headache). Rate them fast and when you have accumulated a couple of weeks worth begin graphing them. Use colored pens!

Experts usually agree that most accidents and mistakes are essentially a manifestation of the wrong thinking and loss of quality consciousness that maladaptive stress produces. Other stressors can include things you eat, drink, smoke, or things you don't do or consume (enough water, vitamins etc.). You will probably see a correlation between nutritional changes and improvement in stress management and quality of life (unless, of course, you already have your nutritional act together).

Quality of life measures can be of many things but usually measure something you love to do. It can even be earning money. It is almost laughably easy for most middle management, sales professionals, and small business people to record an increase in income from this kind of program that is great enough to pay for the total investment with money left over! This increase in productivity probably can be attributed to the transformation of lifestyle that usually accompanies vigorous application of stress science principles and strategies. One amusing example is the used car salesman who underwent a biofeedback assisted stress management program and had a transformation of life style which resulted in the achievement of his dream. He became a Mercedes salesman. To my mind, economics (which translates for most of us as freedom and energy) is a legitimate quality of life measure. Obviously, many forms of work do not lend themselves to quick changes in income. Sports, art, and quality of life measures usually respond fast. Sometimes the ability to shift time orientation and spend more time with loved ones and doing what is most important to you is a valuable measure.

Out of the graphing of symptom and quality of life ratings a creative journal emerges. Symptom and quality of life rating only takes a small amount of space on the page, leaving plenty of room for journaling. Part of the reason that this kind of training works is that the combination of all of these techniques generates enough movement and energy to break through inertia and change the status quo.

## ELMER GREEN'S MIND/BODY PRINCIPLE

*"Every change in the physiological state is accompanied by a corresponding change in the mental-emotional state, conscious or unconscious; and conversely, every change in the mental-emotional state, conscious or unconscious, is accompanied by a corresponding change in the physiological state."*

## THE SENSE OF MISSION

I wonder if we share what a sense of mission means. It implies passion doesn't it? It implies wanting to do something with all your heart. There is the quality, as Joseph Campbell put it, of 'following your bliss'. Assuming we understand what a sense of mission is, have we as individuals got one now? Do we remember having had one? If we have lost our sense of mission, what does it take to get another one back?

We are going to present some ways of looking at this idea that might seem controversial at first. But hang on, we are going somewhere! If we make statements that do not work for you, jot them down and see if they make more sense later. **Intelligence = sensitivity.**

## LEARNING DOES NOT TAKE TIME!

Of course, there is a kind of learning that does take time, practice, and conditioning such as playing an instrument, driving a car etc. We are not denying the value of that, but the kind of learning that breeds freedom, and which therefore affects all of the lower orders of learning, is usually based on quick insight (the 'Aha—Eureka Phenomenon'). This is some-times called insight learning. Furthermore, the mind that is actively engaged in this kind of free-flowing, non-linear learning has an altogether different relationship to time than the mind that is engaged in the more common, linear, processing, mechanical learning. We intend to show how these different types of learning at least partly define third and fourth dimensional consciousness.

Scientists, including Norm Don at the University of Chicago, have used brain mappers to measure the electrical activity of the 'AHA—Eureka Phenomenon' which is usually accompanied by an almost involuntary exclamation and is common to all cultures. It is an area of considerable scientific interest sometimes referred to as the psychophysiology of insight. The 'AHA' or insight phenomenon almost always appears to 'ride' a theta (4-7hz) brainwave and seems to sweep from the rear and middle of the brain forward. There is an elegance to this brainwave movement which implies first perception and visualization and then action. The front of the brain is that part that is involved with making things happen…the 'materialization' of 'works'. This description of what this apparent 'movement' means is, of course, still hypothetical. But if it turns out to be true, it is quite neat, don't you think?

Now, a lot of effort may take place before that flash of insight occurs. Of course, hard work is important but real progress, especially the levels of excellence implied by our adventure together, is based on insight and not on time spent trying or 'efforting'. A Zen master noticed that one of his students had been sitting for a particularly long time, brow furrowed, struggling to meditate. So the master picked up a couple of bricks, sat down next to the young man and began to noisily rub them together. Finally, the frustrated student could stand it no longer and he asked what the venerable teacher was doing. 'I'm making a mirror', he answered. 'But Roshi, you can rub those bricks together forever and they will never become a mirror'. Gently the master answered, 'I know, my son. And you can sit there straining, struggling, making a great effort, and torturing yourself for the rest of your precious life and never learn to meditate.'

## A SENSE OF MISSION. THE ULTIMATE GOAL.

It may be presumptuous to call a sense of mission the ultimate goal, but to my way of thinking it is certainly an ultimate goal because it is the means whereby enhanced human performance and quality of life is usually achieved. We must understand the art of goal setting. It is a vital skill. But having a sense of mission is different from goal setting. So, let's stay focused on mission now.

Barriers to the emergence of a sense of mission include comparing oneself to another. Thinking that one is superior or inferior to another is irrelevant to the task of doing the best I can with what I have. Common additional barriers include limiting self-talk, and a dysfunctional view of time such as; ' I'm too young, I'm too old, I've got too much time, I don't have enough time, if I could do it, I would have done it already,' etc.

Think of Sense of Mission as Process rather than goal orientation. High achievers are usually more process oriented than goal oriented. They often express the feeling that the goal is changing and emerging out of the process. The means are more important than the end. Probably the actual achievable goal, in a sense has already been realized, so long as the quality of the process is as high as it can be for a particular individual.

Psychologists have developed tests that determine relative happiness. They suggest that people who are functioning close to their highest potentials and are not comparing themselves to others usually rate much higher in terms of these 'happiness scales' than others who might be richer, more recognized by society, and so on.

Mindfitness is a term I use because it implies that understanding and improving the way the mind works is a goal, an art, a science and a process. Mindfitness implies a clean, properly energized, flexible, healthy brain. MindFitness programs are designed to advance one's ability to self-regulate and make mental processes clearer and healthier. Some people think of mind as basically brain, but we use a classic, and we believe more accurate, definition. As already mentioned, 'All of the body including the brain is contained in the mind, but not all of the mind is contained in the body.'

## MINDFITNESS IS THE REAL SUPER INFORMATION SUPER HIGHWAY.

MindFitness implies order, and that is why we are working so hard to understand physical, psychological, economic, creative, sexual and other types of order. We must understand the relationship of order to the environment (field) in which we are living out our lives as best we can. It is a critical component of our success that we realize we are using language ( aural and visual thought) to work in an area which has its root, its source, beyond thought. One of the exciting things about this time that we are living in is that English, as well as other 'living' languages, is growing, evolving, maturing. We are creating better ways of communicating about illusive subtleties (such as qualities of mind, thought, insight and consciousness) that are usually difficult to share. So at times we may have to go slow in order to define words, and even request that you accept our definitions for now so that we can go forward. This is not easy but it should be rewarding.

Since before the turn of the century, research has been conducted into the relationship of high quality mindfulness to insight. Of paramount interest is: By what means can we increase the amount (amplitude, power, depth), the frequency (how often it occurs) and above all the quality of insight? If the quality of the insight is great enough the entire life is immediately transformed; a literally unstoppable sense of mission emerges and an extraordinary quantity and quality of energy is released which burns away and breaks through barriers and inhibiting factors...including the worst of them all...The Inner Enemies. The result is an increased sense of psychological freedom. So, the first key to gaining a sense of mission is realizing that meaningful change is possible. Most of us cannot resist 'going for it' once we see that true growth and unfoldment is within reach, is possible for me personally, and not just for someone else.

Twenty nine years ago I had what was for me an immense insight, and it immeasurably enriched my life, and exploded a life long intense dedication to learning all I could about the mind and body as well as the way science, technology, and consciousness form an integrated whole. This insight ignited a burning sense of mission which seems to be growing, and which I expect to carry through to my death...and if I allow myself to play in the field of Thanatology...beyond. But I'd rather spend time immersed in the here and now. I'll have eternity to deal with the ultimate mystery. On the other hand, insight into death probably does more than anything else to empower and unfold the highest possible quality sense of mission.

*"All the world is going to die. Perhaps, even I too!" Italian proverb.*

*"If something should happen to either one of us I plan to retire in Florida." Archie Bunker to Edith*

So, we are looking into our minds and hearts and saying do I have a sense of mission now? Can I deepen it, make it stronger and thereby release greater energy...open the window so more and better insights can come in? Do I remember having had a sense of mission? Can I restore, renew my sense of mission? Can I bring about a new sense of mission as though for the first time ever?

How can I express to you the insight that has brought so many benefits to me and countless others? It is paradoxically both the easiest and most difficult of all things to describe and to employ in one's life. The insight may be defined as making contact with, attending to 'what is'. Think about that. If these words seem too forceful, uncomfortable, we can soften them by saying 'relative contact' with 'what is'. Or in psychological jargon, association of a high order.

That is why we place a high priority on assisting those who do not consider themselves to be scientists in learning enough about the best of the scientific process and the technologies of self-knowledge to measure what is so and what is not...what works for you and what does not.

*"You can look at life in two ways: As though nothing is a miracle or as though everything is." Einstein*

One of the most fundamental aspects of science is that it deals mostly with the measurable. This is not to say the immeasurable doesn't exist. The things which count most in life are those things that cannot be counted. In fact, most of the great thinkers who have my deep attention love to contemplate the immeasurable, the infinite, the unlimited...that which lies beyond the known. But that is a potential that emerges from mind-quietness. A potential that takes care of itself and unfolds by itself. If we do a good job of the down to earth work we are exploring together, who knows what miracles might materialize?

*"The most beautiful and most profound emotion we can experience is the sensation of the mystical. It is the power of all true science." Einstein*

May I suggest again (if you haven't already) that you write down as best you can your sense of mission? Perhaps you have more than one, but writing it down should help you gain clarity and set priorities.

## THE PSYCHOPHYSIOLOGICAL STRESS PROFILE

Another way to enhance your progress is to get a PSP (Psychophysiological Stress Profile) from a qualified biofeedback practitioner. A PSP measures the amount of change stressors cause in terms of muscles, autonomic system, breathing etc. A PSP also measures your ability to recover from a stressor. We suggest that you try to get it done as early in The Process as possible so that you can set a scientific baseline. A PSP makes it easier to determine how big a barrier or drag the unhealthy stress response exerts (yes, there is a healthy stress response) on your day to day well being, the actualization of your potential and the unfoldment of your sense of mission. This measure can help determine what types of strategies and training techniques are most likely to produce the best and fastest results for each individual. Furthermore, this kind of a baseline makes for more effective evaluation of progress later on in the training, as well as being a correlation with other indices of growth. Doing a PSP can lead to increased insight, and head off the tendency to backslide into the mysterious yet common problem of forgetting what has produced success. Other types of biofeedback instruments can further accelerate learning, and we integrate them whenever time permits into our MindFitness programs including the Process.

# Neuro (EEG) Feedback

We repeatedly emphasize that The Process is a way of understanding and applying the perennial principles better; and neurofeedback is entirely optional and obviously unnecessary for some. We also emphasize that neurofeedback has been a highly valued learning tool for many including those who have developed this program. Therefore, we are making our best effort to give you insight into the role neurofeedback might play in your personal self-teaching work. We will come back to this subject later in the book; however, the following thoughts may prove useful at this point:

1. Neurofeedback is not a panacea. But it *is* an awesome development in the science and art of self- knowledge, voluntary control and applied psychophysiology.

2. When we change the electromagnetic activity of the brain, we change the field. 'The field is the sole governing agency of the particles.' That means we change the brain cells including the glial (neuronal support) cells, and all of this together implies there must be a brain chemistry change. It seems to us the question really is how much and what kind of change—not whether.

3. Since neurofeedback seems to reduce the effects of psychological conditioning it provides benefits as well according to one of the most important psychodynamic models. Which is when you reduce conditioning there is a tendency for the sense of mental freedom to increase (remember, we are defining mind as much more than the brain). Reduction of unhealthy, unnecessary psychological conditioning is widely believed to increase creativity. Reduction of these complex and often illusory self-images makes it easier for the mind to move in the direction of a deeper, wiser understanding of who and what one actually is.

4. Another psychodynamic model is that fears in the subconscious (or unconscious depending on your orientation) contaminate, restrict, and

limit the quality of moment to moment consciousness. So, the ancient strategy of bringing those fears up so they can be 'burnt up in the fires of consciousness' (or integrated according to psychological jargon) seems to work well. Moving into slower brainwave states may trigger memories of earlier developmental periods when our brain moved slower. Nancy White suggests this is due to state dependent memory. Dealing with these fears is a critically important aspect of cognitive and other cutting edge psychological theories. Therefore, many believe neurofeedback is extraordinarily powerful at both the psychodynamic and organic level. As we have suggested before, there are a growing number of brain chemistry specialists who believe that this kind of self-regulation training is affecting at least some neurotransmitters, neuromodulators and neuropeptides including but not limited to endorphins, serotonin, dinorphins, enkaphalons, acetylcholine, and dopamine etc.

The term 'influence' is somewhat of an understatement. For example, it is widely believed that endorphins make you feel good. Those of us who are runners, athletes, meditators, conscious breathers etc., might say increasing endorphins can make you feel real, real good. If my understanding is correct, dinorphins can make you feel 7 times as good as endorphins and enkaphalons 70 times better than that. Delgado's experiments showed that animals will starve to death when given the option of stimulating certain parts of the brain rather than eating. Experiments with humans are much better science in my opinion, since animal and human consciousness appear to be vastly different. However, in this case, 'pleasure point' brain stimulation has shown similar results in humans.

Finally, if it is true that neurofeedback can substantially assist human understanding of thought, then this technology must be of the highest order imaginable. We believe that NFB is a manifestation of Herbert's vision as described in the introduction and again:

*"One of the greatest scientific achievements imaginable would be the discovery of an explicit relationship between the waveform alphabets of quantum theory and certain human states of consciousness." Nick Herbert, Quantum Reality.*

## BELIEFS AND THE PROCESS

How does the Process deal with different belief systems? If you are going to hang on to your beliefs, then you are! Call yourself what you will: Christian, Buddhist, Muslim, Hindu, Catholic—Christian, socialist, agnostic, reverent agnostic, atheist, etc. From our point of view that's OK. Like the song says, 'It's all rock and roll to me'. The Process is NOT about telling you what to believe. It aspires to be about assisting you in understanding so much as possible how the mind/body works better. It seeks to understand the nature of belief itself. How to be crystal clear about what you believe, and how to live more effectively. How to be truer to yourself. How to discriminate between healthy and unhealthy beliefs for yourself, and not according to some outside authority. How to be aware of the ways beliefs change, mature and transform. How to see if there are beliefs which are limiting your ability to live according to your own highest values. How to break out of and go beyond those beliefs you believe are not good for your soul, mind, body and those you love.

Three men were having a rather heated discussion about spirituality. Each one belonged to a different faith, and naturally believed his religion to be the truest, the best. Finally, they noticed an old man sitting in the corner listening to them. So they asked him if he could help them out since the situation was deteriorating into an argument. The old man thought a minute and then said, "Well, I used to haul cotton for a living and there were three routes you could take to the cotton mill. You can take the northern route and its smoother but takes longer; then there is the southern route—its shorter but much bumpier and hot as hell. Of course, there is the mountain route and it's the shortest of all but it is very dangerous. You can loose your brakes, lose control and easily get killed. But when you get to the mill all they ask you is how good is your cotton!"

"It seemed to me that a critical moment in Pransky's life was when his belief about the quality of life changed. He previously thought that we all had to carry some extra weight (stress and anxiety) around as a membership fee in the club of life. After spending a summer with people who had apparently transcended that limitation, he saw a better way of life. His subsequent vertical jumps were a result of a high level of interaction with those who were already experiencing the benefits of self—actualization. To make a vertical jump, its important to see that the higher level exists and is there for the jumping." David Cascino after reading *The Renaissance of Psychology.*

*It seems to me that beliefs are more like structures. They can be true or untrue, beautiful or ugly. Faith seems to have more of a day to day, massive action, 'do what it takes' quality about it. Faith is action. Bucky Fuller said, "God is a Verb."*

## Session Three

## Thriving on Stress (Change). The Physical Equation. How the Mind and Body 'Landscape' Each Other.

*"Body is that portion of Soul that can be perceived by the five senses."* William Blake

## Thriving on Stress Is Thriving on Life. Stress Basics.

One of the most important basics of Life Enhancement is learning how to thrive on stress. Stress is defined as change and life is constant change. Therefore, learning to thrive on change means learning to thrive on life.

As a result of assisting health care and educational professionals in improving their stress management skills over the past 29 years, I realized that properly applied biofeedback can dramatically increase the learning curve of stress management for most people.

Let's see if we can gain deep insight into stress science within the shortest time possible. Stress is an engineering term, which simply means change, and it was made popular as a psychophysiological term by Canon and Selye. Stress is not good or bad, positive or negative. As our skills as cartographers of consciousness mature, richen, we want to move away from confusing use of positive and negative and other language which triggers dualistic thinking. Stress may be healthy or unhealthy, productive or counterproductive.

Unhealthy stress is professionally referred to as distress or maladaptive stress, and healthy stress as eustress from the Greek euphoria. You are all already skillful at stress management or you wouldn't be alive. The issue is what happens if you increase that skill?

Peak Performers do the basics very well. Life Enhancement takes energy and clarity of mind. The first place to get that energy is from the reduction of the maladaptive stress response. And if you have already reduced it, reduce it further! If you find you cannot control your mind the way you like, start with the basics and control what you can, such as muscular and autonomic nervous system tension. You are then, to a substantial degree already regulating the mind! If you doubt this, then biofeedback can dramatically prove it to you. See how simple this pathway is? We move according to our own pace from the easy to the more difficult.

## Stress Is Energy. Use It or It Will Use You.

Imagine you are a bucket and your life force is water. If the bucket is full of holes (poor stress management) it doesn't matter how much life force you pour into your bucket, you are going to wind up empty. Excellent (not just fair) stress management is like repairing almost all the holes in the bucket. Now it doesn't take very much water to fill it to overflowing. As life force 'overflows,' creativity happens. As you read, are you watching the unnecessary tension in your body? Are you breathing easily and fully from the diaphragm? How is your posture?

Some people make an argument that the fight or flight response works well in fast moving, emergency, unusually challenging situations. We feel that there is a superior response even in those circumstances, and as enthusiastic Life Enhancement students we must discover what that is. One of the astronauts who went to the moon told me that he and other astronauts had done biofeedback training in order to improve their ability to stay calm and focused during fast moving, emergency situations. The astronaut said, "For example, you can be flying along at 17,000 MPH and a couple of indicators on your instrument panel can suddenly tell you that you have a few seconds to make all the right decisions. One mistake and you will become a shooting star." Of course, fight or flight response is better than no response at all. But realize that the fight or flight response actually reduces the types of sensitivity and energy we most need for highest possible performance. Sustained fight or flight drains the body of energy, produces disorders and causes overthinking (psychothenia). It clearly reduces both quality of attention and consciousness, and increases mistakes. By the way, the same astronaut also told me that brainwave training was part of a program to teach deep meditation skills because NASA believes that the ability to profoundly alter consciousness will be critically important during prolonged stays in space.

## ENERGY

You know, I hope this enormous effort we are making together has helped us all get clearer about what to do. However, being clear about what to do is only part of the problem isn't it? The kind of people who come to this kind of a gathering (or read this kind of book) are usually already filled with ideas about what to do, and have considerable motivation to get things done. But there are three substantial problems which most of us find so frustrating that we could spit nails. These three problems are also completely interrelated, which means that we have to somehow work on all of them at the same time. Come to think of it, that's a good definition of The Process...how to effectively work on these three problems at the same time.

The three problems are ENERGY, TIME (measurement of energy), and MONEY (stored energy). When we look at the entire material world including all those considerations which we deem practical and necessary for any decent quality of life, we can see that they are all manifestations of energy, and some of it is organized energy (which is a physics definition of matter). We can see that energy traveling in a pattern is matter; therefore, thought is matter and a material process, and we are usually ruled by our thoughts. But energy is even more fundamental than thought. In fact, one of the miracles of Thinking of the Third Kind is that thought realizes that the source of its life is energy (see session four); and enhancing the quality of that energy (or allowing a higher quality energy to operate in one's life) is of the highest priority for all of us. Isn't it?

*"Matter is a form of stored energy." Einstein.*

When we look at our lives from the most practical point of view we see that the problem is usually not lack of ideas but rather lack of energy, that is the power required to carry out those ideas. Furthermore, there is a lack of the energy required to harmonize our lives according to the principles, concepts, and values we already have. Haven't you wondered at times if possibly you might have chronic fatigue syndrome? Don't most of us have long lists of projects that we feel would improve the quality of our lives and the lives of the people we love...projects which could lead us into the unknown and into great adventures of the soul? But somehow we just run out of gas before we can get very far with them. Probably, reading about The Process is a step in the direction of trying to solve this energy problem. After all, energy is power. And we want to be more powerful, more free, don't we?

By the way, I've never really understood the oft-quoted statement, 'Power corrupts and absolute power corrupts absolutely.' I think it is one of those clever little cynical homilies which is devoid of Emotional Intelligence. Perhaps it is true that self-centered use of power is corrupting but absolute power is another matter. No human being ever has had absolute power. If God does have absolute power does that mean God is absolutely corrupt? Why do we insist on confusing ourselves and our children with unquestioning, misuse of language this way? Perhaps it is because we are afraid to question the very conditioning that has created those illusions that bind, torture and sabotage us (and which The Process aspires to break through). Another silly saying is 'What you don't know (or won't face) can't hurt you'. I wonder how many Ostriches hid their head in the sand only to be eaten by some carnivore—butt first. I guess the idea is that we should make sure that we all have only a small amount of power so that we can only be a little bit corrupt. When we speak about empowering the downtrodden, empowering those of us who feel weak and powerless, does it make sense to invent the term 'em-corrupt' those who feel powerless? I think not. Ultimate kinds of power are the transcendence of conditioning and the actualization of one's potential. Nothing is more powerful than the law of love or less corrupting in its exercise.

The first step, and possibly the last step, required to solve the three energy problems is to understand who and what we actually are and what we really have to work with. Right? We have to work with what we have. We must bloom from where we are planted. The key is self-knowledge. When we see the facts of the situation, we see that we have to make priorities. We must eliminate the unnecessary. We have to learn how to let go. True love is letting go. This leads to voluntary simplicity, which is a way of getting energy. As we have discussed, stress management is another way. And of course there is a sense of mission and attention, and right sleep. High quality energy, life force is a miracle isn't it? How can we bring this miracle about within our own lives?

## CAN YOU SPARE TWELVE MINUTES PER DAY TO CHANGE YOUR LIFE?

We are going to suggest that you practice 3—7 minute deep relaxation techniques four times per day. Reduction in frequency and amplitude of both graphed symptoms and quality of life measures will probably parallel how well you integrate this concept (pausing for 3 minutes minimum at least 4 times per day, and during that pause going all out to reduce the fight or flight response). Healthy stress (arousal) is essential to life enhancement. See how reducing unhealthy arousal releases energy and clarity, producing healthy arousal?

There are at least two 'magic bullets' that can profoundly enhance the quality of moment to moment living. They are attention and the breath work. Think (meditate) on it. Attend to (watch) shoulders, temperature of hands, and breathing. Warning! Relaxation may be dangerous to your comfort level at first. Relaxation induced anxiety is common. But to go further we must go through it. By the way we are thinking about adding a third 'magic bullet'...healthy, adequate sleep (See session 6).

## INTELLIGENCE, SENSITIVITY

Healthy stress arousal increases sensitivity and ability to accomplish your mission—unhealthy stress dulls it. One of the most creative ways to think of ourselves is as an energy transformation and generating system. Look at the common sense of it. We take into ourselves all kinds of energy such as food, air, what we see, hear, feel etc. Then we transform that energy and radiate it out again as movement, thoughts, communication, emotions, work, etc. Often the subtler forms of energy are more important than the grosser ones. For example, thinking can make a bigger difference in health sometimes than quality of food. Chaos Theory holds that subtle activity can have far greater effects than is usually realized. One of the ways we sabotage ourselves is to waste or bleed away central nervous system (CNS), autonomic nervous system (ANS), and voluntary nervous system (VNS) energy. In biofeedback we call this dysponesis. If we find a way to reduce that dissipation, energy builds. Where does it go? Eventually it explodes, and that explosion is the creative process. Most of us probably do not have to reduce the fight or flight response by more than 15 to 20% in order to bring about creative explosions.

Perhaps it is appropriate to discuss the way this kind of a process seems to go as well as some of the pitfalls. Obviously, we don't need to spend much time working on how to handle everything going beautifully, because things going well take care of themselves, and the most we can say is, 'Don't wake me, this dream is wonderful'. Or should we say,' This reality is wonderful'? Anyway, things going well are easy to handle and do not require effort.

## *"The wise see trouble coming from afar"* Lao Tzu

We are better off using our time to look at the problems. The first problem is almost laughable, and commonly plagues peak performers. Simply put, when you do a good job of applying these principles there is a huge energy release, and you blast yourself up to another level of activity, responsibility and challenge. We are forced to deal with this in the professional biofeedback community. As the fight or flight response is reduced there is an energy build up, release and concurrent self-actualizing lift. There seems to be a kind of octave—like character to it so that it feels to some almost musical, as though one raises to the next logical, sort of 'frequency/energy determined' level of activity and achievement. And then there is a plateau.

So far so good. No problem. The problem arises when one sees that the level of skill, competence, responsibility, attention, awareness, mindfitness that triggered the explosion, the blast off, is inadequate to meet the challenges encountered at this new higher plateau of action. In order to do that one must develop stress management skills much further. We could tell you hundreds of stories of stress management professionals who brought about a transformation of their own lifestyles and assisted many clients in transforming their lifestyles as well, only to find themselves breaking down from the increased rate of change (stress) they had brought on themselves by just being successful and achieving their goals. I'm reminded of the story of the secretary who had done such a great job for a California company that she was promoted to vice president, thereby increasing her salary from $28,000 per year to $45,000. She then sued the company because the stress of her new responsibilities caused her to develop stress-related disorders. She collected $650,000.

There is usually a period of shame, self-incrimination, and embarrassment when someone raises himself or herself to a new plateau only to discover that their old level of stress management skill is no longer adequate to meet the new challenge. Sort of reminds me of a cat that misses a leap, crashes to the floor and then confidently saunters away as though the crash is part of a clever plan to outwit a hidden opponent or stalk an invisible prey. If we are fortunate, the benefits of our stress management successes clarify. We realize that there has been enormous progress, and we have created a super school for ourselves, enabling us to grow even more. I have personally experienced this phenomenon a number of times. The only solution is to recognize this trap quicker so you can just get on with the consolidation and refinement that plateaus are all about, and from there build up the energy for the next leap, for raising the bar. Integrating this phenomenon gracefully with aging is itself a most interesting and daunting challenge, and one of the reasons 'aging ain't for sissies'.

*"The man will be, by then, at the end of his journey of learning, and almost without warning he will come upon the last of his enemies: old age!*

*This enemy is the cruelest of all, the one he won't be able to defeat completely, but only fight away." Carlos Castaneda*

## A CLEAN MACHINE

So then, what are the ways that the senses can be made more acute so that perception is enhanced? If it is intelligence we want, we have to increase sensitivity. Once again, the easiest way to make progress is probably eliminating, in a balanced, common sense way, those things that dull perception. Making the senses as sharp as possible increases the size of one's slice of the Pie of Life. More sensitivity means more aliveness doesn't it? Then the right exercise for each person emerges as a relatively easy way to increase aliveness. Over the years I became fairly proficient at both helping clients find out what is the best exercise for them, and assisting them in developing a sense of mission about it. Some of the most popular included martial arts, running, walking, tennis, golf, yoga, tai chi, swimming, dancing etc.

One of the most enjoyable and efficient exercise strategies is yoga, and many have made exceptional progress from simply doing a beginner and intermediate class. The reason is that stretching and breath work are critical to advanced stress management; and advanced stress management skills are critical to The Process of Life and Performance Enhancement. You might want to read Beryl Bender's book **Power Yoga**. The Iyungar Yoga Association has a national network of certified instructors and an excellent reputation for quality and consistency. (Iyungar 800 889 9642 www.comnet.org/iyungar.)

Stretching is key to cleaning up and maintaining a clean machine because of its detoxifying effects and the way it reduces anxiety by reducing tension in the muscles. Stretching combined with the breathwork can produce astonishing results.

*"I discovered the middle path of stillness with speed, calmness within fear, and I held it longer and quieter than ever before." Steve McKinney when he broke the world downhill ski record.*

## BREATHWORKS

Breathing is one of the most difficult things to teach because we all take it for granted. But it is one of the easiest ways to bring about healthy physical and psychological change. We cannot spend the time we would like to in this short seminar doing the breathwork; however, we may be able to make enough progress so that those of you who need it will be inspired to make sure you have given adequate attention to this critically important basic. Interesting, the word 'inspire', no? To breathe in, the inbreath. And in probably every language, breath (also wind) implies and is often interchangeable with the word spirit.

Biofeedback practitioners are usually stress management experts, and they understand that breathing correctly is critically important to learning to thrive on stress. Therefore, most of us were extremely surprised to find out that we knew relatively little about how to harness the power of breathing until Eric Peper and Bob Fried began doing their workshops in the early eighties. If the breathing dynamic is important in treating disorders, please see how much more important it is in Life Enhancement. The challenge is how can I assist you in looking at your breathing as though for the first time? If you can do that and you discover that your breathing is optimal, then good, go on to the next thing.

But I suggest that most of us are significantly underbreathing, and the reason we are can be a bit scary. I believe that an unconscious form of self-sabotage whereby we prevent ourselves from becoming too aware, too intelligent largely causes underbreathing. This particularly widespread, insidious and debilitating form of self-sabotage is accomplished by simply reducing the quality of consciousness by reducing the efficiency of the brain. Chronic underbreathing prevents the brain from getting the oxygen it needs as well as the right mix of gases. This in turn causes disregulation of the brain chemicals and electrical activity.

I assert that the reason for this rejection of intelligence, awareness, 'the light,' is because if we see too clearly we realize that we must take full responsibility for ourselves. Beyond that, some part of the brain is trying to resist seeing the inevitable—that we are all connected, so we must take responsibility for even more than ourselves. I would rather not realize that I am my brother and my sister's keeper. Or that in fact, in some sense I AM my brother and my sister. Going further, it seems thought is trying to prevent our realization that the image of the 'me' is an illusion, and we are not who or what we think we are (at least not so long as we perceive ourselves through the distorting lens of common, heavily conditioned states of consciousness). A word of caution: over-breathing, hyperventilation, and the so-called 'locks' can be dangerous, just like too much or the wrong kind of exercise. Over breathing and over exercise should be categorized as another form of self-sabotage.

Isn't it interesting that humans are the only animals who develop paradoxical, thoracic (up in the chest) breathing patterns? Furthermore, we start these dysfunctional breathing patterns at somewhere between about six to ten years old. Therefore, one of the secrets of stress management is the restoring of natural breathing, which will usually cause excellent results all by itself with most clinical symptoms. Subclinical symptoms are equally responsive. You will recall that subclinical symptoms must be dealt with in order to enhance the quality of life. Another thing about the breathwork is that it seems to deliver results along a seemingly infinite continuum. Restoring natural breathing not only reduces symptoms, it affects the brain chemistry, and can enhance deep levels of homeostasis, attention, reverie, and meditation.

One of the problems with attention is trying to do it: forcing yourself doesn't work very well. Attention needs to flow easily, naturally. One of the most effective ways to bring that about is to become aware of inattention. Improving breathing is similar. Becoming aware of thoracic, rapid, shallow breathing and its consequences helps motivate us to correct that situation. However most adults who have been breathing inefficiently for a long time may find that they have to make relearning deep, slow, abdominal breathing a high priority in order to succeed. Falling back into the old patterns is for a time much easier than waking up. In addition, there is great resistance to acknowledging that I have been 'asleep', even relatively.

Watch yourself to see if you stop breathing when you get up or sit down or something catches your interest. Probably, we should never stop breathing unless there is good reason such as walking behind a bus or swimming underwater etc. A great exercise for restoring natural breathing is to sit outside on a lovely day when the air is clean and sweet, and listen to the wind and let it teach you (this is also a neat atmosphere for doing brain wave training).

Perhaps as you read this you can scan your body and notice what is happening with your attention, your thoughts. Remember, resisting thoughts doesn't work, but just watching thoughts does. Notice your posture, and if you find that your breathing is too shallow and up high in your chest, just fix it easily, naturally. Don't try too hard. Trying too hard is counterproductive. Easy breathing, easy!

Recapping, we can only barely introduce you to the breathwork in this book, but if you will do a good hatha yoga class you will get substantial training in the 'full breath' and other breathing techniques which restore natural breathing (estimated at about 9 -12 bpm and about 600 to 800mls of air per breath). If you calculate that you are probably breathing 18-22 breaths per minute at about 300 to 500 mls of air (especially if anxious) then this simple shift will amount to approximately a 400% increase in breathing efficiency without even taking into consideration that the balance of the gas mix will be better. It might take a couple of years for this kind of breath pattern to become a new, super healthy habit; however, practicing it usually brings immediate, often dramatic benefits. This alone can change your life, and at the very least profoundly reduce fight or flight response and 'clean the machine'.

## GETTING MORE BY GIVING UP

Surrendering something of less value, even though one may be attached to it, in order to gain something of greater value is one of the most classic of all growth strategies. But most of us have to learn how to do it. There are some remarkably interesting and effective ways to help oneself get the hang of this 'letting go' concept. I was amazed at the power of the simple shavasana yoga technique. You lie on the floor on your back and let everything go. Imagine sinking into the floor and sort of pretending like a kid that you are peacefully dying. It may sound silly if you haven't sincerely tried it. It is also extremely relaxing. It can lead to a kind of ability to practice 'dying' as part of the creative process. This kind of surrender does not mean physically dying, of course; but it does mean one is learning to do a kind of psychological dying which clears the mind and allows a space for the new to be born.

## THE FUTURE IS NOW

*"Seek above all for a game worth playing. Play as if your life and sanity depend on it, because they do!" Robert de Ropp*

**The Lord of Tomorrow is Profound Attention to the Present.** We have heard all our lives that living each day as though it is the last is wise. Notice how the standard, conditioned, third dimensional consciousness tries to argue with this, saying 'you would not plan for the future'? But those who do live each day that intensely (interestingly enough) seem to have superior ability to plan for the future. Because the seeds of the future are in the present, and that which empowers the present also empowers the future. What did the novelist Samuel Johnson say? *"Nothing sharpens the mind so much as knowing one will be hung in the morning"*.

Think about how much one has to give up in order to give birth. A sense of mission implies one truly loves what (s)he is doing. True love is letting go. Can I say to myself, 'I have The Beginner's Mind. My mind is empty. I know nothing. I am ready to learn. I am ready to be both the teacher and the student?'

## REMEMBERING I'M FORGETTING

One of the difficulties inherent in learning stress management skills is forgetting to use them when you most need them. Paradoxically, it is unnecessary to become aware when I am aware because awareness takes care of itself (and much beyond itself as well). An explosion in growth happens when I can become aware that I have lost awareness. There are all kinds of techniques for remembering to scan the body for signs that unhealthy stress is building...holding the breath or underbreathing, shoulders lifting, bad posture etc. A strategy I like recognizes that we usually underuse one side of the body, especially if we are right handed; and this mechanical behavior is linked to doing many things unconsciously like dressing, eating, driving, brushing teeth etc. It seems clear that more mechanical means less human doesn't it? And less mechanical means more human, no?

So, I take these small mistakes as opportunities to wake up the brain and make it more flexible. For example, if I always put my belt on one way, put it on the other. If I always put a shoe on the left foot first, then put it on the right first. In the seminars we always ask everyone to put their watch on the opposite wrist and attend to the feeling. Most find it uncomfortable. This is the kind of discomfort which also accompanies many of the most effective life enhancement strategies. The person who can consistently handle small discomforts in the interest of learning and progress can usually achieve extraordinary things.

We can carry this further. For example, some of us are orally compulsive, which makes us eat too much, too fast, and swallow without chewing or even savoring. So switch to eating with the left hand. It's astonishing how fast one gets with the left hand. I decided to try chop sticks and became lightening fast; and finally switched to chop sticks with my left hand with which I can now pick up single grains of rice at warp speed. I guess I don't need to spend much energy generating a sense of mission about eating.

About six months after I started brushing my teeth with my left hand my dentist began saying, 'At last you have stopped damaging your teeth by brushing too fast and across the dentine. Whatever you are doing, keep it up.' Don't switch hands if unsafe as when driving or operating dangerous equipment. But do fix posture and practice shoulder relaxation and breathing while driving. All of this like right exercise and stretching contributes to brain flexibility (dimensionality) and should improve your control of whatever equipment you are operating.

One of the problems which arises during stress management training is resistance to relaxing the face muscles and abdominal breathing. In the case of the face muscles there is often a fear that relaxing them will make the face seem expressionless and dull. Actually, the opposite is the case. Tension in the subtle muscles of expression in the face prevents the nuances of feeling from playing on the mask of the face. This is often unconsciously interpreted by the other person as withdrawal, which triggers anxiety, which in turn can trigger anger or suspicion. Relaxed face muscles allow the true personality to play on the face and this tends to engender a feeling of inclusion and closeness on the part of the other person. In fact, this physical skill can be used irresponsibly in order to take advantage of people as in the case of con men. By relaxing the face muscles and smiling they can engender trust. Caveat emptor. Awareness is the key.

The same kind of an issue sometimes arises with people who have a bit too much fat around the middle, and are afraid that abdominal breathing will make them seem less attractive, less sexy. Remember Scarlett O'Hara in Gone with the Wind? She was obsessed with maintaining her eighteen-inch waist and she went crazy. It's a good metaphor. In the first place, breathing correctly increases energy which then burns fat, secondly it strengthens the stomach muscles, thirdly it is actually a strategy for enhancing sexual dysfunction. Just as I've never known a woman who really cared whether her man was bald or not, so I've never known a guy who felt a woman had to have a wasp waist in order to be delicious in bed. You ladies who believe all is lost if you are not skinny with a narrow waist might take a hint from the belly dancers. They breathe real good, they love their tummy muscles and are very much in touch with them. Although many of them are a little Rubinesque, maybe even a bit chubby, they give most men fever. The anorexic model look may be all the rage in fashion, but most of the guys I know say, "I just don't get it" when they see these skinny, drugged out looking waifs.

## THE BIG PICTURE

The standard as far as to what is a good quality of life in the United States and some other countries has been increasing for many decades and is a formidably complicated subject. However, we feel that there is a big picture which can be relatively easily understood by us all. Since 1900 life expectancy has almost doubled. All of us are probably delighted to observe the extension of middle age which has happened in our lifetimes. I'm sure we all feel fortunate to be living in a time when it is possible to have a wonderful quality of life even though we are in our fifties, sixties, seventies, and for an increasing number, eighties and even nineties. Indeed, some of us wonder how much further the prolongevity revolution can go. Prolongevity has been of paramount (and increasing) interest to me ever since I was in my twenties. One of the primary reasons that I made a career out of self-regulation technology is precisely because I believe it to be one of the most powerful technologies ever developed in terms of enhancing The Process of extending and enriching the quality of life through all stages of life, especially late middle age and beyond.

Recently, on CNN, a world class genome researcher and prolongevity expert stated that he is virtually sure we are going to double the life span again within the next hundred years. Whether this becomes a blessing or a curse depends on the quality of mind and sense of responsibility of this highly functional, increasingly wealthy and powerful segment of the population. Many factors are contributing to this incredible evolutionary leap which is taking place within a moment of anthropological time. Factors such as wealth, leisure time, nutrition, genome research (including organ replacement), and thousands of medical and drug advancements are contributing to a mind-numbing explosion of the average life span. Some of the research is taking place literally out of this world on space stations, as recently dramatized by the international hero John Glenn.

In our view, none of these factors is as productive as the modification and transformation of the way the mind is used. We assert The Process can bring out such enhanced use of mind in a dramatic and cost effective way. In fact, we believe careful return on investment analysis of the true benefits to the community of this kind of learning should exceed several hundred percent (much more if we factor in the individual and cultural benefits we receive when we turn away from certain kinds of mistakes and significantly improve our creative process). Furthermore, the ability of the Learner to practically apply these principles can be further enhanced, and made much easier to understand, with the assistance of neurofeedback self-knowledge technology.

Most scientists who are experts in healthy aging strategies agree that there is probably nothing more important in terms of improving the quality of life and the very process of aging than vigorous application of stress management. Traditional biofeedback is known to be unusually powerful as a stress management super tool. However, neurofeedback is widely believed to be even more effective for many people. Stress management is where The Process begins because learning curves turn upward in proportion to reduction of the maladaptive stress response. Remember, the classic definition of stress is simply change. Whole heartedly and whole mindedly meeting the challenge of inexorable change is key to aging healthily.

The Process continues far beyond classic stress management and teaches practical, relatively easily learnable strategies for understanding at the functional level how the mind works. In addition, The Process (enhanced with the adjunctive use of EEG self-knowledge technology) further trains the Aging Learner in how to think more coherently, reduce counterproductive dysfunctional thinking, worry and fear. Beyond that, we accept the challenge of assisting the learner in rediscovering and renewing their creative thinking and action capabilities by the scientific cultivation of usually underutilized potential in the vast field of the mind. One of the world's leading neuroscientists, Nunez, observes that most people decrease in alpha as they grow older. But there is a relatively small percentage whose alpha holds at youthful levels. We speculate that there should be a correlation between sustaining alpha, ongoing brain cell growth and a vigorous, relatively happy old age.

Although much more research must be done, there are already many clinical reports by well-respected neurofeedback researchers detailing successful application of EEG biofeedback (used adjunctively) for the numerous disorders of aging including but not limited to dementia, stroke rehabilitation, head injury, depression, hypertension etc. Substance abuse is another NFB application among the aging. As you are aware there is a major problem of unwise and dangerous mixing of medications that have been prescribed by different physicians, often unaware of the total combinations of drugs the patients are taking. Obviously, the clinical application of neurofeedback for these medical problems should be done within a proper clinical environment, and under medical and psychological supervision, by appropriately qualified practitioners.

However, The Process focuses on the vastly under recognized, under treated, and often devastating (especially among the aging) problem of subclinical symptoms. Please see excerpts from the two articles included from the Science Section of the New York Times regarding the work of Martin Seligman, past president of the American Psychological Association, on performance and life enhancement, as well as the necessity for addressing subclinical symptoms, and an article asserting that adult brain cells can reproduce. Since it has long been established that rats and birds can reproduce brain cells if their environment is enriched, it has also long been believed by many responsible scientists that human brains should be able to do what rats and birds can do in this regard. We believe The Process is an extraordinarily powerful set of principles and strategies for 'enriching the environment' of the human brain. Brains which have seen a lot of life, and are thereby heavily conditioned, can renew themselves and learn to look at life 'through fresh eyes'.

Any program to assist anyone in improving the quality of their life needs to integrate specific knowledge pertaining to truly holistic approaches to self-regulation, including knowledge about stress management, nutrition, exercise (physical and mental), economic management, improvement of relationships and other factors. However, in a surprisingly large percentage of the population the knowledge is already there. Take the case of substance abusers, including smokers and overeaters who really want to adjust their unhealthy behavior. They often know full well what they should do or stop doing, but cannot take the appropriate action. The Process goes right to the heart of that problem by focusing on how the mind works and by applying relatively simple, learnable strategies for enhancing the performance of the mind. The Process seeks to produce these benefits by applying the perennial principles, scientific advances in psychology and the design and delivery of cutting-edge biofeedback and self-knowledge technology protocols.

*The student asked his teacher, a Zen master, "How do you put enlightenment into action?" "I put enlightenment into action," replied the master, "by eating and sleeping." "But everyone sleeps and everyone eats," replied the student. "Quite so," says the master, "But it is a very rare person who really eats when they eat and sleeps when they sleep."*

## Session Four

## Practical, Relatively Easy Ways to Understand Thinking—Its Powers and Limitations.

We are going to go as deeply as we can into thought and thinking, and we are going to make as clear as possible what we believe to be the truest, most revolutionary view of the structure, the physics, and the uses and misuses of thought. Beyond that, we intend to go into those principles, concepts and insights we can use to influence our own thinking in a healthy, even transformative way. We will also look at the methods of using EEG to gestalt thought and make clearer the way thought operates. From there we may come to qualities of mind that are beyond and superior to thought, capabilities which enhance emotional intelligence. In this session we consider the ways of looking at thought that seem most accurate and useful to us.

## Thought & Thinking

The word is not the thing, the description is not the described. Is there That Force, Ground, Influence which is beyond thought, and within which all thought takes place? And is there anything a human being can do or not do which will bring about a fixing of thought gone wrong? What might the principles be whereby this Ground, this Influence, this Field brings thought to a sane, coherent condition in which creative, living intelligence, emotional intelligence, love can emerge, can flower?

So, if you are still taking this journey with me, let's carefully approach this problem, this barrier to our relative liberation from another angle. We have suggested that thought is matter and a material process. It is both necessary and usually a barrier to the natural unfoldment of our creativity, our intelligence. AHA, so our mind clears; we see that there are at least two orders of thought. Careful here! Is this truth or another game of duality? If ever thought is going to trick us this may be the critical moment.

*"When a thought springs in the field of the mind, let nothing interfere with it, influencing it, altering it, nor find a substitution for it. The past, with its fears, traditions, prejudices, and with its so-called ideals, is ever trying to mold thought, so that there is never a fulfillment but always a conditioning. Let all thought and emotion complete themselves in the flame of awareness." Krishnamurti, Thoughts on Living*

Could this be the way it is? There is a necessary, powerful, useful, functional kind of thought. But what do we call it? Since we have already said that we must create language to help us on this journey, let's call it creative, rational, coherent thought, at least until we come up with more appropriate descriptors. Another way to gain insight might be to use the terms 'free flowing' mode, and computer-like or 'processing' mode, to differentiate between two vastly different kinds of thinking. Certainly, there are times when the computer, mechanical, 'processing' mode of thinking may be relatively functional. However, computer-processing mode may also include an often-destructive kind of psychologically mechanical thinking. The implication in all of this is that there is a kind of thought which simply sees the facts of a situation as best it can, and proceeds to take the most rational, coherent action (or non—action). Later, as we look into the concept of the dimensionality of consciousness we will make a case for coherent thought's relationship with fourth dimensional consciousness (4DC) and perception. Beyond that we will make a hypothetical case for the relationship and usefulness of EEG biofeedback, including synchrony training, to thinking of the third kind and fourth dimensional consciousness.

There is a further implication that thinking 'mechanically' is the source of almost everything that goes wrong with the minds, and indirectly the bodies of human beings (especially in regard to psychological and relationship issues or matters requiring creativity). If that is true, then it follows that this 'wrong turning' of thinking is also at the root of most if not all that is wrong about the culture. The difference seems to be that whereas conditioning is critically important in one direction, it can be catastrophic in another direction. When we use the computer-like processing mode of thinking to think psychologically we are moving in the direction of loss of emotional intelligence (EQ) and probably IQ as well. We are certainly sacrificing our humanity.

Of course, one of the assumptions of The Process is that thought, even coherent thought, is still at least relatively mechanical, because thought is defined as image making process based on memory. Gordon Pask, Von Neuman and numerous other scientists and philosophers have been saying for decades that computers are thinking. We hasten to add that we think there are orders of human thought that are far beyond anything the most powerful computers can do. Yet, even fairly small computers can 'out-think' almost all humans when doing a wide variety of tasks.

Examples of coherent use of processing thought might be language itself, how to read, drive a car, organize a project, build a house, read a map etc. Now coherent thought is really no problem; although, we must be careful not to confuse it with higher orders of perception which are 'pre or beyond' thought such as insight and creative (archetypal) imagery. We should think of rational, coherent, creative thought as a kind of tool of these higher orders of perception (into the actual nature of 'what is'). Creative coherent thought is relatively energy efficient. In fact, when operating properly (coherently) it probably generates more energy than it uses.

Then there is the Mother (and Father) of all problems: mechanical, heavily conditioned, computer-like thought and its effect on psychological events, especially relationships. The difficult problem we are trying to get at here is that mechanical, computer-like, processing mode of thinking does a very poor job of thinking rationally about psychology. In fact, in this cartography scheme we would say that thought that thinks rationally about psychology is really creative, coherent, free flowing, and probably non-linear thought. Examples of typical dysfunctional, psychological thought are: 'I am superior, I am inferior, I am smart, I am stupid, I don't have enough time, I have too much time, I'm too old, I'm too young,' and so on. It is lost in the corridor of opposites and the illusions of comparison. Dysfunctional psychological thought reinforces dissociative trances.

We realize that discussing these categories of thought is to some degree complicated and confusing, and that is partly because our language, psychology, education and priorities have ill prepared us to understand this critically important aspect of our lives. Please be patient, we will look at this elephant in many different ways throughout this book. We believe a much better understanding of the orders of thinking and the principles which lead to the enhancement of the quality of thinking will emerge as we go deeper into The Process together.

Careful here! Don't be thrown off the chase by thought nullifying the possible insights that may be unfolding, because thought can claim it sees some contradictions. All of the examples above could also be actual sane perceptions of coherent thought, but this would be the exception to prove the rule. This destruction of potential insight, because of the appearance of superficial contradictions, is an old and dangerous game of the self-destructive mechanical mode of thinking. It seems helpful to us to think of this as 'The Old Thought Circle Game'. The closer we come to breaking through the illusion (the facade of thought) the more active 'The Inner Enemy' aspect of thought becomes in preventing us, by any means possible, from gaining these insights.

This game like quality of thought gives rise to the notion that thought has a kind of independent, 'mind- like' quality of its own, trying to exert its will. It would appear that thought and thinking has its own agenda which is, at least in part, to dominate the mental activity of the human being (even though there are potentially more intelligent capacities available). Can we watch this together?! This preceding piece seems to imply that thought is blowing the whistle on itself. Interesting, no? This is getting arduously subtle isn't it. We are challenged to see the truth within the false, and the false within the true.

Stay with the hunt here! Let's try to clarify with an example. When you are trying to cross the railroad track and thought calculates the train is coming and you don't have enough time...that is coherent thought and is very useful. So you stop and let the train pass. But when thought says, 'I'm late for my appointment, I may get fired, I don't have enough time to wait for the train because of all of the consequences that may happen, so I'll step on the gas and try to beat the train.' This is likely to be irrational, incoherent thinking, and it can be deadly because it is replacing and not paying attention to logical, sane, rational, coherent thought. The power behind mechanical—psychological thought is a self-image, which is just that, an image, a construct projected like a movie from memory, and essentially an illusion. This self-illusion acts like a barrier preventing the actual, true individual and emotional intelligence from emerging.

There are probably many secrets to living a wonderful life; but for me now, there is one insight so astonishing, stunning and immense, that I almost can't believe I have been so fortunate as to have found it. Let's try to put it in simplest possible formula form: When attention (awareness) gets clear, sensitive enough, it sees that thought runs along two pathways. One pathway leads to heaven and one to hell. Those two pathways are rational, sane, coherent, free flowing, nonlinear and creative thinking and linear, processing, mechanical, conditioned, ego—oriented thought (especially when it is applied to psychological phenomena including relationships).

To repeat, the terms coherent and psychological are intended to help gain insight. Coherent in this sense does not mean 'mechanical' or 'processing' mode of thinking; although, when appropriate such modes may be integrated with the wider field of coherent thinking. Coherent thought thinks rationally about psychology, technology and other things. But thought thinking in heavily conditioned and mechanical ways about psychological issues tends to be much too self-referencing, comparative, energy binding. It is losing its rationality and insightfulness into psychology and relationships.

The more one becomes aware of the mechanical (electrochemical) nature and makeup of thought, the more one is freed from the illusory, self-defeating psychological constructs of thought. Like, for example, the 'me'. As this vast waste of energy is decreased, there is a corresponding increase of 'direct' perception of that which is actual. This perception leads to, and is that, which is actually creative, not thought itself. Such a person becomes evermore skillful at sustaining the perceptual mode of mind rather than being everlastingly stuck in the thinking mode. The person who can somehow diminish mechanical, psychological thinking experiences a huge release of bound-up energy. This energy may be of a high order. The feeling of this phenomenon is one of freedom and excitement because one is like a child surrounded by toys (tools) and unlimited potential for play, work, and creativity. As you read this can you watch your own ego play? See if things don't seem to bog down and get stuck as ego considerations enter your mind, such as 'I'm above this, how do I compare to others reading this, etc.'

The key to withering inappropriate thought is attention (profound attention). This kind of attention also allows the flow of the previously bound up energy along best possible lines…in best possible direction. At this stage of wisdom the individual begins to feel and have insight into what Jung called synchronicity (the spontaneous unfoldment of events in a serendipitous way).

*"Of Magic Doors there is this, you do not see them even as you are passing through."*

As we have discussed before, there are many things one can do to enhance this process (being aware of others, their needs, exercise, eating right, meditation etc.) However, for most of us progress is probably largely dependent on what we can let go of (La via Negativa).

Pressing to get clearer about this healthy and relatively wise kind of thinking, perhaps we can call it 'adequately observed thought', since the act of attention seems to shape it best. Invoking quality thinking seems to be accomplished by attending to it, by adequately observing it. This heavily conditioned, dysfunctional mechanical thought can change, and as it does so does the value system of the individual who has been able to correct this 'wrong turning'. For example, isn't it obvious that creative, non-mechanical thinking is the source and foundation of powerful culture-enhancing forces like the women's, ecological and voluntary simplicity movements? Another example might be that the perception that arises when there is awareness of the limits and mechanicalness of thought sees that learning, or understanding love is the most profitable mission of all.

Remembering that thought is matter, and thinking is a material process, then combining that with the Heisenberg principle (what is observed is changed by the observation itself) the following seems reasonable:

1. Adequately observed thought is 'slowed down' as in peak performance or being in the 'zone'. This causes thought to clarify.

2. When thinking is clearer discrimination is easier. One becomes aware of thinking which does not meet a high standard and which is leading the mind/body in the wrong direction. Remedial action can be taken.

3. Thinking is changed in some fundamental and profound way by the act of observation itself. Since thought is matter (and thinking a material process) it follows that it exists at the photon (and apparently at the subatomic and molecular level). The logical next step suggests that observation and awareness of thinking not only changes thought but also transforms thought. This change may be of such a magnitude as to qualify as a kind of healthy mutation. In my opinion, awareness...profound attention to thought...actually is the true 'Philosopher's Stone.'

### Simply looking at something affects it: Quantum Theory Demonstrated from the Weizmann Institute

It has always been a problem to measure something without affecting or changing it somehow in the process. One of the most bizarre premises of quantum theory, which has long fascinated philosophers and physicists alike, states that by the very act of watching, the observer affects the observed reality. In a study reported in Nature (Vol. 391) researchers at the Weizmann Institute of Science have now conducted a highly controlled experiment demonstrating how a beam of electrons is affected by the act of being observed. The experiment revealed that the greater the amount of 'watching', the greater the observer's influence on what actually takes place.

When a quantum 'observer' is watching, quantum mechanics states that particles can also behave as waves. This can be true for electrons at the submicron level, i.e., at distances measuring less than one micron, or one thousandth of a millimeter. When behaving as waves they can simultaneously pass through several openings in a barrier, and then meet again at the other side of the barrier. This 'meeting' is known as interference. Strange as it may sound, interference can only occur when no one is watching. So, how is this known (other than theory) if even a mechanical device is an observer?

Once an observer begins to watch the particles going through the openings, the picture changes dramatically: if a particle can be seen going through one opening, then it's clear it didn't go through another. In other words, when under observation, electrons are being 'forced' to behave like particles and not like waves. Thus the mere act of observation affects the experimental findings.

To demonstrate this, Weizman Institute researchers built a tiny device measuring less than one micron in size, which had a barrier with two openings. They then sent a current of electrons towards the barrier. The 'observer' in this experiment wasn't human. But it (the detector) was observed by humans and, of course, the detector is merely an extension of the human senses. Scientists used for this purpose a tiny but sophisticated electronic detector that can spot passing electrons. The quantum 'observer's' capacity to detect electrons could be altered by changing its electrical conductivity, or strength of the current passing through it. Apart from 'observing' or detecting the electrons, the detector had no effect on the current.

Of course, it could be argued that even though the reputable scientists had a well-designed experiment; however, as it is described, it appears that the detector had mass. They also passed a variable current through it and placed it in close proximity to the electrons. So, how do they know that none of that affected the electrons? Certainly a lot of quantum physics is non—intuitive but this seems to be stretching it.

But look again. The scientists found that the very presence of the detector 'observer' near one of the openings, caused changes in the interference pattern of the electron waves passing through the openings of the barrier. In fact, this effect was dependent on the 'amount' of the observation. When the level of the observation went up, the interference weakened; in contrast, when the observation slackened, the interference increased. Thus, by controlling the properties of the quantum observer the scientist's managed to control the extent of its influence on the electron's behavior.

## THOUGHT AND THANKING II
## CAN EEG BIOFEEDBACK HELP CLARIFY THINKING FUNCTION?

The essence of the Process is learning heuristically (how to teach ourselves) to use knowledge and acquire the right kind of knowledge efficiently, while at the same time learning how to uncondition oneself. This means one gets more efficient, more powerful in terms of being more functional, more able to make one's way in the world responsibly. While on the other hand one is becoming freer, discovering the wonder of greater psychological freedom—implying access to higher orders of

**intuition, creativity, fulfillment, and actualization of one's truly human, humane potentials. 'Being in this world but not of it.'**

Our view of what thought is and its relationship to perception is not (yet) held by most of the scientific community. We are constantly revisiting and upgrading our understanding of neurophysiology, including neurochemical and structural electronics. We are doing all we can to keep as open-minded as possible and to look with 'fresh eyes'. However, the deeper we go the more we are struck with the feeling our now ancient model is and always has been on the right path. We assert that thought has a mechanical, although potentially glorious capability, analogous to an arm or leg, yet more powerful than either. Of course, the analogy is limited and should take into consideration that motor neurons of the muscles also do a form of thinking. However, perception is of a much higher order of intelligence than thought. The more one intuitively (or through usually heuristic learning strategies) realizes this, the less thought makes a 'wrong turning', and the more it becomes a happy servant of a much more energized creative process. Further, we believe that normal people not just geniuses, can achieve this insight with immeasurable profit to their lives, health and relationships. Nothing, but nothing seems more fun to us and more useful to the tribe than to seek out ways to assist people in perceiving this for themselves in their own ways.

## THETA, "AHA", INSIGHT THINKING

The term 'Theta Thinking' is emerging among neurofeedback professionals. It refers, as we have already said, to the perception that a burst of theta brainwaves seems to accompany the 'aha' or insight phenomenon. There is a bit more to it than that. 'Unhealthy' theta brainwaves seem to be associated with dissociation and some types of seizures. That is one of the reasons that we encourage alpha training per se. Because mid range (8-13hz) alpha training in 'alpha R's' tends to suppress the unhealthy theta while opening the 'Window of Opportunity' to bursts of the healthy theta, insight, and creative (hypnogogic/hypnopopic/archetypal) imagery.

One of the characteristics of this type of 'insight' thinking is that it draws on seemingly unrelated material and concepts in order to arrive at unforeseen, and usually superior solutions to problems. There is a delightful synchronicity in the realization that this insightful kind of theta burst apparently starts in the back of the head (vision) and sweeps forward to the front of the head (bringing the vision into practical, real world manifestation). Remember, one of the meanings of the Greek word problema is to be thrown forward into the solution to the problem. Probably asking the right question is the same thing. Doesn't it follow that if a key to problem solving is asking the right question (Profound Knowledge) then the key to asking the right question is to see 'what is' (Profound Attention)?

*"I think the one lesson I have learned is that there is no substitute for paying attention." Diane Sawyer*

This does not mean we don't have to do our homework. For example, the people who invented the jet engine had studied everything they could about the internal combustion engine and then a whole new insight occurred. It doesn't mean that linear thinking doesn't work. Indeed, it is necessary, and at times it is all we have. It may clarify things to compare linear thinking to the fight or flight response. As you know, the fight or flight response is a largely mechanical, conditioned, and instinctive response to challenge. Probably fear is always present during this challenge. However, when we look at the complex set of psychophysiological events which take place when the fight or flight response is triggered, we see that many of them can cause us to do the wrong thing at just the moment when we can't afford to make a mistake.

Of course, we all understand that the nature of the fight or flight arousal/response is to help us meet fast moving, threatening emergency situations. And we further understand how it is disastrous for us to use fight or flight response as a way to meet ongoing psychological challenges. Because if the fight or flight response is sustained over days, weeks and months, it poisons and exhausts our system and we begin to break down in the order of the weakest genetic link first.

It is usually a big surprise to find out that the fight or flight response is NOT the best way to deal with fast moving, emergency situations. It is better than nothing, of course, but there is a much superior way to deal with both short term and long term crisis and that must be one of the basics of any quality heuristic learning program. When we carefully examine ancient and contemporary martial arts and elite athlete coaching strategies, we see that one of the most effective things the athlete can do is to learn how to reduce or eliminate the fight or flight response and replace it with relaxation, calmness, awareness and attention. This then appears to invite another kind of subtle energy which is faster, more powerful, and far, far more sensitive and intelligent (including emotional intelligence).

Just as the fight or flight response seems to be what we fall back on when we can't do something more effective, so linear thinking is a fall back capability that is exercised in the absence of holistic, holographic, fourth dimensional thinking. Fundamental conditions for producing this high order thinking during crisis are relaxation, homeostasis, balance and profound attention.

Great therapy is a high form of true heuristic education, and I have been constantly taken by how often quality therapists say that when they are working at their best, the client virtually tells them what to do in order for healing to occur. And then, by making themselves into a kind of mirror, the therapist reflects back the problem, the question, and the solution to the client.

*Problema in the Greek also meant something is hurled at you. Sin in the Greek had a martial arts connotation as well in that it referred to anything less than the bull's eye (as in archery or spear throwing). It simply meant mistake. There was no guilt—laden, moral burden attached to it. This was the way Jesus used the term. "Let he who is without sin cast the first stone…go and sin no more".*

If we can conceive of the problem as a living thing, if we can see it clearly, the problem will reveal to us 'how it is going'. We can see it's status now and the direction it is moving in. Then by listening very carefully, the problem itself can tell us what to do. The problem may/will probably surprise us. We must be ready to hear what it says, including:

1. The problem we defined is not really the problem.
2. The problem is much bigger than we thought.
3. The problem is not really worth solving.
4. The function of the problem is simply to guide us, and build up our muscles so we can work on a deeper problem.
5. We should resist forcing a solution now because more time will yield more information and probably a better decision. If it is not necessary to make a decision, it is necessary to not make a decision. The timing may be wrong for making our move now.

The insights required to work at this level are often associated with a natural increase in theta brainwave activity. However, as we have stated before, we think that theta training per se may not be as natural and productive as alpha and other EEG strategies, which 'open the window so the breeze (theta) can come in when it is ready.'

As we have suggested before, one of the problems inherent in EEG biofeedback is the confusion over theta brain waves. The model we feel comfortable with holds that unhealthy theta relates to a kind of trance-like behavior, the result of which is a kind of detachment from 'what is.' These are generally not good trances. I assert that this dissociative trance-like trap may be broken out of by Profound Attention. Indeed, awareness and quality attention to one's own dissociation may be a prerequisite for breaking through. Prolonged attention/awareness may be the only way of not falling back into the dissociative trap. To reiterate, alpha training seems to attenuate the unhealthy theta while opening the 'window' for healthy theta to emerge. And Profound Attention increases sensitivity to subtle internal imagery such as the fast moving archetypal, insight imagery associated with healthy theta. A popular alternative strategy is to downtrain theta that is suspected of being unhealthy. Of course, that should work. However, we prefer the other strategy best because it seems to us that up training alpha may activate a kind of internal governor which 'decides' what theta to attenuate. Downtraining unhealthy theta requires knowing how to clearly identify which theta is unhealthy and which is not. That may be more easily said than done.

So, a strategy which seems to bear fruit is to produce the 'window' with prolonged alpha training. This window appears to be a condition where healthy theta emerges, constructed visualizations have enhanced effect, and consciousness—contaminating repressed psychological material rises up...to be, as it were, burnt up by insight, energy...a kind of fire in the mind.

*"...Look, acting according to knowledge is a prison; you will never be free; you cannot ascend through knowledge. And somebody like K says; look at it differently, look at action with insight—not accumulate knowledge and act, but insight and action. In that there is no authority...can one observe the actual anger without any conclusion, without saying right, wrong, good, bad? Can one observe holistically? Self-knowledge is not knowing oneself, but knowing every movement of thought. Because the self is thought, the image, the image of K and the image of the 'me.' SO WATCH EVERY MOVEMENT OF THOUGHT, NEVER LETTING ONE THOUGHT GO WITHOUT REALIZING WHAT IT IS. TRY IT. DO IT AND YOU WILL SEE WHAT TAKES PLACE. THIS GIVES*

*MUSCLE TO THE BRAIN." From Exploration Into Insight by J. Krishnamurti*

## THOUGHT AND THINKING III

A famous zoologist recently said that certain dinosaurs developed feathers on their little three towed, clawed arms. Then one of their three toes turned around backwards and their teeth got smaller. Their bones began to get lighter and they developed extremely powerful chest muscles. Yet these mutating creatures were not even close to flying. Mysteriously, the evolution continued until they were soaring in the skies. But you would never have been able to guess where all this weirdness was heading until one of them actually flew and was able to grab hold of branches (because one of those toes had turned around). I believe thinking function is like that. It is an unfinished evolutionary miracle like a bird before birds could fly. We are still in the in-between stage before thought becomes a winged creature, able to fly, free in eleven dimensions, and we are able to enter into literally unimaginable relationships with the universal creative process.

Fear is a form of thought and is at the root of most, if not all, psychological disorders. When adequate masses of brain cells are quieted, fear in general is cut off. One of the most interesting definitions of pain I have ever heard is that pain is a sensation with thought added to it in the form of fear. Probably we are also creeping up on an insight into suffering, which the dictionary defines as the feeling of pain. Attention/awareness deals with fear now, in real time, replacing it with increased sensitivity to what is....and creative, or as Jung would say, archetypal imagery. Pain becomes sensation, information. No wonder neurofeedback is being applied to pain management. Even if only the perception of pain is reduced there are benefits (including the system becoming more homeostatic, which would by itself accelerate the recovery process).

I have read that traditional cognitive psychology holds that your thoughts determine your reactions to reality. This was considered to be a big advance in its time, and indeed it was. We and others whom we consider to be leading neuroscientists and neurophilosophers hold the view that your thoughts *are* your reality. We suggest that this perception is critical to practical understanding of how the mind works. There is an even more extreme and popular New Age model which holds that your thoughts can change external reality. For example, how many of your friends have told you that they can think themselves a parking place? It seems obvious that our thinking can influence external reality; although, just how it does and what the actual result may be is for most of us unclear. Furthermore, there are plenty of examples that show that influencing our external reality is not as easy to do as it is to talk about doing. For example, I used to be slightly over six feet, one inch. But I shrank as I grew older. No matter how hard I think about it or how much I wish it could be so, I cannot even get back to six feet.

Therefore, we wind up with a correlation of 100% with the cognitive and the even more advanced thought = reality perspectives. Many of us even feel that there is something to the New Age view, but it is difficult to prove and the correlation is certainly low. Also, if you are wishing or thinking it so, it means that at the moment you don't believe it is so; therefore there is an inherent contradiction that the New Age model has yet to work out.

A powerful model for helping to understand thought is that there is Thought with a big T and thought with a small t. Thought with a big T is the Stream of Thought within which individual human thought is caught, and is being swept along like a toy sailboat on the surface of the Mississippi. Whereas, thought with a small t is thought that is generated from within ones own brain, i.e., image making process based on memory (and at least partially conditioned into us by socialization). Thought with a big T is Thought that is thinking you...the Stream of Thought that drives your thought and conditions you. Seeing thought in this way has been a great help for many of us, realizing that we are not in control of our thoughts nearly as much as our thinking would like to believe. Further, there is a certain illusory quality to the idea that we, 'I', (actually the thought formed image of the me) is doing the thinking. This leads to the questions: Are there orders of intelligence, consciousness, awareness, available to the natural man or woman that are not dominated, conditioned by thought, and are actually outside and independent of this Stream of Thought? Are they worth reaching for? Is it possible to grasp them...or It?Do the winds of thought blow through me conjuring up a kind of magical 'spirit' that generates the illusion that I am doing the thinking? Of course, I (the image) am thinking...the thinker is the thought. Then is Thought the Thinker and the thinker? If the ending of sorrow is the beginning of wisdom and only wisdom can teach us how to end sorrow, are we trapped? Or is there a kind of wisdom that can operate before sorrow is completely ended, and which can teach us how to think well enough, how to understand thought and its progeny sorrow? Is there a latent intelligence (quality of consciousness) in us which can teach us how to use thought, how to think and how to go deeply into thought, so deeply that we see the limitations of thought...the source of thought and perhaps glimpse the beginning of something else...another dimension possible for the human mind?

## CLOSE ENCOUNTER TO SUPER FUNCTIONAL THOUGHT (DIFFERENT KINDS OF THINKING)

### THINKING OF THE THIRD KIND

The late David Bohm was a genius and a physicist who devoted his incredible talents to the integration of the physics, the math of consciousness, perception, and those principles by which the mind naturally unfolds itself. He worked hard to get scientists of different disciplines to make communicating with each other a high priority. He also made a

Herculean effort to help get a movement started which will integrate all sciences in the task of bringing about a holistic world view as a critically important scientific paradigm. We became friends towards the end and I am still wrestling with all he taught me. One of the most interesting concepts he had was a way of categorizing thinking as types a, b, and c. He may have gotten his original insight from Plato. In my efforts to make it my own, I changed the terminology to thinking of the First Kind, Second Kind, and Third Kind...sort of a play on the movie Close Encounters, because thinking of the Third Kind implies contact with a higher order of intelligence. By the way, Bohm's work has blossomed into an international movement of a sort, and you can get connected easily and find thousands of pages to read, books, tapes etc. on the web.

**Thinking of the First Kind** is the condition in which a person is lost, not a good thing. The individual is not aware he is thinking and cannot observe himself think. Therefore contact with 'what is' is lost. All that she sees, hears, or feels is distorted by this condition of unconscious over-think...'Psychothenia'...usually leading to one form of disaster or another. Extreme psychothenia would be typified by a panic attack, complete dissociation and inability to see 'what is,' the creation of much too many 'thought-felt' images and virtually all of them wrong.

**Thinking of the Second Kind** is the condition where the thinker begins to watch himself think. This begins the capability for the thinker to discriminate. The good engineer emerges because he can reject those thoughts that do not conform to natural law as he understands it. Of course, when his wife scolds him for forgetting to take the trash out, his ego is activated (fear and panic emerges) and he falls back into thinking of the First Kind.

Remember the Heisenberg principle? This observed thought is being changed by the simple dynamic of the observation itself; although, the nature and degree of the observation is probably usually outside the awareness of the observer.

**Thinking of the Third Kind** is the highest order of thought. In this condition a kind of 'quickening' of thought occurs as thought awakens to its own structure and composition (**What Is**). This leads to awareness by the thinker that his self-image or ego is constructed of images based on memory and that (s)he is not who (s)he thought (s)he was.

*"If I am not who you say I am, then you are not who you think you are."*
*James Baldwin*

Further, thought becomes aware of its own limitations. At this point thought stops trying to be all things. For example, perceiving its limitations, it stops behaving as though it were unlimited. This produces a kind of shock, and in this shock relative neural silence, greatly enhanced sensitivity, and creative or archetypal imagery emerges. This 'higher' order of thought is quite aware that as it is observed it changes. It is also aware that that which is doing the watching is not thought itself but a function of intelligence that is much greater and more creative than thought. It may be said that when thought achieves these levels of silence there is the possibility that some aspect of the mind (but not thought itself) can make 'contact' with the 'unlimited'.

Thought sees that it must build it's structures on the insight provided by this higher order of intelligence rather than thought itself (thought building it's foundation out of thought.). The foundation must be this insight, this archetypal 'contact' with the creative source. This is all very traumatic for thought in the beginning and the 'trauma' itself can provide the shocked silence so necessary for insight. Sort of a creative giving up tends to ensue. This can result in profound value changes, actualization along Maslow's hierarchy of needs, and the emergence of a pervasive, non-specific sense of well being, peace, energy, and happiness…even euphoria.

# THE THREE KINDS OF TIME

We are learning together in real time (as though our lives depended on it because they do) how to make thought/thinking our friend. How do we develop our minds and bodies so we can handle the heat in the kitchen, and make contact with the reality, the fact, the actuality, the 'what is' of our lives, our opportunities, our problems, the specific and the general? Are you aware now as you read—of your thoughts, feelings and all that is going on inside and around you?

You know, when we say we must learn now, in real time as though our lives depended on it, it is true isn't it? If we are aware we can see that most accidents and most mistakes are the result of misuse of thought and lack of attentiveness/awareness. Certainly, it is obvious to all who have looked even superficially, that wrong thinking is the primary cause of premature deterioration of physical and mental health. 'As though our life depended on it' has another even more immediate meaning doesn't it? If thought, when it is operating incoherently, destroys our sensitivity and blocks us from following our hearts, having beautiful relationships, and developing emotional intelligence, then it is reducing the quantity and quality of our living isn't it? It is eating our share, our slice of the Pie of Life.

So, how do we gradually, or preferably quickly, bring our thinking to our bosom like a friend? What are those actions and principles whereby thought becomes sane, rational, whole, coherent, free flowing? Whereby thought becomes silent or absent when appropriate? Thinking more does not mean thinking better, it usually means psychothenia which is thinking too much and thinking wrong kinds of thoughts which block contact with the fact of the situation, the problem. Relaxation is the basis of quieting the mind so attention can emerge. Attention to thought makes thought coherent, reduces unnecessary thought, and allows moments of non-thought to occur. This leads to insight, AHA, archetypal alpha/theta imagery.

## IMAGERY

May I suggest that you allow your eyes to fall closed, easily and naturally, as we look into this vast field of imagery. It is, of course, also OK to allow your eyes to be open if they want to; however, it is easier for most of us to listen and absorb this kind of material with eyes gently, ever so gently closed. We have asserted that one of the most important, perhaps the most important, thing that an adult can learn is how to increase the ability to watch thought as it happens. Some call this 'thought recognition'. One of the strategies which we believe can assist in this area is to use imagery and to understand as best we can as much as we can about imagery. One of the first things to realize is that many of us tend to visualize differently from others, and that is fine. Some see pictures clearly, even in color. Others visualize verbally and don't actually see a picture. Others may see pictures in black and white. Others may combine a kind of verbal and black and white or even occasional color imagery and still others may 'feel' imagery kinesthetically.

What matters is that you are aware of and comfortable with your method of 'seeing' imagery. One of the remarkable aspects of NFB (especially alpha) training is the effect it seems to have on imagery. For example, imagery which is modestly effective in standard 3D, conditioned consciousness becomes far more effective for most if 'implanted' or observed during periods of high alpha production, whether using instrumentation or not. This conjures up the ancient notion of 'meditation with seed'.

There are powerful reasons why we want to become as sensitive as possible to the imagery that is constantly going through our minds. One of the most obvious is that a great deal of that imagery, perhaps most of it, is thinking function imagery. And the more a person realizes that 'I am what I think' the more actualized or wiser (s)he becomes. So learning as much as possible about the way I make images appears to be one of the most intelligent strategies with which I can understand how healthy (or unhealthy) change may be brought about in myself, and by extension, those I love.

Now the way we watch our imaging activity is also extremely important, don't you agree? Another reason that neurofeedback training (especially alpha) seems to have exceptional value is that it seems to assist many of us in being able to view our imagery more clearly. And clarity leads to coherence, doesn't it? We believe there is a relationship between the ability of people to watch themselves think and the speed with which those same individuals can actualize themselves (according to the model of Maslow's scale of needs leading to higher orders of actualization). May we suggest that the kind of visualization that takes place in standard third dimensional (beta) consciousness is already quite effective. In fact, one of the ways that we get ourselves into trouble is that a kind of uncontrollable visualization is going on almost all of the time (psychothenia again) and this imagery is often leading our minds in a counterproductive, mechanical, unhealthy, less human direction. Those who have relatively wonderful lives seem to be those who have found ways to influence this imagery and turn it in a more productive, creative, life affirming, and human direction.

So, gently and easily, just continue watching your own imagery now. May I suggest that a most important benefit of this will be an increase in your own self-knowledge? Who are you? What are you? Is it becoming clearer that I must look in the direction of thought in order to find out who I am? Or should I say in order to find out who I think I am? If this is true then who I think I am is a complex of images projected by memory. The implication is that most of these self-images are illusory. This movie—like representation of who you think you are may be relatively accurate or extremely far from the truth. Either way, more or less, this illusion prevents the actual you from being able to emerge…be born…again. I hope this is not too difficult, but in order to become more free it appears this kind of work is necessary for most of us. Notice how your imagery and your thoughts are flowing by. Notice how apparently completely unrelated thoughts enter in, and then when you look for them again they are gone or have changed. Notice how multiple thoughts can crowd themselves into your mind simultaneously or in a short passage of (linear) time.

We suggest some guided imagery (constructed visualizations) may be more appropriate. As easily and gently as you can, just allow the show.

There is something like going to the movies about this isn't there? Just allow the show to flow by. Resistance usually doesn't work very well. The thing which seems to change imagery easier for most of us is simply watching it flow. Resisting it can make it repeat; however, if you are looking carefully you will see that each iteration is at least slightly different. This is a very good time to be aware of the breath. Is it flowing easily and naturally? If the waist is pressured by your clothes, loosen them.

Remember, one of the apparent effects of alpha training is that constructed visualizations that are brought into the consciousness at the same time the alpha is flowing seem to take on additional power and focus. This focus, this clarity, translates into enhanced ability to materialize that which you are visualizing. Is the relationship between mind quietness, coherent thinking, deep relaxation, alpha training and profound attention becoming clearer?

You may not want to visualize some of the things that I am suggesting. That is perfectly OK. What is important is that you get to know your own mind better and better. As I suggest the following imagery you may be thinking something altogether different. That is fine. Just think it as clearly as you can. Remember, we are doing this merely as an exercise, a kind of mindfitness workout. We want you to increase your ability to recognize and be more aware of thought and the power of your own imaging processes when they are happening.

You may be thinking, 'I don't care what he is saying, what I am really interested in is this stream of thoughts and perhaps other-than-thought images that are coming up from my heart and flowing through my brain, my mind.' That is good. Some of the things I say may trigger completely different ideas for you. The most important thing is that your awareness, your ability to profoundly attend to this stream, increases. One of the most useful 'fourth dimensional' visualizations is: 'Now I am aware of.'…and you fill in the blank. Now I am aware of the sound of the jet over head. Now I am aware of my breathing and my shoulders. Now I am aware of new unexpected thoughts coming into my mind etc. Try it. Notice how it calls the mind back again and again into the here and now.

Another interesting visualization is to scan down your whole body and make sure it is deeply relaxed. Then allow yourself to look down on your self from about six inches above your head. Now about three feet. Now go all the way up to the ceiling and notice how you can see the whole room. Now you are on the roof. Now look down from about fifty feet above the house and see the yard and the neighbors' houses and the street and some buildings in the distance and the activity all around the block. Now soar up to about 500 feet. You can see the whole town and the river in the distance. Continue to about 1000, then 10,000 feet, then 5 miles then 50 miles, then 500 mules, you can see the whole earth, now 100,000 miles and you can see the earth as a ball like the famous photos taken during the moon shot. Notice how this changes your perspective, maybe your priorities.

When you feel ready to let that visualization go, you might want to try this one: If I could change some of my relationships, which ones would I change and how would I change them? If I could change my consciousness how would I like to see it change?

There are apparently unlimited ways to use imagery. Try this one:

*People are unreasonable, illogical and self-centered.*
*Love them anyway.*
*If you do good people will accuse you of ulterior motives.*
*Do good anyway.*
*If you are successful you win false friends and true enemies.*
*Succeed anyway.*
*The good you do today will be forgotten tomorrow.*
*Do good anyway.*
*Honesty and frankness make you vulnerable.*
*Be honest and frank anyway.*
*People favor underdogs but follow topdogs.*
*Fight for some underdogs anyway.*
*What you spend years building may be destroyed overnight.*

*Build anyway.*
*People really need help but may attack you if you help them.*
*Help people anyway.*
*Give the world the best you've got and you may get kicked in the teeth.*
*Give the world the best you've got anyway. Words found in a Peet's coffee*
*house located in Northern California.*

Sometimes the power of imagery can be amplified by mixing 'journaling' with the natural flow of your imagery.

A potent and basic form of imagery is to aggressively search for the best questions. Try some of these:

Who you would like to be? How would you like to change? What things, behaviors, and physical characteristics would you change about yourself if you could? List them. Who are you? What would love do? Do I already have the resources to follow my heart? Can I afford not to do what I love? I should comment that most of the people that have come to The Process seminars so far are middle-aged and have some resources; therefore, many of them have the potential to live much more freely than they do, but they do not yet realize it. Obviously, relatively strong economic circumstances are not shared by everyone who reads this.

Another classic imagery strategy is to imagine you have died. A peaceful happy death at, of course, some time in the distant future. What would you want people to say about you? How would you hope they felt about your life? Reminds me of the three men attending a friend's funeral. One of them said, "when I die, I hope my friends will talk about what a fine doctor I was and how I helped a lot of people get better. What would you two like folks to say about you?" The second man said, "I would like folks to say what a fine teacher I was and how many people were able to live better lives because of what I taught them." The third man thought a moment and said, "I would really like for people to say, look, he's moving!"

Amazing how many of us believe that somehow every one else is going to die, but I will miraculously escape?

*"A beautiful woman took me out to a lovely field and showed me an open grave. And in that grave was a skeleton and it was me. But the strange thing about it was that the skull had a smile. I immediately knew what the smile meant. I had died a happy death. So I asked the beautiful woman does this mean that it is possible to die a happy death? To be happy in death? And she said, ' yes'. Then I asked her how one does this and she answered, 'you accomplish this by having adventures'. 'Do you mean that I travel to lots of different countries and do all kinds of dangerous things, etc.?' She said, 'no, it means that you open yourself up to people. You just be with and have real relationships with lots of different people. That's how you have happiness when you die...in death."*
One of Steve Martin's dreams.

So visualize that you have died and you are looking back and what is really important to you now? What, when you look at the great sweep of your life, what were (are) the things that really mattered? Do they matter at this moment? Does this make you want to make changes?

## Session Five

### PROFOUND ATTENTION. ENHANCEMENT OF DIMENSIONALITY/FLEXIBILITY IMPROVES QUALITY OF LIFE.

### ADULT BRAIN CELLS ARE REPLACEABLE, STUDY SAYS

Over thirty years ago it was discovered that 'enriching the environment' by giving them more toys and fellow mice to play with caused adult mice to grow more brain cells. Similar findings demonstrated that adult birds who learned new songs could also grow new brain cells. I was delighted to read this because for decades I had believed it would eventually be proven that the long held scientific belief that humans begin losing brain cells soon after birth, and those cells can never be replaced or in anyway be renewed is untrue. It seems to me that this notion and the implications that go along with it is an example of our scientific establishment doing tragic psychological damage to untold millions of people. It seemed to me that either there was no relationship between numbers of brain cells and intelligence (including wisdom and creativity) or a whole lot of people were growing new brain cells as they aged; because anyone using simple common sense can observe that many people get wiser, more productive, more creative as they grow older.

I am aware that research shows that younger people perform cognitive tasks far better than older people, although older people do it more efficiently because they have more strategies. Further, that short term memory is also better in younger people. It may also be true that intelligence is unrelated (at least relatively) to numbers of brain cells. Some suggest that how well brain cells are organized may be the key to intelligence. However, the general impression that the public has held for decades is that the brain and its latent intelligence deteriorates after thirty in a way that leads to decreasing quality of life.

So, from the late sixties on, until the studies described herein were released, I have been asserting that humans ought to be able to do what mice, birds, and who knows how many other creatures can do. I really don't mean to gloat. I'm just so relieved because I hated the implication that our minds are probably deteriorating throughout our lives. And intuitively, I knew that this notion, along with numerous other 'sacred cows' of science, are not good science at all and point to the need for the scientific establishment to take a much more humble approach. Science and scientists, it seems to me, influence our thinking too much, considering how often they're (our) findings are wrong. After all, as you think, so you are, and science (as it is commonly practiced) is but one of many pathways toward truth.

Therefore, it gives me great pleasure to share the following synopsis of a NY Times Science section article written by Holcomb B. Noble. "Through a rare glimpse inside the human brain, American and Swedish scientists report that they have discovered the generation of brain cells in adult humans for the first time, opening an important area of investigation into possible new treatments for such debilitating neurological disorders as Alzheimer's disease, Parkinson's disease and stroke."

"The finding is one of a series of recent discoveries that have overturned years of conventional 'wisdom' about the human brain: that, after birth, once brain cells die off, they could never be replaced. In one such finding last spring, scientists reported substantial new cell growth in the brains of developing children under the age of 6."

"Now, with the discovery in adults that cells are continually dividing and producing mature cells, the potential arises that this regeneration may be used to mend a brain damaged by disease, or treat a disease caused by a damaged brain. 'The door has been opened', said Dr. Fred Gage, team leader at the Salk Institute, whose work will be published in the journal Nature Medicine."

"...The new growth was discovered in the hippocampus, a center of learning and memory in the brain." The ingenious study was accomplished by performing autopsies on cancer patients at Sahigrenska Hospital in Sweden. Prior to their deaths the patients were given injections of a marker, or tracer, and "After the patients died, the researchers used advanced imaging techniques to find the markers and confirmed that undeveloped primitive cells had in fact divided and continued to divide and produce new, mature neurons as well. They also found indications that this process continues until death....It provided science, its first real retroactive look at a live human brain in the process of creating new cells....the conclusions are absolutely incredible."

"The conventional thinking that humans could not grow new brain cells was based on lack of scientific evidence: no one would choose to cut open the brain of a living person to prove it. Dr. Gage believes that studies done and underway indicate that there may be a way to manipulate the new cell growth in humans and make some difference in their physiology and brain function. 'Once you know the chemicals and modulators that control division, you can imagine that under disease or trauma conditions you might be able to control this with beneficial results.'

"The scientists emphasized that the hippocampus is one small area of the cerebral cortex where a vast number of brain functions occur. But it is the area where cell loss occurs in Alzheimer's patients, so its importance is real. Why this disease, and other neurological disorders, would occur despite the creation of new neurons replacing the old is one of the many questions now to be investigated." An editorial in Nature Medicine said the discovery "opens the possibility of autologous repair and regeneration" in the brain. It noted that Parkinson's disease, Huntington chorea, and Alzheimer's all share a gradual loss of certain categories of neurons, and that 'these losses might reflect not only the insult that causes the neurons to die, but a failure of an otherwise expected regeneration that ordinarily repairs the loss.'

"Dr. Shankle, a neurologist at the University of California, reported in the Journal of Theoretical Biology that his research indicated 'tremendous growth in the number of cells in a child's brain from birth to age 6, adding some 400 billion. To him, that phenomenon, coupled with the Gage study, indicates that new cell growth may be found in areas of the adult brain outside of the hippocampus.' Dr. Shankle said experimentation might now begin with attempts to use the newly created hippocampus cells in treating asphyxia, caused by oxygen deprivation to hippocampus brain cells in drowning or smoke inhalation victims, or treat some forms of memory loss."

Many of us involved in the neurofeedback field have been intrigued by this concept of 'enriching the environment' and its relationship to enhancing latent intelligence in humans. We believe that applying the principles upon which The Process is founded creates a life style which is a de facto enriched environment, or as some scientists are saying, 'produces healthy changes in the landscape' (Another application of Einstein's maxim, 'The field is the sole governing agency of the particles'). We assert that powerful agents for producing these kinds of beneficial changes include true meditation, thinking of the third kind, fourth dimensional consciousness, profound knowledge, and profound attention. In so much as neurofeedback can enhance the learning of these skills, it is indirectly assisting in the development of an enriched environment. There are even some of us who would suggest that changing the electromagnetic activity of the brain through voluntary control may be directly enriching the environment.

## ATTENTION

*"The intention with which you approach the problem is more important than knowing what to do about it". Krishnamurti*

Lawrence Edwards, a psychologist, sent me the following email: "What is the most valuable commodity in the world? Some say time. Now think, what do you do with your valued time? Whatever you do with it, there is something more basic which makes 'time' so valuable. What is that most basic thing which is most valuable and by which all other activities, events or objects gain value? ATTENTION. ATTENTION is the most valuable commodity in the universe. Entertainers are highly valued because of the attention they command. Advertisers pay millions of dollars per minute to put on a commercial during the Superbowl. Why? Attention, they're buying the attention which sports figures command in the hopes that some of that attention will go to their product. When we pay a top notch professional, surgeon, or consultant, we're paying for their attention and the attention they invested in developing the skills and knowledge which inform that attention.

To assess what is truly of value to you, look at what you invest your attention in, not what you wish you could pay attention to or would like to think you value most, but what you would really like to invest your attention in. Then develop a plan to change your allocation of this most valuable resource. When you develop consciousness processing skills—meditation, deep relaxation, alpha, dream work, altered states exploration etc.—you are investing attention in attention, thus vastly improving the quality of your attention. You develop the ability to bring your full awareness to what you want to attend to, when you want to attend to it, and in the state you want that attention to operate in."

## How Is Attention Enhanced?

Thirty years ago I had a vision—insight. It was that the most important thing to understand and apply is attention. In fact, I even began to substitute the term 'attention—learning' for meditation, because I think it communicates the nature of meditation (the real thing) as different from many other (and in my opinion, less functional) views of what meditation is. Of course, claiming that I understand better than others what this ultimate expression of human wisdom (meditation) is seems uncomfortable and somewhat arrogant. However, everyone from the Dalai Lama to Daniel Goleman seems to agree that one of the fundamental aspects of meditation is to train the attention in order to use it to gain better fundamental insight into the nature of being! So, there is great support within the 'meditating community' for this concept that Profound Attention to 'What Is' is the beginning and possibly the end of all that a human being can do to maximize the quality of life. Perhaps I can soften the statement and suggest that 'attention—learning' better expresses my understanding of that capability which can unfold extraordinary hidden potentials within the meditator. There is so much about being a human being that seems unchangeable, or only changeable in an unhealthy way. That's the bad news and that bad news points to a crisis…a crisis of consciousness.

However, the good news is that there is something which is changeable…at least in a substantial percentage of human beings. And it is changeable in a healthy, sane, coherent and potentially incredible way. It is the quality of attention. Not just, can we increase the amount of time in seconds or minutes that we attend to 'what is'…but also the depth and the quality of that attention CAN BE enhanced. There is a sense that more than the brain is involved. In this sense the heart also becomes involved. 'The heart enters into the brain'. Or to put it another way, the whole mind includes also the heart-both metaphorically and literally. This notion is powerfully supported by the hot, relatively new, emotional intelligence (EQ) concept.

If we follow this stream to its source, we see that some human beings come to make attention to attention (polishing the mirror of the mind) one of the highest (perhaps the highest) of priorities. Such people, it seems, break through conceptually and actualize their potential for coherent thinking, insight, and dare I use that word compassion?

This quality of 'profound attention' (at least during the time it is 'turned on') seems to render unhealthy conditioning relatively innocuous. There is a belief that many, if not most, infants and small children have this capacity, but it gets conditioned out of them. Our job is to recover that capacity. To bring ourselves and as many others as possible back to what has been lost. "Unless you be like children you cannot enter the kingdom…" Perhaps the time will come when our culture places the highest priority on making sure that our children do not lose this ability Then, of course, the crisis in human consciousness is resolved before it happens. And the most imaginative among us cannot say what kind of world we will have then.

In the meantime, it is our privilege to enter ever deeper into perhaps the greatest adventure or Odyssey of all time…up to now. Technology wears many masks and is ever a mirror, a catalyst. We have, in our eons long pilgrimage of seeking our highest destiny, come to one of the most incredible manifestations of technology ever. A tool or set of tools which can assist the natural man or woman in learning about and deepening the quality of his or her attention…a technology which can assist us (like a telescope) in looking into the brain and seeing thought in vitro, as it happens, in action....and in learning ways in which thought can be slowed—unnecessary thought reduced, and at least indirectly, allowing us to gain insight into orders of intelligence which lie beyond thought.

We think The Process will gradually be recognized as the beginning of a new art form. It is not that we are creating a new art form but rather that an ancient art form is being discovered 'as though for the first time ever' and emerging in ways that are appropriate for our time. The Process is one of many expressions/manifestations of it. Of course, it is also true that there is 'nothing new under the sun'. And the deepest hunger of the human heart has always been to wring the most life out of life, to touch the unlimited, eternity, to die well, to merge with love.

We see that the more successfully a person can live according to these principles the more (s)he tries to share and assist others in finding this treasure. And The Process can be seen as simply another way of accomplishing this goal of active assistance. However, it is also true (in the sense of the new science, chaos and turbulence theory, the new physics, attractors and the like) that *everything* is new under the sun and there never has been a moment/time like this on earth before.

As a metaphorical example, think for a moment about the phenomenon of flying. Man had always flown in his mind/heart and spirit. There are even many accounts of human beings levitating; although, I have never seen it nor have I seen a credible photograph of it. I heard somewhere that Roger Penrose, the legendary mathematician and physicist, said that in principle it should be possible. Something about the human changing the fields around the body creating conditions similar to a room temperature super conductor. But then the invention of the balloon, the glider, the airplane, and finally the space ship, turned the ancient concept of 'levitation' into hard science and giant industries. And we have extended our senses using radio telescopes to the far edge of our universe which cosmologists tell us amounts to traveling virtually 15 billion or more earth years back in time. So, there is much that is new under the sun. We are at the threshold of an era so staggering in its scientific and spiritual immensity that we must build up the muscles of our brains and hearts to 'super human' or should we say 'more fully human' levels just to handle the excitement.

I believe that a growing percentage of the population is realizing that 'having more toys when you die is not necessarily winning'. It may be, in fact, losing. This trend setting segment of humanity is increasingly turning its attention to the enhancement of the quality of consciousness instant to instant, second to second, minute to minute, hour to hour, day to day, week to week, month to month, year to year, life stage to life stage. And so far as I can see, nowhere is more talent being brought to this task, nor is there more opportunity to make this holistic mind/body leap happen, than at this moment right here in the US. Of course, this 'voluntary simplicity' idea is already a worldwide phenomenon, and the last thing we want to do is be nationalistic. After all, this perspective places a high value on world citizenship and understanding society from a holistic perspective. I only mean to emphasize that the time is now, the place is here. Great expense and risk and travel are not required. We can bloom here where we are planted. And if you are reading this in another country, chances are that you can and must bloom where you are planted.

A poem from Christopher Fry's play The Prisoner says it beautifully....

*The human heart may go the length of God*
*Dark and cold we may be*
*But this is no winter now*
*The frozen misery of centuries*
*Cracks, breaks, begins to move*
*The thunder is the thunder of the flows,*
*The thaw, the flood, the upstart spring*
*Thank God our time is now*
*When wrong come up to meet us everywhere*
*Never to leave us till we take the greatest stride of soul folk ever took*

*Affairs are now Soul Size*
*The enterprise is expiration into God*
*But what are you waiting for?*
*It takes so many thousand years to wake*
*But will you wake, for pity's sake?*

## TRANSFORMATION OR MUTATION?

The way we see it from an anthropological point of view is as follows: Neanderthal was an incredibly successful early human being. The earth had never seen an evolutionary miracle like this. His brain was as big and sometimes bigger than our own. His technology, artistry, and social development were awesome and couldn't have been predicted by anything we know of that had lived before. Neanderthal reigned supreme for at least a million years. And then Cro-Magnon exploded upon the earth and within the last three thousand years or so Homo Sapiens actually began to take charge of his/her own evolution. Now we are on the threshold of a mutation, an evolutionary leap that is even greater than the leaps between Neanderthal, Cro-Magnon and modern man. Perhaps another way to think about it is that Homo Sapiens may be returning to it's own original promise and evolutionary destiny.

The Process, as conceived, should be compatible with most of the mindfulness psychological models, Quantum Theory (including the Eleven Dimensions String/Membrane Theory), Chaos Theory, Relativity etc. The Process, as we see it, is also compatible with Bohm's Hidden Variables Theory. We believe 'Hidden Variables' will play an important role in revolutionizing Quantum Theory in the next century. If Bohm is correct, then following the Hidden Variables to infinitely subtler levels below the quanta takes us 'closer' to the Source of the Stream which is a 'right turning' for the mind of humanity, individually and collectively.

The best strategy I am aware of, for application of the principles implied, is Profound Attention. To see as best we can that the observer is the observed, the thinker is the thought. You are the Process. The enfolded unfolds in proportion to the quality (energy?) of Profound Attention to What Is. So, the most appropriate action is Profound Attention to what is and then hidden variables manifest as phenomena, which in turn can lead, motivate, and empower us. As Bohm would say, 'the implicit becomes explicit, the enfolded unfolds'.

The Hidden Variables principle holds that there are subtler and subtler 'causes' or laws operating below the presently observable quanta, and there always will be because these causes stretch on to infinity. Infinity and zero are legal, even essential physics and mathematical concepts. This ever subtler play of 'variables,' or laws stretching into infinity, gives a perspective to the quantum theory that dissolves the problem of preordination (which is seen as arguably the greatest problem in physics, and the source of the famous conflict between Einstein and Nils Bohr). Also, this Process takes place in 'real time' which includes the past and the future in the Infinite Present.

When I told this to my wife she asked if it was possible to release the need to do this trip, that is follow the trail towards the source. I believe her insight is important although incredibly subtle because letting go of the need to make this journey may be essential in order to acquire the quality and quantity of energy necessary to make the journey. The realization that the application of the principle of La Via Negativa (elimination of the unnecessary) is necessary in order to reach towards the highest aspirations of the heart pushes thought, like a good Zen koan, beyond its limits. This opens the possibility of something more intelligent than thought influencing the thinker. Dr. Soutar reminded me that this notion expresses the principle of the Bodhisatva vow. In Buddhist teaching the Bodhisatva is believed to be a human being that 'evolved' spiritually to the level that it is released from the cycle of deaths and rebirths. But this being rejects the highest heaven in order to reincarnate and work among mortals until 'every sentient being can also achieve the highest liberation.'

## Attention Unfolds the Enfolded. The Implicit Becomes Explicit.

*Consciousness,* the state of being aware especially of what is happening around and within one. Having a feeling or knowledge of one's sensations, feelings, etc. Being able to feel and think...awake. Aware of oneself as a thinking being. The totality of one's thoughts, feelings, and impressions... mind. William James defined consciousness as a stream of awareness.

## What Is Consciousness?

**I suggest that consciousness has the properties of a multidimensional field. The cleaner, the less conditioned the field is, the richer the consciousness. We divide this field into the conscious and the unconscious, which is possibly a mistake leading to unnecessary confusion. Even profound consciousness is probably limited. Yet it appears that the more conscious a person is, the greater the possibility of something which transcends the limitations of consciousness taking place, emerging, spontaneously combusting.**

Are there *levels* of consciousness? Psychology tends to look at consciousness in a relatively limited, rather mechanistic way. The text book overview of consciousness would be to think in terms of stages of neural activity from deep sleep to wakefulness. This perspective views these levels as 'artifacts' representing changes in consciousness which are characterized by changes in EEG. In this model deep sleep beyond dream is represented by delta and the 'highest' level is represented by beta. We think this model is quite limited but is all (at least the conservative) psychological establishment has.

We think the term levels of consciousness is not adequate, and that thinking about consciousness in terms of its many dimensions is far more productive. Does our mind move along a continuum from unconscious to superconscious? If that is so, where on the continuum are we? Can we watch ourselves move 'up' and 'down' that continuum in real time? Can we do anything about improving the quality of that 'movement'? What role does desire or need play in this process? Is it possible that nothing can be done, and we are helpless to increase the quality of our moment to moment consciousness? I know how I feel about these things, but we must ask the questions somehow innocently without knowing the answer.

## THE LITERAL DIMENSIONS OF CONSCIOUSNESS

Obviously, there are many ways to think about and construct mental models of consciousness. As we have asserted, we can understand consciousness better by looking at it from a multidimensional perspective rather than thinking about it in terms of levels (like different colored oils of different viscosity's layered in a beaker). Probably, there is a perspective that is better than the dimensionality model, and when I can find it and understand it I will try to pass it on as best I can; but for the past twenty years or so the dimensionality model seems to me to be the most practical way to think about and understand consciousness (which by necessity includes acquiring insight into that which is pre or beyond thought...literally the 'unthinkable').

Of course, all of this stems from the premise that the most important thing we can do to improve the quality of our lives is to understand in a practical, common sense, readily applicable way, how the mind works. Understanding the dimensionality model is only one way, but for me it has been a breakthrough, and I hope it can be for you too. In addition, the dimensionality model seems to help integrate the understanding of consciousness with the 'new science' including math, physics, biology, cosmology, psychology, medicine and art. The search for the understanding of consciousness has become the most challenging and promising frontier, a kind of 'end point' for some of the world's best scientists. Please remember that we are striving to create better ways to communicate, better language. Some of what we say may not work for you. If so, forget about it. Take what works and throw what doesn't away. As we will continually remind you and ourselves, a fundamental aspect of The Process is to work experimentally and heuristically. This means you take your best shot and see what works and what doesn't, and then go to work making what doesn't work, work better.

**EMOTIONAL DIMENSIONS** are an even less visible aspect of consciousness than thoughts. Of course, emotion, feeling etc. also runs along a continuum that includes and is enveloped by thinking, and which may include feelings which are quite beyond thought. David Bohm said that he felt we should invent a new word for thought-feelings which he termed 'felts'. Although, attending to feelings as intensely as you attend to thoughts, and in fact seeing that feelings are a form of thinking (most of the time) seems obvious. We have found that many, if not most of us, tend to separate thoughts and feelings. Probably, those explorers who really care about this sort of thing are about to mount a challenge to the whole notion of unconsciousness. I believe we are going to begin to think in terms of the many qualities, properties, conditions, and dimensions of consciousness. If the whole of consciousness is a continuum, then artificially drawing a (specific) line between consciousness and unconsciousness is dualistic thinking, and is counter productive, leading in the direction of illusion instead of productive understanding.

One of the most important and compassionate things to remember is that we all move along this continuum. If we find ourselves spending less time in the more dysfunctional forms of consciousness, and more time in the functional (even ecstatic forms) we can only be grateful and deeply humbled by the grace of such a blessing. The challenge becomes how to parlay such good fortune into the assistance of others who are caught in the web of sorrow and struggling to know themselves better.

**FIRST DIMENSIONAL CONSCIOUSNESS (1DC)** corresponds to the first dimension in the sense that it is like a straight line without width or depth. It seems useful to think of minimal, fragmented, disassociative, heavily conditioned, mechanical, self-centered, dysfunctional, dull, incoherent consciousness as one-dimensional. It might also be said of one 1DC that it is relatively unaware of being conscious. However, this idea is problematical because there are some 'superconscious' states which also seem to have dropped the need for consciousness or awareness about consciousness and awareness. As long as we are still using the term unconsciousness we must differentiate between dysfunctional, unhealthy unconsciousness, and healthy, functional unconsciousness. For example, most would consider healthy delta and alpha/theta sleep a form of highly functional unconsciousness. Shallow, unrestfull, delta and alpha/theta sleep, coma, being knocked out through injury would be examples of unhealthy unconsciousness. On the other hand, there are a growing number of scientists and neurophilosophers who believe that a form of awareness may exist in quality, deep delta sleep which is never, or almost never, stored in memory.

In any case, first dimensional consciousness may be said to correspond to extreme fear states, as in a panic attack (we view anger as having its root in fear). It is characterized by psychothenia (overthinking) and virtually all of the thoughts are dissociative and extremely prone to error. The organism, in general, is losing sensitivity (as innate intelligence). However, some senses may actually become more acute, such as hearing; but unfortunately the overthinking condition causes the brain to convert what is heard into something other than the fact, bringing about a distorted perception of what is actually happening. Actuality in this model is different from and closer to the 'truth' than reality. Essentially, out of control and distorted thinking is dominating the reality of the organism and producing a deep, dissociative, dysfunctional trance like condition.

This distortion and loss of sensitivity to 'what is' means a major decrease in quality of consciousness, and is clearly a movement in the direction of unconsciousness (or decreased quality of consciousness). As previously suggested, 1DC probably should be thought of as a stage of highly automated and a mechanical/reactive mode of processing and relative unconsciousness (especially by those who believe the term unconsciousness still has validity). 1DC is characterized by thinking of the first kind.

**SECOND DIMENSIONAL CONSCIOUSNESS (2DC)** corresponds to a line with width and length but no depth. It is 'bigger, wider' than first dimensional consciousness and that much closer to functionality and association. Consciousness which begins to be a little less self-centered, more flexible, but is still rigid, conditioned, delusional, stuck in limiting beliefs, may be considered two-dimensional. However, it is still a tragically distorted perception of actuality, and easily subject to catastrophic mistakes. One of the nastiest aspects of second dimensional consciousness is that it appears that there is a loss of understanding of the connection between actions and the consequences of those actions (or non—actions). There is a hypothesis that this is at least partially due to a limbic or thalamic disregulation often caused by brain damage due to injury or drugs etc. As in first dimensional consciousness, powerful emotions (usually counterproductive) can be present as can depression and a feeling of 'no feeling'.

For me, second dimensional consciousness also implies a kind of dysfunctional rationality such as efficiently, and skillfully committing war crimes. One who is 'stuck' in second dimensional consciousness is easily conditioned, exploited and manipulated. He is constantly battered between the poles of pain and pleasure, and therefore doomed to live a second hand life unless (s)he can break out by exercising breakthrough thinking based on insight and understanding. Probably, the most successful strategy for finding the way out is self- knowledge which means seeing that one is in this sad condition. The image of voluntarily waking up from a bad dream seems appropriate here. 2DC is also characterized by thinking of the first kind.

THIRD DIMENSIONAL CONSCIOUSNESS (3DC) corresponds to a line with both width, length and a certain relatively limited depth. It is relatively comfortable with third dimensional phenomena such as material objects appearing to be solid and 'unchanging'. In fact 3DC is locked into a rigid belief in linear, psychological time (past and future), has difficulty understanding and relating to matter which is outside the limited sensitivity of senses which are themselves limited by 3DC. 3DC does not realize that its perception of the present is severely distorted, fragmented and limited because 3DC is viewing 'what is' through a kind of memory based, active (image-filled) 'lens' that distorts. Sort of like depending on the movies to teach us the truth about life. They can be very entertaining but, with the possible exception of the relatively rare great work of art, there are more effective ways to understand how to live life to its fullest.

In fact, looking at life from 3DC is similar to projecting a movie onto an actual landscape and winding up with a confusing, energy wasting, hodge podge of a movie. We are not saying that this is bad or good. We are only trying to see it as it is. As one moves towards 2DC the movie seems more 'real' and energy and truth fade. As one moves towards 4DC the truth emerges, the movie fades, and one gains energy.

Third dimensional consciousness may be relatively functional but is quite error prone. There is a certain capability for getting what is necessary for survival done, but life is just not much fun. There is a feeling of the same old, same old. Thought dominates everything. There may be a relatively constant, agitated effort to break out, but it is somewhat like an animal trying to break out of a cage. Sometimes 3DC can at least appear to generate a kind of dysfunctional creativity, but in general it is uninspired. 3DC is characterized by thinking of the second kind. 'Doing one's best' in 3DC can set up conditions conducive to spontaneous 'leaps' into 4DC.

For purposes of our adventure third dimensional consciousness is the standard sort of heavily conditioned consciousness most of us are in most of the time. As we suggested, it can be relatively functional although severely limited by conditioning. When unhealthy stressors are present we 'sink' towards the danger zone of second dimensional consciousness, and when we are balanced and using our mind and body well we 'rise' toward the much more rewarding 'edges' of fourth dimensional consciousness.

We are fluctuating along this continuum all the time. It is as though consciousness is a kind of light bulb and correct or incorrect living, and use of one's capabilities, causes energy to flow or not flow into this light bulb. When we are trapped by mistakes the energy flow is minimal and the light is minimal; therefore, it seems that one is surrounded by darkness. The brain is in retreat. But when one is able to live rightly (and be oneself) the light is great because the energy flow is great. Therefore, the sense of darkness is dissipated and one can see and understand much that was once hidden. 'Seeing' what had previously been hidden may be a defining characteristic of 'happiness'.

**FOURTH DIMENSIONAL CONSCIOUSNESS (4DC)** corresponds to a line with width, length and depth, except there is apparently no limit in any of those directions. One important characteristic of 4DC is that it senses time and space differently. For example, 4DC can see that there are at least three types of time (psychological, chronological and real). 4DC recognizes **psychological time** as a distorting complication and an inner enemy. **Chronological time** in this model is simply measurement of energy (light on the rotating earth). **Real time** is the eternal, infinite present, the 'place' where the actual action happens. 4DC may be characterized as 'being in the zone' or 'flowing'. It is common for there to be extreme shifts in the perception of psychological time during 4DC. For example, things can seem to be happening very slowly when that is beneficial (as in an athletic event or emergency) and yet hours of immersion in work can seem like minutes, and years can seem like weeks etc. The attitude towards time tends to be that if it is worth doing, then whatever time it takes, it takes.

Another property of 4DC is that phenomena lie 'in wait' as enfolded potential, and the quality of mind (attention) brought to that potential allows the unfolding to occur. Attention might be equated to sunlight and rain on a seed. Therefore, 4DC begins to pay attention to attention, seeing it as the source of quality action. As 4DC pulls the brain into contact with the present actuality, 'what is', the brain becomes relatively quiet, and in that quietness insight tends to flash much more often. This flash becomes the 'governor,' the foundation and the seed of thought rather than the 3DC tendency for thought to govern thought. This relative neural silence allows a sense of immensity or opening, and it is experienced as relative freedom; also, there is less unnecessary thinking which means less fear. 4DC loses psychological time pressure, has a sense of space, freedom and a reduction of self-centeredness. It increases archetypal imagery, compassion, inspiration and healthfulness.

Space stops seeming to be empty, and instead takes on the properties of a charged immensity, often becoming much more important than the objects within that space. There can also be a feeling that there is no space. For example, the distance and separation between the observer and the observed may seem to dissolve, resulting in a feeling of oneness. 4DC is characterized by thinking of the third kind.

To me 4DC seems like a kind of 'end point'. Of course, there is the notion that it is possible for the human mind to go beyond 4DC. However, 4DC is by its nature and quietness an open doorway inviting…open to the flow of the highest orders of intelligence possible to a human being. Interestingly, advanced physics considers the fourth dimension a kind of 'end point' in the sense that the other seven dimensions (as in String Theory) are 'collapsed' into or contained by the fourth dimension. Might it be that 4DC actually is an 'end point' because the essence of all other dimensions of existence are contained within and at the service of 4DC?

**Emmanuel Swedenborg,** the celebrated 18th century genius, scientist, and mystic, based much of his work on what he termed correspondences.

The use of correspondences may be just as valuable today in helping us make leaps of understanding and insight. It is amazing and beautiful to me to watch the correspondences play out relative to the dimensionality of consciousness, physics, math, chaos theory, as well as ancient yet widely respected theories of phenomenology such as arevedic medicine, Chinese medicine, the chakra concept, etc. The term correspondences takes on profound and difficult meanings for those familiar with Swedenborg's work. However, a brief and simple way to get a handle on it would be to see the way fractals reflect the microcosm in the macrocosm etc.

Some of the most powerful 'correspondences' from my point of view include the resonant relationships and points of agreement between the classic metaphysical and aggressively holistic science of the ancient and contemporary wisdom schools and modern science. It seems obvious to us that there are areas where the ancient wisdom and the best of modern science and philosophy seem to overlay, support, and even mirror one another. These incredibly exciting ancient/modern 'correspondences' are often beautifully functional 'application maps'. One of David Bohm's enthusiasms was assisting modern scientists in getting the hang of thinking holistically or holographically. Bohm believed that a science that is not holistic was tragically and dangerously flawed regardless of the magnitude of its perceived accomplishments.

**TIME AND 4DC.** Perhaps it will be helpful to go a bit further into the three types of time; because 4DC tends to understand and relate to time much more productively. To reiterate, it appears that there are at least three kinds of time: **psychological time, chronological time** and **real time. Psychological time** appears to be the enemy of man because it is an opinion about time which is rarely accurate and moves the mind away from the present and contact with 'what is'. Characteristic of psychological time is: 'I am too young, I am too old, I don't have enough time, I have too much time.' All of which reduces one's ability to be all one can be in the moment now.

**Chronological time** probably should not be called time because it is actually a form of measurement of energy. It is based on the measurement of light and dark projected onto a rotating sphere (earth). It is extremely useful for bringing events together in real time and space and is not a problem so long as we do not obsess on it. Because if we do, it stimulates psychological time and now we are in a mess again.

4DC perceives and thinks in terms of **Real Time** which is to say that it sees time accurately and is not fooled by the illusion of psychological time. 4DC perceives that there is only one eternal moment and within that vast infinity energy is moving in different ways and different directions. Scientists think of Real Time as the fourth dimensional perspective which Einstein discovered and called the time/space continuum. 3DC sees some of that energy as moving from the past to present to the future (usually left to the right, at least in western cultures). 4DC senses and tends to perceive timelessness, infinity, eternity as the greater truth, the greater actuality. The 3DC's distorted view of time may be necessary until the mind can handle the implications of past and future being enfolded into the infinite present...everything happening, in a sense, at once.

So 4DC tends to be patient. It sees the futility and danger of psychological time and seeks to avoid it. 4DC also becomes aware of the importance and beauty of space. Probably one of the reasons artists are driven to create art is because good art breeds right relationship with space and time, and this in turn engenders 4DC. Think about the way musicians manage the distance between notes, and how that space, these micro moments of silence, have everything to do with the beauty of the music. Van Gogh's work was rejected in his lifetime because it was perceived as not accurately reflecting nature. Many years after his suicide people began to realize he was a genius at visually communicating aspects of life as energy. This is similar to the 4DC perspective.

One night after discussing the relationship between the dimensionality of consciousness, neurotransmitters and 'bio—balance' with Ron Ruden, I lay awake for hours looking at a metaphorical way of describing dimensionality. I hope you find it useful. The flowing of water from left to right (in western cultures) is like 3DC and adding more of the multi-directional properties and 'life' to the water is like 4DC. That is, the 3DC conditioned view of time as flowing from the 'past' to the present to the 'future' is similar to the way 3DC looks at a stream. The 3DC sense is that the stream of time (a name and an abstraction) is flowing down from the left (and the past) to in front of me (the present) to the right and further downhill (the future). 4DC recognizes the 3DC perspective as 'true' but relatively unimportant. Just like linear time is true but it is a truth of less importance than real time. The relationship of the 3DC and 4DC perspective is similar to the relationship of Newtonian physics to Quantum physics. The lesser truth is contained by and shaped by the greater truth. The lesser truth becomes the particle and the greater truth the field (the terrain or the 'landscape').

Continuing the metaphor, 4DC is filled with the aliveness, the meaning and miracle of water. It sees water as many potentials actually unfolding all at once. For example, water is home for innumerable living creatures with vastly different time senses than we have. Also, water is a source of aliveness in every living thing we know. 4DC sees water dancing on the edge of great waves, changing the earth and wearing down and nurturing everything in its path. The molecules of water, so necessary for life, are alive themselves as they explore and nurture the dark earth. They turn to snowflakes (each one a perfect star) and great seas of ice and icicles sparkling, flashing all the colors of the spectrum in the sunlight. The living molecules of water become quiet and meditative moving slowly in the deep. As they warm they find themselves becoming excited in a new way—rising lighter and lighter until they break free like liberated souls. Lighter than air they drift gently upward, at first slowly, then sweeping higher and higher where they meet others like them and unite to become droplets. And sunlight shining on them and through them creates rainbows. Soon, they grow heavier and more solid and fall like tears, rushing 'home' to earth again to begin the cycle of nurturing anew.

So, 4DC sees that water, like energy, moves in all directions, and what it was in the past and what it will be in the future, is an abstraction and not all that interesting compared to what water is now, this precious moment of perception. 4DC feels that water's past and future somehow, mysteriously depend on its present. This 4DC feeling of oneness with the aliveness and multidimensionality of water leads to an even deeper understanding, an awareness that water's past and future as well as it's eternal present is forever changed by the quality of the observation…the quality of the awareness itself, now in real time!

*"Without love you cannot wipe out the past; with love, there is no past. Love and time is not." Krishnamurti*

The reason we are being so aggressive about 'alpha enrichment' is because most of the time most of the population, in our opinion, are suffering from alpha deprivation. The result of this alpha deprivation, we suggest, is a loss of flexibility, dimensionality, sensitivity, aliveness and what we (with reservation and until we can come up with a more apt description) term 'micro moments of pleasure'. When the alpha mix (and other electrochemical activity) is right, it's like the gas mix being right in an engine…the whole thing hums along at peak efficiency and is maximally responsive to changes in the 'throttle'. This means as in Profound Attention and Open Focus concepts, there is a high order of integration at all functional and superfunctional levels (including both long and short-term memory). Now this memory issue gets tricky because a characteristic of 4DC is that it is better able to reach in and grab a memory when it is really needed; however, 4DC also has the characteristic of transcending the need for (and at times 'abandoning') memory as it seeks greater depth within the present and more heuristic learning. Actually, we are thinking about upgrading 'micro moments of pleasure' to 'micro moments of delight or aliveness', because the precise meaning of the term pleasure may suggest a lower order of consciousness than we are aiming for. Interestingly, Buddha felt that pleasure was more like a 'nice' form of pain.

Pleasure and pain, strictly defined, are actually two sides of the coin of thought interpreting sensation. One of the problems that fourth dimensional consciousness resolves is freeing the individual from the constant battering he is taking because of the oscillation or bouncing between the two memory based poles of pleasure and pain. 4DC sees everything as related, and dualistic thinking as ineffective. By means of attention pleasure and pain are reduced to their residual sensation, which is then used as an information system. This liberation makes a 'space' and provides energy for more functional orders of feeling and emotion. The word pleasure is inadequate to describe the essence of these more functional orders of intelligence and humanity, nor can it even hint at the power and beauty accessed by the accompanying flashes of perception of 'what is', the actual.

Surely, we can all see that consciousness ranges along a spectrum from no consciousness (unconsciousness) and corrupted or perverse and fear-ridden-consciousness (rage, hate lust, jealousy, greed, selfishness etc.) to exceptional awareness and so called superconsciousness. Krishnamurti has discussed consciousness as a kind of friction; and that implies that there is something that is frictionless that enfolds consciousness…something that includes those aspects of consciousness which we feel are beneficial properties without the limitations that consciousness itself may have. If we follow this mode we see consciousness probably always has a center and requires memory in order to be; then it would follow that we can improve the quality of this consciousness by being more 'centered'.

As we look into the dimensionality of consciousness we are forced to consider whether or not we have a definition of consciousness which really works. In general, we tend to think that there is either consciousness or unconsciousness, and that is all that is possible for the mind of a human being. However, consciousness itself may be a limited phenomenon in the same way that thought is limited. Remember, thought itself has a very difficult time recognizing it's limitation. (If you can see the deliciousness of thought thinking about its own limitations, you are probably smiling). In fact, recognition by thought of its limitations implies that such thought is of an extremely high order. We have asserted that those who see the limitations of thought (including thought-feelings or 'felts') clearly actualize their potential at much greater rates than those who allow thought to convince them that thought can do anything, and can operate competently in any sphere.

It seems likely to many that there is a phenomenon which transcends consciousness, yet is not unconsciousness. In fact, it is generally referred to in English as superconsciousness. We feel better words are emerging in English, and probably other languages as well. The debate about what consciousness is and how it is enhanced is going to go on for centuries; however, we must arrive at our best possible understanding now. It seems to me that consciousness is like a kind of 'friction'; and it moves along a continuum of great 'friction' to imperceptibly subtle 'friction' and that continuum correlates with extremely dysfunctional to maximally functional dimensions of consciousness.

I realize that suggesting that consciousness implies a kind of 'friction' is pushing the envelope, but like a good koan, considering that possibility might lead the mind to a new way of looking. If the concept of consciousness as friction seems too arcane for you, just drop it for now. Although, you might want to revisit this notion later.

### *"Consciousness is friction." Krishnamurti*

Staying with this arduous process, an awareness begins to warm our mind like the faintest glimmer of dawn; and this stunning, incredible intimation suggests that when we have become truly 'centered' in the highest meaning of that concept, we are standing before a door, beyond which is another dimension...a dimension which has no center and is far beyond being 'centered'. We have little language for this yet but the concept is upon us, and we must meet this challenge also as the new century unfolds before us.

There is an implication that this other dimension is one in which there is infinite creativity and aliveness and a loss of 'friction'. Somehow the image and properties of the superconductor seems like a good metaphor. This other dimension defies description, yet is the birthright of the natural man and natural woman...a dimension in which 'you' and the 'image of the me', the ego, stops trying to solve all problems, because it sees that only truth solves problems (thus increasing the motivation to handle the 'pain' of some truths). This other dimension welcomes the love hungry 'warrior of the mind' like a mother welcomes her infant. A dimension where conflict is resolved and the miraculous explosion of life flows like a river. We think that the term fourth dimensional consciousness (4DC) is a responsible symbol for this 'end point' of aspiration.

We realize that exploring this incredible issue is extremely arduous. It is somewhat like trying to think about what was there before the universe began, and what is there beyond the outer edge of the universe, and what will be after the universe is gone. Perhaps these concepts cannot be expressed in words. They are more easily considered in mathematics because math comfortably uses zero and infinity. The concepts of 'basins' and 'attractors,' as in chaos theory, seems applicable here as well.

As we have mentioned, one of the miraculous pieces of literature that appeared about 500 BC is Patanjali's Sutras (meaning stitches). It appears that each of these Sutras is attempting to describe a state or aspect of consciousness that is possible for at least some human beings. There seems to be an instructive, progressive flow to it. Yet that may be illusional because early in the Sutras 'time' as we know it falls away. There is great excitement among modern cartographers of consciousness about the first four or five levels of consciousness that have been researched and which, it is hypothesized, most human beings are theoretically capable of attaining. Of course, who isn't a cartographer of consciousness? Some maps are better than others, but we all are mapping our own consciousness, trying to find our way back home, trying to locate the treasure we have lost.

The peculiar thing is that Patanjali seems to describe the same four or five levels of consciousness that modern neurophilosophers and scientists are so excited about in his first four or five Sutras. This implies that there may be at least one hundred more 'levels' or dimensions of consciousness beyond the highest level we are presently aware of today.

Fifth dimensional consciousness (5DC) is about as far as even the most ambitious modern cartographers of consciousness seem to go. And the going (hypothesizing) gets extremely difficult here. Some suggest that 5DC may have something to do with original archetypical creativity. A human being in 4DC is relatively egoless...at least able to watch the ego and be so aware of it that it doesn't screw things up all the time. 4DC sees the image of the me, the ego, as a psychological construct of thought and, as such, a necessary but somewhat dangerous tool which must be understood until the mind can free itself (at least relatively) of the limitations and liabilities of an ego-oriented mind and life.

Could 5DC be a frictionless state where ego is truly gone and the individual is a conduit for some kind of pure creativity...an incredible, almost, maybe literally unimaginable manifestation of the human potential? These very words are painful to think about because we are naturally repelled by anyone who implies that (s)he is relatively free of ego orientation. However, grappling with this problem is at the very essence of The Process...so face it we must, with all the courage and love we can muster.

We have suggested that there is a way of using language and symbols so that we can better understand different qualities or states of consciousness. We have used the example of third level (third dimensional) consciousness representing the standard, relatively functional, limited, highly conditioned state that most of us are in most of the time. Therefore, it seems obvious that if we want a bigger slice of the actual, the vital, original life, we must somehow break through into what may be termed fourth level (fourth dimensional) consciousness (not to be confused with thinking of the third kind which we suggest corresponds to 4th dimensional consciousness).

As we mentioned, the neurofeedback community has begun adding the term dimensionality to the existing concepts of flexibility and plasticity in order to describe fundamental goals of EEG biofeedback training. We find that encouraging; however, it seems clear that this concept of dimensionality goes much farther.

It seems clear that enhancement of the quality of our consciousness, moment to moment, is the most healthy and creative thing we can do. But how do we do it? What are the best questions we can ask? Within the question rests the answer. How do we use our consciousness so that we learn how to improve the quality of that consciousness second to second, minute to minute, hour to hour, day to day, year to year? Hard experience has taught us that there is a superficial and relatively useless kind of learning. And then there is profound knowledge and insight. It seems certain that the latter virtually guarantees the kind of healthy transformative experiences that we all are hungry for. We want to understand consciousness in a practical way...a way that will lead us to a huge improvement in our ability to sustain quality consciousness as much of the time as we possibly can.

As we have noted, most textbooks show us EEG readings when they talk about consciousness. They show the slow delta waves of sleep, and explain that as we awaken and move up through theta and alpha into beta, we progress through different qualities of awareness until we are actively thinking and maybe even aware that we are aware. Awareness of what is happening around us is often lost in the thought—processing of information and the memory searches of beta or the dissociative imagery of theta in unhealthy mode. Remember that we have dubbed this Utheta (unhealthy) as different from Htheta (healthy, well behaved, associative, creative theta.)

If we are going for totality we would have to agree with Fehmi's Open Focus notion of attention. Attention that is as inclusive as possible of all available activity. Interestingly enough this is what Zen teaches as well. This form of attentional activity seems to be correlated with an EEG signature rich in alpha (at least for alpha R's). This supports the idea that the neurofeedback community add the term 'alpha enriching' to the clinical jargon. The brain is probably always generating the whole spectrum of brain waves from delta through beta. *It's a matter of how much and what combination of brain waves are appropriate at any given moment.* What we want is to make the brain more flexible so it generates just the right combination of electrical activity to meet the challenge of this instant, and then instantly change to meet the challenge of the next instant. This is what we mean by flexibility (dimensionality) being the essential foundation for a tremendously alive, infinitely sensitive brain.

It seems choicelss then that we are living our lives so we can sustain 4DC as much as possible...or are we? If not, why not? Is it because we are discouraged? Is it because we cannot resist the degenerating effect of our environment? Is it because we do not understand it well enough? Are we in a state of denial about possibilities? Are we happily asleep in our habits and grumpily pushing away those who are trying to rouse us? One of the great barriers to achieving the best quality of consciousness we can and staying there is the fear that we can't succeed, that these principles may work for someone else but not for us, that we are too old to begin, that our brains are already too damaged by suffering and conditioning. This is a classic example of the ego at work, blocking us from our potential...our natural birthright. Focusing on the present and doing our best even if it is in little steps is one of the best ways to 'just do it'. Awareness...deep, profound awareness in the present is the essence of the psychology of awareness (a true paradigm shift) and probably the 'secret' to self-actualization. Learning heuristically and by just doing it is critical.

## Eleven Dimensions Makes the Hair on the Back of My Neck Stand Up.

May we return for a minute to one of the latest, hottest concepts in physics, the so-called String Theory? It predicts there are ten dimensions in the physical universe. Except that recently it has been expanded to eleven dimensions in order to include the notion that the so called 'strings' are 'hollow' and have a 'membrane' around them. The idea is that these strings are sort of like strings on an instrument playing 'notes' and these 'notes' become sub atomic particles. Now, although these dimensions exist in physics and math, the seven dimensions above the fourth dimension are 'invisible', or as Bohm might say they are 'hidden variables'. So, as previously suggested, the physicists are now proposing that the reason for their 'invisibility' is that they are 'collapsed' into the fourth dimension.

When I read this, a chill swept up my spine, because this supports the feeling I've had for some time that fourth dimensional consciousness is a kind of de facto and practical 'end point' for human beings. The implications are that fourth dimensional consciousness may actually be an end point, because 'all that is' is appropriately present within 4DC, active and doing its job, even though it is invisible and beyond the 'friction' of what we call consciousness. Isn't it reasonable that the other seven dimensions of existence are also dimensions of mind (even though it may include states for which we have no words) since there is no separation between mind, meaning and matter? Could it be that just as in physics these seven 'extra' dimensions of mind are 'collapsed' into fourth dimensional consciousness, and are 'at its service' even though 'invisible'?

This might help explain the kinds of epiphanies that humans feel when they (we?) finally come to a time and a place when we can say and feel 'It's all over but the quality of the thank you.' (S)he can just sit back and enjoy the drama and infinite beauty of love and life. This powerful principle corresponds to something called passive volition in the science of self-regulation. One gains this kind of 'control' through allowing the organism to operate more intelligently. Athletes and artists will also talk about this important principle of not trying too hard in order to do better. So, the peace and power that comes from 4DC seems to give us the sense that the universe is unfolding as it ought, and one's enfolded potential is unfolding. I'd like to try and 'head off at the pass' the comments that such a cosmic sense of security and self satisfaction will lead to lack of motivation to actually do what needs doing. It does lead to lack of motivation to 'do something even if its wrong'. But my reading of history indicates to me that those minds I treasure most harbored this mystical sense that the Universe is unfolding as it ought.

Perhaps we have already come very far. We hope not too far. One of the goals on our map seems to be emerging. We want to understand how to bring about 4DC as much as we can, because that implies the unfoldment of our human potential. Furthermore, the implication is that if our minds are that clean, that clear, we are surely capable of finding our own unique way from here on. Implied in 4DC is the attention, the navigating equipment (the calibrated compass), the heart, the spirit, the character required to find one's way home…to merge with the truth (at least relatively).

*"The only prayer one needs to learn is Thank You." Meister Eckhardt*

I quote here a brief passage from a scientific presentation that my brilliant friend, the late Charles Stroebel, MD, Ph.D., delivered in 1998, a week before he unexpectedly died.

"…Over my years of medical practice I have marveled at the general wisdom of persons with heightened mind/body intelligence. They magically seem to anticipate the 'big picture' without being told, apparently using extra insights or dimensions not available to most mortals. What dimensions might these be?

Eleven dimensions are required for Hawking's 'unified' theory to explain 'everything' in the universe. Most of us are familiar with the three dimensions of space needed to describe our physical world…namely length, width, and depth. We also can visualize time as the fourth dimension when we think of 'snapshots' taken in succession. Einstein called this 'space—time.' But what of the other seven dimensions? Since we cannot directly visualize them, these extra dimensions are puzzling mysteries. Could these seven extra dimensions be the realm accessed by the mind/body prodigy?

Amazingly, there is indirect evidence (this is not necessarily evidence, but certainly a basis for a working hypothesis) for exactly seven extra dimensions in the mind/body domain! A prism (along with our eye and brain) resolves white light into a rainbow spectrum of seven component colors: red, orange, yellow, green, blue, indigo, and violet. These seven colors may be said to correspond to seven energy vortices/force fields called 'chakras' by the Arevedic system of medicine for optimizing mind/body health. Seven is also the number of 'color—dimensions' needed for constructing a three dimensional brain image so, that no two adjacent regions in the body have any overlapping border of the same color. This is the famous color map theorem in mathematical topology which was solved by Appel and Haken in 1976.

Ironically, under conditions of symmetry and balance, all eleven dimensions 'simplify' to become just four—our familiar dimensions of length, width, depth, and time! A parallel for this simplification might be a prism coalescing the seven colors of the rainbow back into a single beam of coherent pure white light…"

To reiterate, I am smitten by the way Dr. Stroebel also perceived that the eleven dimensions 'simplify' or 'collapse' under conditions of adequate symmetry and balance to become just four, lending support to the staggering implication that 4DC really may be a kind of practical end point…a kind of gateway to 'all that is'. Once through that gateway the rules as we know them may or may not apply as in a singularity, or perhaps more easily understood, Bohm's Hidden Variables Theory. Or to say it another way, using Swedenborg's concept of correspondences, other dimensions (seven more?) of consciousness may 'simplify', 'collapse into', 'precipitate,' 'become accessible and usable' under conditions of fourth dimensional consciousness.

This may allow the properties and qualities of these other dimensions to operate; although, they might not be subject to registration (memory). Since these dimensions of consciousness exist in real time, and memory may not be applicable in the same way, it seems reasonable to see them as having no quality or less quality of 'friction' (again the superconductor metaphor seems useful). For most of us the beauty, truth, love, creativity, accomplishment, peace, even ecstasy inherent in 4DC may be quite enough at least for this lifetime. But it seems reasonable to speculate that there are some who have and will go even further.

It is also intriguing that in the ancient chakra system of psychophysiology the first three chakras seem to correspond with the first three dimensions of consciousness, as well as Maslow's first three stages in his brilliant hierarchy of needs. The opening or energization of the fourth 'heart' chakra may be seen to correspond to the 'emotional intelligence' that is characteristic of fourth dimensional consciousness and the gateway to the natural energization of the last three chakras. We would like to take this opportunity to acknowledge that the above is not hard theory but rather a working hypothesis and an example of the kind of thinking implied and inspired by the work of Krishnamurti, Bohm's Hidden Variables, Swedenborg's principle of correspondences and many other teachers.

*Hypothesis, from the Greek hypothesis meaning groundwork, foundation, supposition. Literally to place under (hypotithenai). An unproved theory, proposition, supposition, etc. tentatively accepted to explain certain facts or (working hypothesis) to provide a basis for further investigation, argument, etc.*

So, the mission of the Process is to cultivate uncultivated parts of the vast field of mind as responsibly, as lovingly, as joyfully as we can.

## Session Six

## AWAKENING TO SLEEP. THE MAGIC, MYSTERY AND POWER OF SLEEP.

Awakening to Sleep is the title of an article in the New York Times Magazine (January 5, 1997) and written by Verlyn Klinkenberg. It presented some of the most advanced research on sleep that I have seen anywhere. Further, it supports ideas that we have been teaching for more than a decade. Some of the highlights of the article are paraphrased or quoted in this session together with our comments.

"The problem of sleep curtailment is so big that people just can't digest it. The vast majority of people are sleep deprived."

What's your sleep IQ?

You may spend eight hours a day doing it, but do you really understand it? Experts say a better understanding of sleep and sleep deprivation can help you make effective use of your waking moments. Try your hand at this true—false test.

1. During sleep your brain rests.

2. You cannot learn to function normally with one or two fewer hours of sleep a night than you need.

3. Boredom makes you feel sleepy, even if you have had enough sleep.

4. Resting in bed with your eyes closed cannot satisfy your body's need for sleep.

5. Snoring is not harmful as long as it does not disturb others or wake you up.

6. Everyone dreams every night.

7. The older you get the fewer hours of sleep you need.

8. Most people do not know when they are sleepy.

9. Raising the volume of your radio will help you stay awake while driving.

10. Sleep disorders are mainly due to worry or psychological problems.
11. The human body never adjusts to night shift work.
12. Most sleep disorders go away even without treatment.

Answers: 1.F, 2.T, 3.F, 4.T, 5.F, 6.T, 7.F, 8.T, 9.F, 10.F, 11.T, 12.F.
(Source. National Sleep Foundation)"

When I was in my teens I was worried because I seemed to need so much sleep. In my twenties I began forgoing sleep in order to work toward my incredibly ambitious goals. And then I began to pay the price. It took a series of dangerous crises for me to realize that in my case I simply had to get more rest. I felt ashamed because I had heard about all those truly remarkable people who only needed a few hours sleep per night. In my thirties, I began to study sleep seriously as part of my passion to understand stress science. From that time until now I have used biofeedback assisted self-regulation training to assist others in restoring natural sleep patterns, and reaping the wonderful physical and psychological rewards that enhancement of sleep brings.

No matter what the symptoms, most expert biofeedback practitioners usually begin with stress management. This includes a combination of biofeedback, breathing, and other deep relaxation techniques, which tend to result in a marked improvement in sleep and rest. This invariably accompanies a reduction in symptoms. The clients usually remark that they feel better, are more productive at work, and gentler on their family members etc. Therefore; it became clear that the sleep dynamic would be even more important in Performance and Life Enhancement Learning, because the very essence of Life Enhancement is becoming as fully awake as I can be. Time and again, executives that I taught how to 'power nap' in order to reduce their symptoms reported that they now found their power nap was often the most productive part of the day because when resting in these deep reverie states they got their best ideas and insights. They also reported being more cheerful and productive during the afternoon and evening, and making fewer mistakes, especially in the afternoon. So obviously, making sure that we understand and can implement the best possible sleep patterns for ourselves is a critically important aspect of The Process.

One of the first things to realize about sleep is that unless you are unusual, you are not getting enough of it. The average American accumulates a 'sleep deficit'" of at least 500 hours per year. According to sleep research, more than one third of people report being so sleepy during the day that it interferes with their activities. While the average adult actually needs between 8 to 9 hours sleep a night, most get only 7, and nearly one third get 6 or less. Sleep needs are biologically determined. There are people who actually do need only 6, others need 10, but for most at least 8 hours is needed to function optimally. When we honestly look at the sleep patterns of extremely accomplished people (including many believed to be geniuses) we see that in the main they need as much sleep as anyone else, and some of the most famous spend 10 hours per day in bed. Since this program is about functioning optimally, we have to face this actuality about ourselves, like it or not. For most of us this sleep problem can easily be a hidden weak link in our life enhancement 'chain', and for many of us it definitely is. Isn't it critically important that we stop thinking of ourselves according to published and often incorrect 'norms', and find out what we really need and make sure we get it? Isn't that a relatively easy way to make true progress?

It is commonly believed in business that most of the work is done in the morning and up to 80% of the mistakes tend to happen in the afternoon. The fact that a good stress management program includes at least short, skillfully done, effective relaxation periods during the work day means such programs probably turn a handsome profit just by reducing mistakes due to tiredness and unhealthy stress.

There is a huge problem of denial regarding this sleep issue, and it may be greater amongst those of us that aspire to be all that we can be. We believe that by driving ourselves harder we are going to accomplish more.

Of course, there is just enough truth in that to make it dangerous. Most of the people interested in this kind of learning do not have to worry about having the ability to work hard. The issue for them really has been for some time, how do I work more intelligently? And if I am not getting adequate sleep (especially delta sleep) then I am probably unconsciously sabotaging myself.

Sleep curtailment not only affects mood, cognition, and performance, but it also affects metabolism, cardiovascular function, and immune function. Klinkenberg suggests that, "Western cultures of work and entertainment aspire to make machines of us all, to create an electronic, robotized atemporality that conflicts with the natural biological constraints inherent in being human". Although no one has done the long term epidemiological studies needed to discover the true dimensions of chronic culture-wide sleep deprivation or its effects on human health, it is widely believed by sleep researchers that those effects have become incredibly costly to society. We seem to really want to stay up past our evolutionary bedtime, but the clock we are trying to fool is our own inherent circadian rhythms; and these powerful rhythms control, among other things, the timing of variations in body temperature, cardiovascular rates, and the secretion of substances like melatonin in the pineal gland, prolactin and human growth hormone in the pituitary, and cortisol in the adrenal gland. Taken as a whole, these variations define not only the internal state of our bodies but also profoundly effect consciousness.

REM (Rapid Eye Movement, alpha/theta) accounts for about 20 to 25% of a good night's sleep. Slow wave (delta) also accounts for about 20—25%. Delta sleep is believed to be beyond dream, and seems to be unusually important in the rebuilding of tissue itself, as well as the rejuvenation of psychological function. Modern sleep is only, at most, a few centuries old. We have come to believe that we can control our own destiny, and that means our own evolution. One of the ways we are trying to do this is overriding our ancient biological sleep patterns.

Allan Rechtschafen at the University of Chicago Sleep Research Lab
has done studies to see if people could really tell if they were sleeping well
or not. He invited self-described good sleepers and bad sleepers to the lab.
When the instrumentation indicated they were in deep sleep he awakened
them and asked them how they were sleeping. The good sleepers said they
were "sleeping just fine" and the bad sleepers said they were "awake, of
course." So, the perception of sleep is a major factor. If I believe that I am
sleeping badly, then I feel like I have been sleeping badly even if I have
actually been sleeping OK (at least from a scientific point of view). Once
again, the quality of thought is determining our reality much more than
most of us realize.

Sleep researchers report an extremely consistent pattern in the adult circadian rhythm. It is called a midday trough, roughly between 1 and 4 P.M.
It is a time when sleep looms, existence pales, and not coincidentally there
is a significant rise in traffic and industrial accidents. A parallel trough,
familiar to anyone who has known the despair of early morning, occurs
between 1 and 4 A.M., the time when humans are most likely to mourn
credit card debt and to die. So, a major improvement in overall quality of
life can be brought about by resting enough to bring up the quality of the
afternoon trough (napping if possible, the siesta is ideal). Meditation can
convert the early morning 'Hour of the Wolf' into a time of creative
reverie and working on deep issues.

In fact, there is more than a little evidence to indicate that the natural
purpose of the early morning 'trough' may be to bring on productive
altered states for the adult. Thomas Wher, a sleep researcher at the
National Institute of Mental Health did a fascinating experiment in which
volunteers subjected themselves to a sleep schedule based on the duration
of a midwinter's night at the latitude of Washington DC, just like our
ancestors did. That is about 14 hours of darkness and 14 hours of light.
Wher and his team measured the usual things: temperature, hormones,
melatonin secretion, EEG patterns, etc. The first night they slept 11
hours, and during the first weeks of the experiment paid back 17 hours of

'sleep debt. After that they settled down to about eight and a quarter hours, but it was not consolidated sleep, and it was not just sleep. Wher says that, "another state emerged (not sleep, not active wakefulness) but quiet rest with an endocrinology all its own."

Each night the volunteers simply rested quietly before passing abruptly off to sleep. They slept about four hours and then awoke out of REM sleep into another two hours of quiet rest, followed by another four hours of sleep and another two hours of quiet rest before rising around 8 A.M. This pattern of sleep and rest is called a bimodal distribution of sleep. Apparently, bimodal sleep is a pattern modern Americans revert to almost as soon as they are given the chance. Traditionalists would view this pattern as a sleep disorder, although the resemblance to animal sleep confirms its naturalness. Also, as people get older they revert to this pattern of bimodal sleep. Perhaps it gets harder to override it.

For anyone who has pursued what I call meditation (the Real Thing) this finding has got to be stunning. Over the decades I have watched sincere people enter into the heuristic super school of learning how to meditate for real (as opposed to the many formulas which usually do not take one very far and are much too slow). There are some phenomena which seem to happen to some people during these periods of rapid personal growth which can be tricky. One example is sometimes called 'unstressing'. It often happens to a person who is burnt out or has become chronically exhausted over a substantial period of time. As relaxation skills are improved and the individual learns to let go of the need to be hypervigilant, a sometimes disturbing need to sleep a lot ensues and may last quite awhile. Our view of this is that it is usually quite normal and healthy. Of course, if it happens to you and you are concerned, then seeking professional help may be a good idea. I have believed that this phenomenon was probably due to the fact that most adults do not begin serious meditation work until we are in a major crisis. The suffering literally drives us to seek a better way. Obviously, the 'unstressing phenomenon' happens at least in part because we are simply sleep deprived (of course, sleep deprivation usually gets worse during crisis periods).

Another phenomenon experienced by people who are really trying to learn is the bimodal sleep pattern. In fact, one of the indicators that The Process is going well is that there is a greater tendency to enjoy these quiet reverie states rather than resisting and lamenting them. They emerge as an extraordinary learning opportunity. For decades I have been trying to assist people in learning this art form. It is encouraging to see that sleep research is now supporting this concept. It is even more comforting to see that this bi-modal pattern spontaneously emerges given movement of the mind in the direction of the natural.

Wher's subjects generally remarked that after having given themselves to this pattern they felt more awake than they could ever remember during the rest of the day. When Wher used the Multiple Sleep Latency Test he discovered that not only did they feel more awake but they actually were. This sleep deprived pattern has existed so long that, as Wher writes, "modern humans no longer realize they are capable of experiencing a range of alternative modes that once may have occurred on a seasonal basis in prehistoric times, but now lie dormant in their physiology". Over time as we have learned how to sleep a less characteristically mammalian sleep, we have also learned to sleep a less human sleep.

*"The breeze at dawn has secrets to tell you. Don't go back to sleep." Rumi*

Wehr writes, " It is tempting to speculate that in prehistoric times this arrangement provided a channel of communication between dreams and waking life that has gradually been closed off as humans have compressed and consolidated their sleep. If so, then this alteration might provide a physiological explanation for the observation that modern humans seem to have lost touch with the wellspring of myths and fantasies." We would take this hypothesis a bit further and assert that these reverie states can lead to meditation, a superschool, and a kind of private 'laboratory' within which the mind can produce extremely powerful insight and creative imagery. Beyond that, we would assert that restoring these natural, bi-modal sleep patterns can play a key role in energy conservation and accu-mulation, as well as enhancing the quality of psychophysiological energy. It has been reported that Einstein dreamt the theory of relativity over a period of thirteen nights.

**The Creative Process** is a little masterpiece of a book written by Brewster Gheslin forty or more years ago. He simply published the thoughts of a number of acknowledged geniuses who had at some time in their careers taken the time to write a description of what happened to them when they produced the kind of work which we call genius. So the book explodes with insights. One of the recurring themes is that these superproductive people seemed to place a great value on what we would call reverie states, and they had developed many clever techniques for pro-ducing them. They also seemed to have a very different attitude about sleep compared to most other people. My spin on it is that the genius class deliberately or intuitively places a high value on listening to at least those aspects and signals coming from their psychophysiology which relate to the creative process. This translates into a wider variety of sleep and wak-ing states, including simply quietly resting modes of consciousness. Many of Gheslin's geniuses were also conspicuously skilled at nap taking.

Throughout this book we are striving to arrive at best use of language we can. This implies coming to definitions which we can agree make sense and allow us to go forward together. One of the most difficult and important is meditation. One of the definitions of meditation that works for me is: the art and science of allowing the mind (including the body) to rise to the highest levels of actual intelligence that it is capable of. This level or quality of intelligence includes emotional intelligence, wisdom, and the capability to love. How one arrives at this happy condition is easier talked about than done. However, for some time it has been clear to me that one of the most natural ways to 'get there' is to allow sleep and these reverie-like stages of consciousness, which take place between sleep and waking, to quietly lead the learner to the 'how.' In short, sleep can serve as a natural path leading towards the discovery for oneself of those spontaneous explosions of profound intelligence which some call meditation.

Furthermore, there seems to be a correlation between awareness of subtle imagery such as dream and archetypal, creative imagery and quality of waking consciousness. It is as though waking up while you sleep means you are more awake when you are awake. As dreams clarify so does waking life. This concept seems to be at least relatively true. However, I know some people who manifest an unusual high level of consciousness and yet claim they remember very little of what they dream. Krishnamurti, himself, claimed that he almost never dreamed (although, some of us who most appreciate his astonishing work would have loved to have gotten him in a sleep lab to check that one out).

One of the yogis who was studying EEG biofeedback and its application to yoga told me that meditation teachers had used alpha/theta trainers for centuries in the Himalayas. He said that when a student seemed to the teacher to be ready he was instructed to cut a board the length of his body and put a hole in both ends. Then he suspended the board from the branch of a tree over an icy mountain stream. He then learned to sleep on that board. I immediately saw what the yogi meant. Anyone doing that would be forcing himself to learn how to put the body to sleep while keeping at least part of the brain awake (as is commonly understood regarding the Reticular Activating System?). Falling into the icy water would be a powerful motivator. By the way, this techmique could be very dangerous. Please, don't try it.

This led me to the technique of training with a brain wave trainer in order to produce a similar effect. By lying down when one is tired and hooking up to a brain wave trainer, and turning on alpha brainwaves, one will probably drift in the direction of sleep. Then there will come a period when the signal stops because the alpha production has dropped and the dream activity (theta) has begun. During this time the consciousness may be skipping along the surface of the unconscious like a stone on the water. Finally it will sink for awhile. However, as adequate rest ensues the 'stone' will rise to the surface again and begin skipping as it gathers momentum in order to 'fly' into waking consciousness. This becomes an excellent way to train for increased awareness in that in-between state.

As the consciousness moves towards waking, the alpha signal will kick in again, further increasing the ability of the individual to build bridges to these alternative modes which integrate creative, archetypal imagery with thinking imagery. This capability is also one of the goals of meditation. Probably, most scientists would hate the term 'The Higher Self', but I'll bet Maslow, Jung and Campbell would find it useful and relevant to their work. In any case, wouldn't it be interesting if it turns out that these afore-mentioned methods of working amount to a kind of bridge building to the 'Higher Self'?

*"Everybody is familiar with the edge between normal waking con-sciousness and sleep: it's often a time of extraordinary feelings, sensations, and insights, particularly as we move from sleep into wakefulness... When the brain is brought to the edge of the world of God, the place of 'true' con-sciousness, a fractal intersection occurs. An unstable and dynamic system is created. Alpha/theta learning seems to enhance this ability to shift states, to move to the edge. At this 'fractal intersection' many aspects of mind may be accessed including wisdom, insight, and awareness of earlier traumas (or 'woundings'). Encountering these hidden fears or woundings in this way seems to make them more accessible to healing". Thom Hartmann*

As previously mentioned, another strategy is to relax towards light sleeping (as in napping) and count the hypnic jerks (muscle twitches which are usually accompanied by bursts of theta and theta imagery). We suggest training to the point of being able to count at least three twitches before waking up and entering back into regular activity. As stated before, one of the most common comments that clients, doing brain wave training report, is that they are sleeping better and they are more aware of their dreams.

One of the strongest arguments against overuse of consciousness altering substances is that they generally reduce the quality of sleep, and probably interfere with delta sleep, bringing particularly devastating consequences. One of the benefits of applying the Voluntary Simplicity logic (see session seven) is that by reducing commuter time, we can sleep later...since probably most of us are getting up too early as against the time we are going to bed. Certainly, we are probably making children (especially teenagers) get up too early in order to be in school by 7:30 or 8 A.M. In fact, there is a growing national movement to correct that problem, and I predict it will gain momentum rapidly as the electorate realizes the costly consequences of sleep deprivation, and forcing unnatural time constraints on ourselves, much less our children.

As we have suggested, the hypothetical reasons for the effectiveness of skilled stress management and meditation are that delta sleep is extremely healing for both mind and body. Most people who are drawn to these intense periods of personal change do so as a result of suffering, and having undergone prolonged periods of stress in which considerable mind/body damage has accrued. Toxins and stressors usually interrupt delta sleep. The most effective way to fix this is to get enough sleep.

*"Sleep is the poor man's wealth, the prisoner's release, the indifferent judge between the high and the low." Sir Phillip Sidney*

## DREAMWORKS

Dream work can be an important tool for some of us. As we have said before, there are different thinking/learning/doing styles. Not everyone needs to or wants to get into the dream work, but it can play a major role in the creative process. Even with conventional stress management it is common for dreaming to change and become much more interesting. As we have mentioned, neurofeedback clients often report a dramatic increase in quantity and quality of dream activity. For that reason we want to go over the basics of dream journaling for those wanting to explore their own field of dreams.

Simply write dreams down chronologically in as much detail as possible. If you feel that there is color, or there is something you are not sure of but think happened in the dream, it is important to write that down also. This process can lead to dreams becoming clearer and even workshop like…actively usable for problem solving and practical work.

When you have one month's worth (even if it's only 1 per week) read them over in chronological sequence. Second month you do the same (read first month then second etc.) Continue with this system for a total of four months. So, at the end of the fourth month you are reading the first month's dreams for the fourth time, second month for the third time, etc. That should do it in terms of assisting you in finding out for yourself that dreams can become clearer, that there are rhythmical repetitive dreams occurring, and that there are practical applications for dream awareness. Oh yes! Your own interpretations and feelings are most important. Other people interpreting your dreams may be interesting, and even helpful, but you must learn to do your own interpretation. For example, some imagery when verbally described may seem frightening, yet the feeling accompanying the imagery may be euphoric, indicating a deeper meaning.

## FLUFF ON THE NEEDLE

We have observed over the decades that as people discover and apply the Principles of Profound Attention and Profound Knowledge, or 'actualize', or restore balance to their lives, or go through a transformation of lifestyle, or 'awaken', or develop breakthrough thinking, or shift from primarily 'processing' mode of thinking to 'free—flowing' mode of thinking or reinvent themselves, or whatever terminology works best for you, there are a

278   MindFitness Training

number of changes or 'signs' that occur. We have already alluded to many of them in this book and we will try to explore this even more deeply as we investigate further. A particularly useful sign which we have already mentioned is the relationship of 'waking up' when we are sleeping, to waking up when we are awake. It seems clear that as one develops awareness during the sleep cycle (including bimodal sleep cycles) one's awareness and 'aliveness' during the day also increase.

Our hypothesis, largely derived from the work of Krishnamurti and Stan Krippner, goes something like this: When we are only semi-aware during the day we are also only semi-conscious. This means that many events are happening which are escaping our attention. However, part of the brain is noticing these events even while we are only being partially (and in this model inadequately) aware of them. The net result is a series of 'unlived' or only 'partially lived' moments. We believe the brain considers 'partially lived moments' to be a form of disorder or dysfunctionality and, indeed, if living life as fully as we can is the goal the brain is right in this regard. Obviously, sleep deprivation is going to exacerbate this problem.

The part of the brain that understands partially lived moments as a mistake may be said to be 'superconscious' or 'emotionally intelligent', and it finds ingenious ways to signal that a mistake (sin in the Greek) is being made and corrective action should be taken. These signals take on a variety of manifestations, including both psychological and somatic disorders. One of the more subtle attempts by this 'superconscious' aspect of the brain to correct the situation happens during the dream life. During dreaming the brain will try to bring order to these many partially lived semi-conscious moments and memories that accumulated during the day. That is why the dream life is usually experienced as trivial and relatively boring. The brain must do the best it can to 'complete' these moments by sort of 'reliving' them. We call that 'fluff on the needle' (hearkening back to the days of turntable stereo systems that were malfunctioning because the needle had accumulated too much dust).

As one begins to become more aware of the small moments in life that were previously missed, there is a parallel phenomenon of becoming more aware of detail in the dreams. When this happens adequately, the dream life begins to take on a far more creative and profound character. We hypothesize that increasing the awareness of what is happening moment to moment in normal consciousness (Profound Attention) reduces the need for this trivial dreaming, and makes a space for a much deeper (and more fun) aspect of Mind to emerge. We suggest that one of the properties of 'true meditation' is to naturally, easily, 'effortlessly' allow this rich, internal unfoldment, and make it possible to observe first hand the phenomena just described.

*"You must sleep sometime between lunch and dinner, and no halfway measures. Take off your clothes and get into bed. That's what I always do. Don't think you will be doing less work because you sleep during the day. That's a foolish notion held by people who have no imaginations. You will be able to accomplish more. You get two days in one—well, at least one and a half." Winston Churchill*

**Power naps are truly powerful.**

Following are some insights taken from a NY Times Science article by Jane Brody. Famous napping enthusiasts include Albert Einstein, Napoleon Bonaparte, Thomas Edison, John F. Kennedy, Ronald Reagan and Bill Clinton. Researchers have proven that no matter how long one sleeps at night the human body is programmed to become sleepy in the early afternoon, even without a big lunch. Dr. James Maas, a Cornell sleep researcher says, "Napping should not be frowned upon at the office or make you feel guilty at home. It should have the status of daily exercise." Trying to jump-start the system with caffeine in the afternoon is actually counterproductive according to sleep experts because it creates the illusion of efficiency and alertness and yet deprives the body and the brain of much needed sleep.

There is growing evidence that restorative naps are making a comeback. Recognizing that most of their employees are chronically sleep-deprived, some companies have set up nap rooms with reclining chairs, blankets and alarm clocks. If unions are actually interested in worker welfare they should make such accommodations a standard item in contract negotiations. Workers should take advantage of the opportunity to sleep for 20 minutes or so during the workday. Those that do report that they can go back to work with renewed energy and enthusiasm.

Companies that encourage napping report that it reduces errors and increases productivity even if it shortens the workday a bit. Studies show that sleepy workers make more mistakes and cause more accidents, and are more susceptible to heart attacks and gastrointestinal disorders. Dr. David Dinges, a sleep researcher at the University of Pennsylvania, is a strong advocate of prophylactic napping—taking what he and others call a 'power nap' during the day to head off the cumulative effects of sleep loss. He explained that the brain 'sort of sputters' when it is deprived of sufficient sleep, causing slips in performance and attentiveness and often resulting in 'microsleeps'—involuntary lapses into sleep which cause many accidents.

Dr. James Maas, author of Power Sleep (Villard Books, 1998), points out that naps 'greatly strengthen the ability to pay close attention to details and to make critical decisions.' A brief afternoon nap typically leaves people feeling more energized than if they had tried to muddle through without sleeping. Studies show that the brain is more active in people who nap than in those who don't sleep during the day.

## Session Seven

## ECONOMIC ORDER. FINANCING QUALITY CHANGE. VOLUNTARY SIMPLICITY. WHAT ARE YOUR ACTUAL RESOURCES?

*"...human beings strive perpetually towards ultimate humanness, which itself may be a different kind of becoming and growing. It's as if we were doomed forever to try to arrive at a state to which we could never attain. Fortunately...there is another truth which integrates with it. We are again and again rewarded for good Becoming by transient states of absolute Being, by peak experiences. Achieving basic—need gratifications gives us many peak experiences, each of which are absolute delights, perfect in themselves, and needing no more than themselves to validate life. This is like rejecting the notion that heaven lies someplace beyond the end of the path of life. Heaven, so to speak, lies waiting for us through life, ready to step into for a time of striving. And once we have been in it, we can remember it forever and feed ourselves on this memory and be sustained in time of stress."*

*"Not only this, but the process of moment to moment growth is itself intrinsically rewarding and delightful in an absolute sense. If they are not mountain peak experiences, at least they are foothill peak experiences, little glimpses of absolute, self-validative delight, little moments of Being. Being and Becoming are not contradictory or mutually exclusive. Approaching and arriving are both in themselves rewarding."*
*Abraham Maslow*

## ECONOMIC ORDER

has always been critically important to the free, creative, original life. And in our culture it is certainly one of the most basic of basics. Ross Perot once said that the absolute worst way to judge a person is by how much money he has in the bank (by last count Perot was reported to be worth about 7 billion). It is good that such a wealthy person said that. Nonetheless, in our world we are consumed by our lust for wealth, and severely psychologically damaged by our fear that we may be worth as human beings about as much as we are worth economically. Strange, since by materialistic measures we have more than any people in history.

Yet only a few of us are wise enough to be happy with what we have…to refrain from torturing ourselves with compulsive ruminations about the investments we should have made, the economic opportunities we should have seized, the endless comparisons with others who earn more than we do, have better houses, cars, clothes, vacations, and most of all more free time.

One of the major ways we bring suffering to ourselves is comparison. See how wasteful this is? Clear sight reveals that we are all incomparable. This does not mean we can't learn from others and encourage ourselves by realizing that if (s)he can do it so can I…that is different from comparison as we are discussing it here. Attention is one of the ways to literally burn through compulsive misuses of the mind which wreck us, like comparisons, money lust, and the belief that greed is good. Attention to the actual situation, the facts of 'what is' make it possible to see what doors are open and which doors are closed.

*"When one door is closed, the other one opens, but the hallway is hell";* *is an anonymous but widely accepted notion. My wife, Dagne, said that if she found herself stuck in the hall for awhile, the solution, for her, would be to decorate the hallway.*

Ask yourself, of the doors that appear open to you, which one most pleases your heart? This is what Joseph Campbell called 'following your bliss.' When you see a door that is open and one you would love to go through, just that perception is capable of generating the energy needed to go through it. So fear of not having enough money is one of the worst of the Inner Enemies and can lull us into a lethargic, discouraged, counter productive trance. This is an absolutely horrible way to live, and most of us are living it most of the time. It is a chain binding us and separating us even further from our life force, our potential for learning and living love, our birthright of a beautiful life—regardless of whether we have a lot or a little at any particular stage of our lives.

*"Follow your Bliss. If you follow your bliss, you put yourself on a kind of track that has been there the whole while, waiting for you, and the life you ought to be living is the one you are living." Joseph Campbell.*

There is a lot to that. But I am impressed with how many times one does not feel like doing something, yet decides it is the right thing and does it any way. Actually, doing things that are correct, yet may not be comfortable, may be one of the most important ways to bring about the full, rich life.

*"Felts are programmed, memory based feelings." Bohm.*

*"Make your bliss follow you. Set up traps for it by the way you live." Dagne Crane*

*"A feeling which is uncaused is bliss." Krishnamurti*

## IN PURSUIT OF AFFLUENCE, AT A HIGH PRICE

is the title of a New York Times science section article written by Alfie Kohn, the author of **No Contest**, a powerhouse of a book we strongly recommend. The principle of economic order implies right thinking about money. It means earning one's living in a way that is truly good for the world. A goal of economic order is to earn your living doing work you love. Economic order carries with it the feeling of being neither rich nor poor; of living happily within one's means, of making what one has work as well as possible, of not envying those that have more. Of course, we all know the old saying that money doesn't buy happiness, but which one of us really believes it? It takes a strong mind, indeed, to bring about those thoughts which are life and love affirming when such thinking conflicts with the acquisition of wealth. That is why we are doing our best to tackle the economics of the self-actualized life and the immense problem implied. Recently, researchers have developed a great deal of scientific evidence in support of the values and principles we seek to understand and apply in The Process. It appears that a huge amount of data has emerged indicating that you simply cannot buy deep or lasting satisfaction.

As Alfie Kohn points out, "Not only does having more things prove to be unfulfilling, but people for whom affluence is a priority in life tend to experience an unusual degree of anxiety and depression, as well as a lower overall level of well being. Likewise, those who would like nothing more than to be famous or attractive do not fare as well, psychologically speaking, as those who primarily want to develop close relationships, become more self-aware, or contribute to the community." It has long been established that income and attractiveness do not correlate with a sense of well being. However, more recent research demonstrates that the problem is worse than previously realized.

Several studies, with more on the way that have been or will be published in leading psychology journals, "sketch an increasingly bleak portrait of people who value 'extrinsic goals' like money, fame and beauty. Such people are not only more depressed than others, but also report more behavioral problems and physical discomfort, as well as scoring lower on measures of vitality and self-actualization." Two leading researchers in this area, Dr.'s Richard Ryan and Tim Kasser provide an insight into..." the dark side of the American Dream, noting that the culture in some ways seems to be built on precisely what turns out to be detrimental to mental health...the more we seek satisfaction in material goods, the less we find them there", Dr. Ryan said. It seems that such satisfaction is fleeting and has a short half-life.

In addition, the unhealthy mental effects of having extrinsic goals is apparently true no matter how wealthy or how old the person is. "The fact that pursuing wealth is psychologically unhelpful and often destructive," Dr. Ryan reports, "comes through strongly in every culture I've looked at...(however) affluence, per se, does not necessarily result in an unsatisfying life." The difficulty arises when one lives a life where the extrinsic values are the primary focus (the mission). For example, the research indicates that unhealthy psychological dynamics occur even in people who have not yet achieved their extrinsic goals but believe they will. This flies in the face of many forms of popular performance and life enhancement training programs. That's why we place such emphasis on aligning the sense of mission with one's own highest values.

### *"This whole culture is circling the drain." George Carlin*

There is a study about to be published which "found that college students who aspired to affluence had more transient relationships, watched more television, and were more likely to use cigarettes, alcohol, and other drugs than were those who place less emphasis on extrinsic goals." Apart from its obvious implications for a culture that thrives on material gain, this whole line of research raises questions about the proclivity of some psychologists to analyze the dynamics of goal-directed behavior while, in effect, ignoring the nature of the goal (that's why we place such emphasis on aligning goals with highest personal values, no matter how difficult it may seem). Likewise, it challenges homespun advice to follow one's dream, whatever it may be. These data strongly suggest that not all goals or dreams are created equal. According to the researchers, pursuing goals that reflect genuine human needs, like wanting to feel connected to others, turns out to be more psychologically beneficial than spending one's life trying to impress others, or to accumulate trendy clothes, fancy gizmos, and the money to keep buying them."

Additional research by Ryan, Kasser, Zax and Sameroff indicates that there is a relationship between people who want to be wealthy and parents that are 'cold and controlling'. There are many stories of wealthy men who had unhappy childhoods, and the conventional interpretations of those stories is that these people turned out well in spite of their early unhappiness. But the researchers suggest that "they may not have turned out so well after all. They just turned out wealthy." Scientists are not sure why a poor psychological profile seems to accompany those whose sense of mission is tied to seeking extrinsic goals. But they suggest the very act of chasing after money and fame may reduce one's sense of well-being, perhaps because it makes you ignore the goals that could lead you to have more satisfying experiences. Another possibility is that unhappy people tend to develop a need to chase after money and fame. In other words, when something deep down has gone wrong we turn to extrinsic goals. That is why we suggest that self-knowledge, seeking insight, and self-healing are fundamental principles necessary to the achievement of true economic order.

Dr.'s Aric Rindflesch and James Burroughs have found that "while people who are more materialistic tend to be unhappy with their lives, this effect may be moderated or even eliminated for those who also have close, caring relationships". But the bad news, according to Ryan and Kasser, is that "close, caring relationships may be among the first casualties of a life devoted to getting rich". Obviously, being rich or poor is not the critical issue, but the quality of being (consciousness?) is. We arrive full circle at the necessity for balance and soul—searching in order to bring about 'economic order'. And we see the choicelss fact that such order is necessary if we are to have the healthiest mental and physical life we can.

*"Fame or integrity: which is more important?*
*Money or happiness: which is more valuable?*
*Success or failure: which is most destructive?*
*If you look to others for fulfillment, you will never truly be fulfilled.*

*If your happiness depends on money, you will never be happy with yourself.*
*Be content with what you have: rejoice in the way things are.*
*When you realize there is nothing lacking, the whole world belongs*
*to you!" Lao Tzu*

## "BOLDNESS HAS GENIUS IT"

It has always been difficult for me to listen to someone who has plenty of money admonishing us to follow our hearts, do only work we love, have faith, God will provide. Especially since most of them (including myself) are requiring that we pay an admission fee to hear them speak, or buy their books and tapes, or are subsidized in some other ingenious way. But like it or not there is some truth in that idea. There is a baby in all that bathwater. And I do not know how any of us can seriously attempt to improve the quality of our lives without bringing economic order into our lives so we can afford to follow our hearts. Of course, just taking the high road with spirit and enthusiasm releases a tremendous amount of energy and intelligence.

*"Until one is committed there is hesitancy, the chance to draw back, always ineffective concerning all acts of initiative (and creation). There is one elementary truth, the ignorance of which kills countless ideas and inspirations: that the moment one definitely commits oneself, then providence moves also. All sorts of things occur to help one that would never otherwise have occurred. A whole stream of events issues from the decision, raising in one's favor all manner of unforeseen incidents and meetings and material assistance which no man could have dreamed would come his way. Whatever you can dream, you can—begin it. Boldness has genius, power, magic in it. Begin it now". Wolfgang Goethe*

Are we willing, like Deming to ask questions which challenge the status quo? Questions that are taboo? In my opinion, unless we can learn to ask those kinds of questions we will fall short of the insight and energy we need to bring about the radical changes we hunger for...dooming ourselves to a kind of conditioned, second hand consciousness. Living a beautiful, compassionate and creative life requires freedom and a big time investment. Being a slave to work is not freedom, and there is little time left over to invest in anything (unless it is work you love to do, in which case you are a 'love slave' which is a different thing).

You may disagree strongly with the following controversial material, but I'll bet that the questions raised are critically important for at least 50% of us if we are to bring about a higher level of economic order. One of the biggest questions all of us face is, how can I invest the time and energy necessary in order to live creatively and still meet my economic responsibilities?

The assumption most of us make is that we must simply make more money. We tend to think that if we could make more money our real problems would be solved. Of course, there is truth in the fact that increasing income can usually mean increasing options...just enough truth to create an entrancing and dangerous illusion. Most of us know people who make much more than they need, and yet are living desperate lives. Probably you are familiar with the studies on people who have won the lottery. Several years later, the majority of them considered it a curse. The vast majority of relatively happy millionaires are people who do simple, usually unglamorous jobs, and run basic kinds of businesses. What makes them millionaires is the care they bring to their work and the practice of voluntary simplicity. They are often frugal people, careful about spending more than they need. If ever there is an urgency to exercise our best intelligence, it is surely in discovering for ourselves how to think coherently about money.

*"We are not rich by what we possess but rather by what we can do without." Emmanuel Kant.*

I know this is scary territory but dare we ask, "Do I already have enough resources to fund the kind of life I long to live"? One of the most important ways we measure how well we are doing in life is by how much money we have accumulated. How much more are we worth this year compared to last year? And that's valid. It's OK as long as I don't become complacent if I had a good year and go into depression if I lose money. After all, the creative life is deeply caught up with risk taking, and real risk taking means we lose sometimes, no? We must make mistakes and recognize those mistakes and recover from them as quickly as possible. And that depends on the quality of our consciousness, doesn't it? How does exploring this area feel? Notice the mind trying to move away from this subject? That is called dissociation and it is the wrong direction.

A mother brought her son to Ghandi to ask him to tell her child to stop eating sugar. Ghandi said come back in one week. She did and the sage lovingly explained to her son that he should stop eating sugar. At which point the mother, being somewhat put out at having to make the long trip to see Ghandi a second time said, "why didn't you tell him last week?" "Because", he answered gently, "I was still eating sugar".

## THE GENUINE PROGRESS INDEX

There is a grass roots movement sponsored and endorsed by many internationally respected economists, politicians, business leaders etc., which has sprung up in Europe and the US, and it is focused on the problem of the GNP (Gross National Product) as a valid measurement. It dares to ask if the GNP measures are accurate or do they propagate an illusion…a deadly dangerous illusion. This blue ribbon group of thinkers proposes that we change the GNP to a much more valid system of measurement called the GPI (Genuine Progress Index).

The way GNP is interpreted is that as long as the GNP is growing, our standard of living and the quality of life is improving. The GPI places real values on things that the GNP ignores. For example, oil left in the ground means little to the GNP, but is considered money in the bank according to the GPI. A woman who works at home has no GNP value, but is valued highly by the GPI. Those of us who live with housewives are usually astonished at what it costs to attempt to replace her services. The GNP only places a value on a primeval Redwood forest when we cut down 2000 year old trees to sell to some other country that has already destroyed its forests, or values them so highly they pay us to destroy ours. The GPI calculates the value of that forest if left standing. Less than 50 years of tourist revenue far exceeds the total revenue brought in by converting these priceless irreplaceable world treasures to board feet of lumber. And these trees live for thousands of years! Hello? Is anybody home? For a few million now, we sacrifice billions, maybe trillions in the future and foul our nest in the meantime.

The GPI scientifically proves that although the GNP has shown a steady growth for more than sixty years, the true quality of life has actually deteriorated steadily and precipitously since 1970. So, mindless growth is not always healthy. A cancer is growth, cells feeding on the host until the host is killed. But there are mindful ways to grow that *are* healthy. Think about it. What happens if every country in the world has a favorable balance of trade at the same time? There are reliable calculations stating that if all countries of the world sustain even a 3% annual GNP growth rate, and growth continues to be measured the way it is now, we will strip the earth bare within 50—150 years.

David Bohm once pointed out to me that we are educated to believe that we must grow continuously in order to be successful, in fact in order to survive. Yet if all countries grow at only 2 1/2% per year, that means we grow ten times in a hundred years, ten thousand million times in a thousand years. We will grow beyond the mass of the universe in 7,000 years. In 1,000 years there will be a trillion people per square mile at the present rate. So we must reconsider the whole thing. The idea of indiscriminate growth is taken for granted. In fact, we have arranged society so that it falls apart if it doesn't grow at a fast rate. We are convinced that our self-interest is dependent on these rapid rates of growth. To understand these facts and ask these kinds of questions takes sensitivity. Society has become desensitized so that it doesn't ask these questions. This lack of sensitivity means we also become desensitized to violence and other things.

Of course, Bohm is referring to growth of a certain kind. He is referring to the kind of growth we have had over the last 4 or 5 hundred years, and especially since the industrial revolution. It is important to keep in mind that the true quality of life could probably grow without any effective limit because that is really based on growth in the quality of consciousness. Of course, that takes a transformation of consciousness by some critical mass of humanity. Possibly a small percentage of the actual whole. And that is the mission of The Process. So, consuming less (of nonrenewable resources) is utterly essential if there is going to be anything left for those that come after us.

In short, if we the people (especially the 'Actualizer' trendsetters) realize how much the GNP illusion is costing us, we will shift our values dramatically and our true quality of life will begin improving again. There is a similar illusion created personally and individually when we equate our happiness and self-worth with how much we have in the bank. Think what happens when a relatively small number of people like us who have had a great education, years of training and practical experience, and relative economic muscle…think what happens to our world if we devote our time and resources to enhancing the overall well being of Spaceship Earth?

*"If we do not reduce the mania for more and more (material consumption) then we will end our species. It is a form of suicide" Paulo Solari.*

By placing a true value on forests, minerals in the ground, leisure time, and by exposing the economic and health costs of the rat race, and for that matter the GNP system of measuring progress, the GPI way of thinking

can contribute brilliantly to a much needed cultural turn around. You can
learn more about the GPI movement by contacting Redefining Progress,
One Kearny Street, fourth floor, San Francisco, Ca 94104.

## VOLUNTARY SIMPLICITY

Wouldn't it be wonderful if we could free ourselves from this endless economic nightmare? Let's approach this problem with carefulness and
respect—the way we would an enemy who really wants to hurt us bad.
Contrary to the screaming message from our culture—greed is not good
because it destroys the mind. But is it greedy to want more than we have?
If you are starving, isn't it reasonable and necessary to want some good
food? Wants and desires then are not in themselves the problem…but
being ruled by them is very much the problem. By the way, at the time of
this writing, America is enjoying an all time record boom, and many people are rich and feeling rich. Many are also complacent. In addition to that
there are some gifted individuals for whom economic order is simply not
a problem. We salute you. You are very blessed. But economic disorder is
one of the most powerful psychological problems preventing most people
from working the Perennial Principles of The Process. That's why we feel
our responsibility is to make sure you are not assuming you have this
Inner Enemy handled unless you really do. But even if you are confident
that you do, realize it can all change in a moment. One of the oldest rules
in martial arts is never turn your back on an enemy you think you have
defeated. It is the last act many would-be victors ever did.

There is a book entitled **Your Money or Your Life** by Dominguez and
Robin. It became a national best seller, and it is a great work because it
details practical ways of breaking out of the money prison even if you
earn relatively little. It is part of a rapidly developing movement in the
US and other countries called Voluntary Simplicity. Some are predicting
that Voluntary Simplicity is going to sweep the United States and some
other countries with astonishing force precisely because the higher value

is quality of life, and that means escaping so much as is possible the economic agony that most find themselves in. According to the principles of Voluntary Simplicity this escape can be relatively easily achieved by most of us (at least in the more affluent countries) if we will employ breakthrough thinking and the strategy of eliminating the unnecessary (La Via Negativa).

Simply put, it means that a growing number of people are looking at their economic lives and discovering that making more money, at least making more money at a job they do not love, is often a mistake. Even worse, careful arithmetic is showing that in many cases making more money is resulting in no gain in real wealth (as in the GPI illustration). In fact, the price many of us are paying in real dollars, commuting time, lost opportunities, taxes, destroyed relationships, deteriorating ecology, and wrecked mental and physical health far outweighs the extra after tax dollars we are left with.

## VOLUNTARY SIMPLICITY PINACHE…ARTISTS OF LIVING.

Therefore, those applying voluntary simplicity concepts often discover that by working less they are winding up with a much improved quality of life and a greater net worth (for one thing they can manage their portfolio and other resources better). Essentially, they are discovering that by exchanging dollars for time they can improve important areas of life including their true economic order. What about you? Oh, this is getting painful isn't it? Time is money and money can also buy time. Remember, if you can live more creatively, more humanely, then you empower your passion and passion finds a way.

Only you can find out what is possible for you. However, most people of our level who go through this exercise, this economic investigation process with a scientific factual mindset, come to an amazing insight. It is that we have far more economic power and the freedom it buys than we realized. Further, if we employ our existing resources differently, and apply breakthrough thinking to our own economic lives, we can bring about a huge improvement in the quality of our day to day living.

## Do I Want and Desire to Change My Wants and Desires?

*"You are what your deep driving desire is,*
*As your desire is, so is your will.*
*As your will is, so is your deed.*
*As your deed is, so is your destiny."*
*Brihadaranyaka Upanishad IV.4.5*

Perhaps this is a good place to look at wants and desires. Can we modify our desires? By what strategy? In the first place we had better be careful what desires consume us because we become what we desire. 'You are what you think' and wants and desires are thoughts. Thought forms are already matter by the best definitions of matter that we have, and the more energy poured into these thought forms the 'thicker' they get until they actually begin to manifest as matter that even standard (3D) consciousness recognizes.

*"We are formed and molded by our thoughts. Those whose minds are shaped by selfless thoughts give joy when they speak or act. Joy follows them like a shadow that never leaves them"* Gautama (Buddha)

Shaping our thoughts is perhaps the biggest opportunity we will ever have. Shaping thoughts is also largely accomplished by La Via Negativa… eliminating the unnecessary. In this case we are particularly referring to unnecessary thinking (reducing psychothenia or over thinking). The most powerful strategy for doing this is Profound Attention. As the attention increases thoughts tend to slow down, decreasing in quantity, and increasing in quality. As we have asserted before, alpha training can be uniquely effective in getting the hang of this.

How can we think about money in a way that leads us out of the hell of the fear of not having enough? Most of us have been conditioned to believe that people with tremendous amounts of money are somehow wicked, and yet we envy them. Those of us who feel we have enough money tend to think of ourselves as entitled; after all isn't our relative wealth proof that we are somewhat superior to the rest of those teeming, desperate masses?

To me, use of the term economic order leads to breakthrough thinking. Economic order is different than being rich or poor per se. It is different than saying I must have a certain large sum of money before I can begin to live the beautiful life. See the hopelessness of this? Basing one's psychological security on having lots of money is building one's house upon the sand. It is only a matter of time before the foundation cracks and the mind sinks.

Remember what it was like to be a child and free of the fear of not having enough money? Some of us probably cannot, but most of us can. Mom and dad took care of us, and our days were too full of learning and laughter and naps and the drama of childhood and endless possibilities and dreams to realize that we were, in fact, relatively poor. Remember how that freedom seemed to be accompanied by optimism and the excitement of endless possibilities for a joyful life full of meaning and love and health and the ability to contribute and participate in the lives of others? Getting that kind of a feeling NOW is part of what we mean by economic order.

This does not mean we do not have to earn a living. Of course we do, but thinking in terms of economic order opens many new options to us because it puts money more in perspective and allows us to apply the principle of relativity to economics more easily. For example, one who is doing work that is fulfilling, who is surrounded by beauty and love, is likely to be in a state of consciousness that has little time or energy for worrying about money. If I may suggest, reducing worry tends to increase energy. Increased energy (along with the optimism that usually accompanies decreasing worry) leads to greater productivity and ability to earn.

Remember, worry is fear-filled thought. This very way of living creates economic order because doing work you love in a healthy environment leads to development of great skill. This skill level usually means that you can earn enough to continue living that way...probably more than enough. Such a mind finds it much easier to learn about economics in a way that is likely to substantially increase the quality of economic order.

Certainly, one is much wiser to reduce expenses to the very minimum in order to devote the maximum amount of time to doing work that is loved. As a practical matter, even a person who has to work a job that is beneath his/her potential is usually happy if he is also doing work that is loved a substantial percentage of the time. So, we must do work we love even if we are not (yet) paid for it. This is a fundamental part of economic order.

*"If you follow your heart your heart sings and you just dance to the music." Lambchop to Sherri Lewis*

What about those of us who began doing work we love, and then it turned into a business and somehow it stopped being fun and became too stressful? To start with, such a person is lucky because he once loved his work and knows the difference. However, there is now a trap. (S)he became successful doing what was loved and then fell out of love with it. Now it must be done again, there must be a reinvention of the work. The trap has been formed because he has gotten used to the income, and there is fear of abandoning the formula that has usually developed over a considerable period of time. And, of course, (s)he is older and fears that the vitality and ability to be happy living minimally is gone with youth. This person once knew economic order but must now recreate it.

Well, what is transformation if not rebirth? And what are the choices? It is clearly unacceptable to limp along without joy in work. So, one must find a way to begin again, because economic order is necessary and implies work that one loves. Living simply is one of the most responsible things a human being can do. Besides buying time to do what we really love, living simply is one of the most effective, accessible methods of improving the quality of consciousness.

Living simply is usually utterly critical if we are going to follow our hearts. What does living simply mean? Obviously, it means getting the expenses down to the minimum, consistent with the true essentials. However, this is different for different people and may include a relatively safe neighborhood, an attractive (although less luxurious house) nature, proximity to cultural activities etc. It seems to us that living simply includes the creation of a psychological comfort zone around ourselves so we can afford to ask the right questions like, 'what do I really want to do with my life?' In any case, for many of us, our lives, maybe even our souls, depend upon it.

## AN AMAZING CHALLENGE TO YOU

When I was about 48, I suddenly realized that I had grossed millions of dollars, yet had a net worth of almost nothing. This was perplexing since I had always intended to have economic order, and thought of myself as reasonably intelligent. When I meditated on it I discovered that my mistake was not realizing that earning money and keeping it are different art forms. Although I have been incredibly fortunate in life, I had to face up to the fact that when it came to accumulating capital and bringing about a higher level of economic order, I was neither wise nor lucky. So I began to search for a way to improve this situation. While reading advice from a financial consultant who specialized in the financially undereducated, I came upon the following amazing challenge:

**1. Calculate your true hourly rate. That means you have to include all of the hours required to do your work including travel time and work done at home.**

2. Begin investing some small amount of time regularly in the most efficient program of economic self-education you can. This usually begins with reading, attending seminars, talking with people who know more than you (finding out who they are) etc.

3. Keep careful records of how much time you invest and how much money you save, keep, earn etc. as a result of the time you invest in economic self -regulation.

4. At the end of one-year divide the money made and saved by the time you spent educating yourself economically.

What everyone whom I know (including myself) who has actually done this has found out is that we made at least as much by studying practical economic strategies and disciplines for increasing our financial base as we did at our regular jobs calculated on an hourly basis. This is usually a big shock since most of us have been putting off doing this kind of research because we felt we just couldn't afford the time. In fact, most people who accept this challenge, and do this experiment, report making far more than their normal hourly rate plus an extra dividend of reducing distress as well as increasing their sense of confidence and freedom.

Economic order means eliminating the unnecessary so we can become much clearer and more skillful at achieving the necessary. Historically, many of the most actualized human beings place a high value on simplicity, and often live their lives as shining examples of how to live simply, and how rich life can be for those who understand and apply the principles of economic order and eliminating the unnecessary.

Certainly this kind of thinking carries with it a sense of insecurity, especially in the beginning. And a sense of mission is one of the most precious yet illusive things to have. Learning to acquire a sense of mission may be difficult, but once we have it, it all but guarantees our success. Of course, there are no absolute guarantees, and it is far more creative to understand that triumphing over insecurity means learning to live with it. Since insecurity is an essential part of life, and since love of life (being an artist of living) may be the mother of all senses of mission, we actually must learn to love insecurity the way we would any teacher who is pointing out the way to enrich our consciousness. One of the most powerful ways to look at economic order is that it is a way to stack the deck in our favor, which in this insecure world is probably the best we can do. For example, thinking coherently about economics can create a situation in which the chances are far greater that we will have what we really need in order to live well; and even in times of economic adversity we will have the internal spirit and life force which enables us to live peacefully and happily.

## Session Eight

### 'La Via Negativa'. Eliminating the Unnecessary. Inviting the Liminal Moment, Insight, the Creative Life Process.

**Living The Process is a strange combination of unlimited patience and unimaginable aggression. One must allow the truth to unfold as it must while taking heaven by storm. Time to clean house, clear the decks, get ready for action!**

Increasing creativity is largely a matter of increasing sensitivity to and recognizing subtle signals coming from the body. Remember, Sensitivity = Intelligence. The songwriter or business executive will often laugh out loud or feel a tear come to the eye as the emotion wells up at the instant of insight. Remember, both Einstein and Bohm talked about feeling the solution to a problem, an insight coming 'in their muscles' long before they could clearly visualize it.

We have explored writing and seen that it is a strategy which can increase our thought recognition and a method whereby we can bring a certain amount of 'control' to our thoughts. We can see our thoughts are changing like the weather second to second. Probably most of us find ourselves thinking about things involuntarily all the time and the more we try to stop it the more it happens. Actually writing can act like a corral, collecting our thoughts like you would wild horses in order to tame them and bring some order. Writing can act like a magnet which attracts thoughts. If the thoughts we are hungry for are like a mysterious fish, writing can behave like a kind of bait. Only this fish does not wind up in the frying pan but instead becomes freer, more beautiful, more alive than ever.

We have seen that there are many priorities necessary to achievement of our mission but the mother of all priorities is probably deeply quieting the mind, because this will make the mind clearer and the thinking more coherent. It will also bring about a release of repressed fear material so that those fears can be addressed, healed, and transformed into creative energy and insight. Facing fear seems to have a most liberating, energizing effect. Understanding how to use La Via Negativa is possibly the mother of all basics.

Where do we go from here? Can we bring about, individually and collectively, the changes that we have been working so hard on together? We have come far, haven't we? Yet, there is a sense that we are at the beginning, isn't there? Don't be worried, the beginner's mind is incredibly creative, and our whole goal is to see if it is possible to live more, much more creatively and originally. We have dared to tackle some of the biggest problems there are.

From recognizing that unhealthy stress, overthinking and wrong thinking are robbing us of our potential, we have studied how to reduce those conditioned and limiting ways of using our minds and bodies. And in the very doing of that something immense, powerful, and life changing is beginning to emerge. And we enter the honorable struggle to put words on it even as we realize that the description is not the described, and we must make contact with the actual, the fact. We must somehow leap from the map to the actual road.

Even though it's difficult, we begin to see that attention and awareness can be enhanced, that the picture is not nearly so bleak as we have feared. Change (even transformative change) is possible, but it hinges on our ability to awaken our capacity for awareness and attention in real time to 'what is'…what is externally, certainly, but what is internally too. And internally we find what? Sometimes, for some of us, the internal world may seem like a paradise, heaven, and for at least awhile we are encouraged. At other times we may find a fiendish amount of fear, pain, sorrow, boredom and a sense of hopelessness.

But perhaps we are beginning to get a handle on the notion that by making contact through attention and awareness we change whatever it is, and there is energy released, possibly enormous energy. It doesn't really matter in a sense if what we are attending to is pleasant or unpleasant, encouraging or discouraging, 'positive' or 'negative', attending is the correct, the healthy, the transformative action, a secret of healthy change.

We have questioned science. We have seen that some science is good science; yet much science is misdirected, fragmented, unholistic, and therefore dangerous and counterproductive. We have used what we can understand of healthy science from journaling and neurofeedback to quantum and chaos theory in order to enhance our learning curve.

We have recognized that some of the barriers to growth, to using the mind better, are extremely subtle, and that vague feelings of discomfort may prevent us from moving in the right direction. Vague feelings of discomfort can also prevent us from moving in the wrong direction. We have gotten more clarity together about the problem of conditioning and how it sometimes makes us uneasy when we move into creative change. And yet we must somehow become more sensitive to intuition and understand when it is signaling us in preverbal, feeling ways. We have perhaps had some insight into the necessity of being at ease with the unknown if we want to live original lives.

When we ask most stress management experts what the ideal time period is in order to produce best results with their clients they usually suggest a two year protocol: Six months at one office visit per week, three months at one visit per month, and the balance at one visit per quarter. This protocol assumes that the client is complying with the 'transformation of lifestyle' homework assignments and strategies learned in the office visits. The two year learning period is important because it allows the client and the coach to ride through a number of cycles in order to strengthen the skills required to handle the natural waxing and waning of symptoms, challenges etc. It is my sense that for most of us The Process and Performance/Life Enhancement learning may vigorously unfold over a period lasting at least as long. Keep in mind that one of the implications in self-knowledge and self-education is that huge leaps of understanding can take place in a very short time. However, the practical implementation of these insights may take a bit or even a lot longer.

Insight can come at any moment. Real learning does not actually take time in the normal sense and there is always the possibility of great progress, huge movement happening very fast. Of course, a great deal of time and effort is often spent setting up the conditions and getting to that moment when insight flashes (and if captured 'real learning' happens). At the same time steadiness, patience, realization that it takes what it takes in order to achieve the goal, the mission is necessary. Setting unrealistic deadlines and other parameters can be counter productive, self-sabotage.

We have studied some of the basic strategies for defining and solving problems and how to think holistically, i.e. brainstorming individually and collectively. And we have looked into the process of dialogue, in particular Bohmian Dialogue. And most importantly we have plunged into the sea of implementation, action. How to implement, get feedback, correct course, implement again.

We have for the most part focused on how we enhance performance and quality of life for our own personal benefit; and further, how to generate a sense of mission and performance enhancement skills in the teams of people that we all must assemble or work with if we are to accomplish our dreams. We haven't adequately addressed the implications of applying these principles to society; however, it seems reasonable to me that that this process must extend naturally into the culture as a whole because the culture is made up of individuals, no? It is important to keep in mind the 'hierarchy of needs'. You know, really hungry people are unlikely to attend to much more than getting food. But once the stomach is full then there is the possibility of the mind beginning to move into deeper channels.

The deeper these channels, the greater the fun. However, like Maslow so brilliantly pointed out, you do not have to force the issue. Actualization proceeds up the scale naturally. Of course, there is the fact that some of us use our power to go in what seems to be a wrong direction. I am still struggling to understand this myself and I think I have some insights into it. But, in general, the best way I know to deal with those who seem to insist on this 'wrong turning' is to offer help but be careful, try to keep from getting hurt by them (people stuck in this way often attack those trying to help), and work with those who really want to unfold themselves according to the highest values they can.

*"All that one does against the truth or for the truth, in the end serves the truth equally well." Frank Lloyd Wright*

In my life I have had, and still have, some wonderful relationships, potentially wonderful relationships that just didn't happen, relationships that once were quite good and somehow went awry, and like most of you, some relationships that are a shambles. It might be reasonable to defend ourselves by saying who in the history of the world did not have some relationships that were dissolved by anger or sorrow or both?

So, like all of you, I am working hard to fix or at least improve all of my relationships. Indeed, the mirror of relationship is probably the most important type of feedback there is and virtually all of the concepts put forth in The Process live or die based on their usefulness in enhancing relationships. There will always be a mysterious aspect to relationships, suggesting that we will never know why they come and go, succeed and fail, flower with great beauty and die. However, there is a learnable art to improving the quality of all relationships, even that rare, love—filled glory of a relationship that all by itself can give meaning to an entire lifetime.

When I wonder at the source of those relationships that have filled and nurtured my life, two principles emerge: The first we can call Grace, and Grace is mysterious. When I contemplate Grace it seems that it flowers in innocence. How one becomes innocent again is itself a mystery, but I believe it is a quality of consciousness that...like love...can come and go. It appears that innocence does very well within the field of Profound Attention and 4DC. 'The shortest distance between two points is innocence'. The second principle is use of that power which almost all of us have to change and to influence our thinking, our health, and our capacity to live creatively. That which we attempt to point to and call deep, quality, 'Profound Attention'.

*"Relationship means to respond...respond accurately...accurate means to take great care...accurate means infinite care. ...when we act or respond according to the image we have about another it is inaccurate, it is not with complete care." Krishnamurti*

This deep attention means that the attender is tremendously interested to see with new eyes as much as possible. Looking freshly at a person implies seeing them as though for the first time ever. Love affairs that last for a long time have this quality. The implication is that somehow, the lovers can see each other without the burden of the past. People in such a relationship will often comment that they can suddenly be astonished and surprised by the depth of spirit of the other. We think of this as a kind of meditative insight. Look, when relationships falter what has happened? Isn't it almost always from the same cause? Isn't it simply that we are looking at the other through a conditioned image (3DC)? And when we are looking that way don't we simultaneously have an image of ourselves? So, the two images are in relationship with each other, but the actual, living human beings are not, because they are hidden behind these conditioned images (projections of thinking function). An example might be the image of 'My wife or husband, girl friend or boy friend who used to be more excited about me and who has hurt my feelings, but who is still my property and better treat me right or there will be hell to pay etc.' We come back again and again to this concept of the images being in relationship instead of the actual living people being in relationship.

*"Metaphors can sometimes have an extraordinary power, not only to extend the thought processes of science, but also to penetrate into as yet unknown domains of reality which are in some sense implicit in the metaphor...i.e. a particle is a wave." David Bohm*

## THE POWER AND LIMTATIONS OF THE IMAGE OF THE ME(EGO)

I'm afraid I'm taking too much for granted when I expect the listener to understand this necessary breakdown of the ego, or image of the me, which must occur if the true uniqueness of the individual, the real person is to emerge. I don't mean that the self-image must completely dissolve, but I do mean that the quality, the accuracy of that self-image must improve. That improvement can happen as a consequence of learning to perceive the image of the me moment by moment as a living, changing series of images rather than as a static, solid, sacred, absolute truth needing to be maintained and defended at literally any cost. The individual is less subject to self-delusion. (S)he is less affected by either insult or flattery, and less energy is lost because of friction between the self-image and 'what is'. This is what we mean when we agree that knowing oneself (self-knowledge) is critically important for meaningful growth and healing to take place. Since the image of the me, the ego is a compilation of thoughts, then the key to self-knowledge is knowing what I think, being very clear about it.

Either I've lost my mind, (taking one's sanity for granted may be the height of foolishness) or there is a fundamental insight emerging here. It seems to me that there are incredibly powerful cultural forces which are defining us. In addition to these external forces, our inner conditioning passed down through tradition (maybe even our genes) is telling us who and what we are. We are believing this image laid upon us, and since believing and thinking can make it so, the image of the me (ego) is formed. The image of the me amounts to a limiting belief pattern. In order to break through our limitations to a 'higher,' less limiting pattern it is necessary to break through the limitations of the ego. I haven't the faintest idea what *complete* freedom from this self-image would be like, since I am constantly struggling with my own shifting ego. But reports of others and my own *relatively free* epiphanies suggest that a powerful characteristic of relative psychological freedom is a sense of merging with the environment, resulting in profound feelings of wholeness, healing and 'empowerment'.

Is there a better, less limiting way than allowing ourselves to be swept along by the mass and momentum of our culture like a chip of wood in a great river at flood stage? Self-actualizing human beings long to reinvent themselves in much more profound, more human, more mystically enriched ways. This means to many of us that we want to be defined by our own souls rather than the culture. After all, what if the culture has lost its mind, i.e. Imperial Rome towards its end, Nazi Germany, Egypt when it enslaved the Jews, our own country when we burned women and healers as witches and slaughtered the Native Americans, Britain when it slaughtered the Chinese because they didn't want to be Opium dealers, and lionized lord Kitchner for machine gunning thirty thousand Dervish (Sufi mystics), Spain during the Inquisition, and so on and on and on? By the way, a historian pointed out recently that the Spanish Empire began its great decline just at the time of the Inquisition, when it drove the Jews and other 'foreigners' from its centers of learning and culture. And Spain's current renaissance has paralleled its opening up its culture and welcoming back those whom it had once driven away.

R. D. Laing, the famous psychiatrist, once pointed out that we consider people healthy or normal by how well they fit into the culture, yet in his opinion our culture is seriously, psychologically ill (so much for population norms). So, the truly healthy, mentally sound people will often not fit in and will usually try to change the status quo. By the way, we all fit in some ways and at some times, or we wouldn't be survivors. It is a matter of degree. Yet, we long to be unified. We hunger to be one: whole, holistic, holy. Can we be true to ourselves? Can we be defined by our own 'Souls', our own uniqueness, and still cooperate as necessary and in truly creative ways? Can we end conflict within us, and will that lead to an ending of conflict within the culture? Sounds like paradise doesn't it?

*"Again and again some people in the crowd wake up, they have no ground in the crowd, and they emerge according to much broader laws. They carry strange customs with them and demand room for bold gestures. The future speaks ruthlessly through them". Rainer Maria Rilke.*

So, what does it mean to be defined by one's own 'soul'? Many will accept this term 'soul' and feel they understand it—that we can go on from here. But much of the world, especially many of the intellectuals and scientists, will resist the term 'soul'. From my point of view that is O.K. The arguments that the soul is unnecessary, and probably a mythical fantasy, are often brilliantly put. Although, I do have a sweat shirt that says, "God is dead"—Nietsche. "Nietsche is dead"—God. I wonder why Canfield's **Chicken Soup for The Soul** books sold over thirty million copies so far? Seems like a lot of us believe soul's are real.

Nonetheless, can we come at this issue of being defined by our innermost true selves in a way which works for those who reject the term 'soul'? I think so. Chaos and Turbulence Theory with its 'strange attractors' may provide another approach to the same phenomenon. Earlier we refered to the late David Bohm as one of the incredible minds of our time. Dr. Bohm worked hard to communicate his view of the explicit and implicit order. His work brilliantly explains deep, mysterious, living patterns of infinite subtlety, in terms of traditional quantum physics, as well as emerging concepts in physics. I hope I am not taking too great a liberty when I offer my abbreviated synthesis of part of his hypothesis. It goes something like this: Psychological Time (past and future) is a relatively superficial way that the human brain organizes energy when it is functioning at a relatively low level, heavily conditioned, 3D consciousness. This probably equates with what is meant when we say we are using only 5% of our potential. When the brain is used at a slightly greater percentage, let's guess, say 10%, it begins to have major shifts in the way time is perceived. At this point the time/space continuum essential to quantum physics begins to be comprehensible (at least from a feeling, intuitive perspective).

One of the delights of being in David Bohm's company was that he was able to explain these concepts in plain language so that anyone who really cared could grasp them. And he did it in a way which seemed to be amazingly devoid of ego. He seemed to begin at the end point, and then see where you were and come back and get you, and take you with him back out towards the end point. When he saw that you had reached a limit of understanding, then he hung out with you there and helped you make the most of the (usually) great distance you had traveled.

Recall, if you will, our earlier look at the three types of time and the critical necessity to think and to live in real time no matter how arduous it is, no matter how much it hurts. Isn't it obvious that the best chance to bend the 'future' in a healthy direction depends upon our capacity to bring as much as possible of our mind, our energy into the Immense, Infinite Present? If the mind can get this far, then it begins to consider the concept of the past flowing into the present, and thence to the future as relatively useful and true. However, an enhanced (4DC) consciousness sees that basing one's life on the flow of linear time does not work as well as putting as much of one's aliveness as possible into the principle that the future is now. Of course, the linear flow of time does exist. If for no other reason than that we believe it to be so.

Another remarkable way to look at this notion, so much as we can, is through the eyes of Hawking, who suggests that entropy, not time, is unidirectional and sustains the illusion of linear time. May we suggest that in order to have the most effective relationship with linear time one must be observing it from a fourth dimensional (Real Time) perspective? This is similar to the concept that Newtonian physics is true, but becomes immensely more useful when enfolded by and applied from a quantum perspective.

So, it is unnecessary to call it 'soul', isn't it? Especially, if using that word builds walls between us. From the point of view of Chaos Theory we can suggest that within the Universe and within the inner space of a human being there is chaos; and when there is adequate freedom an innate, implicit order becomes explicit. It does so by producing a pattern which might be called 'a strange attractor' (taking a little poetic license). The nature of these patterns is that they (like snowflakes) are always different and always the same. When indescribably huge numbers of these beautiful six pointed stars fall on the earth they produce wondrous forms which are themselves attractors. And when human beings allow their own true nature to unfold they produce cultures that are also true...true to humanity, true to nature.

*"...the word soul having come back into vogue of late, resurfacing from years of being drowned in scientific thought. Soul, after all is what Kierkergaard, Freud, Jung and so many others struggled to find. Soul—filled lives are what we are called to live. The hero's journey is the journey of finding and actualizing soul...." James Hillman, Soul Code.*

Call it...allowing ourselves to be soul defined, or setting up conditions allowing our 'strange attractor' to form...the result is that our uniqueness emerges. This enhances our relationships, and by extension the culture, forming unions which in themselves are beautiful. Living this insight is easier said than done; but when done it works and conflicts between us are resolved. Our relationships flower.

Another problem which arises is that relationships may change. Relationships (personal, business etc.) held together by fear are really not held together by the right kind of glue. Also, following one's bliss and developing a strong sense of mission means that one eliminates the unnecessary. Sometimes we have become addicted to relationships, behaviors that are, like substance abuse, entrapping us and preventing actualization of our potential. Dealing with the ending of these can be one of the most traumatic sections of the 'Royal Road'. There are many dangerous places on this road. La Via Negativa (and sometimes survival) dictates slowing down and going very carefully. For example, we tend to collect friends who think like we do. But if we are changing in big ways, we may lose some of these friends. Most people who go through major leaps of consciousness tend to value their quiet time alone much more. In addition, living more simply becomes one of the easiest ways to gain energy and clarity.

This kind of program is useless unless it is concerned with education in the deepest, truest sense. Education means to unfold from the inside out that which is already there. Of course, we respect knowledge, and realize that knowledge really is power. But there are all kinds of knowledge and all kinds of power, and some kinds of power are extremely unhealthy. The kind of power we are most interested in derives from knowledge which recognizes that all knowledge is limited and is usually a projection from the past into the present. Further, the greatest hunger and highest aspirations of the human being rest in freedom, the concept and actuality of freedom, and freedom's power to make contact with the unlimited.

So, there is a special kind of knowledge which we have tried to get insight into and which we've alluded to in the Profound Attention discussions. A kind of knowledge which sees quite clearly its own limitations; and, therefore, begins to set up the conditions for allowing another form of intelligence to emerge. This healthy form of knowledge sets up and makes way for the recognition that attention to 'what is' is of the highest order of functionality. Further, that this attention uses knowledge like a set of tools to construct or allow best possible, most creative life to emerge. It seems reasonable to suggest that information is not necessarily knowledge.

**LA VIA NEGATIVA** is the first way to get the energy we need. We have said before that we are cartographers (mapmakers) of consciousness as we enter into the Real Work/Play of Life Enhancement. Remembering that we must use language very carefully, we probably want to stop thinking of positive as good and negative as bad. Precisely because La Via Negativa, the negative way, is probably the most 'positive'...oops, I mean productive principle there is. It means simply that one of the first things to do when high achievement and excellence is the goal, is to eliminate the unnecessary. Clear the decks, strip down for action. Also, negative is often associated with female while positive is associated with male, and that can lead to further confused thoughts and 'felts'.

One of the reasons we often fail to achieve our goals is that we refuse to give up those things that are preventing us from reaching them. Even more fundamentally, we don't even allow ourselves to ask the kinds of questions we need to because we are terribly afraid that the answer may be that we have to give up something we are attached to. Denial of what we must do or not do in order to achieve our objectives is a Great Thief. Living without letting go is like driving with the brakes on. It uses more fuel, wears things out, slows you down.

According to the New York Times, what follows is a transcript of the ACTUAL radio conversation between a US naval ship and Canadian authorities off the coast of Newfoundland:

**Canadians:** Please divert your course 15 degrees to the south to avoid a collision.

**Americans:** Recommend you divert your course 15 degrees to the north to avoid a collision.

**Canadians:** Negative. You will have to divert your course 15 degrees to the south to avoid a collision.

**Americans:** This is the Captain of a US Navy ship. I say again, you divert YOUR course.

**Canadians:** No, I say again, you must divert YOUR course.

**Americans:** THIS IS THE AIRCRAFT CARRIER U.S.S. LINCOLN, THE SECOND-LARGEST SHIP IN THE UNITED STATES

ATLANTIC FLEET. WE ARE ACCOMPANIED BY THREE DESTROYERS, THREE CRUISERS AND NUMEROUS SUPPORT VESSELS. I DEMAND THAT YOU CHANGE YOUR COURSE 15 DEGREES NORTH. I SAY AGAIN, THAT'S ONE FIVE DEGREES NORTH, OR COUNTER MEASURES WILL BE UNDERTAKEN TO ENSURE THE SAFETY OF THIS SHIP.

**Canadians:** This is a lighthouse. Your call.

When we look at the muscle system and the concept of highly precise movement, of say the fingers, we see that finger dexterity and precision is gained by the motor neurons we *don't* fire. In the case of muscle speed, control and precision, the key is relaxation of everything except that which is necessary. So as we focus on goals, including the goal of maximizing moment to moment quality of consciousness, it becomes clear that one of the first goals is to identify what activities contribute to success and what detract from it.

When we look at those people who work hard but don't seem to accomplish much and those whose performance curves are steeper, we see that one of the most common characteristics of the high performance group is that they understand something about La Via Negativa...what not to do. Of course, we are practicing this principle all the time by making a choice to not do something. But we want to become far more skillful at using this major tool/technique.

Stress management is a classic example. We gain energy, power, focus, health by reducing muscle tension, fight or flight arousal, rapid thoracic breathing, and perhaps most important of all—over thinking. In a very real sense it can be said that the potential within life unfolds because of what we don't do as much as it does because of what we do.

## MIND MOVIES

You know, we are going deeper and deeper into the mind, aren't we? And this negating of the unessential is kind of like cleaning house, isn't it?

(Insight into the way the creative mind works.) Well, hang on, this gets much more exciting. One of the most important treasures we are searching for here is a clearer understanding of thought. One of the goals of this training is to help clarify the notion that thought is not the only capability of the brain/mind. We must see the importance of activating another order of intelligence (part of whose function is to direct thinking). Further, that thought/thinking is an image-making process based on memory similar to a computer or movie projector. See if the following constructed visualization helps.

If you will, close your eyes and imagine that you are sitting in a room looking at a large white wall, and this wall is washed with powerful, bright lights. Behind you there is a movie projector projecting a movie against the large wall but you can't see it because the powerful lights are washing it out. This is like the condition of thinking of the first kind. The thinker is not aware that he is thinking. The thoughts are going on but they are 'invisible'. However, quieting the mind is like turning down the lights, and gradually it becomes possible to make out that the movie is playing on the wall. At first it's just a lot of flickering, meaningless images; but as the brain gets quieter it's as though the room is getting darker and the movie becomes clear and comprehensible. As the engineers would say, the signal to noise ratio is increased, the gain is being turned up. Sometimes the movie is entertaining, sometimes boring, sometimes fun, but mostly it gets scary. At first you don't realize that it is a movie and you really believe it is real. And of course, it is a perfectly valid form or expression of a relatively low order of reality.

But as you attend to it more vigorously you see that it is merely light play on the wall. (Remember Plato's metaphor about people chained in a cave in such a way that they could only see the shadows of people moving around a fire as those shadows played on the wall of the cave? Lacking the liberty to go to the actual fire and see the real people, the prisoners believed that the shadows were all there was to reality. And of course, unless they could free themselves, the prisoners were, in a sense, tragically correct). So, you follow the source of light back to the projector. The projector is like the brain cells in thinking mode. The light shining through the sequential pictures on the film is like the light source in the brain animating images made from the material of memory. This leads to the realization that thought is by nature mechanical, and although interesting and useful in its own right, it is illusory. So, you ask the question, 'Is there another kind of capability of the brain? What is the source of the power of this projector, this thinker?' In the relative dark you follow the power chord back to its source, an outlet in the wall. You decide to experiment with pulling the chord out. This is like very deep meditation. The movie shuts down and you are in total darkness.

But since thinking function is temporarily silent you are not afraid (fear is a form of thought). Somehow, you touch the outlet (The Power Source) and receive a shock so powerful it knocks you clear across the darkened room. Stunned and overwhelmed, you decide to plug the movie projector back in and watch the movies for awhile longer. But now you know too much. So even though the movie projector is continuing to run, you use the peripheral light to examine the rest of the room. Suddenly you come upon a door. Carefully, you open it and are amazed to step forward into another, immensely greater dimension of reality. A dimension which easily includes, as a small part of Itself, the room and the projector, a dimension in which the colors are far brighter and more beautiful. It is a spring morning and the air is unimaginably sweet and the sounds and beauty of nature uplift your spirit and fill you with energy, a sense of purpose, and joy of living. You wonder how you ever survived that dark closed room and all of those watered down, illusory images, and separation from the miraculous beauty of The Actual.

It is already obvious that what we think has everything to do with achievement of our goals, improving quality of life. Yet one of the greatest factors in failure is psychothenia (over thinking) and here we come to the most powerful expression of La Via Negativa of all. If over thinking is one of our greatest problems (some say our greatest problem) and since it automatically causes much less accurate thinking, then it follows that reduction of unnecessary thought is equivalent to bringing about an engineering change so powerful that it will transform the mind. To reiterate, one of the most important principles of the Process: As *the quality of attention to thought increases, thinking itself appears to slow down (as being in the 'Zone') and as the quantity of thought decreases, the quality of thought tends to increase.* Further, using the mind in this way implies a reduction in impulsiveness which is often a sign of maturity of function i.e. a high level of self-regulation. This is one of the fundamental principles of the so-called meditation model. It is also an ultimate example of Deming's Profound Knowledge strategy applied to the human being as an organized energy system.

The Problem is, the harder we try to slow thought down, and the more we struggle with it, the more anxious we become, the more overthinking happens. It's like over-steering a car, liable to cause a wreck. That's why we are working on all these different strategies, because taken together they decrease psychothenia while increasing the quality of the remaining thought. Think about this: what if brain wave training is an extremely efficient way to help a person get the hang of practicing the most powerful form of La Via Negativa there is....healthy reduction of unnecessary counterproductive thought? What a concept! We reduce our barriers to success by reducing thought...at least some kinds of thought. And one of the many ways to do this is skillful brain wave training (at least for some of us). One more thing. This is a test. If you are able to think in these ways, what kind of thought is that?

## MISSION PRIORITIES

So as we focus on our goal, even better our mission, we must set priorities:
  A. Actions that definitely contribute to achievement of your mission.
  B. Actions which might contribute to achievement of your mission.
  C. Actions which do not contribute to the achievement of your mission.
  D. Actions which are clearly antagonistic to achievement of your mission.

Huh?, Oh. Things may be getting a little uncomfortable here. What do you think? What am I doing that is preventing my success? Let me give you a personal example: I used to enjoy a little smoke. I appeared to be quite functional and healthy. But I realized unequivocally that if I wanted to go deeper into the nature of the mind and improve my health and energy I would have to give it up. When I saw that in my case the superior 'high' road, first class, meant giving up some of the things I drank, I ate...I gave them up. This was much more difficult than I expected it to be, and the process continues as I learn more about what enhances the quality of my life. This is only an example, and I'm not say-ing you should do exactly the same. I personally believe in moderation, while others whom I respect might say complete abstinence is better. Only your own intelligence can determine what is right for you. That is the essence of heuristic learning. Giving up some of my addictions was and continues to be tough, but my performance has gone way up and my economic order has become much more orderly. And it was worth it many times over. By the way, brainwave training played an important role in my personal success.

Another personal example is The Process itself. As my sense of mission about it got stronger I saw that I would have to give up a lot of my marketing time. This translated into the loss of hundreds of thousands of dollars of gross income to my business. Of course, I feel I will probably make it up but, whether I do or not, I've followed my heart and that feels like the right road to me. Although I've been working on it for years, I feel as though this project has only just begun, yet it has already paid off psychologically since I feel healthier as well. I am having a huge amount of fun. I feel like my fire has been lit, and The Process itself is increasing the passion and the sense of mission. The very fact that working on the development of The Process has made my life work better and dramatically increased my fun ratio means I have already achieved my first level of goals, and consider the substantial investment in The Process already profitable in the deeper sense of that word.

Here we have to warn you about a problem, or perhaps you are already aware of it. One of the primary causes of overthinking is that the brain needs to keep itself busy, even if it is just chattering with irrelevant trivia. The reason for this drive for chattering is because if the brain gets quiet, it will see more truth, and some of that truth is threatening. It will have to deal with difficult paradoxes like the necessity for a certain amount of emptiness in order to be fulfilled. And the realization that you must give up some things you have become extremely attached to if you are to grow. One of the most difficult paradoxes is the notion that insecurity is inescapable in life, and therefore happiness depends on learning to live with lack of security.

Probably most of us will agree that the pathway to the richest possible life lies in being as intimate as possible with the truth, 'what is', the way things actually are. We do not mean to imply that we know what the absolute truth is and we are going to hand it down. On the contrary, it seems to us that the nature of the human mind implies that it will always be limited to relative truth at best. Further, there are certainly altered states of consciousness in which at least some human beings have felt they are 'in touch' with a kind of absolute truth, an 'end point', but communication from that state appears to be at least extremely arduous, if not impossible.

There are buried fears that are so threatening that when we sense our relatively quiet mind is opening the basement door and letting some of those fears come up into consciousness, we turn on the movies and create chattering and illusion again so we can put off dealing with this unfinished business. Sorry, but we cannot ignore our inner enemies and at the same time improve the quality of our lives. We must find a way to deal with them. Remember, as we relax deeply these subconscious fears tend to come to the surface and get processed in a way that works and is healthy. We hasten to add that this book is intended to be used by people who are learning about these concepts in order to enhance already functional lives. There are, of course, many of us for whom the crisis has already become so dangerous that competent help from a mental health practitioner must be sought before taking on the challenges implied by performance enhancement.

## SIMPLIFY—FOCUS—CREATE

Now the means to quiet the mind are everywhere and they certainly do not require EEG biofeedback. We hope we have made that clear. However, we intend to assist you in learning this most practical of art forms even faster and maybe better (unless you don't need this kind of assistance which is cause for celebration). Remember, just trying harder isn't enough. In fact, as we seek to use language in a way that works better we have to watch the use of the word try. It may be a subtle way to allow ourselves to escape the necessity of actually doing.

When EEG training works as best it can it obsoletes (negates) itself. By this I mean that once you learn it, you can leave the training equipment behind. How long this obsolescence takes is still unclear, and may vary enormously with each individual. For example, I still feel I benefit from EEG training from time to time (with biofeedback instrumentation as different from internal 'natural' feedback). This is true even though I have trained with equipment for many hundreds of hours, and have learned how to increase the desired brainwaves and sustain them for substantial periods of time using only internal feedback.

A great way to learn is to do some EEG training outdoors during different times of the day...a beautiful morning, afternoon, or evening. The senses become more acute, while obsessiveness, compulsiveness and anxiety tend to fade. Space and time can seem to open up, and a sense of immensity may emerge. If the brainwave training is working for you then there will come a time when you find yourself spontaneously falling into these delicious states. States that are sometimes reveries, sometimes electrifying awareness of the astonishing moment to moment miracle of creation taking place with you in the middle as an essential part of it. One Process participant was describing her sense of renewal, the freshness and beauty of the present. "When driving into the city yesterday morning everything was so alive, possibilities seemed endless. I felt like I was in a rock video." The 'goal' is for these spontaneous moments of clarity (4DC) to take place ever more frequently without even giving a thought to using the biofeedback instrumentation. The instruments will have done their job. Although, as we suggested, 'refresher' sessions from time to time may prove helpful.

You will probably find yourself asking, 'why didn't I do this before? Why have I not allowed myself this silence, this peace, this aloneness?' Aloneness is quite different from loneliness, isn't it? And then insight is likely to come, and that means change, healthy change. And if you have your creative journal at hand the ideas begin to get written down, including strategies and lists of things to do, steps to take…and perhaps most important, things not to do, things to let go of…La Via Negativa.

## HIGH ACHIEVERS USE LA VIA NEGATIVA

Life is filled with paradoxes and the wise understand how to deal with them. First thing is to realize that the nature of standard conditioned consciousness (3DC) is to see things in terms of opposites. This is called dualistic thinking and it is usually counterproductive because it cannot see the problem clearly. You already realized that, yes? Watch your breathing now. Are your shoulders relaxed? Ask yourself if they can drop. This may become a little threatening. So, the Greeks and others said that wisdom lies beyond the corridor of opposites; or to give it a more upbeat spin, the corridor of opposites lies at the threshold of truth. Sounds like 4DC doesn't it? And we are passionately interested in bringing more truth into our lives aren't we? 'Peak Performers do the basics very well.' One of the basics is to break out of the trap of dualistic (either or) thinking. The key to that is seeing that dualistic thinking exists and watching (attending) to it.

We continue being as careful as we can with language. So, negation means elimination of the unnecessary in personal growth and Life Enhancement. We are being careful not to confuse ourselves with the creative opposites which are necessary for nature to exist (north and south, east and west, positive and negative charges, male and female, up and down, matter and antimatter, light and dark, yin and yang, etc). They are necessary descriptors. Dualistic thinking is different and it is not necessary and it is not good. In fact, it destroys the mind's ability to have right relationship with nature's 'opposites'.

When a reporter asked Edison to comment on his 10,000 "failures" to develop a working light bulb, he reportedly said something like, "What do you mean failures? Discovering what does not work was critical to our success! We had to learn what not to do." La Via Negativa says that by eliminating those things that don't work we come to those that do. By eliminating the untrue we come to the truth. Truth does not lend itself to being grabbed by the throat. Probably the most aggressive way to come to it is by negating the untrue. This can be tricky because a misguided version of this concept can lead to a dysfunctional, intellectual arrogance, and a tendency to criticize others in a counterproductive way. But we never said it was going to be easy (Except when it is. We must always be ready for things to happen correctly, effortlessly. In fact, it is a characteristic of 4DC to operate just like that. Recall the notion of free—flowing thinking? Of being in the zone or 'flow'?)

So, by reducing, negating unnecessary thought, the necessary emerges. By reducing and negating unhealthy stress the system becomes quiet and balances itself. When the system is balanced, it naturally stops wasting energy and begins accumulating energy. This opens up the possibility of the high-energy condition of Profound Attention arising. Attention to external phenomena leads the mind to awareness of and attention to internal phenomena. Attention to thought reduces the quantity of thought while increasing the quality. As thought decreases moments of relative neural silence increase. As these moments of relative neural silence increase, a higher order of intelligence can begin to operate, and it uses creative, hypnogogic, hypnopopic, theta, aha, insight imagery in order to seed thinking. This gives thinking a vitality, aliveness, productivity which fuels a sense of mission and meaningful accomplishment. This kind of thinking sees how to reduce (negate) conflict and the unnecessary, so the necessary can emerge. By negation we create a silence, a quietness; we allow a space, an emptiness in which something may emerge. We bring about a balance, like a teeter-totter in which things can shift either way. We invite the Liminal Moment, that space/time when the old is dying and something as yet unnamed and unformed is being born.

*"I could not face the world's pain until I faced my own. Paradoxically I could not pass through that narrow place until I was willing to attend more deeply to the pain of others. Most important, certain experiences are included in order to show—in ways that I have only begun to discern— that we are always guided, always cared for, always healing, moving inevitably toward wholeness, even when we cannot yet see it for all the pain and difficulty that surrounds us.*

*There is a goodness, a Wisdom that arises, sometimes gracefully, some- times gently, sometimes awkwardly, sometimes fiercely, but it will arise to save us if we let it, and it arises from within us, like the force, that drives green shoots to break the winter ground, it will arise and drive us into a great blossoming like a pear tree, into flowering, into fragrance, fruit, and song, into the wild wind dancing, sun shimmering, into the aliveness of it all, into that part of ourselves that can never be defiled, defeated, or destroyed, but that comes back to life, time and time again, that lives— always—that does not die. Into the Divine."* **The Bond Between Women.** *China Galland*

Technology is a finger pointing to the Sun. Rejoice in the Sun. Do not get hypnotized by the finger.

The first duty of love is listening.

## Session Nine

### AWAKENING 'EMOTIONAL INTELLIGENCE'. LOVE AS PRINCIPLE, CHALLENGE AND A 'FIELD' BEYOND THOUGHT.

*"It is not that there must be an end to seeking, but rather the beginning of learning. Learning is far more important than finding."*

*"As long as education is concerned merely with the culture of the outer...the inner movement with its immense depth will inevitably be for the few and in that there lies great sorrow. Sorrow cannot be solved, cannot be understood when you are running with tremendous energy along the superficial. Unless you solve this with self knowing you will have revolt after revolt, reforms which need further reformation, and the endless antagonism of man against man will go on."*

*"The heart of the matter is education, it is the total understanding of man and not an emphasis on one fragment of his life...All the enthusiasts for outward change always brush aside the more fundamental issues."*
*Krishnamurti,* **Beginnings of Learning.**

I'm going to talk to you intimately about the most difficult of all principles. In so doing I must become vulnerable. I cannot deny that sometimes discussing love makes me feel like a fool. So be it.

*Once the Sufi saint Nazrudin was carrying a 'lazy man's load' of fine crystal glasses stacked way to high across the cobblestone street to his house. He slipped and all of the fine crystal glasses smashed to smithereens on the cobblestones. A crowd of villagers gathered around, astonished at the accident and genuinely concerned about Nazrudin's great loss. The sage stared in dismay at the pile of glass for a few moments and then shouted at the crowd, "What's the matter with you fools, haven't you ever seen an idiot before?"*

To me the most interesting, scary, dangerous, beautiful, intelligent, life changing and enhancing, mysterious, illusive, mystical, innocent, complex, simple, humbling, wisest, infinite, timeless, important principle that exists is the Law of Love and Compassion. It is the soul of The Process, but I resisted doing an actual session on it because it is so fraught with complications and difficulties and potential for major misunderstanding. Probably, most of us, especially the guys, feel better dealing with Love (The Real Thing) from the condition of silence. It seems clear that the problem with Love is not with Love itself as Love, The Principle. The problem is with the language. It is so difficult, painful, exhilarating, wise and stupid to verbalize it at all.

### *"Talking about love is like dancing to architecture."*

On the other hand, I have seen many pieces of architecture that made me feel like singing and dancing.

When I was young I believed that the noble way to deal with the Principle of Love was to do all I could to live by it, but never talk about it. Then a moment came when I caught my beloved quietly weeping. She didn't want to say why at first, but when I prevailed she said, "Because you never say you love me." Suddenly, I realized that for the rest of my life I would be learning how to talk about love without making it go away. How very messy! So, much for my lofty philosophical theories. A significant part of loving her is clearly saying so.

If it is true that life on earth can be either a heaven or a hell, then it seems obvious that the more love fills your life, the more life is a heaven, and the less love fills your life the more life is a hell. Recently, I was moved by a NY Times story about the visit of an Indian woman who taught by touching people in a special, healing way. Like other 'Bhakti' (heart awakened) teachers, there are many who believe she can effect the healing process of those she touches and there is much anecdotal evidence indicating that may somehow be true. If it is true, wouldn't that be incredible? Wouldn't you just love to be able to smile at someone and perhaps touch them and they would be healed physically, and perhaps more importantly, psychologically? My wife devotes a lot of her time to the hospice movement. She has taught me how it is possible for a person to be dying of a terminal disease while being 'healed' in the sense of the mind and spirit finding peace, love, and a guiding light within themselves, a sense of fulfillment while letting go. Anyway, I believe that there is more to lose than to gain if we fail to at least try to deal with this Infinitely Immense Force (Love) in the best way we can; because if we make even a tiny amount of actual progress in this area we may exceed every thing else we have attempted in terms of bringing about meaningful change at the individual level. To me, definitions of love are laughable, probably futile, yet since we are using words as tools of communication we probably can start there. We have to start somewhere no matter how daunting and risky it may be.

**Love,** (Luve, Lufu, luba, liebe) to be fond of…a strong affection for or attachment to a person or persons…a strong liking for or interest in something…a strong usually passionate, affection for someone of the opposite sex, (This would probably be socially incorrect today) sexual passion or its gratification…God's benevolent concern for mankind…man's devout attachment to God…the feeling of benevolence and brotherhood that people should have for each other. To like or desire enthusiastically.

**Compassion,** from compassio (sympathy), com—together + pati, to suffer…to feel pity (Compati), sorrow for the sufferings or trouble of another or others, with the urge to help, pity, deep sympathy.

These Webster's definitions provide a point of departure, but for me the departure eventually gets really really big. I have been amazed at how often, as you track down the root meaning of a word, there is an humbling shock at the realization that the original meaning of the word is consistent with the highest modern understandings of the word, both scientifically and philosophically. Stunning examples of this might be anu, a 7,000 year old Sanskrit word for atom which has tiny, moving, charged particles whirling around it. And bedingen, the German root of thinking which means 'thinging'. Thoughts are things, meaning material. You may recall one of our favorites, Intelligere, the Latin root for intelligence, and it means to see between the threads finely woven. In other words, sensitivity. The implication is sensitivity to the subtle actuality of 'what is.' But the dictionary definitions for love and compassion seem to me to be only a starting point at best.

Scholars say the Greeks had twenty-eight words for love, each one expressing a different dimension of it. The greatest of these as I understand it, the kind of love that is far beyond any of Webster's definitions, and the kind that will probably enhance the quality of our lives the most, was called Caritas. Interestingly, Webster doesn't even try for a definition of Caritas, even though it is often used by English writers. This bears out the hypothesis that I am working from which holds that English is a very young, immature language, and as it matures the most important additions and deepening of the language will relate to qualities of mind and consciousness (including feeling). Meanwhile English is borrowing the words it needs from other more mature languages like Greek, Sanskrit, German, French, Spanish, Hebrew, Aramaic, Chinese etc.

## COMPASSION, SIMPLE AND PRACTICAL

*"The true state of affairs in the material world is wholeness. If we are fragmented, we must blame it on ourselves." David Bohm*
*"A mind once stretched by a great idea or new understanding will never fully return to its original dimensions." William James*
*"Just to be is a blessing. Just to live is holy." Rabbi Abraham Herschel*

Can we begin with our best attempt to understand compassion? Surely, its essence is the understanding and reduction of suffering. The result of a lifetime of study of the most interesting and actualized people I can find is that the ones who had the greatest quality of aliveness are those who really had and lived by the principle of compassion. If that is true, then getting compassion, however that is done, has got to be the wisest quality that a human being can acquire. Some say that artists are born, not made. But I have a problem with that notion because it implies the denial of the possibility of learning and transformational change. Of course, some people are miraculously gifted from the beginning, and that includes some artists of living (which is surely the ultimate art form). Some people seem to be born with an intuitive 'handle' on compassion and love. But the rest of us can make all the difference in our lives and the lives of others by focusing our powers of learning on this great opportunity, this ocean of possibility.

It follows then, that one of the most practical things we can devote our attention to is the principle of compassion. In fact, my belief is that if one invests enough Profound Attention in compassion, compassion will spontaneously combust in that attender's heart and brain. How's that for getting down to the short strokes? Since that is so much easier said than done, perhaps we can explore this vast territory, and see where we wind up (by getting lost we may find a great treasure).

The first problem is that many of us think that compassion is inconsistent with mental toughness and the achievement of one's practical goals. Nothing could be further from the truth. Compassion has nothing to do with soft headedness, or being a doormat or martyring oneself for the intended benefit of others. It has nothing to do with being a victim. Many of the greatest martial arts masters are known for their compassion. According to legend, Gautama Buddha was the martial arts champion of India when he was young.

Compassion has everything to do with understanding the human condition and the horrible predicaments we all get ourselves into. It has everything to do with creating an environment which allows people to work happily with a feeling that they are appreciated and understood and will not be taken unfair advantage of. As Deming has so brilliantly taught, this should be the first order of business of truly great business leaders; because this kind of an environment tends to produce a stronger, more durable, more resourceful, more creative organization. It is fun to work in such an environment and in business, the more fun we are having, in general, the more productive we are. If you look at the essence of the Bohmian Dialogue concept, it is compassion...really understanding the other, supporting the unfoldment of their intelligence and reaping the rewards. I'm sure Edward's Deming, Jean Monet, Sir John Templeton, Mary Wells, Margaret Wheatley and many other business geniuses would agree that true compassion is the ultimate profit system, especially if maximum quality of life (and true scientific responsibility) is an ultimate goal, an ultimate form of wealth.

*"...Right relationship means right relationship with the elements, the land, the sacred directions...The seed of pure mind is within all people. It is always there. It is not made impure. Our actions may be impure and set up a stream of reactions, but always we can come again to the seed of pure mind and right relationship...it is time now for people to choose. The first step is to see the power of your own consciousness...The common kernel is care for all beings, good relationship, cycles of reciprocity, generosity, giving of oneself, being an empty bowl so you can know what is." Dhyani Ywahoo*

Since compassion is understanding, it is obviously intelligent. It is not compassionate to become the victim of a scam. Compassionate understanding sharpens the mind and increases the ability to perceive what is actually going on. Therefore, the ability to avoid being taken in by faked suffering is improved. Compassion looks for the innocence that usually exists in the heart of the wrongdoer; but like the proverb, 'Trust in God while tying the camel.' Compassion is careful. Compassion is not sentimental. Perhaps the most important thing to see is that compassion is not suffering along with the sufferer. It is not sympathizing. I realize this material sounds way too preachy but somehow the subject must be addressed. It is difficult and painful for me to even attempt this, but it seems the right thing to try rather than shrink from the effort because of fear of disapproval from those who think it is untidy and awkward. The soul of The Process is compassion, or at least the attempt to understand, live by and help others learn it. There is nothing more practical nor important than the issues of love and relationship. I wonder what a better way of approaching it might be?

It seems to me that compassion emerges in direct relationship to the individual's ability to reduce or possibly end his or her own suffering. Doesn't that make sense? Who is the person who is most able to assist another in ending suffering? One who is caught up in his own suffering or one who has learned how to reduce and sometimes, for substantial periods of time, actually end personal suffering? Who is going to make the best tennis teacher? One who is expert at tennis or one who does not know how to play? So the first thing about compassion, it seems to me, is to understand what suffering is, and then how to personally end or at least reduce it. Then one is in position and highly motivated to assist others in getting the hang of reducing suffering. I realize that it is outrageously bold to assume that compassion can be understood even relatively; but to my mind the risk is worth even the chance that we can grow in this way. I do not claim to thoroughly understand it; but I am deeply interested to learn. And I am sure I have tasted it. Is it too much to hope that we can be learning about this together?

The essence of The Process is enhancement of our capacity to make contact with the actual. Such contact breeds wisdom. A primary manifestation of wisdom is real relationship, unfoldment of the most practical life and performance enhancers there are—love and compassion.

Compassionate understanding and sympathizing are, to me, two very different things. I think confusing the two is one of the most common mistakes we all make. Sympathizing is, I believe, extremely disempowering and ineffective. Essentially, the helper is pulled down toward the usually dysfunctional condition of the sufferer. On the other hand, understanding empowers the sufferer and shows him or her the steps that must be taken in order to reduce the suffering and restore the sufferer's peace of mind, functionality and, yes, humanity. It is true that the human condition includes suffering, but it is also true that extended suffering is dehumanizing as it drains the individual of life force, intelligence, energy, and eventually can destroy the mind. If everyone understood that compassion produces warmth and exhilaration on the part of the 'listener', can you imagine how ubiquitous compassion would be?

*"Joy is prayer—Joy is strength—Joy is love—Joy is a net of love by which you can catch souls. She gives the most who gives joy." Mother Teresa*

A more accurate translation from the Sanskrit of Buddha's first noble truth, 'Life is suffering', is 'There is no lasting satisfaction'. From a Buddhist point of view the flaw in the notion that life is suffering should be immediately obvious. The ending of suffering is one of the fundamental tenets of Buddhist teaching. If the first translation were true, then carrying it to its logical conclusion would mean putting an end to life. Strange how reluctant we are to question translations of ancient 'sacred texts' even though we know the translators were often mistaken, and sometimes paid to put a spin on the teachings which served the special interests of management.

## LOVE

Love of something is the essence of a sense of mission. Love includes but is not limited to the properties of a field. I want to build my house in the Field of Love and be surrounded, enfolded and unfolded by it. I know if I am to deepen my relationship with love I must forgive myself for having so little of it. I must be willing to ask the hard questions…any questions about love. I must not pretend to know the answers, but rather listen carefully to see what love…if love will teach me now. Some of the questions coming to me are:

Is love intelligent? Is love wise? Is love sensual, sexual? I have been dumbfounded and astonished by the feminine. Does love accommodate this indescribable attraction and cosmic conflict that permeates man/woman relationships? And while I am at it, what about love and homosexuality? Is love not also there? Does war play any role in the Great Dance of Love?

And what about speaking of love at all? Is that dangerous? Love may be one of the most used words in any language. Yet does using it, saying it, drive the real thing away—so lull the talker into sleep that love slips away while we are entertaining ourselves talking about it?

But do I presume to know anything at all about love? Is it just another four-letter word? Yet, in the end, I am called to it like a moth to the flame, like an arrow to the heart of the target.

## RAGS

*"We called him 'Rags.'" He was just a cur,*
*But twice, on the Western Line,*
*That little bunch of faithful fur*
*Had offered his life for mine.*

*And all that he got was bones and bread*
*Or the leavings of soldier grub*
*And he'd give his heart for a pat on the head*
*Or a friendly tickle and rub.*

*But we mustered out, some to beer and gruel,*
*Some to sherry and shad,*
*And I went back to Sawbones School*
*Where I was still an undergrad.*

*One day they took us budding M.D.s*

*To one of those institutes*
*Where they demonstrate every new disease*
*By means of bisected brutes.*

*They had one animal tacked and tied*
*And slit like a full dressed fish,*
*With his vitals pumping away inside*
*As pleasant as one might wish.*

*I stopped to look like all the rest, of course,*
*And the beast's eyes leveled mine:*
*His short tail thumped with a feeble force*
*And he uttered a tender whine.*

*It was Rags, yes, Rags! who was martyred there,*
*Who was quartered and crucified,*
*And he whined that whine which is doggish prayer*
*And he licked my hand and died.*
*And if there's no heaven for love like that,*
*For such four-legged fealty-well!*
*If I have my choice, I tell you flat,*
*I'll take my chance in hell."*
*Edmund Vance Cooke*

There is this agonizing pressure to fit the Universe into the small, conditioned, linear, goal oriented (3D) consciousness of most human beings most of the time. We want a nice logical, step by step plan for becoming…some ideal ideal of who we want to be. This is the path of infinite suffering. As Cher said in Moonstruck, "snap out of it". The Universe, life and death, and this world are operating according to laws, levels of order which are not linear (or linearity is a tiny, probably short sighted, relatively illusional component). The Natural Order does not seem to be logical (although I believe it is coherent) and is mostly beyond the normal consciousness of most humans. To paraphrase Einstein, the most incomprehensible thing about the universe is that it is comprehensible.

Realizing this and adjusting one's life so that it harmonizes (merges) with this Great Process is the ending of suffering and the beginning of real mindfulness, meaningfulness, truth, beauty, love—MindFitness. It also implies transcending the limitations of 'normal' conditioned consciousness.

*"Common sense is that set of prejudices we acquire before the age of 18." Einstein.*

Taking Dagne to the train this morning, we saw the river and the mountains on the other side covered with snow. The icebreaker had cleared a path in the river. Found myself saying I love winter, while she said she longs for spring (She is at least mildly affected by seasonal affective disorder- SAD). She rails against the bitter cold, the loss of her beloved color, short days and long nights, the apparent death of all of her plants, the bareness of the trees, and I understand her feelings.

But as for me, I have always felt a kind of excitement in the cold and the snow...perhaps it is the promise of spring soon. But there is more. The emptiness and 'death' of winter is beautiful to me, and seems to open my heart with gladness. Especially a morning like this with a foot or more of fresh snow on the ground and the crisp, blue sky above and everything sparkling...that curious quality of the air as though it is stuffed with molecules of oxygen. Somehow the pain and discomfort of winter seems like a hard workout...pain at first, then a strange high which leads often to a nice, fat, juicy meditation.

Beauty of the long icicles and fantastic shapes in the snow. Our tables and planters on the deck provide a perfect measure of the depth of the snowfall. Now, at February 18 1996, there is a virtual rumbling under the ground and in the trees. We are only several inches away from an all time snowfall record (we broke it by six inches). La Nina sings. Spring will be explosive this year. I must get my heart in shape because the eruption of life this spring will demand much from me. By the Grace of God, I will be ready!

There is eternity in the cold of winter. I love to look up on the cold clear nights and feel the Presence, even the distant Promise of the Presence. There is strength in the cold...a whisper, a shout calling the soul to take heart...suck it up and take joy in sucking it up. We are on our way and it is a good Way.

We are free in the midst of this beautiful, snowy winter even if it is only relatively free. Our failures and successes are illusion, and falling away in the face of this astonishing Present. All that matters is doing the Work with all your heart. Let go...in this crisp air...let go the sorrow, the attachments, the ambitions, the envy, the fear, the anger, the comparisons. What right have they to cloud your mind and drag you down? There is only truth and beauty and love and unfolding. What a privilege to be in it...invisible yet watching. What happened? Where did I go? I am weeping. Swept away by happiness. How does that happen? Did I really let go for a moment? Seeing the death in life and the life in death seems to open the heart. The last line from the Cliff Robertson movie Charlie, was 'True love is letting go.' That line is a continuing epiphany for me.

The essence of learning love is, surely, that I have to be a light to myself...NOW! And speaking of now, is there a timing to meditation, or 'sitting' as some would call it? Here again it is important to listen to the heart. Sometimes, a feeling that 'this could be a good time' may come over you...do it then...make space as best you can to do it when you feel like it, whenever possible; and if the meditation doesn't go the way you want, don't be discouraged. And if you do get discouraged sometimes, then just look at that fear and discouragement. Quietly watch it. It will change and that is just as much a part of The Process as when things go well.

How does the capacity to attend affect our lives, our ability to love...the realities, frailties that are contaminating our moment to moment humanity? How does attention affect self-centeredness, envy, greed, fear of not having enough, fear of not being able to be truly creative, fear of death, fear of growing old, anger, lack of recognition, fear of not being able to really help others, fear of being wrong about self-knowledge technology and its relationship to humanity and quality of consciousness, fear (and anger) for all the suffering of others and their madness, fear that we are all doomed and God doesn't care...in fact doesn't even exist? And for some of my esteemed colleagues, fear that possibly God does exist?

## MAXMUM POWER...SAFELY

*"The conclusion is always the same: love is the most powerful and still the most unknown energy of the world." Pierre Teilhard de Chardin*

*"From a hidden place unite with your enemies from the inside, fill the inner void that makes them swell outwardly and fall out of rhythm; instead of progressing, step by step, they stop and start harshly, out of time with you. Bring yourself back into rhythm within. Find the moment that mates with theirs—like two lovers creating life from the dust. Do this work in secrete, so they don't know. This kind of love creates, it doesn't emote." Neil Douglas Klotz (From the Aramaic of Jesus' words "Love your Enemies...")*

Is this Profound Attention Principle as real, as immense as it appears? Does it have the healing, the transformative power that it seems to have, or is this great insight just another cruel illusion? If it is The Great Tool then by what means do we employ it, use it to solve problems, and dissolve those barriers to living fully?

Is there an art form emerging (perhaps long existent) which focuses all of it's energy on the 'leap' of mind that lies dormant within us? Is there a form of direct assistance like a kind of play, superplay (The Greeks called this kind of play 'Leyla') that coaxes open the door...that shows a way for us to blast our consciousness into a much more true, vital, fun, life-filled dimension?

As Krishnamurti says, *'The problem is to make the mind go very, very deeply into itself.'* Therefore, the highest value must be meditation; how can there be anything more important than that? Is there a better way to remove the barriers to love? 'Letting go' is like bait inviting love to bite.

We search for the keys to healthy change. Surely, nothing is more important than love. But love is such an abused, misused word. Yet in spite of all the illusion obscuring it, It Is. A key to allowing and inviting love to 'take over' is the ending (or reduction) of inappropriate thinking. Certainly thinking can produce…build…develop…solve problems… materialize dreams. But there is a kind of thinking which seems, in the main, to be devastating…creating powerful, often comparative images which lead to energy dissipation, fear, and loss of contact with one's 'heart.' This psychological image making is so subtle, so strong, it appears to be impossible to change. But is it impossible? Or, put another way, is freeing oneself from this kind of thinking as much as one can the only game in town? The most valuable thing to do with one's precious life? Because the quality of our relationships and living according to our own personal highest values depends on it?

*"The system does not produce change. The will does not produce change. The truth produces change." Krishnamurti*

Although words are tricky, dangerous, we must somehow learn to use them correctly. We learn by doing…so let's look again at some of the dynamics that we have already discussed. Heuristic learning demands that we do our best to look as though we are looking for the first time. Let's see what we can do: We are remembering that no matter how compelling these models are, no matter how they may seem to be philosophically harmonic with advanced psychological and learning theories, it is wise and responsible to call them hypotheses…perhaps, working hypotheses.

336	MindFitness Training

Coherent and creative thought is not a problem. In fact, we are using it to work together now. But dehumanizing, mechanical, incoherent, irrational thought is, perhaps, the whole problem. What can we do to change it? 'Watching,' attention to mechanical, incoherent thought changes it. Full stop. Watching thought is far different than 'grooving' on it.

Beyond that, this kind of awareness (according to the laws of physics) must produce a change in the brain itself at the subatomic, atomic, molecular and cellular level. This kind of awareness produces a condition in which the unnecessary begins to drop away, leaving the essence. Contact with the essential sparks a sense of mission. Dropping or 'losing' the unnecessary releases energy which then fuels the sense of mission.

As the mind (including the 'heart')…always remembering that profound attention implies the 'heart' is also involved…as this mind attends to this psychologically maladaptive, 'mechanical thought' this seemingly endless construct of conditioned images, the rigidity of these self-defining, conditioned images begins to break down.

These images operate like a kind of 'personality mold' into which energy is poured. It 'solidifies' and the person(ality) is now 'stuck'…locked into a second hand and mechanical manifestation which is born of conditioning and illusion. As quality observation burns away at this 'mold,' the locked up 'solidified' energy 'melts' and begins to be formed by something else. This 'something else' can be said to be much closer to the true, unique, individual being. Chaos theorists might say we have allowed the actual 'Strange Attractor' to emerge. For those comfortable with Jungian, archetypal language, the 'Soul' begins to emerge. Such a person is 'actualizing,' if we use Maslow's terminology.

Continuing with the Chaos and Turbulence Theory model provides another way to use creative thought to break through the limiting structure of mechanical thought. To wit, as the awareness of the psychological construct…as the quality of attention to thinking function itself is improved….the rigid mental patterns (conditioned constructs) break up into essence (energy) and the underlying 'strange attractor' emerges from the chaos. This attractor behaves somewhat like a carnivore at the top of the food chain, 'eating' or using the energy released by the dissolving, illusion—producing psychological constructs (which are, after all material). So this energy is available for the production of something (someone) new, rather than sustaining that which is relatively dysfunctional, what we might term the 'second hand person'. The archetypal language uses the term 'reborn'. And like all attractors in chaos theory, each attractor is one of a kind, truly unique; the real person (like a snowflake) is definitely different from all the rest. In the same way that a snowflake is always a six-pointed star, so this human being is also like all the rest.

Curiously, as human beings progress up Maslow's hierarchy of needs they become evermore aware of the unity of all things, and usually are quite good and somewhat aggressive at expressing this concept. They (we) also become more capable of expressing and manifesting our uniqueness.

## MASLOW'S HIERARCHY OF NEEDS...PYRAMID

1. **Physiological. Hunger, thirst, elimination, warmth, fatigue, pain avoidance, sexual release.**
2. **Safety. Protection from environment, housing, clothing, crime security.**
3. **Love and belongingness. Intimate relationships, social groups, friends.**
4. **Esteem. Achievement, competence, approval, recognition, prestige, status.**
5. **Self-Actualization. Fulfillment of unique potentials.**

Now, how does this manifest when it really happens? It seems that we can see at least two products of this process fairly clearly:

1. Such a mind begins to make lists and has the energy to accomplish a relatively large part of what is on these lists. This is a fairly obvious, relatively mechanical manifestation. Less obvious is the enhanced sense of mission implied. The implication is that those lists and the sense of mission are of a much better quality than they would be if put together

by a mind stuck in the relatively narrow vision afforded by common, often dysfunctional, 'mechanical-processing' mode of thinking. Interestingly, one of the goals of The Process is to use 'mechanical-processing' thought only when necessary.

2. Much more difficult to express is the notion that a mind working in this way activates or 'allows' an unfolding of phenomena which is far more powerful than the list making function. This phenomena can be said to be the usually unseen (yet often felt) potential within any situation. This phenomena is characteristically transformative in nature and is the 'goal' that lies at the root of creativity...or perhaps better put, the creative hunger in most, if not all of us. My own experience is that the feeling accompanying this kind of attentive thinking is not always comfortable. In fact, it really is work...The Work. Sometimes, of course, it feels indescribably wonderful, but we don't need to do much more than acknowledge that because it takes care of itself and is not a problem. Most of the time this attention is arduous yet rewarding. The old adage that genius is 5 % inspiration and 95% perspiration seems applicable here.

*"Let the beauty of what you love be what you do." Rumi*

We are becoming more aware of awareness and more attentive to attention while striving to maintain our sense of humor. Krishnamurti, the teacher who has provided the most inspiring insight into attention for me, describes a car trip during which he and several articulate teachers were discussing the power and beauty of the attention/awareness principle with such passion and absorption that they did not notice that the driver had run over a goat.

The 'heart' must open up. Stories, songs, poetry and many other forms of art can open (at least a little bit) the heart. Perhaps it is better put to say almost anything done well enough becomes true art, and the measure of it is how much does it open the heart...how healthy is it for the soul? See what an important role La Via Negativa plays here? We must eliminate the unnecessary. True Love is…letting go.

*"Can this movement ever stop—the inner creating the outer environment psychologically, and the outer, the law, the institutions, the organizations, trying to shape man, the brain, to act in a certain way, and the brain, the inner, the psyche, then changing, circumventing the outer? This movement has been going on as long as man has been on this earth, crudely, superficially, sometimes brilliantly—it is always the inner overcoming the outer, like the sea with its tides going out and coming in. One should really ask whether this movement can ever stop—action and reaction, hatred and more hatred, violence and more violence. It has an end when there is only watching, without motive, without response, without direction. Direction comes into being when there is accumulation. But watching in which there is attention, awareness, and a great sense of compassion, has its own intelligence. This watching and intelligence act. And that action is not the ebb and flow. But this requires great alertness, to see things without the word, without name, without any reaction; in that watching there is a great vitality, passion." Krishnamurti to Himself.*

## SURVIVAL OF THE 'FITEST'?

*"The mechanical model of the universe makes nature a means to an end. It implies that nature is there for us to get whatever we want out of it. I say this model is not adequate. A part has no meaning except in terms of the whole. The idea of treating everything as only parts may work in the short run, but it doesn't work when you follow it through."* **David Bohm**

Stephen J.Gould, the zoologist, has implied that evolution is a valid theory, but survival of the fittest is only partially true. Recent studies of apes indicate that the dominant members are those who cooperate the most in a process which results in the building of a consensus as to who is most fit to run the show. There is considerable evidence that many of the fittest have not survived. Either some other dynamic or force contributes to evolution in the main—or you can call it 'luck'. This has extraordinary implications for the concept that competition is all-important.

Just as some of the 'fittest' do survive, so some of the most competitive do dominate. But many business leaders feel that competitiveness is over-rated as a principle that causes the long term healthy success of a business, of a family and of a people. Of course part of the problem is that competition is too general a term, and does not adequately communicate all of the virtues and vices that are attached to that concept in most of our minds. It is questionable as to whether competition is anywhere near as effective as cooperation for bringing the greatest true benefits to the greatest numbers of people, or creative excellence, or improved quality of life. Competition as it is normally defined probably does not guarantee compassion, nor wisdom, nor those things that most of us believe are good for ourselves and humanity.

We are not denying competition as a necessary part of what is, especially considering the states of consciousness most of us find ourselves in most of the time. We are saying that overrating it blinds us to even greater and much more productive possibilities. Competition unchecked doesn't do much for family values. We do think that there are honorable, healthy forms of competition, but we want to make a case for careful discrimination and balance. We, and a growing number of at least relatively enlightened business leaders would like to suggest that some of the holy fervor that our culture attaches to competition needs aggressive challenging. It is delightfully ironic, isn't it? Powerful forms of unity, 'oneness awareness' and cooperativeness are successfully competing with the largely self-centered, inappropriate worship of competition as the best way for humankind to flourish.

Biophysicist Rupert Sheldrake's theory of formative causation and morphogenetic fields may have much more to do with those changes that have been hitherto attributed to Darwinian evolution. By the same token this type of field theory may be much closer to the truth about what's shaping our culture than is the theory of competition. Somehow there seems to me to be a relationship between this model and Gould's notion that survival of the fittest does not always apply. This kind of thinking seems to me to be much more compatible with multidimensional string theory, chaos and turbulence theory, hidden variables theory and correspondence theory.

You may be asking how this relates to The Process. And the best that I can do is suggest that the essence of the Process is arriving at your true highest values. We want to challenge you to ask the most important questions you can, even if asking feels uncomfortable and the answer is difficult to reach. If you believe that beating the hell out of the other guy (or gal), having the most toys when you die, being the top dog or the fattest cat, being the fastest rat in the rat race, is the most profitable thing for you, is going to give you the best quality of life, then go for it, you'll have loads of company. But in my opinion, you just don't get it yet. And that may lead to unnecessary suffering and wasted energy for you and your family. Of course, only you can determine what is true for you. I am merely suggesting that you should make sure that you answer these questions for yourself and make sure you are not living at least a relatively second hand and unnecessarily limited life because you have been conditioned to believe in a model which is not in the best interests of those you love (including yourself).

## Is Consuming the World What We Want…Really?

If *"The field is the soul governing agency of the particles"* and if what we think and feel is a kind of field, then what we think and feel is what is creating our society, our culture, our world….whether it is heaven or hell. And which is it? We have allowed….no let us take responsibility….we have created media which constantly bombards us….let's be kind, informs us of the horrors in the world. And that has its value, but it is also true that stimulating fear and appealing to the lowest and dumbest instincts in humanity creates anxiety disorders, leads to over—competition, and contributes to unthinking, rampant consumption...an unnecessary and self-destructive orgy that scientists tell us is eating up the earth.

It is a simple, extremely effective marketing principle: the more afraid and insecure we feel, the more we will try to acquire to quench that insecurity. But does having more really prevent insecurity? Is it possible to consume less while living better and actually feeling more secure? Look for the Voluntary Simplicity Movement to explode across the US and the world as the realization sinks in that for most of us consuming less and living simply is a necessary step to achieving the actual riches of life we are so hungry for.

As earth can be said to be a hell and getting worse, so there are places and people who are experiencing a kind of heaven on earth...at least some of the time. This breeds contentment, peace, the sense that one has enough, the desire to take more leisure time to enjoy the world, to develop one's mind, to reach out to help others, to work to reduce environmental damage, to stretch what one has to the limit which means be more efficient...waste nothing. Note the majority of the media which depends on advertising dollars (and in general is motivated to stimulate over consumption) considers the enormous good news that also exists in this world to be worthy of only token airtime. That is going to be difficult to change because the growing Voluntary Simplicity Segment of the population probably uses more economically efficient strategies than TV commercials for arriving at purchase decisions. However, since this group is also an important part of the Actualizer segment of the VALS survey, there is at least some influence which can be exercised, because Actualizers are trendsetters and because there is a vital role for quality, responsible advertising to play in a more human and nature friendly world.

Science is defined as systematic knowledge of the physical or material world. Note, however, that David Bohm and other physicists have virtually proven that there is no separation between mind, meaning and matter. Science is nothing unless it is the pursuit of the truth. This means that a science imbued with wisdom, a true science, will understand when to say no, and take responsibility for making sure the public understands, so the politicians will manage government accordingly. Science has given us the means to destroy all life on earth. Just because it can be done, does not mean it should be done. Are we so guilt ridden, so afraid that love has abandoned us, that we must martyr ourselves as a species in an orgy of illusional atonement? Atonement for mistakes or 'sins' which were a necessary part of The Work the Creative Source had to do to get this far?

When we refuse to go through one door, it means we will go through another. Because go we must. The physicist Freeman Dyson thinks our destiny may be to populate the galaxy. This requires a science that knows what not to do. For example, a wisdom oriented (rather than short term profit oriented) science can educate the public as to the true costs of over consumption, environmental destruction, and unnecessary military action. That relatively small but powerful part of the scientific establishment that is honest can help us see what is possible, what is probable, and what is a waste of time and resources, thus liberating that time and those resources for more productive use.

What breeds that kind of wisdom? Caritas? Ahh, 'La Via Negativa' again. By elimination of the untrue, the truth emerges. OUR ABILITY TO SAY NO MAY ALLOW SOME OF THE GREATEST YESES OF ALL TIME TO UNFOLD!

## FEAR

So then we have to look closely at fear because it is guiding our thinking, our science, our technology to a grave degree...an extremely dangerous degree. And fear destroys love. And love destroys fear. Are beings governed by fear fit to populate the galaxy?

Fear is a form of thinking. Love can imbue thought (from our mouths to God's ears), but love as a principle reaches far beyond thought and thinking. Since thought already is a material process, the more energy that is pumped into it, the more it 'materializes'. This computer, this book, this beautiful airplane I am flying in as I write are literally thick thought. As we think, so we are. Descartes was a catalytic thinker, triggering science's penchant for the mechanical view of the Universe. He said, "I think therefore I am". Once he walked into a bar. The bartender said, "what will it be?…a glass of whiskey?" Descartes answered, "I think not", and disappeared.

Of course I respect the contribution of Descartes and Nietzsche, but scientists and esteemed philosophers are just as funny as everyone else, aren't they? We tend to take ourselves much too seriously, don't you think? Now even the revered scientific saint Stephen Hawking seems to believe that with the development of String Theory (the theory of everything) we are almost at the end of the quest to understand the physical universe. Meanwhile a number of physicists studying Bohmian mechanics believe Bohm's Hidden Variables theory will eventually prove that even String Theory and its eleven dimensions is only explaining the outer layers of the onion of creation.

So if we are putting more and more energy into fear, it must materialize. Although fear may have a place, it seems clear that we must materialize much more than fear thoughts—or put the other way around—there are certain deep fears in the psyche of the race that we had better not materialize if we really want to improve the situation here on this earth…much less extend ourselves into the galaxy. Conversely there are thoughts deep in our hearts, indescribably sublime, which can also materialize. But will we? As we let this question go deep into both inner space and outer space at the same time, what will the answer be? The first Duty of Love is listening. Talk about suspense thrillers!

*"Gravitation cannot be held responsible for people falling in love."*
*Einstein*

# SEXUALITY

is incredibly, explosively, sublimely, ecstatically, enlightening, deadly dangerous, destructive, transforming, creative, immense…the list may go on until we run out of words and continue uninterrupted, nonverbally into infinity, and maybe beyond. So sexuality is important; and any attempt to bury it, sublimate it, or avoid dealing with it will result in suffering, and if the suffering is ignored, may lead to catastrophe. So how to meet this life-shaping phenomenon head on? To me sexuality moves so quickly from the relatively superficial to the mystical that writing about it carries a sense of crisis…a sense of danger and opportunity. Discussing details about my own sexuality is tasteless, counterproductive, and probably dishonest since I am anything but objective, and incredibly emotional about it. However, if The Process hopes to be real and truly useful we must do the best job with this aspect of life that we can. Of course those you who are happily ensconced in celibacy may want to skip this section.

To begin with, we all are dealing with the intense power of our sexuality whether we are aware of it or not. Probably the less aware of it we are the more dangerous is our situation and the greater our suffering. Now there may be some for whom sexuality is simply not a problem. In my view such individuals are far more actualized in this area than I and, quite frankly I cannot, at least in normal consciousness, comprehend what that must be like. Or can I? Remember, one of the properties of 4DC is that the previously impossible (like ending substance abuse, smoking etc.) can suddenly become strangely easy.

Let's see, what makes of sexuality a problem? Hmmm, could it be that when I am one with my sexuality (profoundly aware of it and attentive in the present, in real time) it is a blessing, and when I think about it becomes pleasure or pain…at times a curse? Could it be that when I attend to the pleasure and/or the pain, I find my way back to a kind of union with it, a wholeness, an integration? We don't know do we? We are finding out together.

A blessing or a curse! Come to think of it, there have been times when sexuality was no problem at all, in fact, it seemed to be resolving problems at very deep levels. And then there are times when it has seemed to be the greatest of problems. So, what can we learn about moving from the Great Problem to No Problem, that can be articulated here? Shall we start at the gross, physical level?

Sexuality is physical and sensual, and thinking about it can make it more so. Most of us most of the time want to look more appealing than we actually are, or think we actually are. Most of us want to look better than we do when we are young, and that problem gets worse as we age. At 90 George Burns said that the reason he showed up at social functions with a beautiful woman on each arm is 'because it is hipper than canes.' So what can help? We must take the steps that are possible, the next ones. We are concerned with being real, practical, working at the level where people actually live.

The resolution of the problem of looks for most of us is obvious, isn't it? We must do the best we can with what we have. I have known many men and women who had well balanced, even beautiful physical features, yet were somehow unattractive and unhappy. On the other hand we all know people who lack many of those features we consider sexy, and yet they radiate sexuality. Could it be that they have come to love their sexuality, and that energy is reaching us? Pheromones are part of a person's field or 'aura'.

So at the physical level it is relatively simple, isn't it? We focus our mind on doing the best we can with what we have. Well, this ties in with all the other Process principles, doesn't it? The strategies we have already talked about such as exercise, 'a clean machine', right thinking etc., all lead to taking concrete steps to make the most of what we have, which is surely the only real solution to the looks part of the sexuality problem.

Sensitivity and physical conditioning are essential to healthy sensuality. Sensitivity is intelligence (including emotional intelligence) and a critical component of healthy sexuality. So, while working on strategies to enhance sensitivity and intelligence, we were being naturally and healthily sexual without directly trying to be. I guess that's serendipity. Does that mean we are finished with this problem of sexuality? I think not. We have only been dealing with gross, relatively obvious sexual considerations. And we could talk on indefinitely about the benefits and liabilities of the physical and superficially psychological aspects of most people's sexuality. However, I think there is a much more important dynamic that emerges for many who delve deeply into the way The Process unfolds in the crucible of a life lived as fully as possible.

Most of us are struggling with our sexuality our whole life. And that gives rise to another dimension. Sexuality is always changing. We are passing through stages. Making peace with and enriching whatever stage we are in is a pathway to true sexual liberation. Most of us probably feel that we did not do such a hot job of one or more of the sequential stages of sexuality that we have lived through. Watch this carefully!! The memory of that can be a barrier to the rich unfoldment of the current stage we are in.

There is a phenomenon that is well-known in peak performance training. From sports we have the example of the skier who crashes and then (with the intention of figuring out what went wrong) goes over and over the events leading up to the accident including reliving the accident itself. This is usually if not always a mistake. It is called rehearsing failure. So, since the Process is about transforming ourselves from where we are now and working with what we have, it is probably counter productive to go over and over the sexual mistakes and disappointments we have lived through. A much better use of that energy is to attend to the unfoldment of our present life...the opportunity we have for a beautiful, natural sexual unfoldment at this time, working with what we have now. Besides, doing it that way can probably go a long way toward 'healing' the past 'mistakes.'

For me, sexuality transcends reproductive function, especially since many experts believe world population growth has been too fast. Of course, that idea is controversial, but regardless of whether or not the world is over-populated, there is an underlying current to sexuality, a deeper stream, a much more spiritual aspect than just having children per se. Make no mistake, I am not putting down having children as a spiritual path in its own right. In fact, I believe having children is a sacred privilege, and is often the salvation of those who can do it with enough love.

Some say that there is a relationship between those who consider sexuality to be immense and sacred, and a natural reduction of average births per couple. Presumably this is because such couples are also concerned about their ability to properly raise more than a few children. This kind of thinking is fairly recent. In fact, when I was born (the oldest of nine) having lots of children was considered highly responsible and great work if you could do it. Also, the population explosion was not generally taken seriously until about 1960. So, in the end, if we are to find a way to naturally bring about the healthiest possible rate of growth in the population, it will probably come from this sense of sexuality becoming more significant, not less. Although the era of sex without responsibility is still very much with us, I believe those qualities of (4DC) consciousness that provide greatest happiness, freedom, and personal growth are also infinitely more responsible.

But can we go beyond sexuality as a reproductive function? Can we press deeper into the nature of sexuality as a metaphysical path to personal actualization? Male and female do appear to be opposites, while each reflects the maleness or femaleness of the other; and there is conflict at many levels…yin and yang. Can we go deeper? Is there a mystical, a spiritual aspect of sexuality? Now, as a man, I am keenly aware that from a purely physical point of view sexuality stands alone, and one can finish consideration of the subject right there. After all, for most men, and I assume most women, sex is usually pleasurable, and sometimes euphoric, maybe even ecstatic.

Let us suppose that the physical, emotional and responsibility aspects of our sexuality are more or less in order. What then, where do we go from there? This question is very interesting although formidable. It seems to

me that a somewhat miraculous phenomenon can potentially take place. It is probably what is really meant by being in love, rather than in lust. Not that robust lustfulness is wrong. On the contrary, it is likely to be there when real love is present. When asked how he accounted for his long and apparently wonderful marriage, Paul Newman answered, "Love, Lust, and Respect." And it would be incredibly dumb and inhuman to judge those who take pleasure in recreational sex. But is there something beyond all that? What is this real love notion?

I realize it is risky to talk like this, but my own sense of responsibility compels me. We have already discussed different ways of dealing with the 'soul' issue. Those that find the following concept difficult might find it more comfortable to think about it in terms of mythology, especially since Joseph Campbell, the mythology scholar, was one of the rare writers who dealt with the notion of Romantic Love as Super School. But for me, this whole idea is about as mythical as the sun on a crystal clear day over Santa Monica beach at 2 PM in the afternoon on July 7th. In other words, for me, as it was for Tielhard de Chardin, there is an astonishingly achievable and emotionally intelligent potential in sexuality. A potential for learning to love in a whole new dimension…a dimension that explodes the rich humanity latent in each of us…a potential that transcends the mythological and presents itself as the embodiment of inspiration, as the actual, the touchable truth in the infinite moment, now.

*"… The mutual attraction of the sexes is so fundamental that any explanation of the world (biological, philosophical or religious) that does not succeed in finding it a structurally essential place in its system is virtually condemned."*

*"Sooner or later then, and in spite of all our credulity, the world will take this step—because the greater truth always prevails, and the greater good emerges in the end. The day will come when, after mastering the ether, the winds, the tides, gravity, we shall master the energies of love, for*

*God. And then, for the second time in the history of the world, man will have made fire his servant."*

*"Such a transformation, of course, cannot be effected instantaneously on the surface of the earth; time is essential. When you heat water, the whole volume does not turn into steam at once—the 'liquid phase' and the 'gaseous phase' are found together for some time, and this must necessarily be so. Nevertheless, that duality covers but one single developing event— the direction and 'dignity' of which are shared by the whole. Thus, at the present moment, physical union still retains its value and necessity for the human race; but its spiritual quality is now defined by the higher type of union to which it has served as the preliminary and which it now fosters. Within the noosphere, love is now undergoing a 'change of state' and it is in this new direction that mankind's collective entry into God is being organized." Pierre Teilhard de Chardin, On Love*

It is clear that some lovers are convinced that they have come to love the soul of the other person. I share the bias that this phenomenon happens sometimes and that when this 'soul love' exists sexuality becomes a way of learning that transcends fun, pleasure, and reproduction. The sense of responsibility can become infinite, and there is a new 'game' revealing a much higher order of relationship...simple, and elegantly expressed by the classic yin, yang symbol...true union. When these conditions exist the great war that seems to be going on between men and women at more superficial levels transmutes itself into an archetypal life and love-affirming relationship designed to assist the other in becoming all (s)he can be. I am not at all dismissing great love between homosexuals. I just feel my understanding of it is too superficial, and I should leave that discussion for those whose insight is deeper than mine. In fact, some of the most important people in my life have been, bisexual, homosexual or androgynous. There may be absolutely no difference, or a little difference or great differences. I just don't know.

The initial stages of one of these relatively rare mystical love affairs unfolds similar to any other. Each makes the other feel better and better about themselves. Each builds the image of the me of the other…and nurtures this self-image or ego to greater health and robustness than ever before. Then in the next stages, the self-images begin to get torn apart as the lovers realize they are interdependent. A sense of loss of freedom and fear that they can never love this much again sets in. So far, so good. We have the standard romantic war, and the relationship is headed for one of the many endings that make up the classic, often sad stories depicted in the movies and sometimes the headlines. Sounds simplistic, doesn't it? But think about it. Isn't that the way love affairs usually turn out? Or is it possible that we are bored when love turns out beautifully and healthily so we entertain ourselves with the 'lover-war' tragedies of literature and movies?

At this point I feel duty bound to report that when I showed this part of session nine to a friend who is also a marriage counselor he said that the whole concept sounds like ignorance and adolescent idealism to him. He said this notion disregards the fact that relationships carry with them all the baggage from past relationships that have been conditioned into them as a consequence of the socialization process. Further, that romantic relationships are eventually informed by cultural and familial patterns of communication and all the confusion that arises from them etc. In defense of myself I would suggest that I am trying to bring to light a deeper current of which most people seem to be unaware. It would qualify in my mind as a kind of Bohmian hidden variable. The notion I am trying to get across implies a more subtle and powerful unseen influence which in turn leads to the more known, more visible conventional dynamics upon which often ineffectual traditional marriage counseling is based. Of course conditioning plays an extremely important role, and I think the model that I am trying to express takes conditioning fully into account. Finally, I know this concept seems ridiculous to some, and maybe it is. Perhaps, if I were a better writer it would take on much more strength. But this is the best I can do at the moment.

In any case to continue, during the crisis when the soul-lovers are destroying each other's egos there is a chance for their romantic relationship to blossom in an almost miraculous way. The result is a kind of transformative rebirth that is sometimes depicted in movies, poetry and mystical literature. It appears to me that the brutal stress that must be endured when an ego (self-image) is challenged in this way provides an opportunity for some lovers to grow up and learn to love in a far more profound way. Under such pressures sexual love can become a kind of crucible where base metals are turned to gold, where self-centeredness and fear can give way to a deeper concern for others, renewed creativity and enthusiasm for life.

This process can be dangerous because there is an extremely unstable, liminal moment in the romantic wars when 'soul lovers' must choose between hanging on to their egos and outmoded values or learning that 'True Love is Letting Go.' This dangerous crisis offers the opportunity for the lovers to put the deepest spiritual, psychological, and physical welfare of the other first. It calls upon all the competence and selfless 'mother—like' giving that the 'Soul Friend' can muster.

This Process can result in the image of the me (as it used to be) being virtually annihilated. If the lovers survive this often-agonizing dark night of the soul there is the possibility of a huge leap and actualization of latent potentials for a more mature love, compassion, Caritas, or something else to emerge. This something else may include gratitude and a whole other dimension of love for the one who assisted in breaking through the self-limiting image of the 'me'. The one who receives their 'execution' of the 'image of the me' from such a beloved, at the right moment is fortunate. As previously stated, I realize that this concept will seem ridiculous to many; however, I have to risk it. Because, in my view, the potential in revolutionary thinking about romantic love may be infinite. And the nature of The Process is to tackle the real problems, the big issues openly, directly.

If we carry this Transpersonal Psychological notion a bit further, logic might speculate that timing is important. For example, if the 'lover wars' produce an 'image of the me' (ego) breakdown too soon, then it will reform again and may be handicapped by the psychological damage of the earlier struggle. If the lover waits too long, then the one whose conditioned, illusory self-image is being destroyed may lack the strength, the life force to survive, and irreparable psychological damage or even physical death may occur. Remember, in standard, conditioned 3$^{rd}$ dimensional consciousness it is difficult for anyone to differentiate between their ego and their living, breathing body. Tragically, the tendency is to think that if the ego dissolves, the body dies.

*"I think you need to become somebody before you can become nobody"*
*Ram Dass.*

Recently, my wife Dagne and I were discussing how the essence of the hot new psychological concept called 'emotional intelligence' is simply love. It suddenly occurred to me that within five years psychologists are going to be talking about mystical or spiritual or metaphysical intelligence in the same way they are talking about emotional intelligence now. (Since I wrote this I've already seen a science article making this exact same prediction). When I asked Dagne what would be a measure of metaphysical intelligence, she answered without hesitation; "Metaphysical Intelligence, that's when the Aliens land, certain housewives will run out drying their hands on their aprons and asking, 'Something to drink? Hot soup? And I'd love to see the pictures of your little ones back home…Oh, there it is, isn't it precious!!! What a big beautiful, darling yellowy green eye it has. Is it a boy or a girl? Are you a boy or a girl?"

*"For fragmentation is now very widespread, not only throughout society, but also in each individual, and this is leading to a kind of general confusion of the mind, which creates an endless series of problems, and*

*interferes with our clarity of perception so seriously as to prevent us from being able to solve most of them...the notion that all these fragments are separately existent, is evidently an illusion, and this illusion cannot do other than lead to endless conflict and confusion." David Bohm*

*" I think of wrapping one's self in a blanket (field?) of love as protection against scary forces (real, maybe evil). If so done, one should imagine the blanket as an Afghan (as knitted by one's grandmother, lovingly woven of yarn and possessed of spaces). The areas between fabrics breathe in and out allowing the free flow of LOVE. Love functions best going both ways.*

*Therefore, I prefer to see my 'blanket' as many, many dimensional. I am one with all of creation. All of 'me' is in every moment of time and space. The note needs the melody as the melody needs the note.*

*My 'blanket' is more like an eternal, all reaching WEB. Love flowing in all so—called directions, at all so—called 'times'. I shut nothing out. That would be an illusion anyway." Dagne Crane*

## FIELD OF LOVES

A wonderful thing happened some months ago. I should preface it by saying that I have been interested in the seemingly infinite and multidimensional properties of fields (electromagnetic, gravitational, visual etc.) as far back as I can remember. And by now the reader is aware of the staggering importance I place on Einstein's maxim, "The Field is the Sole Governing Agency of the Particles." So naturally, a long time ago I began thinking about the way love includes (but is not limited to) the properties of a field. Haven't we all known people who, at least at times, seemed to radiate love and be surrounded and permeated by it, almost like a kind of electromagnetic and subtle energy field?

*Abraham Maslow, the humanistic psychology pioneer, apparently believed that there were possibilities open to the human being beyond self-actualization in which it was possible to transcend the customary limits of identity and consciousness. In 1968 he concluded, "I consider Humanistic, Third force Psychology, to be transitional, a preparation for a still 'higher' Fourth Psychology, transpersonal, transhuman, centered in the cosmos, rather than in human needs and interests, going beyond humanness, identity, self-actualization, and the like."*

Often, it seems this 'love field' effect is strong with certain children, giving rise to the notion that there is probably a relationship between 'love fields' and innocence. This poses the question: can the mind of an adult which has been brutalized by wrong conditioning and a society gone mad with lovelessness, can such a mind somehow become innocent again? A fundamental of the Process is that such a miracle is possible. Of course, we have all seen these 'love fields' wax and wane (and even completely disappear) to be replaced with other kinds of fields like fear, anger, incoherent, confused thinking, suffering, dissociation and illusion. It seems reasonable to say that the quality of a life depends on the ability to break out of the prison of these emotionally unintelligent thoughts and feelings and restore one's 'Field of Love.'

Anyway, some months ago I had drifted into a dreamy, gentle kind of meditation, and found my mind considering the field properties of love for the umpteenth time. Suddenly I realized something remarkable was happening, and like the proverbial 'out of body' experiences, I knew I must handle this special vision very gently, stay in the moment, not focus too directly, and let the imagery flow, or it would go away. At first I began to smile, then broke into soft laughter as a literal field began to materialize. It seemed to be a beautiful huge green meadow lined by forests, filled with flowers, and with a sparkling happy stream flowing through it. It felt like the safest place on earth. There was bright sunlight and a few white clouds floating overhead.

I had been struggling for some time with a series of particularly intractable, frustrating problems. You know, the kind that make you want to hand in your problem solving credentials? I had been rather hard on myself because I thought I should be able to do a better job of meeting these challenges. One of them was a business relationship that was going down the tubes, and taking the friendship with it; and there are several members of my large family that I cannot seem to get through to. Collectively they were causing me an inordinate amount of pain. During my 'Love Field' reverie I found myself moving to the edge of the vast meadow and gathering up these frustrating and painful relationships. Then I carried them deep into the field. And I left them there.

Upon coming out of this delightful meditation, I realized I felt much better, lighter, and somehow freer. Over the course of these last few months I have found myself taking more and more problems into the 'field' and 'leaving' them there. Of course, I understand that everyone's imagery is unique and personal. But I think something archetypal happened, something that is common to what Jung would term our collective unconscious, and I am having a wonderful time playing with this way of visualizing and thinking. One of the most striking and liberating aspects of it all is that I don't have to carry the burden of being smart enough to figure everything out. The feeling I have is that the 'Field of Love' knows what to do with these situations even though It doesn't always tell me what It is doing or how It is doing it. I must believe Love is very, very Intelligent.

Remarkably enough, many of these problems seem to have taken a much improved turn all by themselves. Perhaps that may have something to do with the fact that I am less worried, or angry and more patient, even amused by the challenges. Sort of like I am interested to see what love will do with them, yet expecting it will be a good solution…although quite likely outside of my original plan. Although I still take action relative to these problems, I find that the nature of the action is changed. For example, I find it easier to be discriminating, creative, and patient. This seems to be improving the timing of some actions. I realize this is magical thinking but there you have it. What am I to do? This is the truth, whether I understand it or not. Furthermore, I have shared this amusing discovery with a few close friends, and some of them have begun spontaneously thinking of love as a literal and metaphorical field within which difficult problems can be safely 'rested'. Some of them have reported similar results. Of course, it won't work every time and for every one but then what does? Truth is one, paths are many.

Plant all you can in the Field of Love. Some of what grows you will recognize...although, it will always be in some way unpredictable. But be prepared. It is the nature of the Field to give birth to miracles that you did not plant there...grace, to the unimaginable, to the unknown, to the longing that never quite reached your conscious awareness, to the plan you have forgotten, to the destiny you did not plan.

*The mystic ascends to the Throne in a moment; the ascetic*
*needs a month for one day's journey...*
*Love hath five hundred wings, and every wind reaches from above*
*the empyrean to beneath the earth.*
*The timorous ascetic runs on foot; the lovers of God fly more quickly*
*than lightning.*
*May Divine Favour free thee from this wayfaring! None but the royal*
*falcon hath found the way to the King. Rumi*

# Epilogue

## GOING A LITTLE BIT FURTHER

Our intention, when it comes to The Process, is to raise the bar as high as we can. Instead of doing market research and finding out what the buying public wants, we asked our hearts, 'What does the world, our brothers and sisters, mothers and fathers, our children and our whole extended family including all of nature, need most? And is there a way, other than through meditation, prayer and doing our best to live a responsible life, is there a way we can assist others to reduce the fragmentation, increase the coherence and significantly enhance the quality of day to day living?' The answer came thundering back to us with such force that we were struck deaf and dumb for awhile, paralyzed by the mind—stunning beauty, exhilaration and sobering, humbling challenge of an adventure in learning (both for ourselves and others). We have come to call this adventure in learning The Process Project.

Our concept was to begin as simply as we could, stay as true to the (Perennial?) Principles as we could (and as we understand them) and from there ask the best, toughest questions we can conceive. Out of that, The Process in its current form has emerged. We haven't the slightest doubt that this is only the beginning, and we haven't the slightest idea where all of this will end. But we are clear about the fact that this book must end. This is really, really difficult because The Process is creating itself and growing every day. And we wanted the book to be the best it could be; but it is time to wrap it up. Perhaps there will be another book some day. Or perhaps we will eventually do an updated version of this book. In any case this epilogue will attempt to provide additional insight into some of the more subtle, hidden, mysterious aspects of the principles upon which this adventure is founded. From the easy to the more difficult, from the gross to the subtle, from the outside in.

We hope that most of you who have found The Process helpful will find this section interesting and fun. Even to the writers some of the material is daunting and mysterious. However, as we see it, that is the actuality of the principles upon which our lives, our minds, our love is built. For most of us, there is no choice but to go as deeply as we can into the nature of our minds, because that is the way to get the most fun (life) out of life. Indeed, we believe, within this century this kind of adventuring will begin to seem like the only game in town, as has already happened during relatively brief, glorious moments in times gone by. I'm thinking of the golden ages of Egypt, Greece, Persia, India, China, Tibet, and lord knows countless other inspired explosions of soul, which like the eagle left no mark in the sky...only a distant rumbling, a nameless, longing, a mysterious flame still burning in at least some hearts, and a new flame which we hope is igniting in many hearts today. Let us be clear, if there is anything to chaos theory, these golden ages qualify as 'strange attractors.' In this case, 'super attractors' seems appropriate. Remember these classic 'attractors' have the enigmatic quality of being always the same and always different (like snowflakes, solar systems, and spiral galaxies). After all, the principles so important to The Process are very, very old and as modern as birth and death and physics and the human struggle to awaken over the ages. And those principles declare that this opportunity, this challenge, this unfoldment, though rooted in the highest aspirations of the human heart and stretching back through countless millennia must be discovered now, in our time...born again as though and truly for the first time ever.

I think Vaclav Havel, president of the Czech Republic, set the stage for this liminal moment when he received the Philadelphia Liberty Medal at Independence Hall on July 4, 1994. I'd like to share some of his poetic wisdom with you:

*"....The way out and something else is painfully being born. It is as if something were crumbling, decaying and exhausting itself, while something else, still indistinct, were arising from the rubble.*

*The distinguishing features of transitional periods are a mixing and blending of cultures and a plurality or parallelism of intellectual and spiritual worlds. These are periods when all consistent value systems collapse, when cultures distant in time and space are discovered or rediscovered.*

*New meaning is gradually born from the encounter, or the intersection, of many different elements.*

*This is related to the crisis, or to the transformation, of science as the basis of the modern conception of the world. The dizzying development of science, with its unconditional faith in objective reality and complete dependency on general and rationally knowable laws, led to the birth of modern technological civilization that spans the entire globe and binds together all societies, submitting them to a common global destiny.*

*At the same time, the relationship to the world that modern science fostered and shaped appears to have exhausted its potential. The relationship is missing something. It fails to connect with the most intrinsic nature of reality and with natural human experience. It produces a state of schizophrenia: Man is becoming completely alienated from himself as a being.*

*Classical modern science described only the surface of things, a single dimension of reality. And the more dogmatically science treated it as the only dimension, as the very essence of reality, the more misleading it became. We may know immeasurably more about the universe than our ancestors did, and yet it increasingly seems they knew something more essential about it than we do, something that escapes us. Today we are in a different place and facing a different situation, one to which classically modern solutions do not give a satisfactory response. After all, the very principle of inalienable human rights, conferred on man by the creator, grew out of the typically modern notion that man—as a being capable of knowing nature and the world—was the pinnacle of creation and lord of the world.*

*This modern anthropocentrism inevitably meant that He who allegedly endowed man with his inalienable rights began to disappear from the world: He was so far beyond the grasp of modern science that He was gradually pushed into a sphere of privacy of sorts, if not directly into a sphere of private fancy—that is, to a place where public obligations no longer apply, the existence of a higher authority than man himself simply began to get in the way of human aspirations.*

*The idea of human rights and freedoms must be an integral part of any meaningful world order. Yet I think it must be anchored in a different place, and in a different way, than has been the case so far.*

*Paradoxically, inspiration for the renewal of this lost integrity can once again be found in science. In a science producing ideas that in a certain sense allow it to* **transcend its own limits.** *I will give two examples.*

*The 'anthropic cosmological principle' brings us to an idea, perhaps as old as humanity itself, that we are not at all just an accidental anomaly, the microscopic caprice of a tiny particle whirling in the endless depths of the universe. Instead, we are mysteriously connected to the universe, we are mirrored in it, just as the entire evolution of the universe is mirrored in us.*

*The moment it begins to appear that we are deeply connected to the entire universe, science reaches the outer limits of its powers.*

*With the 'anthropic cosmological principle,' science has found itself on the border between science and myth. In that, however, science has returned, in a roundabout way, to man, and offers him his lost integrity! It does so by anchoring him once more in the cosmos!*

*The second example is the 'Gaia hypothesis.' This theory brings together proof that the dense network of mutual interactions between the organic and inorganic portions of the earth's surface form a single system, a kind of mega-organism, a living planet, Gaia, named after an ancient goddess recognizable as an archetype of the earth mother in perhaps all religions.*

*According to the Gaia hypothesis, we are parts of a greater whole. Our destiny is not dependent merely on what we do for ourselves but also on what we do for Gaia as a whole.*

*If we endanger her, she will dispense with us in the interests of a higher value—life itself.*

*What makes the 'anthropic principle' and the 'Gaia hypothesis' so inspiring? One simple thing: both remind us of what we have long suspected, of what we have long projected into our forgotten myths and what perhaps has always lain dormant within us as archetypes. That is, the awareness of our being anchored in the earth and the universe, the awareness that we are not here **alone,** nor for **ourselves** alone but that we are an integral part of higher, mysterious entities against whom it is not advisable to blaspheme.*

*This forgotten awareness is encoded in all religions. All cultures anticipate it in various forms. It is one of the things that form the basis of man's understanding of himself, of his place in the world and ultimately of the world as such.*

*The only real hope of people today is probably a renewal of our certainty that we are rooted in the earth and, at the same time, the cosmos. This awareness endows us with the capacity for self-transcendence!*

*Politicians at international forums may reiterate a thousand times that the basis of the new world order must be universal respect for human rights, but it will mean nothing as long as this imperative does not derive from the respect of the miracle of being, the miracle of the universe, the miracle of nature, the miracle of our own existence.*

*Only someone who submits to the authority of the universal order and of creation, who values the right to be a part of it and a participant in it, can genuinely value himself and his neighbors and thus honor their rights as well.*

*It follows that, in today's multicultural world, the truly reliable path to peaceful coexistence and creative cooperation must start from what is at the root of all cultures and what lies infinitely deeper in human hearts and*

*minds than political opinion, convictions, antipathies or sympathies: it*
*must be rooted in self-transcendence.*

*The declaration of independence states that the creator gave man the*
*right to liberty. It seems man can realize that liberty only if he does not*
*forget the one who endowed him with it."*

In summary. Is there a Crisis in the Consciousness of Mankind? Yes! Is
there both danger and opportunity? Yes! Is technology contributing to the
resolution of that Crisis? Yes! (One way or the other). Is technology forcing us to deal with this challenge? Yes! Does that make technology friend
or foe? Yes! Can the quality of our attention transform our enemy into our
teacher? Yes! Are these interesting times? (the best of times and the worst
of times) Yes! Are we cursed or blessed? Yes!

## SCIENCE VS RELIGION?

As a child I was puzzled by the general, cultural notion that science and
religion seemed to be so at odds with each other? Both are supposed to be
devoted to the pursuit of truth. Could it be that there are two great truths
that are mad at each other?

Or is the schism artificial? Perhaps we have become polarized by religious
leaders who are not open minded enough, and scientists who believe they
alone hold the key to the truth and that knowledge is the only way. For
example, the really good religious minds that I find inspirational do not feel
it dilutes the Sacredness of Life one wit if evolution is one of the tools and
principles of creation, any more than the fact of the earth revolving around
the sun is somehow inconsistent with the miracle of creation. And all of the
scientific minds that have my deep attention are extremely humble about
what they do not know, and the glaring limitations of science. Virtually all
of them that I can think of at the moment would consider themselves religious or 'reverent agnostics', or have an obvious (or thinly disguised) mystical core…although some of them would vigorously protest any attempt to
label them as anything other than scientists.

We see science as a truly indefinable art form...and when practiced honestly, *one* of the many wonderful paths we use in our pursuit of the truth. However, appropriate understanding and application of science is seen by many as possibly the greatest challenge of our time. (Personally, I am beginning to see the enhancement of mystical channels of truth, compassion, love as the greatest of all challenges). Many of us have become too confident in the status quo version of science to the exclusion of other strategies leading to even deeper truths. In fact, these other pathways must be wisely integrated if our science is to be sane, healthy, coherent instead of the means whereby we extinct ourselves.

*"The most beautiful and the most profound emotion we may experience is a mystic sensation. It is the seed of all true science. The one to whom such an emotion is unknown is as if he were dead. My religion consists in a humble admiration toward a super-spirit, limitless, who reveals itself in the smallest details we may perceive with our fragile and limited facilities. The deep sentimental emotion of a powerful and supreme Reason, revealing Itself in the incomprehensible universe, such is my idea of God." Albert Einstein*

The problem is, it seems to me, between organized religion and the scientific establishment, rather than the truly religious mind and the truly scientific mind. Of course, many will disagree, but for thousands of years there has existed conflicts which seem to me to be unnecessary and counter productive. On the one hand you have the religious fundamentalists who virtually always believe their religion is the one true, most superior religion of all time. They often use a selective, literal interpretation of one holy book or another to justify their equally selective condemnation of science and technology (while embracing those aspects of science and technology that serve their purposes like printing, microphones, TV and radio, computers, explosives, guns and money). On the other hand you have atheistic scientists who deny the validity of mystical and religious experiences probably because they have not yet had one (at least that they can remember) and feel that if it hasn't yet happened to them it cannot exist. The ultimate logic of this position is that if it cannot be counted, it doesn't count. They believe that ultimately everything will be explained by science. It seems to us that a growing number of thoughtful people feel that they have ' been there done that' and found it far from adequate.

Surely, the integration of the truly religious mind and truly scientific mind is an idea whose time has come. Such a mind does its best to bring about manifestation of both highest possible (mystical) values and responsible science. This concept is one of the fundamental premises of The Process.

## ON SAVING THE WORLD...FOR REAL

*"You are the World." Krishnamurti*

If we take the view that we are utterly insignificant and nothing we do matters, or that the explosive development of technology will by itself save us, or that some outside agency (God, beings from outer space or a combination of the two) will in the end rescue us from the destruction our mistakes are bringing on, then probably the following will not make much sense. I realize that many of my more conservative Christian friends believe that any valid 'rescue' will come from an 'Outside Agency', and I love them and in no way disrespect their beliefs. My own saintly aunt sent me pamphlets for years explaining that the 'Rapture' (when all good Christians will be taken up from the earth so they won't have to suffer through the end of the world) was coming in a year or so and I had better prepare, and make sure all my sins had been forgiven. The pamphlets would almost always name a specific date and offer an incredibly convoluted explanation of why the previous specific date had been changed. Usually it was because God had changed His mind and was giving the world more time to repent. Damn! If I hadn't taken those pamphlets so seriously I might have taken my portfolio more seriously and invested heavily in Microsoft and Berkshire Hathaway. With that kind of money I would have been able to build my own space ship and space station allowing me to help God out by snatching up as many saved souls as I could just before Armageddon. Of course, my conservative friends do not believe God needs any help; but if that is so why does He keep demanding that we do a better job or else? It's all so confusing. Perhaps if I could get Mrs.God to talk me through it she would explain these apparent contradictions so even I could understand.

Anyway, some of us believe that we must be as responsible as possible and do our best to correct our own mistakes. We think the way to do that seems clear although difficult. It is grounded in fixing thought that has gone awry. The beginning of this is enhancing the ability to observe thought. I know I am repeating this notion over and over in different ways. But we keep returning to the source as we try individually and collectively to get the hang of living easily, happily, responsibly on this earth. Never mind that it is difficult like waking up from a deep sleep. Never mind that we must forget what we know and must discover this as though for the first time ever. Never mind that it seems to require a leap of creativity that springs up from a source outside of time, beyond knowledge and even consciousness as we generally know it.

*"....Is it possible to teach students and ourselves to free the mind from knowledge and yet use knowledge without causing the mind to function mechanically? If I were a teacher here, I would be greatly concerned how to bring about this unconditioning in myself and in the student...in the very act of teaching I learn about my own conditioning and see the conditioning of the child and learn how to uncondition the mind. Now, can we go into the question of whether knowledge conditions the mind, and if it does, how to prevent it; how not to shape the mind in the very act of teaching and giving information." Krishnamurti, Beginnings of Learning*

If I told you that there is a technology which will transform society (and maybe eventually the mind and body of humans as well) what would it be? Air travel? The Web? Reasonable idea? Virtually everyone agrees that the web is changing the world in ways and at speeds that were utterly unforeseen. Air travel has already vastly changed humankind. By the early twenties there were over 400 airplane manufacturers in the US. Of course, most built planes way below an acceptable standard. It is reported that there was one company in New England (which like most of the others, advertised in magazines) and which persuaded, I think, 129 customers to buy their planes before they were finally shut down. Their technique was to take the enthusiastic would be aviator's money and 'train' him for a short while in his shiny new single seater plane (without ever actually taking off) and give him much assurance that the plane will fly itself once he is in the air. The hapless aviator who had zero or minimal experience, but obviously plenty of courage and naiveté would then climb into the plane and take off. Apparently all 129 crashed, almost always killing the pilot, usually conveniently close to the little flying field. The owner of the business and his son then went out and salvaged all the parts they could and used them to build the next plane. Of course, there was no licensing then, nor FAA, nor any other kind of regulation.

Now, a true technology of self-knowledge should ultimately enhance the well being of humanity much more than air travel. Yet, it is relatively difficult to hurt anyone with proper use of biofeedback…although, improper use could produce problems. For example, quickly producing super deep levels of relaxation in a diabetic patient with a heavy dose of insulin on board could produce insulin shock. The use of biofeedback is, of course, good for the diabetic patient in so much as diabetes is stress related; the problem arises because as a diabetic is quickly and deeply reducing the maladaptive stress response there must be a corresponding reduction in insulin. Getting this right requires the supervision of a physician. There is evidence that theta training can trigger seizures (similar to flashing lights) in some epilepsy patients. One of my friends who was learning to sky dive decided to do a half hour of alpha training just before a jump. Apparently, once he was in the air he became so euphoric and fearless that he wanted to extend his free fall beyond the 5500 feet mandated by his instructor. At 4500 feet his instructor (falling alongside) reached over and pulled his rip chord for him. My friend says that he was going to do it at 3500 feet (the chute is designed to open automatically at 1000 feet). I've been scratching my head over that one. Of course, performance and life enhancement does mean pushing the envelope. Obviously, pushing the envelope can have unforeseen consequences.

Coming back to our metaphor. Air travel changes things for both the pilot and the passenger. The Process is about becoming your own pilot. Now having good equipment (plane or car) is important, but once that condition is met you need a good map. Then the journey begins and a new mind is the destination. And when that destination is reached, the next destination is a new mind (fresh eyes) again; and so profound attention leads to—that is produces a way of life—a way of using the mind which does all it can to constantly renew itself. The first step is the last step. Transformation is a verb in the sense that it is The Process of grabbing as many opportunities as possible to transform the moment before you the way smiling at a stranger or petting a dog or opening the door for someone does.

Just as some of those committed to air travel saw opportunity and accepted the challenge of doing their best to develop competent, safe, professional flying schools, so we are doing the same relative to The Process and Biofeedback.

*"You ask me of God: to define the Nameless, to place in your palm the ultimate secret. Do not imagine that this is hidden somewhere far from you. The ultimate secrete is the most open one. Here it is: God is all… What we truly are is God manifest in time and eternity. Know this, live well, and die easy." Reb Yerachmiel Ben Yisrael*

*"Truth is a pathless land." Krishnamurti*

The essence of learning, of relationship, of the operation within any-one's life of The Immense Intelligence is…listening…actually listening outside of time (psychological time). Therefore, one of the best ways to bring about the domination of the Process by that Intelligence (The Field of Love?) is for us to actually listen. This quality of listening can breed the natural unfoldment of The Process. But actual listening carries with it the quality of not knowing, because it transcends knowledge based systems. Of course, the Intelligence can use knowledge based systems but they are not what must run the show. As this 'high order' listening takes place Mind can operate and it uses the brain as an instrument.

This means The Process is not dependent on acceptance by anyone. The Process must and will make its own way (with or without any of us) and let the chips fall where they may. The Intelligence must supply the economic order; although, it is OK for the brain to do its best as long as it is actually listening. Furthermore, there are the issues of mutation, goodness and evil. Transformation implies something is being changed to something else. Mutation carries a different quality of meaning, and implies something new is being born. Goodness is not the opposite of evil. That is dualistic thinking and is caught in the web of psychological time. Good has no relationship to evil, as evil is so far as I can, see a projection of the human brain and 3DC, or a certain conditioned, limited con-sciousness. So, quality of consciousness is the means to right relationship with goodness, intelligence, love and freedom from fear, as well as man's invention…evil. Curious how evil is live spelled backwards. Sounds like something a relatively unimaginative social engineer would do, doesn't it? Wonder what their motivation was for inventing evil? Fighting and fund-ing the war against 'evil' could be a lucrative and easy method of control-ling the masses, don't you think? What did Jesus mean when he said, "Do not resist evil…Take no thought for tomorrow for sufficient unto the day is the evil thereof" Was something lost in the translation?

Maybe we are getting closer, except that in that state of true listening something other than consciousness as we define it, may be operating. It is so hard to conceive of that which is alive, aware, intelligent but is not consciousness. Krishnamurti and Bohm discussed this problem in many ways. Once they seemed to just give up and referred to it as a different kind of consciousness. Years later they were still struggling with the problem and limitations inherent in the use of the English word consciousness.

Following is one of the most extraordinary paragraphs I've read about meditation ever. most will find it tough going. We suggest you use it as a 'seed' for your own meditation and let go of the need to understand it completely.

*"Most of us do not seem to give sufficient importance to meditation. For most it is a passing thing in which some kind of experience is expected, some transcendental attainment, a fulfillment after all other attempts at fulfillment have failed…what happens can never be told to another. Even in the telling things have already changed. It is like describing a storm. It is already over the hills, the valleys, and gone beyond…Obviously certain powers are released but these become a great danger as long as the self centered activity goes on, whether these activities are identified with religious concepts or with personal tendencies…But thought is very cunning, extraordinarily subtle in its activities and unless one is tremendously aware, without any choice, of all these subtleties and cunning pursuits, meditation becomes the gaining of powers beyond the mere physical ones. Any sense of importance of any action of the self must lead inevitably to confusion and sorrow. That is why, before you consider meditation, begin with understanding of yourself, the structure and the nature of thought Otherwise you will get lost and your energies will be wasted."* Krishnamurti, Beginnings of Learning.)

As for me, I've had enough of humanity bashing. It is true that as a species we have made and are making many mistakes. But so what? Where is the manual for operation of spaceship earth (Bucky Fuller's brilliant book of that title aside)? Where are the instructions for how to live a perfectly transformed life, for how to manage the evolutionary challenges, the explosive, tsunami of technology? The Creation ain't for sissies. We have to suck it up. Sure, like any creative being we make 'mistakes' and we pay for them. We are all connected. We are a family. If you believe most religious leaders, some of our family have paid and are paying with their souls. But I say, if there is a price to be paid for this Immense Journey, we can and will pay it, and by the highest standard that exists we shall succeed and are succeeding. We are collectively a heroic creation, and we can pay the price because the true Source of our wealth is infinite. And because there are at least barely enough souls on this earth who have been touched by Love.

## J. Krishnamurti and David Bohm

It is obvious to the reader that we have been mightily influenced by Krishnamurti and Bohm. The following material will provide further insight into the reasons why we place so much value on their work. First, a few comments by David Bohm from his preface to The Limits of Thought.

"…the general disorder and confusion that pervades the consciousness of mankind. It is here that I encountered what I feel to be Krishnamurti's major discovery. What he was seriously proposing is that all this disorder, which is the root cause of such widespread sorrow and misery, and which prevents human beings from properly working together, has its root in the fact that we are ignorant of the general nature of our own processes of thought. Or, to put it differently, it may be said that we do not see what is actually happening when we are engaged in the activity of thinking. Through close attention to and observation of this activity of thought, Krishnamurti feels that he directly perceives that thought is a material process which is going on inside of the human being in the brain and nervous system as a whole.

Ordinarily, we tend to be aware mainly of the content of this thought rather than of how it actually takes place. One can illustrate this point by considering what happens when one is reading a book. Usually, one is attentive almost entirely to the meaning of what is being read. However, one can also be aware of the book itself, of its constitution as being made up out of pages that can be turned, of the printed words and of the ink, of the fabric of the paper, etc. Similarly, we may be aware of the actual structure and function of the process of thought, and not merely of its content.

How can such an awareness come about? Krishnamurti proposes that this requires what he calls meditation. Now the word meditation has been given a wide range of different and even contradictory meanings, many of them involving rather superficial kinds of mysticism. Krishnamurti has in mind a definite and clear notion when he uses this word. One can obtain a valuable indication of this meaning by considering the derivation of the word. (The roots of words, in conjunction with their present generally accepted meanings, often yield surprising insight into their deeper meanings.) The English word meditation is based on the Latin root 'med', 'to measure'. The present meaning of this word is 'to reflect', 'to ponder' (i.e. to weigh or measure), and 'to give close attention'. Similarly, the Sanskrit word for meditation, which is 'dhyana', is closely related to 'dhyati', meaning 'to reflect'. So, at this rate, to meditate would be 'to ponder, to reflect, while giving close attention to what is actually going on as one does so'.

This is perhaps what Krishnamurti means by the beginning of meditation. That is to say, one gives close attention to all that is happening in conjunction with the actual activity of thought, which is the underlying source of the general disorder. One does this without choice, without criticism, without acceptance or rejection of what is going on. And all of this takes place along with reflections on the meaning of what one is learning about the activity of thought. (It is perhaps rather like reading a book in which the pages have been scrambled up, and being intensely aware of this disorder, rather than just 'trying to make sense' of the confused content that arises when one just accepts the pages as they happen to come.)

Krishnamurti has observed that the very act of meditation will, in itself, bring order to the activity of thought without the intervention of will, choice, decision, or any other action of the 'thinker'. As such order comes, the noise and chaos which are the usual background of our consciousness die out, and the mind becomes generally silent. (Thought arises only when needed for some genuinely valid purpose, and then stops, until needed again.)

In this silence, Krishnamurti says that something new and creative happens, something that cannot be conveyed in words, that is of extraordinary significance for the whole of life. So he does not attempt to communicate this verbally, but rather, he asks of those who are interested that they explore the question of meditation directly for themselves, through actual attention to the nature of thought.

Without attempting to probe into this deeper meaning of meditation, however, one can say that meditation, in Krishnamurti's sense of the word, can bring order to our overall mental activity, and this may be a key factor in bringing about an end to the sorrow, the misery, the chaos and confusion that have over the ages been the lot of mankind, and that are still generally continuing, without visible prospect of fundamental change for the foreseeable future.

Krishnamurti's work is permeated by what may be called the essence of the scientific approach, when this is considered in its very highest and purest form. Thus, he begins from a fact: this fact about the nature of our thought processes. This fact is established through close attention, involving careful listening to the process of consciousness, and observing it assiduously. In this, one is constantly learning, and out of this learning comes insight into the overall or general nature of the process of thought. This insight is then tested. First, one sees whether it holds together in a rational order. And then one sees whether it leads to order and coherence, on what flows out of it in life as a whole.

Krishnamurti constantly emphasizes that he is in no sense an authority. He has made certain discoveries, and he is simply doing his best to make these discoveries accessible to all those who are able to listen. His work does not contain a body of doctrine, nor does he offer techniques or methods for obtaining a silent mind. He is not aiming to set up any new system of religious belief. Rather, it is up to each human being to see if he can discover for himself that to which Krishnamurti is calling attention, and to go on from here to make new discoveries on his own.

It is clear then that an introduction such as this can at best show how Krishnamurti's work has been seen by a particular person, a scientist, such as myself. To see in full what Krishnamurti means, it is necessary, of course, to go on and to read what he actually says, with that quality of attention to the totality of one's responses, inward and outward, which we have been discussing here."

I feel tremendous excitement as a result of these insights about thought—this sense that one can see its structure. Bohm's metaphor is so helpful. The notion that when reading a book we are usually caught up in whatever the content of the writing is saying. In fact, there is a tendency to believe it is true just because it is in writing. But that one can go much further and also be aware of what a book is, the ink, fabric of the paper, glue and binding making the pages come sequentially one after the other etc. The fact that it is an expression of the thinking of the writer which could be (and often is) very far from the truth, the actual. In the same way we can become aware of the structure of thought, what it is made of, how it is operating, and so free ourselves from domination by the content of thought. If one can reject the thought which is untrue, what is left? If one can see the limits, and nature of thought one can use it like a tool and so much more easily, perhaps choicelessly, allow thought to fall silent when it is not necessary. And this can (must) lead to 'activation' of an order or orders of intelligence (and aliveness) superior to thinking itself. Part of this excitement gives rise to what feels like almost a ravenous hunger to be free of the problems incoherent thought has caused. It seems so much clearer. It's as though I can see the operation of incoherent thought and how it does not run true. How the truth can make it run true, run in parallel with, and be reflective of the truth. Also an equal 'soul screaming' for the 'clean energy' that comes along with that freedom.

To my way of thinking Krishnamurti understood fear and what to do about it better than any other that I have read. Following are a few lines from his talk on fear as documented in **Freedom from the Known.**

*...This craving for position, for prestige, for power, to be recognized by society as being outstanding in some way, is a wish to dominate others, and this wish to dominate is a form of aggression. The saint who seeks a position in regard to his saintliness is as aggressive as the chicken pecking in the farmyard. And what is the cause of this aggressiveness? It is fear, isn't it?...Fear is one of the greatest problems in life. A mind that is caught in fear lives in confusion, in conflict, and therefore must be violent, distorted, and aggressive...But to run away from fear is only to increase it....*

*Therefore, our question now is, is it possible for the mind to live completely, totally, in the present? It is only such a mind that has no fear. But to understand this, you have to understand the structure of thought, memory, and time...Thought, like memory, is, of course, necessary for daily living...So thought is essential at certain levels, but when thought projects itself psychologically as the future and the past, creating fear as well as pleasure, the mind is made dull and therefore inaction is inevitable.*

I think I became aware in the early seventies of the value of asking the right question. So I went into the best meditaion I could and, in fact, a wondrous question did emerge. Thirty years later I am still waiting for a better one. It is—what **would love do?**

Earlier we mentioned that application of The Process principles leads to maximally responsible and successful business models. In support of that assertion we present Edwards Deming's:

**Condensation of the 14 Points for Management**
W. Edwards Deming from his book, **Out of the Crisis.**

**Origin of the 14 points.** The 14 points are the basis for transformation of American industry. It will not suffice merely to solve problems, big or little. Adoption and action on the 14 points are a signal that the management intends to stay in business and aim to protect investors and jobs. Such a system formed the basis for lessons for top management in Japan in 1950 and in subsequent years.

The 14 points apply anywhere, to small organizations as well as to large ones, to the service industry as well as to manufacturing. They apply to a division within a company.

1. Create constancy of purpose toward improvement of product and service, with the aim to become competitive and to stay in business, and to provide jobs.
2. Adopt the new philosophy. We are in a new economic age. Western management must awaken to the challenge, must learn their responsibilities, and take leadership for change.
3. Cease dependence on inspection to achieve quality. Eliminate the need for inspection on a mass basis by building quality into the product in the first place.
4. End the practice of awarding business on the basis of price tag. Instead, minimize total cost. Move toward a single supplier for any one item, on a long-term relationship of loyalty and trust.
5. Improve constantly and forever the system of production and service, to improve quality and productivity, and thus constantly decrease costs.
6. Institute training on the job.
7. Institute leadership. The aim of supervision should be to help people and machines and gadgets to do a better job. Supervision of management is in need of overhaul, as well as supervision of production workers.
8. Drive out fear, so that everyone may work effectively for the company.

9. Break down barriers between departments. People in research, design, sales, and production must work as a team, to foresee problems of production and in use that may be encountered with the product or service.

10. Eliminate slogans, exhortations, and targets for the work force asking for zero defects and new levels of productivity. Such exhortations only create adversarial relationships, as the bulk of the causes of low quality and low productivity belong to the system and thus lie beyond the power of the work force.

11a. Eliminate work standards (quotas) on the factory floor. Substitute leadership.

b. Eliminate management by objective. Eliminate management by numbers, numerical goals. Substitute leadership.

12a. Remove barriers that rob the hourly worker of his right to pride of workmanship. The responsibility of supervisors must be changed from sheer numbers to quality.

b. Remove barriers that rob people in management and in engineering of their right to pride of workmanship. This means, **inter alia**, abolishment of the annual or merit rating and of management by objective.

13. Institute a vigorous program of education and self-improvement.

14. Put everybody in the company to work to accomplish the transformation. The transformation is everybody's job.

If you want to learn more about this business and human relationship genius I suggest you contact: SPC, Inc., 5908 Toole Drive, Suite C, Knoxville, TN 37919 ph 615 584 5005

## SUGGESTED READING

Some of the books which we feel can further enhance understanding of and which we believe support the underlying principles upon which The

Process is built are listed below. This list is by no means complete and like the Process is dynamically changing all the time. The list includes some books that will be of interest to health care professionals.

Basmajian, John V., Biofeedback, Principles And Practice For Clinicians, William and
Wilkins, Baltimore (1989).
Bohm, D., Wholeness and the Implicate Order, Ark, 1983.
Bohm, D. and Peat, D., Science, Order and Creativity, Bantam 1987.
Briggs, J., Peat D., Turbulent Mirror, Harper And Rowe 1989.
Covey, Stephen R., The 7 Habits of Highly Effective People, Fireside, 1990.
Crick, Francis, The Astonishing Hypothesis, Touchstone, 1995.
Criswell, Eleanor, Ed.D., Biofeedback and Somatics, Freeperson Press 1995.
Deming, W. Edwards, The New Economics for Industry, Government, Education,
Massachusetts Institute of Technology Center for Advanced Engineering Study,1993.
de Ropp, Robert S., Warrior's Way, Merloyd Lawrence, 1979.
Dominguez, Joe, and Robin, Vicki, Your Money or Your Life, Penguin, 1993.
Evans, James and Abarbanel, Andrew, An Introduction to Quantitative EEG and Neurofeedback, Academic Press, 1999.
Garfield, Charles, Peak Performers, William Morrow and Company, New York, 1986.
Garfield, Charles A., Ph.D. and Bennett, Hal Z., Peak Performance, Jeremy P. Tarcher,
Inc., 1984.
Ghiselin, Brewster, The Creative Process, University of California Press, 1985.
Gleick, J., Chaos, Penguin 1988.

Green, Elmer and Alyce, Beyond Biofeedback, Dell Publishing, 1977.

Horgan, John, the Undiscovered Mind, Free Press, 1999.

Kohn, Alfie, No Contest, Houghton Mifflin, 1986.

Krishnamurti J., The Awakening Of Intelligence, Harper and Rowe 1973.

Krishnamurti J. and Bohm D., The Ending Of Time, Harper and Rowe 1985.

Krishnamurti J. and Bohm D., The Limits of Thought, Rutledge 1999.

Levey, Joel, Ph.D. and Michelle Levey, Living in Balance, Conari Press 1998.

Levey, Joel, Ph.D. and Michelle Levey, Wisdom at Work, Corporate Edition, Conari Press 1999.

Maas, James. Ph.D., Power Sleep, Villard Books, 1998.

Maslow, A.H., The Farther Reaches of Human Nature, Viking, 1971.

Nierdermeyer, E, M.D. and Lopes Da Silva, M.D., Electroencephalography, Third Edition, Williams & Wilkins.

Peat, F. David, Infinite Potential: The Life and Times of David Bohm, Addison-Wesley, 1997.

Peck, M. Scott, M.D., The Road Less Traveled, Touchstone, 1978.

Pransky, George S. Ph.D., The Renaissance of Psychology

Ruden, Ronald, M.D., Ph.D. The Craving Brain, Harper, Collins, 1997.

Russell, Peter, The Global Brain, J.P. Tarcher, 1983.

Teilhard de Chardin, Pierre, On Love, William Collins Sons Ltd., Glasgow.

Schwartz, Mark S. and Associates, Biofeedback, A Practitioner's Guide, Guilford Press, 1995.

Schwarz, Jack, The Path of Action, E.P. Dutton, New York, 1977.

Shah, Idries, The Way Of The Sufi. London: Jonathan Cape, 1968.

Wheatley, Margaret J., Leadership and the New Science, Berrett-Koehler, 1994.

# About the Authors

R. Adam Crane BCIA Senior Fellow, BCIAEEG, NRNP Diplomate. President American BioTec, Director of BioMonitoring International and Biotec Corporations, Founder of Health Training Seminars. Since 1971 Adam Crane and the companies he has founded or cofounded have played leading roles in mainstream medical/educational biofeedback, and applied psychophysiology.

Because of inspiring benefits he received from biofeedback training and his belief that a technology of self-knowledge could do much to relieve suffering, resolve the crisis in the consciousness of humanity and lead to life long life enhancement, he committed to the field full time in 1970.

The Process is part of a long term strategy to helping make those perennial principles of life enhancement he has discovered (and practices)
understandable and usable to those drawn to self-actualization or as he
prefers to call it—MindFitness. He believes The Decade of The Brain is
opening onto a vast new landscape—The Millenium of The Mind. Adam
lives in Ossining New York with his wife Dagne—simply. He can be
reached at *www.MindFitness.com*.

**Richard Soutar, Ph.D.** recieved his doctorate from Oklahoma state
University and has taught at Arizona State University, Northern Arizona
University, and several local community colleges. He is Director of
Biofeedback Services for the Neuro Performance Center in Phoenix where
he lives with his wife and four children. Dr. Soutar lectures and gives
workshops on social psychology and clinical neurofeedback.

Dr. Soutar was inspired to develop the Neuro Performance Center
because of the results he achieved while undergoing neurofeedback training on himself and personally applying those principles described in The
Process. He can be reached at *www.npctalk.com*.

# Appendix

Following is a list of studies for those readers who may want to delve more deeply into the scientific literature as it relates to neurofeedback. Again, new studies and papers are coming out steadily and this list is by no means complete. These references are intended to support further investigation on the part of the reader. Taken individually, some of the studies do not necessarily support the model(s) described herein. Although, from the writers point of view, they all have their place in the whole and fit comfortably into the practical, evolving, dynamic models which make up The Process. Respect for differing views seems fundamental to any sincere pursuit of 'a better way'. In fact, taken all together and considering these papers and studies are all different ways of 'touching the elephant', they all contribute to The Process from the authors' point of view.

## BRIEF OUTLINES OF SOME KEY STUDIES
*By permission of Richard Patton, MSSW.*

Title-EEG Biofeedback Training for Attention Deficit Disorder, Specific Learning Disabilities, and Associated Conduct Problems. Author-Siegfried Othmer, Susan Othmer, and C. Marks. Source-EEG Spectrum, Los Angeles, CA, 1992, pp 1–20.

The authors examine the efficacy of neurofeedback in the treatment of attentional deficits And learning disabilities in school age children using psychological and academic testing.

The neurofeedback training involves the enhancement of SMR (sensori-motor rhythm) activity of the brain (15–18 Hz) while suppressing excessive theta waves (3–7 Hz) and beta waves (22–30 Hz). Significant improvements in cognitive skills, academic performance and behavior were found and even confirmed in further follow up studies. Among those children studied the average improvement in IQ was 23 points. Based upon the author's work they have determined a preference for 15–18 Hz training versus the 12–15 Hz training common to the Lubar protocol.

Title-Discourse on the development of EEG diagnostics and biofeed-back for attention-deficit/hyperactivity disorders. Author-Joel Lubar of the University of Tennessee, Knoxville. Source-Biofeedback and Self Regulation, 1991, Vol 16, pp 201–225.

The author reviews his 15 years of work and study in the development of a method of diagnosis and treatment of ADD with EEG biofeedback (neurofeedback). He does an excellent job of presenting his research and that of others for understanding the development of neurofeedback proto-cols for learning disability disorders such as ADD and Hyperactivity. The neurophysiological and neurological basis for ADD is thoroughly discussed. In this presentation the author notes the safety and efficacy of this treatment approach based upon his own casework.

Title-Wechsler (WISC-R) changes following treatment of learning dis-abilities via EEG biofeedback training in a private practice setting. Author-M. Tansey, Private Practice, New Jersey. Source-Australian Journal of Psychology, 1991, Vol 43, pp 147–153.

The author presents IQ profiles and changes following neurofeedback training for neurologically based learning disabilities. The children were trained to increase SMR activation (sensorimotor rhythm-14 Hz). This training regimen resulted in increased verbal-expressive and visual motor skills for the children in this study. Improved and normalized academic abilities were not only reflected in brainwave patterns but also IQ testing using the WISC-R. An inverse relationship was observed between theta brainwave production and pretreatment IQ levels.

Title-Differences in semantic event-related potentials in learning-disabled, normal, and gifted children. Author-J. Lubar, C. Mann, D. Gross, and M. Shively of the University of Tennessee, Knoxville. Source-Biofeedback and Self Regulation, March 1992, pp 41–55.

In this study the authors compare 15 learning-disabled, 14 gifted, and 13 normal children of ages 8–12, comparing brain wave patterns in each group to determine differences in each groups responses to language and complex cognitive functioning. This study clearly demonstrates that there is a neurological basis for attentional disorders. An increase in theta activity in learning disabled children has been repeatedly demonstrated, especially for children with Attention-Deficit Disorder, with or without hyperactivity and with or without associated learning disabilities. This study reinforces the strong rationale for the use of neurofeedback procedures based upon cortical electrical activity.

Title-Righting the rhythms of reason; EEG biofeedback training as a therapeutic modality in a clinical office setting. Author-Michael Tansey, Private Practice, Livingston, New Jersey. Source-Medical Psychotherapy, 1990, Vol 3, pp 57–68.

In this article the author reviews the use of neurofeedback with attention deficit disorders both from an historical and current perspective. After making the case for neurofeedback in treating attention deficit disorders, Dr. Tansey turns to an exposition of how advances in electronics and computers make it possible to bring this treatment to larger populations served on an outpatient basis in the clinicians office.

Dr. Tansey explains his own simplified approach to neurofeedback in a manner that helps to remove much of the technological mystique from the treatment process.

Title-State-dependent processing of strings of characters. Author-R. Schmitt of the Humbolt University of Berlin, Germany. Source-Zeitschrift fur Psychologie, 1990, Vol 198, pp 363–380.

The author examines the relationship between psychophysiological states reflected in EEG pattern and performance on a mental task of identification. Seventeen young adult East German males and females were examined in this study. Their task was to identify the first number in each of 120 strings of numbers. Each string of numbers contained 40 digits. The study examined the interaction between alpha band patterns of brain wave activity and each individual's reaction time. High amplitude alpha activity was associated with rapid reaction time. SMR (sensorimotor rhythm) activity (13–15 Hz brain waves) was associated with successful identification of the first number in each string.

Title-Brainwave signatures as an index reflective of the brain's functional neuroanatomy: Further finding on the effect of EEG sensorimotor rhythm biofeedback training on the neurologic precursors of learning disabilities. Author-Michael Tansey of Livingston, New Jersey. Source-International Journal of Psychophysiology, 1985, Vol 3, pp 85–99.

In this study the author examines the impact of neurofeedback on learning disabled boys ranging from 7 to 15 years old. The results of this study indicate that the main effect of neurofeedback is an increase in 14 Hz brain wave activity and substantial improvement in the learning disabilities of all the boys examined. Each boy displayed a tendency for decreased slow brain waves with increased fast brainwaves following neurofeedback training. The boys studied had IQs ranging from below average to above average. The author noted an increase in brainwave amplitude for those boys of above average IQ following neurofeedback training.

Title-Electroencephalographic (EEG) and brain stem evoked responses from learning-disabled and control children. Author-Grant Morris, John Obrzut, and Linda Coulthard-Morris of the University of Northern Colorado. Source-Developmental Neuropsychology, 1989, Vol 5, pp 187–206. In this study, the authors examined the EEG patterns as indicators of brain dysfunction in 15 children with learning disabilities and 15 normal children ages 9 to 12 years old. The normal children displayed more orderly progression of EEG development across all bandwidths of brain activity when compared to the learning disabled children. The authors conclude that the lack of development in brainwave activity in the learning disabled children is related to impaired cognitive performance.

Title-Cognitive determinants of the postimperative negative variation. Author-N. Kathmann, L. Jonitz, and R.R. Engel of the University of Munich, Germany. Source-Psychophysiology, 1990, Vol 27, pp 256–263.

In this study the authors examined slow brainwave patterns (theta waves) associated with aversive, controlling, and demanding stimulus in timed tasks. In short, this study examines the impact of stress on tasks that are demanded to be performed in a given amount of time. The individuals studied were essentially an average representation of the general population, and it can be fairly assumed that the results can be transferred to all groups of people. The authors discovered a trend to produce stronger powered theta waves (3.5–7 Hz) under conditions of stress. This is important in developing an approach to Learning Disabled children as it means that aversive techniques of discipline are likely to encourage the child to produce even more theta waves as a neurophysiological benchmark of attentional problems.

Title-EEG Biofeedback Training for Hyperactivity, Attention Deficit Disorder, Specific Learning Disabilities and Other Disorders. Author-Siegfried Othmer and Susan Othmer of Los Angeles, CA. Source-EEG Spectrum, Los Angeles, CA, 1991, pp 1–11.

The authors review nearly 20 years of research in the techniques of EEG biofeedback. Uses of neurofeedback for conditions such as hyperactivity, attention deficit disorder, endogenous depression, sleep disorders, closed head injury and epilepsy are explored. It is concluded that neurofeedback appears to be exceptionally successful in those areas. The fact that most research indicated permanent improvement in most cases is clearly underlined. The generality of the technique suggests that it affects a fundamental mechanism of brain regulation.

Title-EEG correlates of the success of verbal-analytic activity in young school children. Author-M.G. Knyazeva and G. Bolshakova of the USSR Academy of Pedagogical Sciences, Scientific Research Institute of Child and Pre-Adult Physiology, Moscow. Source-Novye Issledovoniya v Psikhologii i Vozrastroi Fiziologii, 1990, Vol 1, pp 75–79.

In this study, the authors examined the EEG patterns of successful performance on verbal calculation tests in 61 normal male and female Russian children ages 7 to 10 years old. The authors established a clear relationship between successful verbal calculation and the brain's production of high amplitude alpha band activity in all ages and sexes of the children examined. This study had helped to further clarify and confirm the relationship between healthy EEG patterns and successful school performance. Title- Is there a possibility of differentiating between children with minimal cerebral dysfunction (Attention Deficit Disorder) by means of computer-assisted automatic EEG analysis? Author-G. Spiel of the University of Vienna, Austria. Source-Advances in Biological Psychiatry, 1987, Vol 16, pp 161–177.

In his study of fifty-one 7–10 year old children with learning disabilities, the author examines the various EEG patterns associated with attentional disorders. A significant difference in the EEG patterns was noted. The results show that left brain process (brain waves) in the posterior were much slower than in normal children. Also, right forebrain processes were frequently slower.

Title-Physiological factors as determinants of pathological gambling. Author-Peter Carlton and Paul Manowitz at the University of Medicine and Dentistry of New Jersey. Source-Journal of Gambling Behavior, 1988, Vol. 3, pp. 274–285.

The authors emphasize biological causes for gambling. This article explores how compulsive gambling shares many biological features with Attention Deficit Disorder and alcoholism. Relation to certain EEG characteristics common to all three problems are discussed. It is notable how theta brainwave activity plays a common role in the behaviors displayed in Attention Deficit Disorder, compulsive gambling, and alcoholism. The authors urge treating professionals to use an interactive biological/social model in providing appropriate treatment.

Title-Task difficulty and EEG alpha asymmetry: An amplitude and frequency analysis. Author-Jonathan Earle of Bradford College, Massachusetts. Source-Neuropsychobiology, 1988, Vol. 20, pp. 96–112.

The twenty college students studied were examined for the effects of three tasks on their EEG patterns. The tasks involved mathematical, spatial and verbal problems. Each student was examined—not only their EEG pattern but also performance anxiety, loss of attention, confusion and a tendency to rely on a guessing strategy. The authors findings show that while task difficulty increased, Alpha wave acceleration was observed. Many of these alpha wave accelerations were noted to be related to specific hemispheric activity.

# Glossary

*arcane,* from the Latin, hidden or secrete, relating to arcanum, arcana, meaning secrete, mystery; a secrete remedy; elixir.

*archetype,* the original pattern or model after which a thing is made.

*art,* to join, to fit together, making or doing of things that have form and beauty.

*ascetic,* one who practices extreme self denial, especially for religious reasons.

*cohere,* to stick together; be united, hold fast, as parts of the same mass. In physics, to be united within a body by the action of molecular forces. To be naturally or logically connected.

*coherence,* the act or state of cohering. Natural or logical connection. Correspondence, harmony, agreement, rationality.

*coherence theory,* The theory of truth that every true statement, insofar as it is true, describes its subject in the totality of its relationship with all other things. Pragmatic theory.

*consciousness,* the state of being aware especially of what is happening around and within one. Having a feeling or knowledge of one's sensations, feelings, etc. Being able to feel and think, awake. Aware of oneself as a thinking being.

*dysponesis,* from the Greek meaning inappropriate and, or unnecessary use of energy.

*empyrean,* the highest heaven, among the ancients the sphere of pure light or fire, the abode of God, *heuristic*, the method of learning in which the student is encouraged to learn for him or herself with as little dependence on past experience or outside authority as wisdom deems appropriate.

*hypnogogic, hypnopopic* imagery refers to that imagery which emerges as one shifts toward sleep (hypnopopic) ar arises during the transition from sleep to consciousness (hypnogogic).

*hypothesis*, from the Greek hypothesis meaning groundwork, foundation, supposition. Literally 'to place under' (hypotithenai). An unproved theory, proposition, supposition, etc. tentatively accepted to explain certain facts or (working hypothesis) to provide a basis for further investigation, argument, etc.

*liminal*, a moment of equilibrium, charged with promise, when the old has not quite passed and the new is just being born. The border, or at the threshold of which, in psychology and physiology implies the least degree of stimulation that produces a response.

*mutation*, an alteration or change. Any heritable alteration of an organism.

*mysticism*, the belief in a direct, intimate union of the soul with God through contemplation and love.

*ontology*, a branch of metaphysics which studies the nature and meaning of existence.

*psychology*, the science dealing with the mind and mental processes, feelings, desires etc. learning, the acquiring of knowledge or skill.

*renaissance*, to be born, to be born anew, rebirth, revival.

*science*, from the Latin sciens, to know. The state or fact of knowing. Systematized knowledge derived from observation, study, and experimentation carried on in order to determine the nature of principles of what is being studied.

*transform*, to change the external form or the inner nature, to change the personality or character of.

*synchronous*, moving at the same rate and exactly together.

*ubiquitous*, being everywhere, especially at the same time.

# References

Anand, B.K., G.S. China, and B. Singh. Some Aspects of electroencephalographic studies in yogis. Electroenceph. Clin. Neurophysiol., 1961, 13, 452–456.

Ancoli, S., and Kamiya, J. Methodological issues in alpha biofeedback training.

Biofeedback and Self Regulation, 1978, 392), 159–183.

Brown, B.B. Awareness of EEG-subject activity relationships detected within a closed feedback system. Psychophysiology, 1971, 7, 451–464.

Beh, H.C., Mathers, S., & Holden, J., (1996). EEG correlates of exercise dependency.

International Journal of Psychophysiology. 23: 121–128. *

Beyer, L., Weiss, T., Hansen, E., Wolf, A., & Seidel., (1990). Dynamics of central nervous activation during motor imagination. International Journal of psychophysiology, 9. 75–80 *

Birbaumer, N., Elbert, T., Rockstroh, B., and Lutzenberger, W., (1981). Biofeedback of event–related potentials of the brain. *Int. J. Psychol.* 16: 389–415. *

Birbaumer, N., Lang, P.J., Cook, E., Elbert, T., Lutzenberger, W., & Rockstroh, B., 1988.

Slow brain wave potentials, imagery and hemispheric differences. International Journal of Neuroscience, 39, 101–116 *

Bird, E.I., (1987). Psychophysiological processes during rifle shooting. International Journal of Sport Psychology, 18, 9–18. *

Bull, S.J., (1991). Personal and situational influences on adherence to mental skills training. Journal of Sport and Excursus Psychology, 13, 121–132. *

Brown, Barbara B. Recognition of aspects of consciousness through association with EEG alpha activity represented by a light signal. Psychophysiology, 1970, 6, 442–452.

Budzynski, T. Tuning in on the twilight zone. Psychology Today, August 1977, pp. 39–44.

Cabral, R.J., and Scott, D.F., The Effects of Desensitization Technique, Biofeedback and Relaxation on Intractable Epilepsy: Follow-up Study, J. Neurol. Neurosurg. Psychiatry 39, 504–507 (1976).

Carlton, P. and Manowitz, P., Physiological factors as determinants of pathological gambling. Journal of Gambling Behavior, 1988, 3, 274–285.

Cassidy, Claire, H. Unraveling the Ball of String: Reality, Paradigms, and the Study of Alternative Medicine. Advances: The Journal of Mind-Body Health Vol.10, No. 1, Winter 1994.

Chase, M.H., and Harper, R.M. Somatomotor and visceromotor correlates of operantly conditioned 12–14 c/sec sensorimotor and visceromotor correlates of operantly conditioned 12–14 c/sec sensorimotor cortical activity. Electronencephalogr. Clinical Neurophysiology, 31, 85–92, 1971.

Chiarebzam G.A., Vasile, G., & Villa, M., (1990). Goal or near miss! Movement potential differences between adults and children in skilled performance. International Journal of Pyschophysiology, 10 105–115. *

Christian, J.C., Morzorati, S., Norton, J.A., Williams, C.J., O'Connor, S., & Li, T-K., (1996).
Genetic analysis of the resting electroencephalographic power spectrum in human twins. Psychophysiology, 33: 584–591.*

Cocteau, Jean. The process of inspiration. In B. Ghiselin, ed., The Creative Process: A Symposium. Berkeley and Los Angeles: University of California Press, 1952. Earle, J., Task difficulty and EEG alpha asymmetry:

An amplitude and frequency analysis. Neuropsychobiology, 1988, 20, 96–112.

Collins, D., (1995). Psychophysiology and Sport Performance. In S. Biddle (Ed.) European Perspective on Exercise & Sport. Champaigne: Human Kinetics. *

Collins, D.J., Powell, G.E., & Davies, I., (1990). An electroencephalographic study of hemispheric processing patterns during karate performance. Journal of Sport and Exercise Psychology, 12, 223–234*

Collins, D.J., Powell, G.E., & Davies, I., (1991a). Cerebral activity prior to motion task performance: An electroencephalographic study. Journal of Sports Sciences, 9, 313–324 *

Crews, D.J. and Landers, D.M., (1993). Electroencephalographic measures of attentional patterns prior to the golf putt. Med. Sci. Sports Exerc. 25: 116–126. *

Cummings, M. & Wilson, V.E., (1989). Psychological profile of competitive athletes under stress. IV International Psychomotor Learning & Sport Psychology Conference, Trois, Rivieres, Canada.*

DeBease, C.F., (1989). Electroencephalogram activity during visual external, visual internal and kinesthetic imagery of a motor performance. Unpublished doctoral dissertation, Temple University.*

Decety, J., Peranl, D., Jeannerod, M., Bettinardl, V., Tadary, B., Woods, R., Mazziotta, J.C., & Fazio, F., (1994). Mapping motor representations with positron emission tomography. Nature, 371:600–601 *

Englekamp, J., (1991). Memory of action events: Some implications for memory theory and for imagery. In C. Cornoldi, & M. McDaniel, (Eds.), Imagery and cognition, New York: Springer-Verlag. *

Ellertsen, B., and Klove, H. Clinical application of biofeedback training in epilepsy.

Scandinavian Journal of Behavior Therapy, 5, 133–144, 1976.

Etiner, J., Whitwer, S., Landers, D., Petrazella, S., & Salazar, W., (1996). Changes in EEG activity associated with learning a novel motor task. Research Quarterly in Exercise & Sport, 67:272–278. *

Farah, M., Weisberg, W., Monheit, M., & Peronnet, F., (1990). Brain activity underlying mental imagery: Event-related potentials during mental image generation. Journal of Cognitive Neuroscience, 1, 302–316 *

Fenwick, P.B.C., and Walker, S. The effect of eye position of the alpha rhythm. In C.R.

Evans and T.B. Mulholland (Eds.) Attention in neurophysiology. New York: Appleton-Century-Crofts, 1969.

Finitzo, T., Poole, K. and Chapman, S., Quantitative EEG and anatomoclinical principles of aphasia (loss of language skills): A validation study. Annals of the New York Academy of Sciences, 1991, 620, 57–72.

Finley, W.W., Smith, H.A., and Etherton, M.D. Reduction of seizures and normalization of the EEG in a severe epileptic following sensorimotor biofeedback training: Preliminary study. Biol. Psychology, 2, 189–203(1975).

Finley, W.W. Effects of Sham Feedback Following Successful SMR Training in an Epileptic: A Follow-Up Study. Biofeedback and Self Regulation 1, 227–235 (1976).

Fontani, G., Voglino, N., & Girolami, L., (1996). EEG frequency variations during a test of attentional in athletes. Int. J. Sport Psychol., 17: 68–78. *

Fontani, G., Tarricone, S., Vigni, L., & Zalaffi, A. (1989). Brain electrical activity during motor performances and competition in athletes. Pflugers Archiv, 414, S54 *

Galin, D. Implications for psychiatry of left and right cerebral specialization. Archives of General Psychiatry, 1974, 31, 572–583.

Galin, D., and Ornstein, R. Lateral specialization of cognitive mode: An EEG study.

Psychophysiology, 1972, 9, 412–418.

Gannon, L. and Sternbach, R. Alpha enhancement as a treatment for pain: A case study.

Behavior Therapy and Experimental Psychiatry, 1971, 2, 209–213.

Gannon, T., Landers, D., Kubitz, Salazar, W., & Petruzzello, S., (1992). An analysis of temporal electroencephalograhphic patterning prior to initiation of the arm curl. Journal of Sport & Exercise Psychology, 14: 87–100.*

Gliner, J.A., Matsen-Twisdale, J.A., Horvath, M., & Maron, M.B. (1979). Visual evoked potentials and signal detection following a marathon race. Medicine and Science in Sports, 11, 155–159.

Gould, D. & Udry, E., (1994). Psychological skills for enhancing performance: arousal regulation strategies. Med. Sci. Sports Exerc., 26, 4, 478–485. *

Green, E.E., Green, A.M., and Walters, E.D. Voluntary control of internal states:

Psychological and physiological. Journal of Transpersonal Psychology, 1970, 2, 1–26.

Greenspan, M.J., & Feltz, D.L. (1989). Psychological interventions with athletes in competitive situations: A Review. The Sport Psychologist, 3, 219–236.

Hardt, J.V., and Kamiya, J. Conflicting results in EEG alpha feedback studies: Why amplitude integration should replace percent time. Biofeedback and Self Regulation, 1976, 1(1), 63–75.

Hatfield, B.D., & Landers, D.M. (1983). Psychophysiology: A new direction for sport psychology. Journal of Sport Psychology, 5, 243–259. *

Hatfield, B.D., Landers, D.M., & Ray, W.J. (1987). Cardiovascular-CNS interactions during a self-paced, intentional attentive state: Elite marksmanship performance. Psychophysiology, 24, 542–549. *

Hatfield, B.D., Landers, D.M., & Ray, W.J. (1984). Cognitive processes during self-paced motor performance: An electroencephalographic profile of skilled marksmen. Journal of Sport Psychology, 6, 42–59. *

Hatfield, B.D., & Landers, D.M. (1987). Psychophysiology in exercise and sport: An overview. Exercise and Sport Sciences Reviews, 15, 351–387. *

Hirai, T. Electroencephalographic study on the Zen meditation (Japan). Folia Psychiatrica et Neurologica Japanica, 1960, 62, 76–105.

Kamiya, J. Autoregulation of the EEG alpha rhythm: A program for the study of consciousness. In M.H. Chase (Ed.), Operant control of brain sciences (Vol. 2). Los Angeles: BIS/Brain Research Institute, University of California, 1974.

Kamiya, J. Operant control of the EEG Alpha rhythm and some of its reported effects on consciousness. In C.T. Tart (Ed.), Altered states of consciousness. New York: Wiley, 1969. pp. 507–517.

Kamiya, J. Conscious control and brain waves. Psychology Today, 1968, 1, 57–60.

Kasamatsu, A., and T. Hirai. Science of Zazen. Psychologia, 6, 86–91, 1963.

Kasamatsu, A., and Hirai, T. An electroencephalographic study on the Zen meditation (Zazen). Folia Psychiatrica et Neurologica Japanica; 1966, 20, 315–336.

Kathmann, N., Jonitz, L. and Engel R.R., Cognitive determinants of the postimperative negative variation. Psychophysiology, 1990, 27, 256–263.

Klimesch, W., Schinke, H., Ladurner, G. and Pfurtscheller, G., Alpha frequency and memory performance. Journal of Psychophysiology, 1990, 4, 381–390.

Knott, J.R., Platt, E.B., Ashby, M.C., & Gottlieb, J.S. A familial evaluation of the electroencephalogram of patients with primary behavior disorder and psychopathic personality. Electroencephalography and Clinical Neurophysiology, 1953, 5, 363–370.

Knyazeva, M.G. and Bolshakova, G., EEG correlates of the success of verbal-anbalytic activity in young school children. Novye Issledovoniya v Psikhologii i Vozrastroi Fiziologii, 1990, 1, 75–79 (USSR).

Konttinen, N., & Lyytinen, H., (1993a). Brain slow waves preceding time-locked visuo-motor performance. Journal of Sports Sciences. 111:247–266. *

Konttinen, N. &Lyytinen, H., (1993b). Individual variability in brain slow wave profiles in skilled sharpshooters during the aiming period in rifle shooting. Journal of Sport and Exercise Psychology, 15:275–289. *

Konttinen, N. & Lyytinen, H. (1992). Physiology of preparation: Brain slow waves, heart rate, and respiration preceding triggering in rifle shooting. International Journal of Sport Psychology, 23: 110–127. *

Konttinen, N., Lyytinen, H., & Konttinen, R., (1993). Brain slow potentials reflecting successful shooting performance. Research Quarterly for Exercise & Sport. 66:64–72. *

Landers, D.M., Petruzzello, S.J., salazar, W., Crews, D.L., Kubitz, K.A., Granoln, T.L., & Han, M. (1991). The influence of electrocortical biofeedback on performance in pre-elite archers. Medicine and Science in Sports and Exercise, 23, 123–129. *

Lantz, DeLee, and Sterman, M.B., Neuropsychological Assessment of Subjects with Uncontrolled Epilepsy: Effects of EEG feedback Training, Epilepsia, 29(2), 163–171 (1988).

Linden, M.K. Electrophysiological validation for subgroups of attention deficit disorder and implications for brainwave biofeedback. Proceedings of the 21st Annual Association for Applied Psychophysiology and Biofeedback Meeting, 1990, 106–109.

Lubar, J. Neocortical Dynamics: Implications for Understanding the Role of Neurofeedback and Related Techniques for the Enhancement of Attention. Applied Psychophysiology and Biofeedback. Vol. 22, No. 2, 1997.

Lubar, J., Mann, C., Gross, D., and Shively, M., Differences in semantic event-related potentials in learning-disabled, normal, and gifted children. Biofeedback and Self Regulation, March 1992, 41–55.

Lubar, J., Discourse on the development of EEG diagnostics and biofeedback for attention-deficit/hyperactivity disorders. Biofeedback and Self Regulation, 1991, 16, 201–225.

Lubar, J.F. Electroencephalographic biofeedback and neurological applications. In J.V. Basmajian (Ed.) Biofeedback: Principles and Practice. 3rd Edition. Baltimore: Williams and Wilkins, 1989, 67–89.

Lubar, J.F. & Culver, R.M. Automated EEG signal detection methodologies for biofeedback conditioning. Behavior Research Methods and Instrumentation, 1978, 10 (5), 607–616.

Lubar, J.F. & Shouse, M.N. EEG and behavioral changes in a hyperactive child concurrent with training of the sensorimotor rhythm (SMR). A preliminary report.

Biofeedback and Self Regulation, (1976b), 1, 293–306.

Lubar J.F., Bianchini, R.J., Calhoun, U.H., Lambert, E.W., Brody, Z.H., and Shabsin, H.S. Spectral analysis of EEG differences between children with and without learning disabilities. Journal of Learning Disabilities, 1985, 7, 403–408.

Lubar, J.F. & Deering, W.M. Behavioral Approaches to Neurology, New York:

Academic Press, Inc., 1981.

Lubar, J.F. & Shouse, M.N. Use of biofeedback in the treatment of seizure disorders and hyperactivity. Advances in Child Clinical Psychology, Plenum Publishing Co., 1977, 1 224–251.

Lubar J.F. & Gross, D.M., Shively, M.S., & Mann, C.A. Differences between normal learning disabled, and gifted children based upon an auditory evoked potential task.

Journal of Psychophysiology, 1990, 4, 470–481.

Lubar, J.F., and Bahler, W.W. Behavioral management of epileptic seizures following biofeedback training of the sensorimotor rhythm. Biofeedback and Regulation, 1, 77–104 (1976a).

Lubar, J.F., Shabsin, H.S., Natelson, S.E., Holder, G.S., Whitsett, S.F., Pamplin, W.E., and Krulikowski, D.I., EEG Operant Conditioning in Intractable Epileptics. Arch. Neurol. 38, 700–704 (1981).

Lubar, J. O., and Lubar, J.F., Electroencephalographic biofeedback of SMR and beta for treatment of attention deficit disorders in a clinical setting. Biofeedback and Self-Regulation, 9(1), 1–23 (1984).

Mann, C. A., Lubar, J. R., Zimmerman, A. W., Miller, C. A. and Meunchen, R. A., Quantitative analysis of EEG in boy with attention-deficit/hyperactivity disorder (ADHD). A controlled study with clinical implications. Pediatric Neurology, 1990.

Mann, C.A., Sterman, M.b. & Kaiser, D.A., (1996). Suppression of EEG rhythmic frequencies during somato-motor and visuo-motor behavior. International Journal of Psychophysiology. 23: 1–7. *

Maslow, A. Toward a humanistic biology. American Psychologist, 1969, 24, 724–735.

Matousek, M., Rasmussen, P. & Gillberg, C. EEG frequency analysis in children with so-called minimal brain dysfunction and related disorders. Advances in Biological Psychiatry, 1984, 15, 102–108.

Morris, G., Obrzut, J., and Coulthard-Morris, L., Electroencephalographic (EEG) and brain stem evoked responses from learning-disabled and control children.

Developmental neuropsychology, 1989, 5, 187–206.

Muehl, S., Knott, J. R., and Benton, A. L. EEG abnormality and psychological test performance in reading disability. Cortex, 1, 434–439 (1965).

Mulholland, Thomas, and S. Runnals. Evaluation of attention and alertness with a stimulus-brain feedback loop. Electroencephalography and Clinical Neurophysiology, 14, 847–52, 1962.

Mulholland, T.B. The concept of attention and the EEG alpha rhythm. In C.R. Evans and T.B. Mulholland (Eds.) Attention in neurophysiology. New York: Appleton-Century-Crofts, 1969.

Mulholland, T., and Runnals, S. Increased occurrence of EEG alpha during increased attention. Journal of Psychology, 1962, 54, 317–330.

Mulholland, T. Objective EEG methods for studying covert shifts of visual attention. In F.J. McGuigan and R.A. Schoonover (Eds.), The psychophysiology of thinking. New York: Academic Press, 1973.

Mulholland, Thomas. Human EEG, Behavioral Stillness and Biofeedback. Suggest contacting Mulholland directly at Bedford VA, bedford, MA 01730 USA.

Okeima, T., Kogu, E., Ikeda, K. and Sugiyama H. The EEG of Yoga and Zen practitioners. Electroencephalography and Clinical Neurophysiology, 1957, 51 (Suppl.9).

Pavy, R., & Metcalf, J. The abnormal EEG in childhood communications and behavior abnormalities. Electroencephalography and Clinical II Neurophysiology. 1965, 19, 414.

Pelletier, K., and Peper, E. Developing a biofeedback model: Alpha EEG feedback as a means for pain control. International Journal of Clinical and Experimental Hypnosis, 1977, 25(4), 361–371.

Peniston, E.G., and Kulkosky, P.J. Alpha-Theta Brainwave Training and Beta-Endorphin Levels in Alcoholics Alcoholism: Clinical and Experimental Research, Volume 13, No. 2, March/April 1989.

Peniston, E.G. and Kulkosky, P.J. Alpha-Theta Brainwave Neurofeedback for Vietnam Veterans with Combat-Related Post-Traumatic Stress Disorder, Medical Psychotherapy, Volume 4, pp. 47–60, 1991. Hogrefe & Huber Publishers, Toronto 1991.

Peniston, E.G. and Kulkosky, P.J. Alcoholic Personality and Alpha-Theta Brainwave Training, Medical Psychotherapy, Volume 3, pp. 37–55, 1990. Hogrefe & Huber Publishers, Toronto 1990.

Peper, E. Alpha feedback EEG and the oculomotor system. Paper present at the American Society for Cybernetics, Gaithersburg, Maryland, October 14–16, 1969.

Peper, E., and Mulholland, T. Methodological and theoretical problems in the voluntary control of electroencephalographic occipital alpha by the subject. Kybernetik 1970, 7(3), 10–13.

Picton, T.W., & Hillyard, S.A. Human auditory evoked potentials: Effects of attention.

Electroencephalography and Clinical Neurophysiology 36, 191–199.

Pimental, P.A. and Kingsbury, N.A., Neuropsychological Aspects of Right Brain Injury, Austin, TX, Pro-ed, 1989.

Poirier, Ferdinand. Traitement de l'epilepsie par retroaction sonore. La Clinique D. Epilepsie de Montreal. Paper presented at the Biofeedback Research Society Conference, 1972.

Raglin, J.S. (1992). Anxiety and sport performance. Exercise and Sport Science Reviews 20: 243–270. *

Ray, W., & Cole, H. (1985). EEG alpha activity reflects attentional demands, and beta activity reflects emotional and cognitive processes. Science, 228, 750–752. *

Rockstroh, b., Elbert, T., Birbaumer, N., & Lutzenberger, W. (19909). Biofeedback-produced hemispheric asymmetry of slow cortical potentials and its behavioral effects. International Journal of Psychophysiology, 9, 151–165. *

Rossi, B., & Zani, A. (1986). Differences in hemispheric functional asymmetry between athletes and nonathletes: Evidence from a unilateral tactile matching task. Perceptual and Motor Skills, 62, 295–300. *

Salazar, W., Landers, D.M., Petruzzellow, S.J., Han, M., Crews, D.L., & Kubitz, K.A. (1990). Hemispheric asymmetry, cardiac response and performance in elite archers. Research Quarterly for Exercise and Sport, 61, 351–359. *

Satterfield, J.H., & Dawson, M.E. Electrodermal correlates of hyper-activity in children.

Psychophysiology 1971, 8, 191–197.

Satterfield, H.H., Lesser, L.I., Saul, R.E., & Cantwell, D.P. EEG aspects in the diagnosis and treatment of minimal brain dysfunction. Annals of New York Academy of Science 1973, 205, 274–282.

Seifert, A.R., & Lubar, J.F. Reduction of epileptic seizures through EEG biofeedback training. Biological Psychology 1975, 3, 157–184.

Shouse, M.N., and Lubar, J.F. Operant conditioning of EEG rhythms and Ritalin in the treatment of hyperkinesis. Biofeedback and Self Regulation, (1979) 4 (4), 301–312.

Shouse, M.N. & Lubar, J.F., Physiological bases of hyperkinesis treated with methylphenidate. Pediatrics 1978, 62, 343–351.

Shouse, M.N. & Lubar, J.F. Sensorimotor rhythm (SMR) operant conditioning and methylphenidate in the treatment of hyperkinesis. Biofeedback and Self Regulation 1979, 4, 299–311.

Simonton, O. Carl, and Stephanie Simonton. Belief systems and management of the emotional aspects of malignancy. Journal of Transpersonal Psychology, 7, 29–47, 1975.

Spiel, G., Is there a possibility of differentiating between children with minimal cerebral dysfunction (Attention Deficit Disorder) by means of computer-assisted automatic EEG analysis? Advances in Biological Psychiatry, 1987, 16, 161–177.

Sterman, M.B. & Wyricka, W.A. EEG correlates of sleep: Evidence for separate forebrain substrates. Brain Research, 6, 143–163, 1967.

Sterman, M.B., Howe, R.C., and MacDonald, L. R. Facilitation of spindle-burst sleep by conditioning of electroencephalographic activity while awake. Science, 167, 1146–1148, 1970.

Sterman, M.B. and Friar, L. Suppression of seizures in an epileptic following sensorimotor EEG feedback training. Electroencephalographic Clinical Neurophysiology, 33, 89–95, 1972.

Sterman, M.B., Kaiser, D.A., Mann, C.A., Suyenobu, B.Y., Beyman, D.C., & Francis, J.R., (1993). Application of quantitative EEG analysis to workload assessment in an advanced aircraft simulator. Proceedings of the Human Factors and Ergonomics Society 37th Annual Meeting–1993. *

Sterman, M.B., Mann, C.A., Kaiser, D.A. & Suyenobu, B.Y., (1994) Multiband topographic EEG analysis of a simulated visuomotor aviation task. International Journal of Psychophysiology. 16: 49–56.

Sterman, M.B., MacDonald, L.R., and Stone, R.K. Biofeedback training of the sensorimotor EEG rhythm in man: Effect on epilepsy. Epilepsia, 15, 395–416, (1974).

Sterman, M.B. Effects of Sensorimotor EEG Feedback Training on Sleep and Clinical Manifestations of Epilepsy. Biofeedback and Behavior, Jackson Beatty and Heiner Legewie, eds., Plenum Press, New York; pp. 167–200; 1976a.

Sterman, M.B., and MacDonald, L.R., Effects of central cortical EEG feedback training on seizure incidence in poorly controlled epileptics. Epilepsia, 19, 207–222 (1978).

Sterman, M.B., and Shouse, M.N. Sensorimotor Mechanisms Underlying a Possible Common Pathology in Epilepsy and Associated Sleep Disturbances; Sleep and Epilepsy, Chapter 3, Academic Press, 1982.

Sterman, M.B. EEG Biofeedback in the treatment of epilepsy: an overview circa 1980.

Clinical Biofeedback: Efficacy and Mechanisms, Leonard White and Bernard Tursky, eds., The Guilford Press, New York, 1982.

Still, G.F. Some abnormal physical conditions in children. Lancet 1902, 1 (2), 1008–1012.

Stoyva, J., and Kamiya, J. Electrophysiological studies of dreaming as the prototype of a new strategy in the study of consciousness. Psychological Review, 1968, 75, 192–205.

Strauss, A.A. & Lehtinen, V. Psychopathology and education in the brain-injured child (Vol. 1). New York: Grune & Stratton.

Strelau, J. (1977). Reactivity and decision making in stress situations in pilots. In C.D. Spielberger & I.G. Saranson, Stress and Anxiety, (Vol. 4) New York: Academic Press. *

Stryker, S. Encephalitis lethargica-the behavioral residuals. Training School Bulletin 1973, 22, 152–157.

Tansey, M.A., EEG sensorimotor rhythm biofeedback training: Some effects on neurologic precursors of learning disabilities. International Journal of Psychophysiology, 1984, 1, 163–177.

Tansey, M.A., & Bruner, R.L., EMG and EEG biofeedback training in the treatment of a 10-year-old hyperactive boy with a developmental reading disorder. Biofeedback and Self Regulation 1983, 8, 25–37.

Tansey, M.A. The response of a case of Petit Mal epilepsy to EEG sensorimotor rhythm biofeedback training. International Journal of Psychophysiology 1985, 3, 81–84.

Tansey, M.A. Brainwave Signatures: An index reflective of the brain's functional neuroanatomy: Further findings on the effect of EEG sensorimotor rhythm biofeedback training on the neurologic precursors of learning disabilities International Journal of Psychophysiology 1985, 3, 85–99 and 4, 91–97 (1985).

Tansey, M.A. Righting the rhythms of reason, EEG biofeedback training as a therapeutic modality in a clinical office setting. Medical Psychotherapy 1990, 3, 57–68. Tansey, M.A. A simple and a complex tic (Giles de la Tourette's syndrome): Their response to EEG sensorimotor rhythm biofeedback training. Int. J. Psychophysiology 4, 91–97 (1986).

Tozzo, C.A., Elfner, L.F., and May, Jr., J.G., EEG biofeedback and relaxation training in the control of epileptic seizures, Int. J. of Psychophysiology 6, 185–194 (1988).

Ulrich, g., & Kriebitzsch, R., (1990). Visuomotor tracking performance and task–induced modulation of alpha activity. International Journal of Psychophysiology,10:199–202. *

Vealey, R.S., (1994) Current status and prominent issues in sport psychology interventions. Med. Sci. Sports Exerc. 26, 495–502. *

Weiss, T., Beyer, L. & Hansen, E., (1991). Motor imagination—a model for motor performances, International Journal of Psychophysiology, 11: 203–205. *

Weng, Q., Chen, Y., Yan, W., Tan, Y, Fang, Y., & Zhang, C., (1987). A study on the computer analysis of EEG in elite marathoners before and after competition. Chinese Journal of Sports Medicine (Beijing), 6(2), 85–90. *

Werry, J.M., Delano, J.G. & Douglas, V. Studies on the hyperactive child. I. Some preliminary findings. Canadian Psychiatric Association Journal 1964, 9, 120–130.

Whittsett, S.F., Lubar, J.F., and Holder, G.S., A double–blind investigation of the relationship between seizure activity and sleep following EEG biofeedback training.
Biofeedback and Self-Regulation 7, 193–207 (1982).

Williams, J.D., Rippon, G., Stone, B.M, & Annett, J., (1995). Psychophysiological correlates of dynamic imagery. British Journal of Psychology, 86: 283–300. *

Wilson, V.E. and Bird, E.I., (1982). Psychophysiological profiles of mental rehearsal. North American and Canadian Associations of Sport Psychology Combined Annual Meeting, East Lansing, Michigan. *

Wilson, V.E. and Bird, E.I., (1983). Psychobiological assessment of junior figure skaters. Canadian Association of Sport Sciences, November, 1983. *

Wilson, V.E., and Hamilton, H., (1983). Psychobiological assessment of track and field athletes. Canadian Association of Sport Sciences, Toronto, November 1983. *

Wyler, A.R., Lockard, J.S., and Ward, A.A., Conditioned EEG Desynchronization and Seizure Occurrence in Patients. Electroencephalography and Clinical Neurophysiology 41, 501–512 (1976).

Yue, G. H., Wilson, S.L., Cole, K.J., Darling, W.G., & Yuh, W.T.C., (1996). Imagined muscle contraction training increases voluntary neural drive to muscle. Journal of Psychophysiology, 10: 198–208. *

Zametkin, A.J., Nordahl, T.E., Gross, M., King, A.C., Semple, W.E., Rumsey, J., Hamburger, S., and Cohen, R.N. Cerebral glucose metabolism in adults with hyperactivity of childhood onset. New England Journal of Medicine, 1990, 323, 1361–1366.

Zani, A., & Rossi, B. (1991a). Cognitive psychophysiology as interface between cognitive and sport psychology. International Journal of Sport Psychology, 22, 376–398.

Zani, A., & Ross, B., (1991b). Psychophysiology, psychological theory, and the study of skilled psychomotor performance. Int. J. Sport Psychol. 22, 402–406.*

Entries followed by an asterisk (*) courtesy of Vietta E. Wilson, PhD., York University, Toronto, Canada, vwilson@youku.ca

p.51 —